To LEE
XMAS 1995
LOVE xxxxx
MAM & DAD

BULL
The Biography

Howard Wright

Timeform

First published in 1995
by Portway Press Limited
Halifax West Yorkshire HX1 1XE

© Portway Press Limited

Printed and bound by
William Clowes Limited Beccles and London

ISBN 0 900599 76 6

It's a beautiful thing to have lived in the sun.
There is nothing static. We never remain
the same individually for two days together.

William Bull; recorded on the occasion of his 80th birthday
and played at his funeral in 1954.

CONTENTS

ILLUSTRATIONS

P HIL BULL decided against chronicling his own story. Yet it is a story worth telling. His life and personality, his passions and disappointments, cried out to be recorded, explored and, where possible, explained.

Born in West Yorkshire in 1910, the son of a miner and a schoolteacher, he gave up his own teaching career and made a living from betting on horses. He built up a publishing firm which gained an international reputation in its specialised sphere. He bred and owned many good racehorses. He campaigned for fundamental changes in the organisation of racing, but walked away from a senior administrative position after only six months. He held strong views on politics, philosophy and religion; he preached communism but practised capitalism. He had four personal partnerships, three children and a number of longstanding friends, but in later years before his death in 1989 he admitted to being alone.

Allowing that a first-hand account of Bull's life and times is unavailable, a second-hand version would not have done him full justice. What follows is a mixture of the two, starting out under the working title of Phil Bull: Mainly In His Own Words, and proceeding through the wealth of personal material he set down and collected. The foundations and framework for Bull: The Biography were fashioned from his accomplished writing in published articles and reports, and extensive correspondence, both public and private; documentaries and feature articles about him; and telephone conversations committed to tape, whether or not those to whom Bull spoke realised they were being recorded.

Bull's original contribution makes up the greater part of the book, hence its prominence in the presentation which follows. Inevitably, though, gaps had to be filled from other sources in order to produce a fuller, more objective picture. Grateful thanks are due to those who helped to fill the gaps:

To Geoff Walton, managing director of Timeform, who first trawled through the mass of material and has masterminded the project; to his predecessor Reg Griffin, for sharing the details of his long and close association with Bull.

To Dick Whitford, without whom Bull's business, Timeform, would not have emerged in its current well established form, for his invaluable recollections and reflections.

To May Watson-Gott, for her memories of the Bull family and the early life of her brother.

To former Timeform employees Derek Adams, Ken Cunningham, Brian and Judith Skirton, and John and Judith Whitley, for their observations and reminiscences.

To current Timeform employees David Newton, who researched Bull's record as a racehorse breeder and owner, and Geoff Greetham, both of whom painstakingly checked the finished product; Wendy Lewis, who with help from Gloria Gallon transcribed hours of taped interviews, as well as Bull's own tapes, Wendy Muncaster, for work on the typesetting and layout, and John Ingles, for compiling the index.

And to Barclays de Zoete Wedd Securities for providing the Cost of Living Index figures, from which it has been possible to measure Bull's financial achievements in relation to today's values.

Bull himself would not have drawn such detailed attention to the facts and figures of his betting activities. In fact, he expended a great deal of time and energy endeavouring to play down the rags-to-riches image. Bull: The Biography faced no such strictures, thank goodness.

HOWARD WRIGHT   August 1995

NOVEMBER 1964: A distinguished horseracing journalist begins to prepare his Sunday newspaper column. His chosen subject this week is Phil Bull, the highly successful punter and publisher, racehorse owner and breeder. The writer picks up a carefully-prepared, wide-ranging set of notes, and reads:

What racing man sports a ginger beard? Few people even casually acquainted with racing would not name him. For more than 20 years Phil Bull has been an outstanding character on the British Turf. Successful publisher of racing books and periodicals; a breeder of international repute, for many years leading owner in the North of England, and commentator on racing matters, Phil Bull has probably done more for racing than anyone else in the last two decades.

His publications present us every week with a wealth of information about every horse in training, without which owners, trainers, journalists, bookmakers and punters alike would be sadly lost. He has put the appraisal of the merit and individual character of racehorses on an entirely new footing, intelligible to everyone.

He has established the most important two-year-old event under Jockey Club Rules. His observations on the pattern of two-year-old racing resulted in the setting up of the Rosebery Committee and brought about a far-reaching change in the Rules of Racing. For someone standing outside the inner circle of racing's hierarchy these are no mean achievements.

Make no mistake about it. Phil Bull has done more than anyone to educate the racing public, and he talks more sense about racing than any man I have ever met.

So let us take a look at this extraordinary man, his background and how he came to apply himself to racing.

Phil Bull was neither bred from racing stock nor born into racing. None of his relatives had any professional connection with racing, nor indeed with horses at all. His father was a coal miner, until he left the pits after being crushed by a train of runaway tubs; his mother was a schoolmistress. From elementary school he had to win his way by scholarships to grammar school and thence to Leeds University. The Board of Education contributed, in return for an undertaking on his part that he would go into teaching after graduating, but it was a struggle for his parents.

He took a Mathematics degree, which, he says, served him well in his subsequent career in racing, in particular the statistics and evaluating the significance of the data. But he admits he did not work at the University. He spent most of his time playing chess and bridge, writing a play or two, and racing.

In the early 1930s he was a schoolmaster, teaching in London. But the seeds of Phil Bull's love of racing had been sown long before then.

As long as he could remember there were *Racing-Up-To-Dates* and *Sporting Pinks* lying around the house. Racing was always meat and drink to the Yorkshire miner. This miner's son had had his first outing on a racecourse at Pontefract when seven or eight years of age. It fired his interest and imagination, like going to the theatre for the first time.

It was not long before Phil Bull's father was apprehensive about his keenness and tried to discourage him from wasting his time on the racing newspapers instead of his school books. It was a losing battle, and he continued to take his son racing, to Doncaster and the St Leger. Phil Bull remembers seeing the flying Mumtaz Mahal win the Doncaster Champagne Stakes [1923]. A sight to spark the racing enthusiasm of any youngster! Viewed from the Silver Ring, of course.

Little did the 13-year-old suspect that 28 years afterwards he would win the same race with a horse of his own breeding, Orgoglio, his 80-year-old father looking on from a private box in the stand. It would not have occurred to him that he might even own a racehorse, since his was a relatively poor family, with his mother and father's income together amounting to no more than five or six pounds a week.

At that time the young Phil Bull's racing horizons encompassed only model racecourses made of Meccano, and race meetings on the living-room floor, complete with race cards, form books and mocked-up racing newspapers. Play, say the psychologists, is a preparation for living. Prophetic indeed, this, for the future owner-breeder-publisher.

Phil Bull's activities as a writer and a publisher did not begin in racing. *The Tramp Among The Tombstones*, a political diatribe in dramatic form, was his first published book. Laboriously hand-set and printed by himself on a small manual press, it was well received, and the limited edition soon sold out. As a commercial proposition it was of no consequence, but it taught its author the printing business.

Thereafter he gave up politics ('You're a fly in the path of a steamroller'). He also gave up teaching. 'Those who can, do; those who cannot, teach,' wrote Bernard Shaw. That impressed him.

He was at first very interested in education, but somewhat idealistic about it. He found the reality vastly different from what he had imagined it would be. And he was out of sympathy with much of what he was expected to teach. He was too much interested in ideas and too little interested in the pupil.

He also became aware that while teachers broaden the horizons of the children they teach, the effect on the teachers is the reverse—their horizons contract and they become progressively more childish. 'From a social point of view,' says Phil Bull, 'education is all important—racing of little consequence. But to me the environment of the school was stultifying. That of the racecourse I found exhilarating. The fault, of course, was in me. I must have been a lousy teacher. But better to do something worthwhile on the racecourse than make a mess of things in the classroom!' So he gave up teaching, and took up racing.

While at the University he had become interested in the statistical analysis of race times. The time a race takes to run a certain distance depends upon many things: the conformation of the track, the state of the going, wind strength and direction, and the pace at which the race is run. Unless all these things are taken into account, the bare time itself is meaningless, he says.

He developed a technique of evaluating the real value of the time performance of a horse, by mathematical treatment of all the times recorded on that particular day on that particular track, and by reference to statistical analysis of previous times recorded on the same track.

It was very successful, and Phil Bull bet on his conclusions with considerable profit. He then began a mail order Time Test service, selling the information to the public. This too was very successful, so he gave up teaching.

Phil Bull made his mark in the racing world first as a writer, with a series of annual *Best Horses* volumes, commencing in 1942, that delighted readers with their terse, crisp, comprehensive, imaginative and rebellious style. He didn't confine himself to the horses. No mere chronicler of events, he startled thoroughbred breeders by destroying with deadly satire many of their long-cherished theories and beliefs.

Here, wrote reviewers at the time, were books that would take their place among racing literature of the century, the most notable achievement in the annals of Turf writing. His arguing of the case for Dante when that horse was a two-year-old [1944] so impressed one critic that he was constrained to exclaim that Mr Bull would have made the best of them look to their laurels if he had gone to the Bar.

The *Best Horses* annuals quickly gained a worldwide sale and had a powerful impact in America. Despite Nasrullah's relative failure as a three-year-old, Phil Bull described him as head and shoulders above his contemporaries, and forecast that he would prove it as a sire. The Americans bought Nasrullah. And Rex Ellsworth has put it on record that it was largely what Phil Bull wrote that caused him to buy Khaled, the sire of Swaps. It is ironic that nobody regrets the loss of Nasrullah and Khaled to British breeders more than does Phil Bull himself.

Regrettably, Phil Bull was unable to continue writing these annual *Best Horses* volumes, which by 1947 had become a real tome, running to nearly 600 pages of small type. What began as a labour of love had become by 1948 a burden of responsibility too big for any one man to carry.

Mr Bull thereupon turned his attention to publishing, and with a staff of handicappers, writers and assistants working under his direction, he launched a new racing publication—*Timeform*. It was another creative achievement.

Hitherto all racing chronicles had been form books, recording races and race results. *Timeform* deals not with races but with horses, with all horses racing under Jockey Club Rules, and provides for every horse a complete dossier on its career and an appraisal of its racing character. The most important item in *Timeform*, however, is the rating of each horse's racing merit.

Handicapping horses is bedevilled by the fact that they begin racing as two-year-olds, when they are immature. As they mature they improve. Their rate of improvement varies too, according to their distance capacity. These complications had previously defeated any attempt to make a comprehensive running handicap, embracing horses of all ages racing over a wide variety of distances.

Phil Bull tackled the problem and solved it by separating from the performance of each horse the weight-for-age element from the inherent merit of the horse. The latter he expresses as a rating—a measure of the horse's real ability. Though few people seem to have appreciated it, this is, in handicapping, a breakthrough of the first order, which could only have been visualised by highly logical and creative thinking.

For this the whole of the racing world is indebted to Phil Bull.

Those are the words of Phil Bull himself.

The third person was really the first person, for Bull prepared this piece in November 1964, in the form of an article which would appear in the *Observer* under the name of one of his most committed followers, the racing journalist Richard Baerlein. Bull provided the questions for an interview, and the answers. He drafted the article. The words were written out on paper, pored over and altered, until he was satisfied they conveyed the meaning he intended. Baerlein used them, virtually word for word, in the course of his feature.

It typified Bull's approach to writing; it is also typical of the way he wanted others to write about him. Letters to *The Sporting Life* editor were sent with the stern instruction that if the words could not be used in their entirety, they should not be used at all. Journalists phoning for a comment, a discussion or a lengthy interview, were implored to read back or submit the final work, and were instructed to do so if Bull did not know them.

After the Baerlein eulogy was put together, Bull gradually drew back from active involvement in the sport of racing. The introduction and growth of betting tax curtailed his betting activity; he could no longer afford to support a band of mares with increasingly expensive stallion nominations, and his horses in training shrunk in numbers; and he largely left the running of Timeform to others. As well as continuing to pursue the social side of the sport, he did, however, move into the political arena of racing, briefly, as the first chairman of the Horseracing Advisory Council. He died on 10 June 1989, rightly acclaimed as one of the most influential figures in British racing of his time.

The following is Phil Bull's story, told mainly in his own words, with observations from his closest family and colleagues. He had prepared the framework for an autobiography, but never put it together. What follows cannot be anything but an alternative. Only Phil Bull himself could have approved the original.

PHIL BULL was born on 9 April 1910 in the West Yorkshire mining village of Hemsworth, the son of a miner, soon to become a sanitary inspector, and a schoolteacher. When he compiled his notes for a never-to-be-published autobiography, he summed up the first thirty-four years of his life in two parts:

ORIGINS & EARLY LIFE   Hemsworth: terrace house: FATHER miner: well read, powerful speaker: politically active: pit accident: sanitary inspector: had to give up politics: would have become MP. MOTHER zest for life, energy and affection: teacher, Barclays Bank, hard time to bring up four children, outside activities, on rural district council: difficult in these labour-saving days to appreciate how hard it was. EARLY RECOLLECTIONS the miner's bath: washday; outside loo: football in streets: Jack, Jack, shine a light. SCHOLARSHIP to Hemsworth Grammar School: usually top of form in science subjects, especially maths: stupid headmaster who thought Latin more important than physics: won bursarship to Leeds University (committed me to teaching later on).

UNIVERSITY LIFE & TEACHING CAREER   Lived in hostel: very earnest: maths, geology, geography, music. DID NOT WORK cut lectures: chess, bridge, snooker, backed horses and wrote two or three plays: very interested in drama, also in education and politics: now feel I took wrong subjects: should have studied law and psychology: came out with poor degree. TEACHING in London: £173 per annum: hard to live: basement room: rats: flat in Kennington: Balham: London unattached staff: war: evacuation to Peacehaven: return to London: work in rest centres during Blitz: courses at City Literary Institute on political economy, economics and drama: bought small hand press: wrote, printed and published a political diatribe *The Tramp Among the Tombstones*. Continued interest in racing, loss of interest in teaching: disillusioned, 'Those who can, do; those who can't, teach'.

Despite keeping a copious amount of material throughout his 79 years—including articles, correspondence and even secretly-taped recordings of his telephone conversations—Bull left behind few references to several aspects of his formative life beyond these thumbnail notes. Yet they still demonstrate some of the influences on his life and thinking—the humble home, Left-wing politics, disillusionment with the teaching profession, for instance.

His father, William Osborne Bull, was one of the youngest children in a family of at least fifteen who lived at Cannock Chase in the Midlands. Born around 1870, he moved to West Yorkshire—to 3 Cemetery Road, Holly Bank, Hemsworth—before the turn of the 20th Century, seeking work. In a letter dated 20 February 1985, at the height of the miners' strike, Phil Bull recalled:

My father was a collier, working at Hemsworth Colliery at Fitzwilliam until he had six ribs broken when trapped in a road by runaway tubs. He was something of an Arthur Scargill and quite an orator. On one occasion, during a strike, when addressing a meeting at Cross Hill, Hemsworth, he was arrested for supposedly causing an obstruction. Refusing to pay the fine, he went to prison, but was released when the Union insisted on paying it.

He was in line to become the next Labour MP for Hemsworth, but after his pit accident he had to give up working as a miner. So he obtained the required qualifications and became what was then known as a Sanitary Inspector, which necessitated his joining NALGO and giving up his political career. Instead he coached his brother-in-law, Gabe Price, for the job, and in due course Gabe became the next Labour MP for Hemsworth with the largest majority (35,000) in the country. Gabe had been a check-weighman at South Kirkby or Frickley Colliery—I forget which. Later he became disillusioned with politics, and to everyone's shocked surprise committed suicide.

I remember the 1926 General Strike very well. It was the present Miners' Strike all over again with Arthur Cook in Arthur Scargill's shoes, Ramsay Macdonald doing a Kinnock and the TUC chickening out, just as they've done today. Everything remarkably similar.

My sympathies are wholly with the Workers Revolutionary Party—the only one that really knows the political scene—but I fear they are wrong in thinking that a General Strike would bring about the revolution today. Given a TUC with guts a General Strike is feasible and would bring the Government down. But the WRP is neither equipped nor organised to take over the nation and it has neither the power base, the popular backing nor the leadership to give it a cat in hell's chance against the Army, which by comparison is well organised, massively equipped and well prepared for such an eventuality. The outlook, my friend, is bleak, nationally and internationally, and the most likely outcome of things is nuclear catastrophe brought about by the Americans. We may escape it. But it's an odds-on chance in the next ten years. Still, you never know.

Phil Bull was devoted to his mother, born Lizzie Jessop Watson but known as Dolly. When Dolly died in Halifax in March 1972, a few months short of her 88th birthday, Phil asked those present at her cremation to remember her 'great zest and energy, bearing her trials not silently, but bravely and with courage':

She was a magnificent mother to us. I remember her scrubbing the pit-dirt off my father's back as he sat in a zinc bath before the fire. I remember her at the rubbing board on wash days. I remember the pride she took in us as children, buying us everything she could afford, and saving up for holidays for us.

For years while teaching she got up early to go and scrub the floors of Barclays Bank to earn a little extra so that the three of us, and Frank Fulwood, could have the best education we could get. I remember how she fought our battles for us too. The maternal instinct to protect her young was strong in her.

Her energy and zest in middle life were inexhaustible. When Bill was no longer working, she set up in business in the markets, an all-weather outdoor job, learning as she went along. She stood for election to the Council, served on an Education Committee. She made her own social life. Was active in the Operatic Society. She even started a swimming club long after she was fifty years of age. She was, I tell you, quite a woman.

Sadly in her later years her health deteriorated badly. She was still capable, on occasions, of flashes of the old Dolly, but the time came when she had difficulty in moving around, and found little to say. Life was slowly ebbing away from her. And now it has gone altogether. There it is, you know: the whole panoramic tragedy of life, from birth to death, with which we are all endowed and from which there is no escape.

Bill, you will remember, put his view in a single phrase 'It is good to have lived in the sun'. Dolly would simply say 'I've enjoyed my life'. She said so many times.

Bill and Dolly Bull had three children—Phil, born in April 1910; May, born in July 1911, and Connie, born in December 1914. But the family took on responsibility for bringing up a fourth child, Francis Fulwood, born in 1916 the son of Dolly's sister Lena, who was committed to a mental hospital when her child was four years of age. The extended family grew up in pairs—Phil and May, Connie and Frank. Phil and May were still playing tennis together in their seventies.

9

May recalls that the young Phil played indoor games—apart from those taught him by his father, such as dominoes, cards and snooker—to his own rules. And he played at racehorses. 'He had a Meccano set but he wasn't content with building castles and so on, like everyone else. He had to build a racecourse. And the little figures of horses, which the family bought him, he painted in reality, in the owners' colours. I was Solly Joel; he was Lord Derby. The horses moved on by throwing a dice. Phil made up copies of the *Sporting Pink* and race cards, and he kept records of the race results. He kept the horses in a large biscuit tin between layers of cotton wool, so that none of them got broken. They all had a place, and they all had to be put back after the game.'

From imaginary horseracing in a table-top game, Phil and May Bull progressed to the real thing, encouraged by their parents. Bill Bull enjoyed going racing; Dolly Bull enjoyed a bet with the local bookmaker.

Phil Bull often told the story, almost certainly apocryphal, of how his father was in the Army—the Salvation Army. In a speech at the annual dinner of the charity organisation the Saints & Sinners Club in March 1976, he explained:

I was bred to be a saint, you know. My mother was a Sunday School teacher, and my father began his career in the Salvation Army. He used to go out in the dead of night with a bucket of whitewash, and paint religious slogans on the walls. You know: things like 'Prepare to meet thy God', and 'The Wages of Sin is Death'.

One night at the Doncaster St Leger meeting in 1901 he went out and painted on the back of the grandstand, 'What shall we do to be saved?' Next morning, when he returned to the scene, he found that some wag had painted under his 'What shall we do to be saved?', 'Back Doricles for the St Leger'.

Whether my father took this as a divinely inspired answer to his question, straight from the Almighty, I don't know. But he backed the horse, and it won at 40/1. That converted him. From that time on he was more concerned with backing winners than with saving souls.

Shortly afterwards he read Tom Paine and Voltaire and became an atheist. He went up in the world. He became a coal miner (over half a century too soon); and eventually he reached the apotheosis of his career as a Sanitary Inspector. He sought sainthood in Sanitation. His remedy for sin was disinfectant. He was a kindly man—to all except bugs, fleas, and cockroaches.

Earlier, at the 1955 St Leger Dinner in Doncaster, Bull gave another insight to his father's interest in horseracing:

On Tuesday 7 September, 1909, the first day of the St Leger meeting, three men set off to cycle thirteen miles to Doncaster races. The first man had a system, an unbeatable system, so he believed; the second man had boundless enthusiasm for this system, which was the familiar one of doubling up on favourites; and the third man had a tin box, strapped to his bicycle, in which reposed £300, the whole of his life savings. He was due to be married in three weeks time, and the £300 was the nest egg with which he was to furnish the home and set up in married life.

You may guess the rest of the story. Not a favourite won! So the three of them cycled back home again, with empty pockets, very much depressed.

I don't know the identity of the man with the system, but the second man was Mr Gabriel Price, who was later Member of Parliament for Hemsworth, and the man with the tin box who lost every penny of his £300 was my father.

When these three amateur punters got back from the races, my father couldn't face the job of explaining to my mother what had happened to the £300 they were to get married on. So the task was therefore delegated to Gabe Price. Fortunately Gabriel had a sense of humour: he must have made a good job of the explaining, otherwise there might well have been no wedding, and I shouldn't be standing here tonight. I believe it was touch and go. I've had some pretty close calls at Doncaster races, but if what my mother tells me is correct, the closest of the lot was the one that arose out of the Leger meeting the year before I was born.

When my father died last year [1954], he left instructions that he was to be cremated and his ashes were to be sprinkled on a racecourse. He specified the course—Pontefract, not Doncaster. Perhaps the memory of the £300 was in his mind. I imagine his saying to himself, 'Doncaster's had the cash, so let Ponte have the ash'.

> Bull recounted the story in a speech to an annual bookmakers' dinner in Liverpool in 1964—though the sum in the tin box had gone up to £400!—and had further thoughts about the inspiration provided by his mother.

My mother was a schoolmistress, and as a small boy I was in her class. Very early she taught me to count correctly—one, 5/4, 6/4, 7/4, two. She used to send me out at playtime to get the *Sporting Pink*. And while other boys learned that a double was a large whisky, a treble was a boy chorister and an accumulator was a device for storing electricity, my mother was at pains to explain to me the true meanings of these words. I think, on the whole, my mother was a more successful punter than my father.

The Bull household was well read. 'The house was full of books,' May Watson-Gott recalls. 'We were brought up on the classics, from which my father would read to us a chapter each night. We had books that people would normally wait to read at school, and Phil and I would take friends home for our father to read to us. That's why we became so good at English, because we had learned from books before we went to school. My father would buy lots of secondhand books and make notes in ink in the margins, so that we would remember passages from Shakespeare and Scott and so on.'

Phil Bull went first to Hemsworth Church School for boys, where his mother taught, and then gained one of the rare scholarships to Hemsworth Grammar School when it opened for the first time, with about 60 pupils, in November 1921. He remained there until July 1928.

In the School Certificate examinations taken in 1926, Bull passed with distinctions in Geography, Mathematics and Art. His achievements in the Higher School Certificate examinations two years later were not so comparable, though he emerged with 'good' in Pure Mathematics, Applied Mathematics and Chemistry, and a pass in Geography.

Headmaster A. G. Jenkinson noted of Bull in 1926: 'He is a boy of admirable character, of whom I have a high opinion, and for whom I predict further success at school and at the university.' A year later Jenkinson commented: 'He is a boy of intellectual ability above the average, with a particular leaning towards the mathematical and scientific side. He has a good all-round knowledge, and thinks for himself. His character is good; he is honest, industrious and loyal. He is a boy who has determination and independence, and he is sure to make his way.'

Grammar school led to university, as Bull continued to break away from the way of life that the majority led in Hemsworth in the late 1920s. He went to Leeds, moving away from home for the first time, for a three-year course in Principal Mathematics, including Pure and Applied Mathematics. He gained his degree but it was not an outstanding result, no honours. As he admitted, he could have worked harder. 'He did his own thing,' sister May recalls. 'He did as little work as he could.'

Followers of Bull's later successes in racing have described him as a mathematical genius; he was not, in the strictest application of the word, though he was happy with the image.

He was good enough to gain a degree, and would have been capable of teaching at a grammar school, but no more.

In March 1932, William P. Milne, Bull's professor of mathematics at Leeds University, wrote a reference to support his application for a teaching post. It was noticeably restrained. 'Throughout his university career, Mr Bull proved himself a competent student,' he wrote, to whoever it may have concerned, 'and may be relied upon to teach the subject from an intelligent standpoint up to the standard betokened by his degree. Apart from his academic qualifications, Mr Bull has played association football for his hostel, Devonshire Hall. He was for two years secretary of the University Chess Club and captain of the chess team also for two years. He is interested in tennis, cricket and swimming. He possesses a pleasant personality and will be found a persona grata on the staff of a school.'

Bull did become a schoolmaster, like his mother and her sisters before him. 'I don't think he particularly wanted to be a teacher,' says sister May, 'but it was expected of him. He went to London because that's where the jobs were. Living in Yorkshire, it wasn't easy, and not having an honours degree didn't make it any easier.' May also became a teacher, but in Hemsworth.

In 1982 Bull wrote: 'I am a maths graduate and an ex-teacher from a family of teachers. I have no pride in that.' A year later, he replied to a correspondent, a former student teacher who said he had worked with a colleague of Bull's, E. S. McInley (Mac):

Sadly my recollections of my time as a teacher with the London County Council are hazy indeed, and although Mac rings a bell, I fear that is all it does. All I know is that from very early in my days teaching in London I had a fairly luxuriant red beard—down to my navel—and have been attached to one ever since.

Bull's correspondent had suggested the autocratic headmaster at Dunraven School, Streatham, told Bull to shave before he returned to school. Bull, he said, vowed never to shave again. And he did not, even though the beard—changing through the years from fiery red to mellowing white—made him appear shorter than the five foot, five and a half inches recorded as his height on a National Service Grade IV Certificate dated 23 June 1941.

One account of Bull's days as a teacher appeared in his foreword to a collection of amusing stories on racing, *The Wit of the Turf*, published by Leslie Frewin:

The wittiest crack I ever heard in my life was made at my expense by a nine-year-old schoolboy when I was a schoolmaster in Walworth just before the last war. Walworth was a rough area: the kids were tough, and maintenance of discipline was part of the job. I was an easy-going teacher and I got on well with the 40-odd rascals in my charge. Only rarely did I find it expedient to play the heavy disciplinarian. One day, I came back to the classroom to find that whoever had been refilling the inkwells had made an unholy mess of the job. There was ink on the desk tops, on the floor, and all over the place. Things had been getting a bit slack recently. A display of authority seemed called for.

I should tell you that this was the time when Mussolini had just invaded Abyssinia. Mussolini was the embodiment of force and arrogance: Mussolini was the great dictator: Mussolini was a household word.

Well, I stood up in front of the class. I glared at them until they were silent in expectancy. And then I let them have it. 'Ink', I said, 'INK! Ink is for writing. Ink is to go in inkwells. Ink is not for spreading on desks. Ink is not for sloshing over the floor. Ink should be made this way. Ink should be handled that way.' And so on and so forth.

For five minutes, in simulated anger and indignation, I lectured them upon ink, the way they were to regard it, the way they were to handle it. Finally, I laid down the law. 'Ink', I said, 'will be respected. Ink will be made the way I say it will be made. Ink will be dispensed the way I say it will be dispensed; without spilling it; without mess'. I threatened dire penalties if it were not so. 'Is that understood?' I asked, finally. 'Is that understood? It had better be!'

I surveyed the class with all the frowning severity that I could muster. They were overawed. There was dead silence; not a movement. Three seconds elapsed. Then from the back of the class came a single word in a sibilant whisper—'MUSSOLINKI'—plainly audible all over the room.

Of course I couldn't keep a straight face, and the situation dissolved in laughter, which I joined. I admired that lad. In a single spontaneously invented word he combined two ideas and demolished my authoritarian posture like a house of cards. That was wit of the highest order.

Bull had too many other interests to devote himself wholly to the business of teaching pre-teenagers—drama, chess, politics, and the theory of greyhound racing and horseracing. The last-named was to fashion his future, not teaching.

W HEN Phil Bull was a schoolboy, he bet in shillings—the equivalent of fivepences today—and recalled collecting from Caerleon at 25/1. In his prime as a punter, between 1943 and 1952, he made net annual profits in consecutive years (1945 and 1946) that would add up to a total of nearly £1.28 million these days; and in two other years his net winnings were the equivalent of almost £550,000. In all, in the years before he gave up serious betting around 1974, he made a cumulative profit that in modern-day terms would amount to over £4.6 million. He was not the biggest bettor on the scene during and for ten years after the Second World War, but he was without a doubt one of the most successful. And he had the lifestyle to go with his success.

At university—thirty years before betting on horseracing was legalised—he narrowly missed being caught in a police raid on a betting shop. Yet he also gave an early indication to those around him that he knew the score. In a letter to the American author Abe Hewitt, dated 1 February 1984, he recalled:

I was very confident Blenheim would win the Derby. I was at the university [in Leeds] in 1930, and I wrote an article for the racing enthusiasts in the Devonshire Hall hostel, in which after a long, reasoned analysis of the race, I finished up by forecasting the result: Blenheim, Iliad, Diolite and Silver Flare—a feat I've never attempted since! I had a good bet on Blenheim, but on the day of the race I was engaged in an exam and, surprisingly enough, I forgot all about the race and didn't remember it until I saw the result in the evening paper. I was treated with a good deal more respect in the Common Room after that!

This was the time that the national newspapers were holding £10,000 competitions for forecasting the result of the Derby. Of course I hadn't sent in an entry.

Had Bull made the newspaper entry—worth a total of more than £260,000 in today's terms—he would have been spared some of the experiences he encountered on moving to London in 1932 to work as a teacher. In autobiographical notes he prepared, he noted that he would occasionally pawn his race glasses, for £6 each time, to take him through those periods when his betting was not so fruitful. Then, he added: 'Success began when I really got down to tin tacks with timefigures. These gave me a valuable advantage and won me far more money than I could ever have got out of teaching. When I gave up teaching and began racing on the courses in earnest and betting in larger amounts, I won really substantially.'

In 1940 he won sufficient money from backing the Derby winner Pont l'Eveque, who romped home by three lengths from Turkhan at 10/1, to buy a house in a sought-after residential area of Putney, in south-west London. Bull had lived in Balham—at 11 Veronica Road, in quite a substantial Victorian, double-fronted, brick, terraced house—from the time of his marriage to Doris Ashley in 1935 and beyond their separation around 1938. When he and Nell Oxley began living together in 1940, they moved further west to 72 Howards Lane, into a five-bedroomed, double-fronted detached house, built of London stone with a large rear garden, which would likely fetch upwards of £200,000 on the market today.

For much of the next thirty years Bull was, according to Reg Griffin, his long-time assistant and managing director at Timeform, 'a very good professional punter. He made a lot of money out of betting, and it was this that kept him going in the lifestyle to which he grew accustomed—a big string of horses and broodmares, living at The Hollins, Rolls-Royces, and so on—and which kept Timeform going through the dark days when the company was short of money. When we didn't have enough to pay the wages during the winter, Phil would tell the bank manager to transfer £20,000, or something like that. And if we needed more when that had gone, he'd get back on to the bank and transfer the same again.'

The winnings also helped to smooth out Bull's family life on occasions. Dick Whitford, his associate in setting up *Timeform* ratings, recalls how in September 1948 Bull asked him about a two-year-old, Hello Spring, trained at Hednesford by Bob Ward, and wondered if it might win a selling race, in which sphere Ward was adept. 'I thought she would do that all right, though she had already been beaten in a seller,' Whitford remembers. 'That was on the Monday, and I thought nothing more about it until the following Saturday, when Hello Spring ran in the opening seller at Doncaster on St Leger day. Phil said I ought to have a little on the horse, and after the race [Hello Spring won by three lengths at 6/1] he told me he had won £12,000.

'In 1948 that was an enormous sum [£220,000 in today's terms], and for Phil it was sufficient to look after Nell Oxley and the children [Anne and Ray] for life, with a nice house in a posh Leeds suburb, a car and an annuity. Phil said he'd been waiting and watching for a chance to make it all happen.

'I asked him why it was on Hello Spring and not one of his own horses, and he replied: "I'm never really happy betting on my own horses. You have to wait for them to come right, and wait for the best race. You can't construct good bets; you have to wait for them to come along. For a real bet, you must have the right horse at the right time in the right race. That's something you can't contrive. But if you watch and wait, the real bets come along of their own accord." He had been watching Hello Spring for several races, seeing how it developed and what sort of race would suit it. He doubted if the stable knew as much about the horse as he did.'

Bull kept an eye on Hello Spring as a three-year-old, too. Having moved from Ward's stable to Barker's at Redcar, she did not run in another seller until the end of August 1949, when she turned out in a hot race at York and, ridden by Tommy Weston, was backed from 7/1 to 9/2 second favourite behind the useful plater Fair Seller. Bull had four bets on Hello Spring—£6,000-£960, £1,000-£140, £2,000-£320 and £1,000-£160. He collected his planned £10,000 by a head, from Fair Seller. In two seasons Hello Spring won just twice: Bull backed her both times and won almost £400,000 in today's terms.

The verdict at York was narrow but, apparently, not close enough for the bookmakers to bet on the outcome, for Bull does not record having bet on the photo-finish. This was a favourite topping-up policy with Bull, who would often be assisted by Alex Bird in the exercise. They were rarely wrong. The following month, for instance, in the race before the St Leger at Doncaster, Nassau upset the odds laid on the debutant Eclat by a short head. Bull won with his £500-£35 bet on Nassau, but more than doubled his winnings by laying out £5,700 to take a further £600 on Nassau in the photo-finish.

To give another example of Bull's attention to detail, at Goodwood the previous year, 1948, he stood to win £4,000 for £1,000 staked on Laurelle II. He invested the full amount of his winnings on the outcome of the photo-finish, and collected an extra £800 when the verdict was officially announced as a neck in favour of Laurelle II over Gremlin.

Bull was not afraid to lay the odds; the weekly betting analysis for 1962 which follows illustrates that the average starting price of his winners rarely rose above 2/1. Returning to 1949, Hello Spring's example was an exception. It was followed a little over a fortnight later by a more typical outcome, as Bull waded in to back the two-year-old Weensland at Ayr. He traded eight bets, starting with an even £1,000 and ending with a bet of £400-£700. Weensland won comfortably and Bull collected £3,700 for his stake of £5,050. Two days later Weensland went on to Bogside and doubled his margin of victory; Bull staked a total of

£5,000 and won £2,000. In both cases he gained 'the value', since Weensland started at 1/2 at Ayr and 4/11 at Bogside. He found the value when Weensland next ran, backed from 2/1 to odds-on in a nursery at York, but lost £720 when the hat-trick was foiled, though the speedy colt still stood Bull in at a tidy profit.

Bull set out his thoughts on the attraction of racing and betting in autobiographical notes he made in 1969:

I'm not a gambler. Betting as such doesn't interest me, I couldn't be interested in bingo or roulette, they are pure gambling. Racing is different. It's a continuing play with a fresh set of individual characters every year. Not a who-done-it, but a who'll do it. There's a challenge to solve, and success or failure is reflected in one's bank balance. You can't kid yourself. It's a colourful and living scene. Fascinating, with a wide selection of people involved. A fascinating challenge to one's skill.

The path was not always smooth. Whitford recalls: 'There were times in the late-Forties when money was very short indeed. Once he asked my wife Julie to order something from a big grocer's in Halifax and she was horrified to be told Mr Bull would get nothing more until he had paid at least something from his bill. This was probably just an oversight, but there were times when he would ask me not to cash my salary cheque "until next week". And there was a moment when it looked as if his fine broodmare Lady Electra might have to go to William Hill as a loan repayment, though Phil was probably saved by "just one bet", as he used to call it.'

Yet whoever else had to wait for his money, the bookmaker was always paid. Whitford again: '"Miss once", Phil used to say, "and you're done for". And he was always impeccably dressed when he went racing, almost to the point of being dandyish. Before leaving The Hollins to go to the races, he would stand in the hall and carefully brush away any dust or lint from his grey trilby hat, and would inspect the contents of his cigar case. "My stock in trade," he would say. "I may be broke, but I mustn't look broke."'

The details contained in his betting books from 1943 onwards suggest there was never much long-term risk of his losing everything, but he did have his bad days. In 1970 he recounted one to Kenneth Hurren for a feature article in the *Daily Telegraph* Magazine. Bull had gone to Hamilton Park to back a two-year-old, but he recalled: 'The more I bet on the horse, the longer the odds became. I lost £6,500 [at least £30,000 in today's terms] and ended up giving myself a lecture on my folly. I had been so carried away with the the horse's theoretical chance that I hadn't noticed the obvious indications that something was wrong with the horse—which everybody seemed to know except me. On the racecourse, eyes are usually more valuable than ears, but on this occasion the ears had it.'

Normally, however, Bull would take little notice of so-called 'information'. Reg Griffin says: 'It was never of any great concern to know a horse was fancied, or what other people had to say. In fact, if he felt strongly enough about a horse, even if he heard something to the detriment of its chance in a race, he would still go and back it. Even if the bookmaker would sometimes appear to know more than Phil did, he would still back his judgement. If he was right, fine; if he was not, fine again. It didn't make any difference to his outlook.

'He dealt with everything with great equanimity. I did once ask him when he would start to worry about his losses, and he said it would probably be when he was £20,000 down, which was a substantial amount to him.

'In fact, there was a time, in 1963, when he was losing about that much just before the Ebor Handicap at York. On the Monday before the race he decided he would take the form book up to the bathroom and look at the Ebor. He loved lying in the bath for hours, reading a book, smoking a cigar, watching television. If he got the opportunity, he'd stay up there for two or three hours, topping up the water when it went cold.

'On this occasion he says he jumped up saying "Eureka!", which is probably one of his apocryphal stories, but he'd found a horse for the Ebor. It was Partholon, who'd run second in the Timeform Gold Cup the year before, had taken time to come to himself as a three-year-old but had 7st 7lb in the Ebor and was due to be ridden by Joe Sime. On Tuesday morning Phil rang up one of the bookmakers and had £20,000–£1,000 about Partholon, and on the Wednesday he won by a head from Lester Piggott and the four-year-old Arctic Vale, with Sime putting up a pound overweight, at 100/6. At a stroke Phil was back level for the season, purely as a result of his study of the form book.'

Since it was a principle to put the bookmakers top of the list for payment, Bull generally had excellent relations with the men who took his hefty investments. He admitted to having been 'welshed' at York in 1929, when a bookmaker made off with his winnings from Flittermere in the Yorkshire Oaks. And he frequently reminded fellow punters that in 1963 he suffered at the hands of a bookmaker 'who debunked to Australia with £6,500 of my money'—yet he was either chivalrous to a fault or believed he might still see his money, for he never publicly named the bookmaker, who was Eli Rose. Otherwise he had many a good word to say about the boards bookmakers—not to mention a few home truths about their rails colleagues—as in a letter to the editor of *The Sporting Life*, dated 24 May 1971:

As a substantial backer of long standing, I know quite well where I can get a decent bet and where I can't. I have not the slightest objection to taking a stroll to the remoter regions of Tattersalls whenever necessary. Let me also say that it's over a quarter of a century since I made it a firm rule never to expect a bookmaker to lay me a bet bigger than he was prepared to lay; that it didn't take me very long to discover each layer's degree of preparedness, and learned to modify my bets accordingly, and to cease knocking on the doors of those who were habitually not at home, or were ill-mannered or prone to cut the odds as a way of declining to bet.

We have in the North (and in the South, too) a number of excellent bookmakers, like Billy Flintham, Leslie Steele and John Joyce, who have been betting on the boards at most meetings for many years without making a song and dance about it, who quote prices for all horses and are invariably prepared to lay them to lose substantial amounts, while their confreres who should be betting on the rails are still enjoying a between-races sojourn in the bar, waiting for the boards to formulate a market for them to follow.

I have not known any of the bookmakers named ever to be discourteous or to indulge in ducking and flimping, the way a few of the preferred-pitch stallholders on the rails (it would be flattery to call them bookmakers) frequently do.

I'm certainly not on the side of the big bookmaker against the small man. Both usefully serve different populations of punters, and I should be the last person to wish to see the small racecourse bookmakers swallowed up by the Hill and Ladbroke leviathans. Indeed, for the big SP betting-shop organisations to gain complete control of the on-course market would be a monumental disaster for all punters, both on and off the racecourse.

Such an eventuality would not have entered Bull's head nearly thirty years earlier. His biggest problem at that stage was not how to get his bets placed with the bookmaker, but how to get the information which led to the bets in the first place. Bull had discovered time as the key to his betting, and based almost the whole of his operations on his time-test calculations, which he passed on to the public as the Temple Racetime Analysis. There were other followers of time—and Bull was involved in a protracted legal case with one such provider from 1939—but he believed his service was most likely to produce more profit. It was based on scientifically calculating a 'racefigure' from a horse's race performance, taking into account the course and distance, going, wind speed and direction, weight carried by the horse and its age, and using this to compile a list of 'top time value' horses, which would be followed whenever they ran. Like his betting, the basis behind it was methodical and mathematical.

Bull himself took the race times on which his workings were based. He made it plain the difficulties he sometimes had to work under in a letter, dated 26 June 1949, to his printer and publisher Bob Charman:

[Royal] Ascot is an impossible meeting. To time the racing I have to be in the Press stand; to see the horses there is a quarter of a mile to walk, and to get round to make a bet another quarter of a mile in the opposite direction. The meeting is an abomination. Added to which I had on this occasion to trim my movements and activities to the requirements of a visitor from Jamaica. Never once did I succeed in getting to the track in time to settle down before racing, and throughout the whole of the four days I was dashing hither and thither in a fury of impotent annoyance.

If it weren't for the necessity of seeing the good horses, I vow I'd never go near the meeting again until the authorities segregate all the non-racing floozies and tailor's dummies and stick 'em in a compound in the middle of the track, where they can show off their fashions without cluttering up the racecourse, and turning it into a damned garden party. Curse the place!

From the late-Thirties, Bull's most successful period of betting was based on a simple theory of time, expressed in his introduction to the Temple Racetime Analysis: 'Since a moderate horse can never record a really fast racefigure, only one such racefigure is necessary to establish a horse as a first-class animal. A horse which has once recorded a brilliant time performance will be capable of reproducing that performance when similar conditions obtain.' The theory highlighted Dante.

Reviewing Dante's first season in *Best Horses of 1944*, Bull wrote: 'Dante's time performances last season establish him as a brilliant two-year-old.' And he argued that despite Dante's being 'the fastest two-year-old seen for a very long time', there was sufficient evidence to suggest he would 'stay well enough to get the Derby distance.' After Dante had recorded the fast timefigure which attracted Bull's attention, at Stockton in May, Bull tried to persuade William Hill to buy Dante, suggesting his owner Sir Eric Ohlson would probably take £10,000 for the colt. Hill's offer of £7,000 was turned down, but before Bull could convince his bookmaker friend that £10,000 was a reasonable sum, Dante had won the Coventry Stakes at Newmarket, and it would have taken much more to prise the colt from Ohlson. Hill had missed the boat by being too slow on the draw, according to Bull, but he himself was not about to miss out. Bull recalled the events of 1945 in an interview with Geoffrey Hamlyn:

The first substantial bet of my life was on Dante for the Derby. I was so certain this was an exceptional horse that I had a serious bet on him in the Two Thousand Guineas but the mile was too short for him and he met a horse who was a little too fast for him in Court Martial. I knew he had been beaten for only one thing, he required further distance. So within an hour of his coming second to Court Martial I went along to the bookmaker Hector Macdonald and took 5/1 about him for the Derby to £1,000 each way. The following day he was advertised in the papers at 10/1! So I went in again and altogether backed him to win about £14,000 [about £280,000 in today's terms].

From 10/1 after the Guineas, Dante started at 100/30 favourite for the Derby at Newmarket and won by two lengths from Midas, with the Guineas winner Court Martial a head away third. It was the first time Bull had ever won over £10,000 on one bet. He was not the only winner, Bull told Hamlyn:

There had been a party of us at the races, and the day after Dante won the Derby we drove away in two cars. I went with Billy [Hill] in his car, and Bud Flanagan and other members of the Crazy Gang went in another, driving in front. We pulled up somewhere for a meal, and as we got out, there were Bud and the Crazy Gang kneeling on the grass verge, paying homage to me. They'd had a good win out of Dante, too.

Tables which follow illustrate the significance of Dante's victory to Bull's betting balance in 1945; it took him towards net winnings of over £36,000 for the year, nearly £720,000 in today's terms. Every year in the ten-year period up to and including 1952 he made a profit, averaging almost £22,000, and twice more he won over £30,000 in the year. In 1952 he achieved his highest net winnings for any year, nearly £38,000, though the steep rise in the cost of living index in immediate post-War years means the sum in today's terms (about £545,000) equates to much less than that for 1945.

Bull began 1952 on a high note when he concentrated his One Thousand Guineas betting solely on Zabara, of whom *Racehorses of 1951* had been most emphatic. At 134, she was rated second only to Windy City—the highest-ever rated two-year-old in *Timeform* history on 142—and her comment stated: 'We think there is little doubt that Zabara will get a mile, and provided she remains well in herself we cannot see what is to beat her in the One Thousand Guineas; the Oaks is another matter, of course, for it is by no means certain that Zabara will stay one and a half miles, and there will be much stronger French opposition in the Epsom classic.'

Come the One Thousand Guineas at Newmarket on 2 May 1952, Bull staked his all on Zabara. He had eight individual bets, ranging from £500-£60 to £3,000-£420, and in total staked £1,700 to win £10,500. Remarkably, since Bull had averaged a little over 6/1 and even took 15/2 in one bet, Zabara started at 7/1. She won by half a length, leading again after being headed by the favourite La Mirambule II in the Dip, and Bull picked up today's equivalent of £150,000.

Bull was much less successful on the other 1952 classics, the races on which throughout this period he prided himself on being able to fathom. He lost £612 on Agitator and King's Bench in the Two Thousand Guineas: he lost £2,940 on the Derby, where only his main bet, Faubourg (third), reached a place among his five horses, all trained in France; and he lost £1,170 on the Oaks. Having doubted Zabara's stamina for Epsom, he did not back her; she finished second while Bull's trio of Arbele II, his main bet, Refreshed and Triangle finished well beaten behind the winner Frieze.

However, the 1952 season ended as it had begun for Bull, with a big win executed at Newmarket. Nearula had run only once before the mid-October Middle Park Stakes, finishing second to Whistler in the Coventry Stakes at Royal Ascot almost exactly four months previously. The length of absence might have deterred some, but not Bull, whose own horses were in the Nearula stable of Charlie Elsey. *Racehorses of 1952* records that Nearula was 'now fit for the first time and greatly fancied'. Bull's betting book records that he had five bets on Nearula—£2,000-£200, £1,000-£140 twice, and £2,000-£280 twice. And the form book records that Nearula, whose price was halved on the day to 13/2, won by four lengths from the hot favourite

Novarullah. Bull's winnings of £8,000 would be worth nearly £115,000 today.

The run could not go on for ever—Bull pointed out to his Racetime Analysis subscribers, 'Losing runs are inevitable, however good a system or service may be'—and in the last week of the 1953 season he reported to his retained jockey Edgar Britt, in a letter dated 4 November:

It has been an exasperating season for me. I was winning £25,000 at one time, but this has dwindled to less than £7,000—the worst season for some years. Partly just bad luck, and partly not having the self-control to pull up when the weather broke. The biggest single factor in my failure this year (relative failure, of course) has been that owing to reorganising my timefigure system, I've had to go through the whole season without timefigures. This is something I have never done for a dozen years, and I've been absolutely lost without them, especially where the two-year-olds have been concerned. However, I'm not going away this winter, and will have everything straightened out for the opening of the 1954 Flat, when I hope to do 'em in style.

Bull admitted to Baron Henry de Gelsey, in a letter dated 11 January 1954, that the events of the previous season had left him 'in relatively low water for cash at the bank. Thirty horses in training and at stud face me with big future liabilities, and although I hope and expect that my betting will be more successful in 1954, I cannot afford to presume on that.'

Within nine months Bull was writing to de Gelsey again, in a letter dated 1 November 1954: 'As I have had a bad season, I have decided to reduce my bloodstock interests by 33 per cent.' His bad season was not simply with his own horses; others he had backed did not come up to expectation, and Bull made a net loss on his betting for the first time since at least 1943. The total was almost £14,000, or around £190,000 in today's terms. Bull managed to sell only one decent horse, Eubulides, but the tide turned again for his betting and he made a profit for each of the next five years, 1955 to 1959, though in the last three the final total was down to four figures. Even 1956, when he ended the year plus-£21,000, might have been better. He wrote to an associate in New York on 7 September: 'We've had a shocking summer here. After being £30,000 in front, I find I have now given half of it back to the bookmakers. I fear I shall never make a success of betting in the rain!'

Lack of timefigures, rain, more competitive racing: Bull could not repeat his pre-war success through the Fifties, and the Sixties were patchy, with three years of losses in the first five but net winnings of more than £30,000 in each of 1962 and 1965. Then came the virtual death knell. On 24 October 1966 the Government's freeze on wages and prices was accompanied by the imposition of general betting duty of two and a half per cent on all bets. Suddenly Bull's average net return of about eight per cent was hit hard.

Whether it was coincidence or not, 1967, the first year of betting tax, was the worst in Bull's betting experience. His net losses amounted to over £25,000, or £230,000 in today's terms. There were high spots—winning £1,692 on Two Thousand Guineas day, with £480 each way on Royal Palace the major contributor; winning on balance nearly £6,000 in a week in mid-June, including £5,300 in two days at Beverley, where an even £2,000 on the three-year-old filly Mary Tudor and a bet of £2,900-£1,200 on Chicago in the Watt Memorial Plate stacked up; and winning £2,311 on the day at Newmarket in early-October, when £290 each way at 17/2 on Quartette in the Stayers Handicap paid off.

But there were too many losing weeks. At the end of May he lost £7,560 over six days, including an afternoon at Catterick when he left behind over £3,000, despite successfully laying the odds (£1,000-£4,200) on his own horse Ovid. On the Scottish circuit in September he lost £6,762 on the week. This time Ovid—or to be more precise, the Ayr stewards—cost him £2,250 in an amateur riders' race, when, starting at 4/9, he was relegated to second after passing the post first. Bull's special betting agreement which would have covered such a ruling was still some fifteen years away.

This was also the year of the Philoctetes betting coup, of which more later, but the figures quoted show that that week's loss of £3,725 was by no means the worst. However, Philoctetes himself more than made amends over the next three seasons, 1968–70, with eight wins. Bull backed him on each occasion; he also backed him when he lost, but not every time. When Philoctetes reappeared in 1968, for the first time since the abortive Yarmouth episode, Bull won £5,000, and a further four handicap successes that season netted wins of £2,500, £2,750, £900 and £1,600. Bull did not back him when he finished third at Wolverhampton—he went instead to Ayr that day and won £1,562 on his betting—but three other defeats cost a total of £2,050, to leave Bull with a net profit of £10,700 on his bets on Philoctetes in 1968, over two and a half times what the colt had cost him in one week the previous year.

In 1969, when Philoctetes stepped up in grade, Bull refrained from backing him at Royal Ascot and in the Northumberland

Plate (where his £100 bets on four horses included the 6/1 winner Even Say). But he collected a total of £3,075 from major handicap wins at Chester and Redcar, though the Chester return was lessened by the £400 he laid jockey Peter Robinson, and £200 and £100 laid respectively to trainers Ernie Fellows and Staff Ingham. After a defeat in the Ebor, Bull ended the year £1,815 in pocket from backing Philoctetes. The following year most of it went back to the bookmakers, as his £850 won in the Northumberland Plate had to be offset against a total of £2,000 lost elsewhere, half of it in the same amateur riders' race where Ovid had been relegated five years earlier. At the end of the three seasons Bull had made a net profit of £11,365 on his Philoctetes bets, a little short of £100,000 in today's terms. The Yarmouth defeat could be put even farther to the back of his mind, though whether those members of the Timeform staff who took part in the failed coup followed Philoctetes quite so closely in the next three years is to be seriously doubted.

On 30 December 1971 Bull wrote to Mr F. Murgett, a correspondent who had inquired whether it might be worth his becoming a professional backer:

Will it help your ego if I told you that two years ago I made about £20,000 profit from my betting and paid (via the bookmakers) about £24,000 tax—leaving me with a net loss of £4,000 after what would have been for me, in the old days, a damn good year? This last two years, one way and another, I have managed to make a few thousand pounds profit after tax. But take my word for it: there's no percentage in trying to back horses for profit these days. Bet for fun—yes! Bet very, very seldom, very, very carefully; with all the resources of skill at your command; and you may, perhaps, make it pay. But it's tough and hazardous, make no mistake about that.

Two years later, in a letter to George Wigg dated 25 March 1973, following a net loss of more than £22,000 on his betting in 1972, Bull mentioned 'a medium-term bank loan of £40,000' and wrote:

I expect I'll be having to sell the more saleable commodities [among his bloodstock] to keep my head above water! I can no longer rely on betting profit. The tax destroys the prospect. It's tough for us capitalists, you know—to keep ourselves in the affluence to which we are accustomed!

Remembering Bull's extreme political views, there is more than a hint of tongue-in-cheek about this observation to a former

Labour MP. But there also exists an indication of the apparent contradictions in Bull's character. He did believe in revolution and the end of modern democracy, but he lived the life of a capitalist, running a medium-sized business, enjoying the fruits of a well-stocked, if never totally financially-stable, lifestyle. He explained this ambivalent attitude to journalist Kenneth Hurren for a *Daily Telegraph* Magazine feature article in 1970:

I have no ethical justification for my position. Superior intelligence, largely an accident of birth, is no more deserving of reward than superior height. But when in Rome, one does as the Romans do, at least until the Roman Empire falls.

By 1974 Bull's serious betting was over. He continued to take on the bookmakers—with his background and reputation it would have been unthinkable had he not—but his betting was almost always strictly for fun, and he no longer stuck rigidly to applying the principles of skill and logic. Gone were the four or five hours of study in the evening; in their place occasionally came advice from one of his trainers based on work on the gallops, which did not carry the authority he had sought in the past and which at times cost him dearly. Advancing age and the betting tax, which by this time had become 4 per cent on-course and 7.5 per cent off-course, saw off Bull as a major player in the betting ring. Towards the end of 1977 he informed George Wigg in a phone call: 'I won about £37,000 and paid about £17,000 to Mr Healey [Chancellor of the Exchequer].'

Bull saw the working of the betting tax at first hand; he feared for the influence of those who were not acquainted quite so closely with its effect. In a letter to Ben Clements, the former editor of *The Sporting Life*, dated 23 March 1975, he wrote:

The greatest danger to racing is squeezing the last drop of juice out of the punter. The worst of it is that the two dead-heads presently running the show haven't a clue, and are indeed actively encouraging the milking. Leverhulme: 'The punter surely won't mind paying an extra two per cent tax for the good of racing.' He hasn't a suspicion that the tax the punter is really paying for his pleasure is not eight per cent but 80 per cent! (Stakes £100. Deduction £18 lost, of which £8 is tax. Real tax £8 on £10 paid for pleasure).

Bull argued his point again in his submission to the Royal Commission on Gambling in January 1977, drawing on normally confidential information culled from the bookmakers to show the real rate of tax. Rates of duty had changed since he put Ben Clements in the picture and Bull calculated the return to the punter at approximately £80 of each £100 bet. About the £20 which punters collectively were actually losing, Bull argued:

This £20 already incorporates Betting Duty of £7.50 so the real price of the punter's exercise with his £100 turnover is £12.50. This is what it would have cost him had there been no betting duty. And it is upon this £12.50 that he is being charged £7.50 by the Chancellor. The punter is, in fact, paying *ad valorem* duty on his betting at the rate of 60 per cent. Those who don't appreciate this, and think the punter pays a mere 7.5 per cent tax on his betting, are not only wrong, they are wrong by a factor of eight.

Some correspondents to *The Sporting Life* failed to accept all Bull's points. One took him up on a statement that 'you can't get out of the punters' pockets what isn't in them' and questioned Bull's suggestion that 'the right way to seek to increase revenue from betting is to increase not the rate of deduction, but to increase the betting opportunities through evening racing and Sunday racing, with betting offices open for both.' Bull replied on 7 March 1977:

The contradiction is more apparent than real. As I put it on one occasion, phrasing it very carefully, 'the overriding fact is that the punter's pocket contains only a finite amount of cash he can afford and is prepared to lose.'

The operative words are 'can afford' and 'is prepared'. They're not the same. What he can afford to lose is what's in his pocket. That's pretty well fixed. But what he's prepared to lose is not.

The position is this: if you increase the take-out from his bets, you discourage him from betting, but if you increase the number of betting opportunities, you encourage him to bet. You offer him more play and he gets more fun out of the exercise. Obviously you can't take out of his pockets more than is in them. But you may take out less. Putting up the rate of deduction is conducive to just that. It discourages the punter and makes him aware that he's wasting his money. That's why increasing the duty and Levy will prove counter-productive, whereas increasing the betting events does not have that effect.

That's the argument. It's an argument against tax and Levy increases, and in favour of more betting opportunities. The former discourages the punter; the latter encourages him. Either way you can't get out of the punters' pockets what isn't in them. But in the former way you'll get less.

Bull was discouraged by the tax (nowadays, no longer applicable on bets laid on the course); it pulled the comfortable rug from beneath his feet. He died four years before betting shops were allowed to open beyond 6.30pm, and six years before they were permitted to open on Sundays. But he did have one final, unexpected shot to play. It came in his pursuit to change Jockey Club minds about Rule 153, relating to punishment for riding offences. It involved his drawing up an agreement with individual bookmakers to pay on first-past-the-post terms, except under three minor circumstances, including a jockey failing to draw the correct weight or a disqualification for horses not running the correct course.

It was Bull's attempt—one of his last—to highlight his belief in the iniquities of the rule. He negotiated with various book-makers from the summer of 1982, and in a letter to each, explaining his purpose, he pointed out that the rules meant that 'no jockey can be disciplined by being fined or suspended for careless, reckless, dangerous or improper riding without the horse itself being disqualified to last place'. He went on:

In consequence, horses which have won manifestly on merit, sometimes by wide margins, are frequently disqualified to last place in order to enable the Stewards to discipline the jockeys for careless or improper riding etc, with no regard whatever for its effect upon the equity of the result, or for the interests of the owners of the horses involved or the punters who bet on them.

This is not the case in France, nor, I believe, in any other country: only in Britain do the Rules of Racing demand that the misdeeds of jockeys have to be visited upon owners and punters in this way.

The most ludicrous example of this was the disqualification of Centurius after he had finished second a neck behind Bustomi in the King Edward VII Stakes at Royal Ascot in 1981. The Stewards decided that Centurius had interfered with Bustomi, and that Walter Swinburn's failure to keep the horse straight constituted careless riding, meriting a six-day suspension. Automatically the Stewards had no option but to disqualify Centurius to last place, regardless of the fact that Bustomi, the victim of the interference, had won the race and that the two horses had finished lengths clear of all the other runners, none of whom had suffered interference from Centurius. The owner of Centurius was thus deprived of second prize money and punters who had backed Centurius each way lost their money. The idiotic injustice of this is obvious.

It is over thirty years since I first drew attention to the unsatisfactory nature of the Rules relating to these things. More recently, as a member of the Council of the Racehorse Owners Association, as the representative of punters and racegoers on RILC, and also as chairman of the Horseracing Advisory Council, I have sought to persuade the Jockey Club to amend their rules so as to separate the disciplining of jockeys from matters concerning alteration of the placings. My efforts have been to no avail.

I am unable to do anything further to advance the interests of owners and trainers who find themselves victims of Rule 153, but the interests of punters and bookmakers can be protected by their entering into a betting agreement designed to circumvent the unfair consequences that frequently flow from Rule 153.

After consultation with many bookmakers and with the Editor of *The Sporting Life*, I have therefore drawn up such an agreement. I regard it as unfortunate that punters and bookmakers should have to have recourse to such action to protect their interests. But I take the view that it is more acceptable for a punter (or bookmaker) to suffer the consequences of interference in running than the consequences of Rule 153 in the stewards' room.

Until such time as the Jockey Club amends its rules relating to in-race incidents and the disciplining of jockeys, I shall bet only with bookmakers who approve of and ratify this agreement. If and when the Jockey Club decides to amend its rules, it may be that the agreement can then be terminated. We shall see.

> Colin Webster was the first to sign an agreement with Bull on these terms; by the end of July 1982 he had been joined by William Hill, John Joyce, Leslie Steele, Tony Unwin, Roy Christie, Michael Geraghty, Ladbrokes and Fordette. The following year Dan Flynn agreed, and in 1984 the pack was completed by Selwyn Demmy, Laurie Wallis, Neville Berry and Kinghorns. Only Francis Habbershaw declined, admitting that he was loath to lose a punter but explaining: 'I do not agree with you on the contents on which the agreement is based. I sincerely believe it would be a retrograde step to retain placings and not penalise the offending parties. I contend it would increase rough riding and standards would drop because of it. I wish to thank you for placing business with us in the past and wish you all the best in the future.'
>
> The future was limited. The Jockey Club largely stuck to its guns over Rule 153; Bull's betting activities continued to decline.

Not until after his death was the rule seriously amended, to take some account of Bull's observations, but it did not go so far as he had been advocating so strenuously and for so long.

THE GOLDEN RULES

It was an indication of Phil Bull's background and outlook that when in 1942 he published his approach to betting, it came in a slim volume entitled *The Mathematics of Betting*. It accompanied the *Temple Racetime Analysis of 1941*, and the early chapter headings reflected the title—Odds & Chances, Trading in Odds, Covering Bets, Making a Backer's Book.

There followed advice when to bet each way, why not to follow systems, and how to set up and use a betting bank. It was a model of its type, at the time, and much of the advice still holds good. Bull summarised most of the points when he compiled his notes—which began in note-form but in the nature of his verbosity, gradually expanded before returning, as if in exhaustion, to one-word observations—for an article which appeared in *The People* in March 1965:

OBSERVATION ON RACECOURSE: Attend to the horses and not to people. Been a rule with me all my life until these last few years. Was racing regularly for twenty years and hardly knew more than half a dozen owners or trainers. Three consequences: people thought me stand-offish, which I'm not; occasionally everyone on the racecourse is aware of something and I'm not; I have time to see what is to be seen.

WATCH THE HORSES IN THE PADDOCK: Don't watch the owners and trainers and jockeys. Look at every horse. If they are two-year-olds, note what sort of individuals they are for the future, whether they're big, backward and not ready, or whether they're fit.

Signs of fitness: if a horse carries a noticeable belly, it's a sign he's short of work: but beware of those exceptionally round-barrelled horses who always look to have too much middle and race with it. Look at the muscles of the horse, particularly those over his quarters. Those of a fit horse are clean and distinct and visible, their edge not concealed in fatty tissue. Look at the horse's coat and skin: is it clean and bright, with a pleasing sheen, or is it dull: it's an indication of the horse's well-being. So is an alert eye and general demeanour.

Watch keenly how the horse carries himself, not slouching around, listlessly, you hope, but walking freely and with purpose and enthusiasm. Don't worry about a jump or a kick. But do worry if the horse starts going round in circles with staring eyes, breaks out into a sweat and fights his lad.

Occasionally a horse is so darned well it jumps out at you: shouts at you. Never miss such a horse, even when you don't give him much chance on the book.

Sometimes paddock appearance isn't matched by racecourse performance: one that looks really well makes no show, and the race is won by an unimpressive-looking thing that slouched round the ring with its head on the floor, showing no interest in the proceedings. It happens. But not often.

THE CANTER TO THE POST: Never miss this. It can be frequently highly informative, particularly when the going is firm.

Action: whether lithe, fluent, strong and purposeful, or cramped, short, scratchy, laboured, shows knee action: is there any snap and zest about it. Look particularly at the movement of the forelegs as they are extended and at the movement of the shoulder when the forefoot strikes the ground and begins to take the weight of the body. Does it do so smoothly and easily, or is there any sort of jerkiness about it. But most of all, get a general impression of the stride. Don't stand too close: better to be on the stand than on the rail, provided the stand is not too far away.

Beware the horse that bolts to the post, takes charge of the rider. He may look an impressive sight but he'll be no better for the wasting of that energy.

BETTING FOR PROFIT: Have heard big bookmakers laugh at the very idea that a punter could win from him, and John Banks described his betting shops as money factories.

There are 15,000 bookmakers and their staff all living on and paying dividends from what they take from the punter. The Chancellor takes £50 million in tax. As a whole the punters lose annually to bookmakers and Chancellor several hundred million pounds. Neither I nor anyone else can reverse that flow.

Punters as a whole must lose, and lose substantially. But not necessarily all punters. It is still possible, by the exercise of skill, for a minority—a small minority—to beat the book. But the few who win can only win at the expense of the vast majority who must lose.

The truth is that backers are not betting against the bookmakers, or against the Tote. They're betting against one another, with the bookies and the Tote as middlemen, taking a rake-off for their services. The rake-off is so big that only a few can win. The question is how to be one of the few.

VALUE: The short answer is—You only bet when you have value: when the odds available are greater than they should be.

If you want to bet for fun, that's fine: you're entitled to go racing, back your fancy in every race and enjoy the entertainment. But if you're betting seriously—for profit, not for entertainment—backing your fancy is out, right out.

You have to discipline yourself to bet only when you can bet with value. This is the crux of the whole thing. It's so important I propose to spend a minute or two explaining it thoroughly.

Tossing coins; rolling dice. Examples of value (odds always evens) and bad value. In roulette with 37 numbers, 0 to 36, the house pays 35/1 any one number. The true odds are 36/1. You get a point under the odds. It's bad value. You can't win at the game (except by sheer chance). There is absolutely no resource available which will enable anyone to ensure a profit in the long run. Skill and judgement count for nothing. The odds are weighted only 2.7 per cent against the backer, but that's enough to skin every player at the table if he goes on long enough.

With horseracing it's an entirely different matter. The overall odds in each individual race are weighted far more heavily against the backer than they are on each spin of the wheel at roulette, but the game of horseracing presents enormous opportunities for the exercise of skill and judgement. That's what makes it possible to win.

WEIGHTING OF THE ODDS: How much are the odds weighted against the backer at horseracing? I worked out the figures for the twelve races at Wincanton and Uttoxeter last Thursday. On one race of four runners the odds were only 9 per cent over-round, on another they were 71 per cent over-round. They averaged 28 per cent over-round. The odds are shorter than they should be in the proportion 100:128. This is the degree to which the odds are weighted against the backer.

On the face of it this looks very severe indeed, compared with the 2.7 per cent at roulette. So it is. But there are two important points to be remembered. First that it is generally the outsiders in the field whose odds are most cramped—12 or 14/1 chances that should be 50 or 66/1. Second that it is the overall odds about all the runners taken together that are heavily weighted against the backer: not necessarily the odds against each individual horse.

FITNESS, JOCKEYSHIP, THE DRAW AND OTHER FACTORS: No backer should underestimate the importance of these things. Fitness: early in year, back end of season. Jockeyship: plays big part in races, never underestimate. Apprentice allowance: well worth allowing for in long-distance races: very valuable on occasions with very good boy. Draw: I have never paid so much attention to it as others.

GOING CONSIDERATIONS: Most important of all. Types of horse suited by each: mostly matter of action: also a matter of build and body weight. Next to fitness and well-being this is the most critical factor in handicaps.

DISTANCE CONSIDERATIONS: Very important with two-year-olds, important with three-year-olds early on. Should mostly have it sorted out for horses by the time they are four years, but not always. Surprising how many first-class trainers (and I mean first class) fail to run their horses far enough. Reason is usually jockey's reports. Breeding is far and away the best guide. Surprising how little notice some trainers take of the horse's dam and her background.

MERIT OF THE HORSE: Not as easy to arrive at as many people think: not a mathematical exercise, not a jigsaw puzzle—the pieces don't fit. Detective work (removing other variables). Interpretation.

EACH-WAY BETTING: Mug punters' idea—bookies welcome it. Best each-way races and best each-way bets—can't get on. Change from one-quarter to one-fifth the odds enough to kill each-way betting from punter's point of view.

FALLACIES:
1. You should never bet odds on.
2. A bet isn't a good bet till it has been hedged.
3. The concept of luck.
4. The fallacy of staking systems.
5. The fallacy of sequences—no help to be got from past record of favourites or second favourites.
6. That you should not bet in every race.

ADVICE: Importance of self-control. Temptation to chase losses. Temptation to regard the race as already won before the horses are off. Allowing yourself to become so mesmerised by a horse that you can't recognise lack of value in its price, e.g. Tudor Minstrel in Derby, and Nijinsky in Champion Stakes [having seen Nijinsky in the paddock at Newmarket, Bull laid £4,500 to £2,000 on him, then went on to the stand to discover Nijinsky did not have the 'zest and freedom' on the canter down that he expected. In a letter to Vincent O'Brien, dated 18 November 1970, Bull wrote: 'I shrugged it off, thinking it was nothing of importance. Heigh-ho! How often we see these things and refuse to accept them because we don't want to. The horse we saw in the Champion was not the Nijinsky we saw earlier in the year: not by 10lb'].

So try to step outside yourself and see what it is you are really doing. Be objective.

Importance of equanimity: win or lose.

THE TEN COMMANDMENTS

Considering Phil Bull's atheistic views on religion, he would have taken great delight in compiling a list of Ten Commandments to accompany a feature on his life and times in the *Daily Telegraph* Magazine in October 1970. Some might have said horseracing was Bull's religion; he would have been appalled at the association. Whatever, he made heavy weather of adding a biblical flavour to his top ten tips and setting them down on paper. He first had to be supplied with a handwritten copy of the Christian version, which he used for guidance in devising a betting equivalent. The resulting piece of work was not published in the *Daily Telegraph* Magazine; the feature article was.

Bull came up with two versions; he took one thought but strained to produce different expressions using his idea of religious wording. Since neither version was published, it is impossible to be certain that the following is the preferred list. It reads slightly more coherently than the other—even if there is a hint of the Lord's Prayer in at least one case—and since Bull would probably have preferred this as the basis for selection, it is included:

Seek where thou wilt for the winners, but bet only when thou seest value; deliver thyself from the temptation to bet in every race.

Put not thy faith in luck, nor in the law of averages, nor thy trust in staking systems, for these are delusions.

Let thy stake be related to the depth of thy pocket and to what thou regardest as the true chance of the horse; that which hath the greater chance deserveth the greater stake.

Thou shalt not bet each-way in big fields, unless thou art well satisfied as to the value of the place bet.

Bet with Book or Tote according to thy judgement: thus shalt thou endeavour to get the best of both worlds.

Thou shalt not bet ante-post except upon horses that are known to be definite runners.

Beware the man who would sell thee a system: if thou knowest a profitable one, preserve it to thyself in silence.

Double and Treble if thou must; but bet not upon objections, for thou hast not the evidence and the stewards know not what they do.

Let thy betting be informed by wisdom and diligence, and tempered by patience and caution, and leavened but a little with boldness.

Let thy bets be well within thy means: he that would make his fortune in a week loseth his ducats in a day.

BETTING ANALYSIS

For the first time it is possible to assess exactly how successful Phil Bull was as a backer of racehorses. His betting records for the years 1943 to 1974 inclusive were kept meticulously, and his net winnings or losses follow.

They show that for eleven consecutive years he made a profit, and had only one losing year in the first seventeen. Thereafter, starting in 1960, he showed a profit eight times, and a loss seven times. He no longer kept comprehensive records after 1974.

In the 1940s (seven years) he made a cumulative profit of around £150,000 (equal to £2.86 million, or an average of £408,256 a year, in today's terms). In the 1950s his cumulative profit was a little over £111,000 (£1.55 million, average £155,289 p.a.); in the 1960s under £30,000 (£257,576, average £25,758 p.a.), and in the first five years of the 1970s, just over £6,000, which equates to a loss because of the rapid fall in the value of money in the meantime. Despite the late decline, Bull's cumulative profit over thirty-two years added up to the modern equivalent of £4.66 million, for an average of over £145,000 per year.

The year 1962, which has been taken as an example for more detailed analysis, was successful in terms of net winnings of £32,679, or a fraction more than £350,000 at today's values.

Bull's biggest bets in the early part of the season were struck on his three-year-old filly Kermene (by Persian Gulf out of Dynamene, a winning sister to Anadem and half-sister to Arietta), who had had one run over six furlongs as a two-year-old and began her second season at middle distances. He lost £2,000 when she reappeared to be second in the Warren Stakes at Epsom (25 April), £2,500 when at 5/2 on she was second in a four-horse plate at Birmingham (21 May) and £2,000 when she was last of five in a £200 stakes race at Lincoln (30 May). She won her next two outings and Bull recovered some of his losses with £1,800 on her when, backed from 2/1 to 13/8, she won a maiden plate at Manchester (13 July), and £1,500 on her when, as 3/1 second

BETTING RESULTS 1943–74

Year	winnings/losses £	1995 equivalent* £	Cumulative £	1995 equivalent £
1943	2,709	54,988	2,709	54,988
1944	12,412	249,462	15,121	304,450
1945	36,142	719,315	51,263	1,023,765
1946	28,106	556,965	79,369	1,580,730
1947	12,577	241,420	91,946	1,822,150
1948	26,720	488,890	118,666	2,311,040
1949	30,924	546,750	149,590	2,857,790
1950	12,337	211,409	161,927	3,069,199
1951	16,859	257,868	178,786	3,327,067
1952	37,892	544,660	216,678	3,871,727
1953	6,171	87,808	222,849	3,959,535
1954	–13,919	–190,530	208,930	3,769,005
1955	10,008	129,378	218,939	3,898,383
1956	21,186	265,837	240,124	4,164,220
1957	3,931	47,136	244,055	4,211,356
1958	8,911	104,932	252,966	4,316,288
1959	8,016	94,393	260,982	4,410,681
1960	–13,848	–160,092	247,134	4,250,589
1961	–12,828	–142,129	234,306	4,108,460
1962	32,679	352,710	266,985	4,461,170
1963	1,046	11,087	268,031	4,472,257
1964	–13,969	–141,227	254,062	4,331,030
1965	30,747	297,588	284,809	4,628,618
1966	21,016	196,170	305,825	4,824,788
1967	–25,501	–232,367	280,324	4,592,421
1968	–1,885	–16,211	278,469	4,576,210
1969	11,205	92,047	289,673	4,668,257
1970	–5,619	–42,794	284,054	4,625,463
1971	3,764	26,290	287,818	4,651,753
1972	–22,089	–143,332	265,729	4,508,421
1973	7,780	45,646	273,509	4,554,067
1974	22,478	110,702	295,987	4,664,769

*Source: Barclays de Zoete Wedd Securities Equity/Gilt study, 1995

CUMULATIVE WINNINGS (1995 equivalent in brackets)

1943–52: £216,678 (£3,871,727); average £21,668 (£387,173) per year
1953-62: £50,307 (£589,443); average £5,031 (£58,944) per year
1963-74: £28,973 (£203,599); average £2,414 (£16,967) per year
1940s (7 years): £149,590 (£2,857,790, at average of £408,256 per year)
1950s: £111,392 (£1,552,891, at average of £155,289 per year)
1960s: £28,662 (£257,576, at average of £25,758 per year)
1970s (5 years): £6,314 (equivalent to loss of £3,488, at average of £698 per year, due to increase in cost of living index)
Accumulative total winnings over 32 years: £295,958; equivalent to £4,664,769 (average £145,774 per year) in 1995 terms.

BETTING ANALYSIS BY WEEK – 1962

Week Ending	Stakes £	Cumulative Stakes £	Net Profit/Loss	Cumulative Profit/Loss	Cumulative % Profit/Loss	Average SP of Winners
Mar 31	1,150	1,150	−575	−575	−50.00	1.875
Apr 7	300	1,450	−300	−875	−60.34	N/A
Apr 14	4,890	6,340	2,165	1290	20.35	1.433
Apr 21	1,400	7,740	880	2170	28.04	0.824
Apr 28	8,040	15,780	−845	1325	8.40	1.234
May 5	8,885	24,665	−2,217	−892	−3.62	3.200
May 12	11,634	36,299	−99	−991	−2.73	1.302
May 19	14,370	50,669	−1,790	−2,781	−5.49	1.169
May 26	7,240	67,909	−1,175	−3,956	−6.83	1.238
June 2	11,432	69,341	1,647	−2,309	−3.33	1.485
June 9	22,920	92,261	3,355	1,046	1.13	1.522
June 16	21,730	113,991	1,908	2,954	2.59	1.265
June 23	21,030	135,021	3,687	6,641	4.92	1.222
June 30	22,911	157,932	−2,722	3,919	2.48	0.654
July 7	20,983	178,915	2,087	6,006	3.36	1.119
July 14	15,534	194,449	−3,081	2,925	1.50	1.021
July 21	21,940	216,389	3,240	6,165	2.85	0.835
July 28	8,675	225,064	−1,777	4,388	1.95	0.834
Aug 4	18,875	243,939	6,249	10,637	4.36	1.892
Aug 11	20,645	264,584	−2,730	7,907	2.99	1.629
Aug 18	21,854	286,438	−1,468	6,439	2.25	0.892
Aug 25	15,000	301,438	2,350	8,789	2.92	2.541
Sept 1	8,937	310,375	1,409	10,198	3.29	1.219
Sept 8	9,786	320,161	1,494	11,692	3.65	1.623
Sept 15	15,995	336,156	11,590	23,282	6.93	2.048
Sept 22	30,454	366,610	8,392	31,674	8.64	1.629
Sept 29	6,700	373,310	521	32,195	8.62	1.407
Oct 6	6,948	380,258	622	32,817	8.63	1.804
Oct 13	5,600	385,858	−77	32,740	8.48	1.723
Oct 20	1,660	387,518	−60	32,680	8.43	0.333

favourite, she won a maidens-at-closing race at Pontefract (9 August).

To Derby week, Bull's cumulative losses were £2,309 on stakes of £69,341. In the next sixteen weeks his stakes totalled £297,269 at an average of over £18,500 per week. The net profit of £33,983 realised a return of 11.4 per cent on the sums invested. This compares with a return of 8.43 per cent on the season as a whole. The most profitable time of year was the two-week period 10–22 September, embracing the Doncaster St Leger and Ayr Western meetings. Stakes of £46,939 yielded a net profit of £19,982, or 42.6 per cent. The major contributors were:

Black King — £1,500 to win £3,150: Rufford Abbey Handicap, 2m2f, Doncaster, 12 Sept, SP 11/8 (from 9/4).

Bonnard — £730 to win £5,500: Doncaster Cup, 2m2f, Doncaster, 14 Sept, SP 6/1 (from 10/1).

Ultima — £2,600 to win £3,825: Ripon Autumn Handicap, 1m6f132y, Ripon, 15 Sept, SP 15/8 (from 5/2).

Islam — £2,200 to win £4,350: Royal Caledonian Hunt Cup, 1m7f, Edinburgh, 18 Sept, SP 2/1 (from 6/4).

Choral Society — £800 to win £3,050: Arran Stakes, 1m7f, Ayr, 20 Sept, SP 4/1 (against the 8/11 favourite).

Some of Bull's most profitable years were characterised by significant ante-post successes, particularly in the Derby, where wins with Dante in 1945 and Sea-Bird twenty years later yielded profits of £13,750 and £2,333 respectively. But that was not the case in 1962, though fate dealt Bull a rotten hand. He won £2,750 from the Derby success of Larkspur but lost his £2,800 investment on Hethersett, one of seven fallers in a pile-up which also claimed Romulus, the best horse he ever bred. Bull's bets on the Oaks showed a profit, largely through the £2,500 he won on Monade. Hethersett went on to win the St Leger; whether he would have given Bull a bigger profit in the Derby with a clear run is anyone's guess.

The overall rate of return on the season was not particularly high, and given the level of stakes, an alternative form of investments would probably have yielded better returns. However, that was not Bull's interest, though he kept no running total of his sums staked to make a comparison. Scrutiny of his winning bets confirms his search for value, and his mathematical approach to beating the book.

However, as he reflected on many occasions, the more information he shared with the growing number of *Timeform* subscribers, the more it weakened his personal advantage. That might further explain why his profits dwindled so significantly from 1966, while the number of people following the advice and information provided by his company increased.

C ONSIDERING that for thirty years Phil Bull made a substantial part of his living from betting, he was curiously unsuccessful on the two occasions he organised a carefully planned strike against the bookmakers. Each time the intended coup involved one of his own horses. He was known to look at his bloodstock through rose-tinted spectacles before they went into training; he sometimes even appeared to hold a higher regard than the facts warranted once they had started racing. In that respect he was no different from many other owners. But Bull generally stood for logic and reason, not flights of biased fancy.

Perhaps he was simply unfortunate in his choices of horse and race in which to mount a coup. He would not say he was unlucky, since luck was not a commodity in which he held any store, not as far as betting was concerned. He told one correspondent: 'When you are betting, you are concerned with known and partially-known things, and judgements and estimations based upon them. Luck will assuredly affect the outcome. But since you can't know how or when, nor can you exercise control over it, you must concentrate wholly upon the things you can weigh up or control.'

When Bull's three-year-old Tudor Minstrel colt Cherubino ran in a maiden handicap over a mile and a half at Pontefract on 27 August 1960, his judgement for backing him was based largely on a piece of work on Charlie Elsey's gallops at Malton. Bull went to Malton regularly to see his horses in training, and those he managed for William Hill, and on this occasion he returned to inform Reg Griffin: 'Cherubino worked every bit as well as Diamantine; he's in a maidens-at-closing handicap at Pontefract and I intend to have a good bet on him.'

Diamantine was a four-year-old filly owned by William Hill. She had won four mile-and-a-half races in a row the year before, and had returned to winning form that summer. Cherubino had not reached the first six in his five races. There were four older horses in the 15-runner field at Pontefract; the rest were three-year-olds, like Cherubino, who was ridden by Edward Hide and carried 8st 4lb, a couple of pounds less than the expected favourite Sagely, who had won since the entries had closed.

Bull was at the height of his betting activity, and his reputation usually went before him with the rails bookmakers. The ruse at Pontefract, however, was to use members of the Timeform staff to put on his bets, after providing entrance to the course and lunch. One of those involved, Ken Cunningham, recalls that about eight took part: 'We were given a few hundred pounds each, about £200 if I remember correctly, and when we were given the signal, we were to make straight for our allotted bookmaker and put the money on at the same time, so it didn't alter the horse's price.'

That was the plan, and Bull's sister May was to give the signal from the grandstand by waving a copy of the *Daily Express*. Reg Griffin takes up the story: 'The one thing we didn't expect was a thunderstorm just before the race, which caused it to be delayed. That meant we had to get into formation again, but the signal came and everybody pounced. There were bookmakers running in all directions trying to lay off the bet, but our part went very successfully.'

Cherubino is recorded as having dropped in the betting from 6/1 to 5/2 favourite, while Sagely was knocked out from 6/4 to 100/30. Cherubino is also recorded as having finished sixth, beaten a total of twenty-three lengths by the winner as Magga Dan and the apprentice Colin Lake romped home.

The scale of Bull's bet was remarkable. If all eight 'punters' were given £200, that would equate to a total of over £18,000 in today's terms. That it was left with the bookmakers on this occasion can probably be attributed to one of those eventualities over which Bull could not exercise control—the weather. The going at Pontefract was officially 'good', but Bull's racecourse reporters returned it 'heavy' for the *Timeform* comments. It seems that Cherubino was not suited by such a surface. Or perhaps he was simply a morning glory, for he failed to win a race and at the end of 1960 was sold for 500 guineas—almost the price of a couple of bets at Pontefract.

Looking back at the day, Derek Adams, another Timeform staff member involved, recalls: 'It was an occasion none of us will ever forget. There we were, on a wet and thoroughly miserable afternoon at Pontefract, standing close to our designated bookmakers, drenched to the skin waiting for his signal, whereupon we were to plunge to a man. The operation was a success. But the patient died! The horse did nothing to suggest the sun was about to shine, either then or afterwards. A few years later he had us at it again, on a caper with just a little more to it. This time the idea was to sprinkle his money around in dribs and drabs so that none of it would seep through to the racecourse.'

Again it was August (1967) and again it involved a maiden three-year-old colt (Philoctetes). This time it was Yarmouth on Thursday 17 August, a maiden plate over a mile and three quarters with nine runners. The planning, based on attacking off-course betting shops, went on for weeks; it was executed like a military operation under the overall command of Bull but with his National Hunt handicapper Brian Skirton given the key role of making it work.

The troops—drawn largely from the Timeform rank and file but reinforced with trusted friends around the country—were armed with town maps and a list of bookmakers' addresses, and sent to reconnoitre locations from Glasgow to Eastbourne, Edinburgh to Southend. The first forays were made on 16 July and the second on 9 August. Some towns had to be ruled out for lack of easy and swift access either on foot or by car, and those 'operatives', as Bull called them on his master-plan, switched to other places that had passed the test for the big day.

In total, forty-two towns and cities were targeted: Glasgow, Edinburgh, Newcastle, Gateshead, Stockton, Middlesbrough, Scarborough, Bridlington, Harrogate, York, Leeds, Bradford, Halifax, Huddersfield, Barnsley, Rotherham, Doncaster, Sheffield, Hull, Nottingham, Derby, Leicester, Coventry, Wolverhampton, Birmingham, Burnley, Blackburn, Preston, Rochdale, Oldham, Manchester, Bolton, Blackpool, Liverpool, Bath, Bristol, Southend, London, Worthing, Brighton, Eastbourne and Harrow.

Members of the Timeform staff were generally paired off, though one or two had the comfort of working with their wives; chief organiser Brian Skirton went with his wife Judith on a memorable trip to Brighton, for instance. Bull also used members of his family—sister May, son Ray and his wife Carol—and various friends, including his current girlfriend Inge Sanders, a longtime London-based betting partner in Danny Cooper-Smith, one of his oldest associates Billie Richardson, and even his chauffeur and general handyman Bill Allen. On Bull's master-sheet, against one of the team covering Doncaster and Sheffield there appears the note, 'overalls and cloth cap'!

Each pair or individual, depending on the size of the territory and number of betting shops to be covered, was given cash in small denominations, a further £12.50 each in payment, and £20 for overnight accommodation for those who left Halifax on either Tuesday, in the case of Southend, or Wednesday (Glasgow, Edinburgh and Brighton). The amount of money given to each group depended on the number of betting shops in the town; with instructions that no single bet in any shop should exceed £4, the biggest sum was £600 to the team covering Burnley, Blackburn and Preston, down to £100 for Bull's sister, who was on holiday in Brighton and popped along to 'work' Eastbourne for the day. It was intended to strike at over 1,230 betting outlets, with a total of £5,750 set aside for bets.

Each team was also given a set of 'operational instructions and advice'. It showed that Messrs Bull and Skirton had planned everything down to the last detail—or almost:

SECURITY

1. It is highly important that complete secrecy should be observed. There should be no mention or discussion of a betting-shop operation either before the operation *or after it*. There may be several such betting-shop operations this season and any leakage about the first will jeopardise the others.

2. The operation is a big one, has been carefully planned, and, if successful, may lead to the establishment of an organisation of great financial benefit to all of us.

3. It goes without saying that the name of the horse should not be mentioned to others, even to close acquaintances. This security is vital. A small and seemingly innocuous leak may have serious consequences, and kill the whole job.

MAKING THE BETS

4. While there is no need for cloak and dagger business, it is necessary that everything should be done as inconspicuously as possible. Actions or remarks which would draw attention to oneself should be avoided.

5. It is undesirable that cars should pull up directly outside the betting shops. A few yards either way is better.

6. Some of the shops will be small ones in working-class areas. So you may think that an old suit (or overalls) will be less conspicuous than a well-tailored affair. In seaside areas one dresses as a holidaymaker.

7. The plan for covering the territory, the route(s) to be followed and the sequence of shops should be established beforehand as firmly as possible, though you may have to improvise at the time. (Town plans showing one-way streets are available).

8. Each team should have its schedule of operations (as supplied) completed beforehand for use on the day to record what is done, and to furnish (if possible) information which might be useful in the future.

9. Betting shops have different methods. Some expect you to write your bet out on betting slips which they supply. Some merely expect you to 'ask' for what you want and the clerk writes it out for you on a slip which he gives to you. There may be other methods. Fall in with their pattern if possible. But it is better to present your bet written out rather than say it out loud. So have some bits of paper in your pocket to use *if need be*.

10.   Never show large amounts of money in a betting shop. Always have the exact amount of your stake ready to hand over.

11.   Be sure, in each shop, that *the clerk records your bet correctly,* and *never* leave the shop without evidence of your bet. Normally you will be given a ticket with a serial number. That ticket should have five things on it: the name of the firm: the address of the firm: the amount of the stake: the name of the horse: the serial number. If any of these are missing *make sure* that you write them on the back of the ticket or betting slip.

12.   It is suggested that a bundle of envelopes be carried, numbered to correspond with the shops on your itinerary, and that the betting tickets be inserted on leaving the shops, the envelopes being transferred from one pocket to another as they are filled. If the envelopes are kept in rubber bands, the tickets will then be available for the pay-out in the correct sequence. Take care of these tickets: you won't get paid out without them!

13.   It is most important that no betting-shop manager should receive a bet of such a size as to lead him to ring up his head office about it (if the shop is one of a chain of shops), or to feel that he ought to hedge it to ease his liability. The critical amount is £5. So *no single bet in any shop should exceed £4.*

14.   If you find yourself in a one-man hole-in-the-corner shop, bet £2. If there are two or more clerks taking bets, bet £4.

15.   Wherever there are three or more clerks accepting bets I wish *two* bets to be made, if possible. These should be made by different people, with different clerks, and should be of different amounts e.g. £3 and £4. It is highly desirable that the bets should be made silently (in writing) so that no-one should be alerted to the fact that two bets on the same horse are being made. It is, of course, even better if the bets can be made at different times.

16.   I wish to get as much money on as possible, commensurate with sticking to the rules and not alerting the bookmakers. So, if your tour of the territory is completed with plenty of time to spare, go back to the bigger and better shops and have a *second* bet with a *different* clerk from the one you gave the first one to. If possible, the second bet should be made *not* by the same person as made the first bet.

ALL BETTING MUST CEASE
20 MINUTES BEFORE
THE SET TIME OF THE RACE

17. It is expected that the members of the team will wish to have an interest and bet their own money on the horse. Such personal bets *must follow the rules, please.* You will simply deduct these personal stakes from the total amount bet and declare by telegram the balance invested on my behalf (see below).

18. On conclusion of betting (20 minutes before the set time of the race) you will drive to the nearest phone box and notify me of the full amount invested *on my behalf* by phoned telegram, *not* by telephone call. To do this the team leader will send a telegram on a *credit card.* You won't need any money. Contact the operator. Say you wish to send a telegram on a credit card. The operator will ask for the card number, which is

37147—Z—063—322

Then send a telegram to

HOLLIN HALIFAX 63322

stating in words the amount invested on my behalf and your name. For example:-

HOLLIN HALIFAX 63322
TWO HUNDRED AND FIFTY
BRAZIER

If you have any special instructions from me regarding each-way or Tote prices, you will, of course, phrase the telegram accordingly.

COLLECTING THE PAY-OUT

Don't forget that you have to collect not only the winnings, but the stake invested as well.

In all probability it will be impossible to collect from all shops on the day of the race. Part of the collection will have to be left for the following day. There is nothing unusual about this. It is quite common. But collect what you can the day of the race, of course.

It is desirable to have a brief-case or other suitable container available to take the cash. This should normally be left in the car, in the custody of the driver.

Obviously it is highly injudicious for it to be seen that you are 'going round' collecting from various shops. Just bear this in mind.

Enter the amounts received, and the tax deducted, on your schedule, or in a notebook for subsequent entry on the schedule.

GENERAL ADVICE

Don't forget that this whole operation will be repeated, and that any information you can furnish regarding the various shops, their status, *modus operandi*, etc will be valuable. Don't hesitate to make notes about the various shops, so far as time allows, of course.

In this respect there are three things to enter on the schedule when you have made each bet. (1) Do they deduct 2½ per cent tax (2) What place odds do they pay, ¼ the odds or ⅕ the odds (3) Have they any limits, as to pay out.

Fill these in as you go round, if possible. But don't jeopardise the success of the operation by spending too much time looking around in the shop.

The one missing item was the name of the horse to be backed. That was signalled late on Wednesday afternoon, 24 hours before the race. It was Philoctetes, a Bull home-bred three-year-old, who had had four outings as a two-year-old, three over six furlongs and one over five, totally inadequate for a horse bred by the Derby winner Never Say Die out of a mare, Orinthia, who had won up to a mile and a half, including the Manchester Cup, and had bred two stayers.

Philoctetes had not run so far that season, which made the plan all the more attractive. To put 'outsiders' further off the scent, he ran in the name and colours of Inge Sanders, and was ridden by Teddy Lambton's second jockey, the veteran Snowy Fawdon, while Peter Robinson made his way to Catterick for four rides for the stable. Nobody, it seems, had warned Philoctetes of the importance of the occasion; he finished third to Gated, beaten three and three quarter lengths. But the game was up long before he went to post.

Derek Adams takes up the story: 'To those not "in the know" the horse had nothing to recommend it but a classy name. One didn't have to be a Sherlock Holmes to detect, long before post time, that we had been rumbled. Sure enough, the opening price of 5/1 quickly became 5/2 and in no time at all he was favourite, only to get beaten in a race in which on any subsequent form it should have won in a trot. Everyone was devastated, everyone except Mr Bull that is. Philosophically he blamed himself for allowing the horse to be sent out "underdone". Apparently he had been kept "quiet" at home in Newmarket, and the only piece of serious work to which he had been subjected had been a gallop on Edinburgh racecourse.'

The meticulously planned betting-shop operation apart, virtually everything else about the Philoctetes gamble proved wrong; it seemed odd at the time, and odder still later, that Bull had managed to leave so many loopholes. Even the unusual name alerted betting-shop staff, as well as the appearance of unfamiliar faces. By mid-morning most 'operatives' knew something was going on, and the word went round the multiple chains rapidly. Some of those involved—this 'operative', for instance—were quite relieved when Philoctetes was beaten; recovering winnings from certain shops might have proved difficult. In the end not all the money was invested and the place return was minimal—the Bradford team came back with £301, the Scarborough rep with £46. With £2,858 lost to betting shops and £830 paid out in wages and expenses, the operation showed a net loss of £3,625, about £33,000 in today's terms.

Peter Robinson rode two winners at Catterick that afternoon. Philoctetes won five trophy races for Bull the following year and the Northumberland Plate in 1970. Despite the grand ideas harboured before Yarmouth, the betting-shop experiment ended at around 4.5pm on 17 August 1967.

A political diatribe in dramatic form, which owed much to the inspiration of George Bernard Shaw, marked Phil Bull's introduction to printing and publishing. In 1937, while teaching in South London, he wrote *The Tramp Among the Tombstones*, and having bought a small hand press, printed copies at his home in Balham, from where he registered the business name of The Portway Press to publish the play. It was available in December that year and sold for one shilling (5p).

A review in the *Daily Worker*, dated 29 December 1937, set the tone by describing *The Tramp Among the Tombstones* as 'the type of play which can be acted by Workers' Dramatic Groups. It has simplicity coupled with freshness and vitality'.

It went on: 'The play takes place in a graveyard. A tramp who has gone there for a "kip" at the haunting hour of midnight is suddenly confronted by the ghosts of a Press Lord [Flagway], a Banker [Bankero] and an Armaments Manufacturer [Ponderas]. These three pillars of capitalist society, in a fierce denunciation, expose the very society for which they are responsible, and the part they play in it. The ignorant Cockney tramp, however, is so bewildered that he finally collapses, and is carried off by a humorous American Devil. The author does not mince words, and in unmistakeable language explains the political issues involved.'

The following month a one-inch, single-column advertisement for the play appeared in the *Daily Worker*, describing it as 'a derisive and provocative attack upon Capitalist Society, brilliant and humorous', adding that it was available 'from all Left Bookshops or Portway Press'. Ironically, on the back of the advertisement there appeared the day's programme for National Hunt racing at Newbury.

A review in a West Yorkshire evening newspaper expanded on the issues contained in Bull's first published work: 'The perversion of democracy by misrepresentation; the impudent parasitic swindle which masquerades as a financial system; the scandalous trade in death; the preposterous relation between "prosperity" and preparation for war; the criminal apathy of the public towards economic and political issues of vital importance: these are some of the social evils which fall under the lash of the author's invective. The book is enlivened by humorous dialogue, and considerable entertainment will be derived from the much-badgered cockney tramp and the wisecracking American devil.'

The identity of the writer of this fulsome review—which reminded readers that the local author 'at one time was a member of the Old Hilmians' Dramatic Society, for which he produced plays with great success'—was not revealed. However, in a letter dated 26 September 1937, Bull had outlined the four parts of the diatribe: '1, an attack upon the Press; 2, a contention that the Banking System is nothing other than a colossal piece of parasitism; 3, an attack on the private manufacture of armaments, and an exposition of the ludicrous connection between "prosperity" and preparation for war; 4, a codetta to round it off.' The similarity of the phrasing in the September letter and the December review hardly seems to be a coincidence.

Bull's letter was to Edwin C. Fairchild, a lecturer at the City Literary Institute, where Bull attended courses in political economy, economics and drama. Bull pointed out that he intended 'publishing three books dealing in short dramatic form with political subjects'. The first was 'a diatribe upon the present pseudo-democratic, politico-commercial madhouse', namely *The Tramp Among the Tombstones*; the second was 'a discussion of the problems attendant upon any attempt to replace this political and economic anarchy by Communism'; and the third was 'an examination of the fundamental problem which will still remain when Communism has been achieved, i.e. Progress'.

Bull's problem, he explained to Fairchild, was that having completed the first work, he was unable to persuade himself that it was convincing enough to justify proceeding with the others; he needed a second opinion:

I am absolutely unable to judge the thing for myself. I cannot read it as a person perusing it for the first time would do so. In fact, I cannot read it at all, for my eye travels over the words, whilst my mind refuses to stick to their meaning and persists in wandering over all sorts of irrelevant detail, arrangement of ideas, construction, faults, memories of working on it, and so on. The psychological explanation of this is, of course, quite simple, but it leaves me with the necessity of seeking some competent outside opinion. I therefore trespass upon your time and take the liberty of presenting you with a copy in the hope that, without sparing my feelings, you will give me your candid opinion and advice.

Fairchild replied a month later. He appeared to have taken Bull at his word, for though he urged him to press on with the trilogy, he made a number of pointed comments about *The Tramp Among the Tombstones*. Fairchild's letter of 22 October 1937 included the observations:

'My opinion as to the Tramp is that he lacks reality. His speech is too consistently explosive and profane. I do not assert that tramps do not use expletives in wealthy abundance; but what may be literally true requires modification if the appearance of reality is to be sustained in literature or by dramatic representation. The tramp's psychology is oversimplified. I think the Tramp should argue in disquisition on the system of private land ownership. As you present him he becomes a mere foil, on whom Flagway, Bankero and Ponderas try their speech. In Life, it is unlikely that either of these gentlemen would trouble to expound their views to a person of the mental order indicated by your Tramp.

'It would, I suppose, be difficult to introduce anything fresh into the presentation of a newspaper owner, but Flagway's speech strikes me as out of style. The dithyrambic 'O', 'O thou', and 'thy', is not in keeping with 'your belly ached'. If one speaks after the Biblical manner even his vulgarisms should be scriptural. The speech as a whole is in the mode of the Socialist criticism of the 1900–1910 period, and dates, I think, in very pronounced fashion.

'No doubt the modelling is unconscious, but all the speeches you construct for the three principal spokesmen seem to me to follow Shaw's general method very closely. The Shavian manner proceeds by eloquent and paradoxical generalisation, rather than by explicit reference to recognised events and the philosophic comment thereupon, which is the Shakespearian process of the historical and chronicle plays. Moreover, you make the three speakers highly self-critical and condemnatory of their own professions as banker, etc. Which is again the Shavian process, especially of 'Man and Superman' and 'Major Barbara'. It is an attitude rarely encountered in reality.

'As to the content of the speeches, take Bankero's. There I think you get nearest to exposition of the idea that the banking system is a 'colossal piece of parasitism'. But I know the purpose you have in writing; and I am in doubt whether I should have perceived that purpose in B's other speeches had I not known your intention.

'Indeed, the Tramp makes me think that your characters are not psychologically clear before you begin, and hence, their speech does not succeed in presenting consistent character nor reveal its depths. Consequently there is not the clash of views or action which drama requires for its movement.'

The Tramp Among the Tombstones sold out the 500 copies printed, but the second and third works in Bull's trilogy failed to appear. Nor did it seem they were committed to paper. Bull remained wedded to the play and its ideals, and more than thirty years later he sent a copy to an acquaintance in Halifax, Albert Hunt, with a letter dated 22 May 1986, in which he reflected:

I find it as relevant, apposite and true today as on the day it was written. Every word of it. Read it. You'll appreciate it, and the fire within that led me to write it two years before the outbreak of World War II in 1939. That zest and purpose I shall never recover. I have shrunk into a mere philosopher who fritters his time away on snooker, chess and the puerile business of horseracing.

Either Fairchild's comments struck home more forcibly than he might have expected, or Bull's enthusiasm for completing the trilogy waned; were the latter the case, it would not be the sole example of his failing to go through with a venture. Whatever, Bull moved on without a recorded explanation and the 'puerile business of horseracing' gradually became the focus of his working life.

As his interest in teaching declined, so his involvement with horseracing and betting increased. He shared his knowledge with the public on a serious basis for the first time in 1938, publishing weekly lists of horses which had set fast timefigures, calculated by Bull from times taken for individual races and adjusted mathematically for each horse, taking account of various factors, including the result, weights carried, going, and wind speed and direction.

The information was published in the name of William K. Temple. Bull's association with the teaching profession precluded him from using his own name, but the choice of pseudonym is poorly defined. One explanation is that it was cribbed directly from the Archbishop of York of the time, William Temple, who moved on to Canterbury in 1942. It would have fitted Bull's anti-Christ belief and might hint at a certain sense of mischief. Another suggestion, made once to Reg Griffin by Bull himself, is that he was passing through Temple tube station in London when the name stuck; he introduced William from his father's name, and added the middle initial in the way that actors of the time—Edward G. Robinson, for instance—adopted an initialled appendage for effect. Bull took care not to disappoint supporters of either theory.

After the first season, Bull produced a statistical analysis of his results for 1938, revealing nineteen winning weeks out of thirty-four, seventy-two winners from 270 bets made, and total profit of almost £166 on a level £1 stake, for a percentage profit of 61.4 per cent on the total money invested. Stop Speculative Gambling! was the order in the introduction to the Temple Racetime Analysis. 'Are you a person who must bet whenever you see a horse you fancy? Without self-discipline a profit from racing is impossible. Haphazard speculation is the backer's scourge. This book will cure you by placing your betting on a business basis. If you insist on unplanned flutters, don't waste your time on it.'

The 'business basis' of 'the first genuine application of science to racing'—the words of Bull's uncompromising advertising literature—involved backing horses on his list of fast-time performers whenever and wherever they ran. He realised that new customers would require a fresh approach to their betting if they were to get the best out of his service; he also knew the bookmakers might not take kindly to a stream of winning clients. In a 'Very Important Letter to Every Subscriber' dispatched in May 1939, he wrote:

Note particularly the fundamental difference between picking winners and following the exceptionally fast horses. This is most important. By making ourselves independent of the owner's intentions, the trainer's intentions, the jockey's intentions, the going, track conformation, bad riding, luck in running, and one hundred and one other factors which confound the form student and the trainer alike, we have placed ourselves at last in the position of being able to beat the bookmaker. However, there are one or two points of importance upon which I must lay stress right at the beginning.

I am well aware that the greatest thrill in racing falls to the people who have a big wager upon a horse which they particularly fancy, and who are lucky enough to see their gamble materialise. It is only human that we should all fall to this temptation sometimes, but we must be quite clear in our minds that this is no way to make a regular income out of the game. By all means have your little gamble occasionally if you cannot help it, but do try to exercise self-restraint. Wait for the horses indicated on the Weekly Sheets. Back them on a level stake. Force yourself never to miss a single one of them however little you may think of its chance. That is the only way in which you will get your regular income.

My acquaintance with the psychology of the backer makes me quite certain that you will be tempted to manipulate your stakes according to what *you* think of the horse's chance. Don't. If you do so, a long-priced winner will eventually turn up and you will find that your stake on it is negligible. What I think of its chance, what you think, what the Newspaper Correspondents think, or even, for that matter, what the trainer thinks, is quite beside the point. The fact is that for a horse to get on my select list it must register an exceptional time performance. Sooner or later, when conditions are suitable, it is going to reproduce that performance, and your business, as a subscriber, is to follow it until it does so. Never miss a horse because its price suggests it is unfancied. Horses only start at long prices because people do not fancy them. That does not stop them from winning.

I know only too well how anxious people are to make huge profits in a very short time, perhaps because they are influenced by the misleading advertisements of semi-honest tipsters. It cannot be done, and anybody who pretends to you that a quick fortune can be made by backing horses is a fool or a knave. The Analysis will make a steady and satisfactory profit over a long period. If you happen to come in on a highly successful week you are lucky, and if you happen to come in on one or two slight losing weeks you are just unlucky, that is all.

It is high time my subcribers had left the childish prejudice against backing more than one horse in a race to the racing infants who follow newspaper tips, and those who still suffer under the delusion that money can be made by picking winners. I hope you will forgive this forcible expression of my views, but I am really reaching the limits of exasperation where this question is concerned.

It is common knowledge that many bookmakers desire to bet only with those who lose consistently, and remove winning clients from their books by closing their accounts. It is possible, if your bookmaker realises that you are backing the Temple Racetime Analysis selections, that your account also will be closed. The risk will be minimised if you split your bets between several bookmakers, and intersperse them with a few small bets upon fancies of your own. I strongly advise this course. However, should your account be closed, I shall be obliged if you will inform me immediately of the circumstances connected with the closure, and if possible send me the letter in which the bookmaker applies the closure.

This was where William Hill entered the picture, of which more later. Undaunted, Bull pressed on, and the Temple Racetime Analysis continued until 1947, steadfastly standing by the instruction to subscribers that all named horses were to be backed on level stakes, to win only, at Tote prices. 'They are not arbitrary instructions,' his literature explained, 'they are the result of careful logical thought as to what is the policy best suited to our purposes.' The main purpose was 'putting betting on a business basis with a certain and reliable income at the end of it.' With six winning years in the first seven, he was able to advertise a rate of profit equivalent to more than 23p for every £1 bet.

Regionalised racing during the war appeared to make no difference to his rate of success. The war did, however, play havoc with a new venture, in which he provided a greyhound service, sent by post or sold direct to punters outside a number of London tracks including Walthamstow, Wembley, White City and West Ham. In July 1944 he was forced to inform clients:

We regret that owing to unfortunate circumstances resulting from enemy action, further issue of Greyhound Ratings for the six London tracks has had to be suspended for one month. The service will be resumed with ratings covering racing on 19 August, which will be despatched on the preceding Thursday, as usual.

When 19 August came around, subscribers had to exercise further patience. A follow-up letter explained:

Owing to the receipt of a buzz bomb a hundred yards from the office, the resumption of the Greyhound Service will be delayed one week.

The initial statistical analysis of Temple's service during 1938 was followed in March 1940 by publication of the *Annual Review of 1939*, Bull's first attempt at getting behind the Racetime figures with interpretation of the horses and their relative merits. He reviewed the classic three-year-olds, the class four-year-olds, the stayers and sprinters, the two-year-olds, and the big handicap winners as groups. He also began to look into Matters of General Interest: Chance and Coincidence in racing; Form versus the Time Test; Tote versus SP.

In 1941, with Bull having moved from Balham to Putney on the strength of Pont l'Eveque's Derby win, the *Annual Review of 1940* moved closer to examining individual horses, with brief opinions on such as 'unlucky Stardust' and 'great little Godiva'. Part III was devoted entirely to Pont l'Eveque. And Matters of General Interest grew to include such as The Charlatan Bookmaker, The Law and Betting, and The Honest Bookmaker.

In 1942, two volumes appeared between paperback covers for the price of one. As well as the *Annual Review of 1941*, Bull published *The Mathematics of Betting*, 'a new book on The Theory and Practice of Betting, written in straightforward and easily understood language, indispensable to anyone who bets with the serious intention of making a profit,' according to advertising for the one-shilling (5p) volume.

In a dozen chapters Bull spelled out his logical outlook on the mathematical approach to successful betting. He talked of

54

Odds and Chances, What the Backer is Up Against, Ante-post Betting, Making a Backer's Book, and When to Bet Each-way; he exposed the 'Law of Averages' and staking systems as being short cuts to avoiding the objective. And in the accompanying Racetime Analysis Review he examined briefly the top horses of 1941, including 'brilliant Big Game' and 'wilful Watling Street'; in Matters of General Interest he discussed Time, Weight and the Rous Scale, a heavy item at the best of times but an obvious precursor to what he had in mind for future publications.

The spring of 1943 signalled the biggest change in Bull's publishing career. He produced an expanded annual review entitled *Best Horses of 1942*; ninety-six pages in a paperback cover which examined individually in essay form the performances of 250 horses, the best of 1942. The written comments varied in length from a few words—St Loe: Needs strong handling; Pontoon: A half-sister to the Derby winner Pont l'Eveque but not of much account—to a posed portrait and three pocket-sized pages on Nasrullah. In both instances the pattern had been set, on the one hand for note-form assessments to be used in another publication, and on the other for an expansion of *Best Horses* into the comprehensive *Racehorses* series.

Though Bull had produced annual reviews for the previous three years, *Best Horses of 1942* marked the start of a unique departure in the field of racing literature. Much later, the *Daily Telegraph* racing correspondent Peter Scott remarked that 'the vigour and clarity' of the annual volumes 'added a new dimension to racing writing in this country'.

Best Horses of 1942 appeared under the name of William K. Temple. For the following two years the author was 'Phil Bull, professionally known as William K. Temple', but when *Best Horses of 1945* appeared, published from Bull's new home in Hemsworth, Temple had disappeared. The annual had also increased significantly in size and scope—from 280 pages and 450 horses in *Best Horses of 1943*, to 354 pages the next year, and 480 pages and 548 horses for the review of 1945. Bull did most of the writing, but he called on the assistance of the *Evening Standard*'s racing correspondent Jimmy Park to cover southern-raced two-year-olds from 1943, when Bull explained:

As I attended racing in the North throughout the season [1943], I was able to see the southern horses only on the few occasions when no Saturday meeting was held in the North, or when they ran in 'open races' at Newmarket.

From the outset Bull stamped his authority on the annual. It was generally received with undiluted praise by the many reviewers who received a copy each year; just occasionally one writer, usually John Loder in *The Irish Field*, dared to put a slightly counter view. One year Loder suggested *Best Horses* lacked dignity and impartiality, to which Bull replied in his foreword to *Best Horses of 1945*:

I do not strive to write a book whose dignity and impartiality 'will gain for it international recognition as an authoritative commentary on racing in England'. I have no particular use for dignity, and I certainly do not propose to pretend to be impartial towards what I consider to be foolish and dangerous misconceptions, any more than I presume Mr Loder to be impartial towards venereal disease or scarlet fever. I write this book annually to please myself; when I feel strongly I shall express myself uncompromisingly, and when I feel disposed to scorn Mr Loder's cherished ideas I shall pour scorn upon them. There are plenty of books on the market in which the authors waltz around impartially with non-committal platitudes to avoid expressing opinions for fear they may turn out to be wrong. I don't propose to add another to the number.

As well as establishing Bull's forthright stance, the foreword to the edition for 1945 contained reference to another feature which quickly became more obvious; the author of the innovative volume was having problems producing it in time for the market. Having swept aside John Loder's observation and acknowledged assistance from every source from the photographers to the printers, Bull opened his heart to the reader:

I should like to apologise for again having failed to get the book out in time for the opening of the 1946 Flat Racing season. The failure lies with myself, not with the printers; the plain fact of the matter being that the colossal amount of work involved has been too much for me to get through in the four months at my disposal.

It is obvious that I am going to be faced with a very serious problem in the future if I am to continue this publication in its present form. This year I have had to drive myself very hard—too hard, in fact—in order to deal individually with the 548 horses, but with the return to normal racing [after wartime restrictions] the policy of including every winner will mean my having to write up more than twice that number, and possibly with less time to do the job in than I have had this last winter. The prospect appals me. Still, I suppose it will all come out in the wash, and I shall get through it somehow or other. We shall see.

Best Horses of 1946 did come out in the wash, but it was a long time in the process. It appeared as published from Halifax for the first time, after Bull moved from Hemsworth late in 1946; it was also minus Jimmy Park's comments, and had been increased in price to £2, from two shillings and sixpence (12½p) for the 1942 equivalent, and £1 for the 1945 review. Previous annuals appeared in the March or April of the following year; the first bound copies of *Best Horses of 1946* reached Bull on 9 November 1947, thirteen days before the end of the next Flat season. Bull was suitably contrite in his foreword:

I have come to the conclusion that in some respects I must be one of the most pig-headed and obstinate people on the face of the earth; otherwise it is beyond my understanding how I could possibly be so silly as voluntarily to tackle a job as big as that which I have tackled in the writing of this book.

In writing the *Best Horses of 1945* I had been under the whip to deal with 548 horses, and I failed to complete my copy in time to enable the publishers to get the book out before the opening of the 1946 Flat Racing season; so how it comes about that I should be so foolhardy as to attempt, this year, to write up no fewer than 1,142 individual commentaries—a quarter of a million words!—I really do not know. The late lamented Edgar Wallace would have done it in a canter, no doubt; but for me, as I should have anticipated, it was impossible. It is ridiculous.

All I can say, dear reader, is that I am very, very sorry about it. The milk is spilt, and there's no purpose in crying over it, but I can assure you, as the Victorian father was wont to assure his recalcitrant offspring, it hurts me more than it hurts you. That, however, is no consolation to either of us. What I have to do is to ensure that the same thing doesn't happen again. I can promise you it won't.

The prolonged delay in publication did not seem to worry reviewers of *Best Horses of 1946*; one actually recommended it as a Christmas present. The *London Evening Standard* applauded Bull for his bravery: 'Phil Bull has done a courageous thing. He has produced his book at the end of the season instead of at the beginning. Even at this late stage it is worth reading.' And the *Glasgow Noon Record* commented on 23 December 1947: 'Old adage of "better late than never" must surely apply to Phil Bull's *Best Horses of 1946*, which has just been published.' *The Racehorse* did question the timing before sweetening the pill: 'Mr Bull's annual has almost every virtue except the dull but important one of punctuality. A book which is designed primarily to guide racegoers through the tribulations of the 1947 season, and which does not appear until Gordon Richards has ridden two hundred and fifty winners, has clearly failed in its main objective. It says a great deal for the author that the book will undoubtedly survive without any difficulty, despite this very great drawback.'

Writing *Best Horses of 1946* singlehanded kept Bull off the racecourse for four months in high summer in 1947. His net winnings from betting were less than half of the previous year, at £12,000. 'If I'd been able to get out racing regularly, it might easily have been £50,000,' he told his printer Bob Charman. 'Blast the book!'

The effort also seriously affected Bull's health, and the entire affair forced him to revise his individual approach, having promised in his foreword to *Best Horses of 1946*:

I am still anxious for 'The Best Horses' to be as comprehensive as possible, but it is evident that in future I shall have to achieve the desired result in a different way. Next year I propose to limit the number of individual commentaries to four or five hundred, and to enlarge the appendix with a new section, in which I hope to summarise, in tabloid form, the merit and the salient characteristics of every horse in training worth bothering about. That should satisfy my obsession for completeness without hewing any memorial stones.

Best Horses of 1946 appeared at the same time as preparation on its successor was due to begin, and the timing prompted Bull to delay any revision of the design. However, he did make one major concession to time; he called for outside help, commissioning Tom Nickalls (*The Sporting Life*), Quintin Gilbey (*Sporting Chronicle*) and Michael Silley (*Raceform*) to contribute essays, while Bull wrote the rest. Richard Baerlein submitted an example essay but was not accepted as a contributor. Bull's reply, dated 4 November 1947, gave an indication of his requirements for *Best Horses*:

Thank you for the specimen copy, but I'm afraid it doesn't help me much. It is a graphic description of a day's racing, but what I have to find out is the manner in which you *interpret* a horse's performances and pedigree as throwing light upon its racing characteristics and peculiarities. Descriptive writing is important, of course, but what I have to satisfy myself about most of all is the deductive, the inferential side of the business, the analysis of evidence.

For example you say that Birthday Greetings has no pretentions to staying. He is out of a sprinting mare, Clarapple. But he's by Blue

Peter, and there is no *certainty* on breeding alone that he won't stay.
Very probably you are right, but to be justified in saying that he has
'no pretentions to staying' you must have other evidence in mind.
That is what I want to get at. I want to see you take a horse, analyse
the evidence provided by his pedigree, style of racing, conformation
etc, sift it, weigh it and then produce a reasoned picture of the horse
as he appears to you and an estimate of his probable future.

> Further proof of Bull's intent came in a letter, dated 13
> December 1947, to Gilbey—who, incidentally, was taken on at the
> equivalent of £6.50 per thousand words, to Baerlein's suggested
> £5.25—following Gilbey's query about upsetting Happy Knight's
> owner if he referred to a possible respiratory problem in the horse:

I hold very firmly indeed that one ought on no account to weigh
an owner's displeasure so heavily as to preclude a mention of
anything that may be true or material, whether it is fact or opinion.
Naturally one does not hurt anyone's feelings, if it can be helped,
and sometimes it is necessary to say things delicately, or by inference
or implication; but, with me, truth and honesty of writing are all
important.

If a point is worth raising I *never* refrain from raising it because
the owner, or somebody else, won't like it. No man of integrity or
fairness would be upset by a reasonable remark about his horse. But
it must, of course, be reasonable.

For example, to state that Happy Knight doesn't stay as well as
he did, because, like all the progeny of Happy Morn, he has gone in
his wind, would be unreasonable, because it just isn't established
with that degree of factual certainty. But to say that you have an idea
that if Happy Knight's distance capacity is now less than it was, it
may conceivably be due to inadequate respiration, and to quote
Happy Morn's previous progeny as grounds for your idea, is
eminently reasonable. No fair-minded man would take exception to
such a remark, because you have stated it as an opinion and quoted
the evidence upon which it is based. You may be wrong, but at any
rate you are patently honest in your opinion, and that is what matters.

Incidentally, if it is a sin to omit a material opinion for fear of
giving displeasure, the making of remarks deliberately designed to
please the owner, or trainer, or *the Mighty*, is a double-dyed sin to me.
At present my pet anathema is Buttering the Rosebery.

I try to write honestly and fearlessly, but always *precisely*, never
going further than is rationally justifiable. So long as your concern is
truth and honesty of writing, say what you like, laddie.

Honesty in writing was an obsession with Bull, as was precision. More than thirty years later he set out his thoughts in a late-night letter, dated 7 May 1979, to Countess Bunny Esterhazy's son Alexander Elliott, who was seeking to become a political writer:

If you use words with regard to their dictionary definitions, or their common currency, they are unambiguous. And verbiage is a disease. Forget other people's writing. You are concerned with ideas. And your concern is to express them concisely, precisely, unambiguously and forcefully.

Words can be used as bullets or they can be used as cotton wool. If your purpose is concealment, mystification, prevarication or obfuscation, what you need for the purpose is long and involved sentences, with subordinate clauses and ill-defined, emotive and ambiguous words. But if your purpose is the pursuit of truth, enlightenment, illucidation and clarity, you will be sharp and sparing and precise in your choice of words, and short and crisp in the sentences in which you embody them.

'Style' is for people who have nothing to say, and wish to wrap it up in impressive verbiage. Real style of writing is a by-product of precision and force in the expression of ideas—a reflection of the passion and integrity and commitment of the writer, of which he himself, in the writing, is absolutely unaware. Frankly, style isn't worth a light. It's what you have to say that's important.

What Messrs Nickalls, Gilbey and Silley had to say in *Best Horses of 1947* might have been important in Bull's attempt to get the book published on time, but nothing could prevent him from having his own say. Quintin Gilbey began his essay on the Gold Cup winner Souverain: 'I unhesitatingly place Souverain among the very few great horses of my time.' To which Bull added, at greater length than these summary extracts:

Quintin Gilbey's opinion . . . is to be respected, but I am bound to say that it is an opinion which I find difficult to accept.

First of all, the remark that Souverain, on his two visits to this country, took on the best the world put up against him may be true enough as a statement of fact, but its implication is hardly reasonable; for where were the American, Australian and Italian representatives? —or are we to assume that in 1946 and 1947 there were no really good horses racing in the countries where Man o' War, Phar Lap and Nearco were bred? Secondly, I wonder whether Souverain's record as a whole really is good enough to demand that he be labelled a 'great' horse.

I remain unconvinced that Souverain is entitled to be regarded as one of the very few really great horses. An exceptionally good horse certainly, but not, I think, a truly great one.

> In the very next entry, for the two-year-old Speciality, Bull took Michael Silley to task for suggesting the horse's 'consistently odd way of running his races was due to lack of physical strength, making it impossible for him to maintain the gallop all the way'. Bull's explanation was longer than Silley's original essay; it included:

I cannot accept the explanation advanced by Mr Silley. Indeed, I think it not merely wrong, but quite illogical. To me there is nothing in the slightest degree 'odd' about the way in which Speciality ran his races as a two-year-old. The phenomenon of a horse's being prominent to halfway, then losing his place, and finally running on strongly in the last furlong without being quite able to get there again, is, in fact, one of the commonest on the racecourse. The import in nearly every case which involves a two-year-old is that the animal lacks pace and requires a longer distance. The correct conclusion (to me) is that Speciality is a trifle short of pace, certainly lacks acceleration, would have been better suited in May by six furlongs rather than five, and in October by seven furlongs or a mile rather than by six furlongs.

> Bull had taken on the trio of writers because their 'outlook on racing' was much the same as his. In a letter to Quintin Gilbey, dated 4 November 1947, he explained:

The difficulty was to find the right contributors: people who not only know horses and look at racing in a truly critical and intelligent way, but who can also write the King's English, and will take the trouble to write it well.

> Yet Bull had no second thoughts about criticising his contributors' comments in the very book in which they appeared, and almost certainly without their being aware until the book was published. It would have been his way of demonstrating the fair-minded stance of Best Horses. However, it happened in only one volume. Despite all Bull's expressed intentions, and the speedy work of his contributors, Best Horses of 1947 was still

late in being published. It ran to 580 pages, but contained no introduction and no apology. In a letter to his printer Bob Charman, dated 31 October 1949, thanking him for his work on the annual, Bull wrote:

The book's a really good job of work and I'm very pleased with it. Too bad the contents are as dead as mutton. Never mind, we'll have things different in the future.

This time things were different. *Best Horses* and its individual essays on the leading horses, set between dark blue binding, disappeared. In its place came *Racehorses of 1948*, with a green back and the sub-title of Timeform Annual. The new volume was slimline; it ran to 192 pages, and contained note-form comments about all 4,728 horses which ran in 1948. The length of each summary varied from a few words for the worst horses— 'good-looking wastrel: usually tailed off'—to about fifty for the best. There were no essays, but there was an important innovation, the introduction of a *Timeform* rating for each horse, along with a timefigure.

Timeform has become acknowledged as Phil Bull's invention; it represents the foundation on which his company's publications became based, the 'marriage between time and form' as he called it. It resulted in a universal handicap being compiled, in which each horse was given a rating in pounds to denote its merit relative to the next one. It was not Bull's invention. Without Dick Whitford there would have been Time but no *Timeform*.

Having been gradually eased to one side in the *Best Horses* series, William K. Temple officially ceased to exist on 1 December 1945, when Bull wrote to the Registrar of Business Names cancelling the registration. The Racetime Analysis service was wound up and went out on a low note, with Bull admitting to 'unsatisfactory results in 1945'. He was to dedicate himself to his own betting, and to going racing when compiling the *Best Horses* series allowed.

By the time William K. Temple was consigned to history, Bull had returned to West Yorkshire. His house in Putney had suffered bomb damage, and he had already spent the summer of 1943 racing in the North. On the proceeds of his betting, and the insistence of a cousin who worked as clerk to Hemsworth council, he bought Windy Nook, a large property in his home village. It had been on the market for some time but Bull was advised that if it was not bought quickly, the council would turn it into flats for evacuees. He made the purchase in 1945, and Portway Press moved into a new home.

Dick Whitford was one of Bull's first visitors on his permanent return to the North. The initial introduction had been made by letter dated 2 April 1943, when Whitford, chief officer on wartime service on the S.S. Slieve Bearnagh, submitted research he had been doing on horseracing to while away the long hours of naval patrol, '95 per cent watchful boredom, five per cent action and excitement, pacing up and down a ship's bridge, day or night, or lying in harbour, wondering what, if anything, would ever happen'.

Before being allocated this posting on the basis of an officer's certificate gained as a youngster in the Merchant Navy, Whitford had been an advertising copywriter with the radio manufacturing firm of Ekco. He sought ways of relieving the 'monotonous, mind-numbing existence', and was pointed in the direction of horseracing—for which he had no inclination and of which he had little knowledge—during a chance meeting with the sports editor of the *Daily Telegraph*. Whitford returned to sea armed with copies of the annual form books and began to examine the results, plotting charts to link the horses and accumulating evidence that 'racehorses were figurable: not approximately or roughly, but almost exactly'. Soon, he explains, the grids filled up with what he called 'ratings', assessments of relative merit.

Whitford explains how he moved on: 'Each horse acquired a row of ratings, showing how he had run in consecutive outings. Taking the best of the runs, perhaps three or four out of seven, it was evident that most horses were astonishingly consistent, so much so that I had to keep reminding myself that I was dealing not so much with numbers but with flesh-and-blood living creatures. As time passed, I became totally engrossed with reducing the chaos of the form book into regular order.

'My first real breakthrough came when it dawned on me that I would get nowhere without at least a broad outline of the racing spectrum, an idea of the full range between the best and the worst of the racing population. I would need something that would measure the difference between a high-class horse and a moderate or poor one. It seemed to be a challenging exercise to devise some means of measuring ability in the racehorse, just as, at sea, sailors over the centuries had devised scales to denote degrees of wind force and cloud cover. And, of course, there were the temperature scales devised by Celsius and Fahrenheit. And, more appropriately for my purpose, there was the scale of Intelligence Quotient (IQ), an open-ended scale ranging from below 20 for 'idiots', 20 to 40 for 'imbeciles' and up to 140 for 'geniuses'—and higher still for perhaps one per cent of the population.

'So I set about the mammoth task of constructing from scratch a single composite handicap of all the runners of 1941. Instead of small sections of stayers, sprinters, two-year-olds and so on, I tried to connect them all up into one universal handicap. The complications became enormous and I would not have persevered but for the fact that I kept making fascinating little discoveries—groups of horses that meshed with each other with astonishing precision.'

By the autumn of 1942 Whitford had compiled the composite handicap to his satisfaction, especially among the two-year-olds, and whenever he could obtain entries and weights for current races, he would translate his 'horse ratings' into 'race ratings' and send his predictions to the *Daily Express* and *Raceform*. 'The ratings covering the second half of the year worked out exceptionally well,' he recalls, 'but in 1943 I was only able to keep in touch with racing in arrears, since I had no access to entries for future races.' Instead, he made a new contact in Phil Bull, who received Whitford's research and in the course of a reply in June 1943 made a remark which Whitford says 'meant little at the time but which was oddly prophetic':

I hope that some day we shall be able to meet and arrange some form of Combined Operations. Time is Time, and Form is Form, but I am convinced that there is some mysterious alliance between them that is still undiscovered.

The correspondence continued as best it could under Whitford's seafaring circumstances. The winter of 1943–44 passed and Whitford and his handicaps were transferred to the Duke of Rothesay, a hospital ship used in the Normandy landings. 'Horseracing and almost everything else was forgotten for weeks to come, as we criss-crossed the Channel keeping pace with Montgomery's advancing armies,' Whitford remembers. But in August 1945 the war was over and Whitford was demobbed; he was free to return to his old job in advertising. 'As I cleared my cabin to go ashore for the last time I debated whether there was any point taking all my ledgers and charts and battered form books. Luckily, I just couldn't throw them out,' he recalls. 'It seemed a good idea to take a week's leave and to go racing at Newmarket before I started work again, so I telephoned Phil Bull and arranged to meet him at Newmarket.'

Years later Paul Haigh, writing in *The Sporting Life*, described the event: 'It was as though Einstein and Newton had met for a little chat about physics.' Whitford says: 'It was nothing like that, of course, but I think it was the first time Phil had met a kindred spirit who could discuss racing technicalities without irritating him. We had a great deal to talk about, and got on well together.'

They talked for much of the afternoon; Bull persuaded Whitford to return with him to spend the night at Hemsworth before returning to Newmarket the following day, and they talked much more. During the second afternoon's racing Bull invited Whitford to become his assistant on *Best Horses*, and after a few days' deliberating—whether to stay in a secure job or whether to gamble on the racing world for three times the salary—Whitford joined Bull.

Whitford, who moved with Bull from his Hemsworth office when he bought The Hollins, at Warley on the outskirts of Halifax, in the autumn of 1946, recalls: 'In the summer we would go racing almost daily, visit stables, studs and sales rings, watch gallops. In my spare time, especially during the Flat, I could continue with making my handicaps. In the winter I would do the donkeywork, produce the facts and figures, collect the photographs, check the proofs and see the annual volumes through to publication. And Phil would write . . .

'Alas for those who drooled over his wonderful books, Phil became a highly volatile gambler in the immediate post-War years, basing his operations almost entirely on his timetest calculations. The scale of his operations was such that ordinary money lost all its meaning.

'He would sometimes wander into my office in his dressing-gown, just out of bed at about 12.30 pm. "Is there a bet today, Captain?" (or Brother, or Admiral). I would reply that perhaps the 4.30 at Beverley or the 4.00 at Haydock might interest him. He would sit down with *The Sporting Life* and *Raceform* and after a while would say: "All right. Beverley. Meet me at the car at half past two." We would drive to Beverley, go into the course at 4.15, have a glance in the paddock and then go backwards and forwards along the bookmakers' lines, taking whatever odds we could get. If the horse won, we would go back to the car and tot up the markings on the two racecards. "Not bad, £2,800 for twenty minutes work," he would say, with a smile.

'If Phil had been less successful in his gambling, racing might have been blessed with perhaps another forty volumes of *Best Horses* as only he could write them. He was probably the greatest writer on racing there has been.'

As well as noting Bull's brilliance as a writer, Whitford saw at first hand his increasingly unsuccessful attempts to meet the deadline for *Best Horses*. He recalls the winter of 1947–48: 'It became obvious that Phil was falling ever further behind schedule. I had completed all the research for the book—press cuttings, pedigrees, timefigure lists, form analyses and so on—and put dossiers for the horses he had decided to include in filing cabinets beside his desk. Everything was ready except Phil. He had, or seemed to have, writer's block. Convinced that everything he said or did was the product of a rational mind par excellence, he would have denied any weakness in his creative ability. But all the signs were there: sharpening pencils, watching birds circling in the sky, putting more coals on the fire or searching for a mislaid gramophone record, re-arranging the furniture—any excuse that could be found to put off the dreaded moment of starting to write.

'It did not help that he kept odd hours. He would rise from bed in mid-afternoon, have his breakfast about 4pm, roust me out of my office to play snooker until it was his lunchtime at seven or eight, and then settle down to his writings, or meditations, at ten or eleven o'clock. Or maybe, if he had a visitor he would play snooker into the early hours and postpone his writing until the next night. When I arrived in the morning, I never knew what I would find on my desk—a neat pile of copperplate manuscript, a few thousand words of elegant and enthralling prose without a single correction or amending phrase—or more often than not, a note: Sorry, Admiral, nothing today.'

Whitford hit on a temporary answer. He had continued to compile his own handicaps, in which Bull had shown only passing interest as an aid to finding winners. He thought that though only Bull was capable of writing *Best Horses*, there might be a case for producing brief comments about the lesser horses, using a shorthand version of the *Best Horses* style to include all the essential facts and figures, with a thumbnail digest of Bull's verdicts on the more worthy horses.

He recalls that he began writing out brief comments about all the horses that ran in 1947: 'Alongside the comments, I inserted as many of Phil's timefigures as were available. For my own guidance in writing the comments I had pencilled in my form ratings. Phil knew of these, of course, and had admitted them in disguised form in previous books, usually in such phrases as 'worth about 7.11 in Free Handicap'. But apart from this he had expressed no real interest.

'I remember the day when, in the late afternoon, I planted the thick wad of foolscap on Phil's desk and proposed it as the shorthand version of *Best Horses*. He read down the first page, moved to the next and then a third. He turned to me with a gleam in his eye. "This is it, Admiral!" he said. "A pocket guide to every horse in training . . . it's what everybody in racing needs. We'll sell this to everyone, not just those who have ordered the book.

We'll sell it not just as an annual but monthly, weekly even. This will sell like a bomb."'

Bull agreed to use Whitford's ratings, giving him ten per cent of the profits, and said the new publication would be called TIME-FORM—'a marriage of Time and Form'. With the clerical help of John Clarke, a new recruit to the office who was to remain with the firm until his retirement in 1988, Whitford produced the awkwardly-named *Best Horses of 1947 Timeform Supplement*. It appeared in April 1948 with Bull introducing *Timeform Ratings* as 'having been derived from both time and form, thereby enabling us to get the best of both worlds'. He went on:

The time basis is supplied, of course, by the racefigures; the form basis is supplied by my assistant, Mr R. S. Whitford, who has for many years devoted most of his time to keeping a 'universal handicap' of all horses in training. Timeform Ratings are a co-ordination of these time and form calculations, translated into simple figures, whose level corresponds with the poundage represented by the equivalent marks in an average official Free Handicap.

So *Timeform* ratings and comments were born, by Dick Whitford's many hours at sea, out of necessity from Phil Bull's long hours at *Best Horses*. In putting together his autobiographical notes, Bull wrote:

Best Horses became an annual chore until 1947. These books put me on the map as a racing writer. They got an international reputation and big sales. But getting a 600-page book out singlehanded in three months was a killing job—almost literally. I had to give it up. So I got together a small staff and began a new publication, *Timeform*, with an annual volume entitled Racehorses of the Year. *Timeform*, an entirely new kind of book, dealing individually with every horse in training; sold well, and we soon had to find new offices: at one time we occupied three separate premises: in 1962 we erected our own building. Shortly afterwards we bought a printing works. We now publish *Timeform* every week, *Race Ratings* for all races, *Timeform* race cards for all meetings Flat and National Hunt, and the magnificent annual book *Racehorses*, without doubt the best racing book in the world.

Nowhere did Dick Whitford merit a mention. But nor did William Hill figure elsewhere in the notes.

The Hollins, new base for the emerging Timeform, was about three miles outside Halifax, down a long tree-lined drive.

Whitford recalls: 'The winter and spring of 1947–48 was one of the worst on record. Snow was still lying in the hedgerows as late as May, and gales and snowstorms often made access impossible. Newspaper and postal deliveries were highly erratic. There were power cuts and no fuel deliveries. Most of the time we worked in our overcoats. Copy for *Timeform*, which had to be updated almost daily, had to be taken into Halifax to go by train to London [where the printer was based] and sometimes in desperation Phil's driver would take late revisions by car to London in the early hours.'

After *Timeform*'s initial appearance in April 1948, it was published a further five times that year, during which *Racehorses of 1947* made its belated arrival. In 1949 *Timeform* was issued twelve times, after the new-style *Racehorses of 1948* had been published on time.

Whitford stayed until the end of the 1949 Flat season. He reflects: 'True to his word Phil left *Timeform* entirely to me and did not interfere with either the comments or the ratings, except sometimes in a good-natured way. I rarely gave more than a passing glance to the times of races; it was useless to try to mix oil with water. Sometimes time gave better guidance; sometimes form came out on top. But there was often a big difference between what they suggested. As *Timeform*'s fame spread Phil began to take a greater interest in its contents. Now and again he would pounce, quite correctly, on loose phraseology in the comments; it was his schoolmaster instinct coming through.

'My relationship with Phil was not always serene and harmonious. He was far from practical in what he thought we could put into a monthly book, but he achieved his wishes for topicality when *Timeform* became a weekly publication and expanded into the famous *Black Book*.

'Running *Timeform* had changed everything for me. I was working twelve or fourteen hours a day and could go racing only by working until the early hours. Phil had the perks of going racing; he was also able to justify his racing expenses, which I was not. Phil knew I was becoming restless and at Christmas in 1948 he tossed me a bone, saying, "We have laid the foundations with *Timeform* and the reward will come. There will be a different story to tell at the end of 1949."'

Bull was thinking of turning the business into a limited company, and Whitford was to be one of the shareholders. As the year progressed Whitford became uneasy: 'However well *Timeform* was selling, I knew it was far from securely based. For one thing, Phil's whole lifestyle had changed. His travels and mode of living when out and about on the racecourses of

England—and France—had blossomed in line with his higher profile. This was not unreasonable but for most of the time he, personally, was short of money. Money was pouring in to Timeform but printing, advertising and distribution were gobbling it up, and the bills were being settled on a hand-to-mouth basis. The business was starting to become bigger than either of us had anticipated and I suspected that Phil was having second thoughts about its future. I asked for a contract of employment, at least. This was promised but never appeared.

'Matters boiled over one day in midsummer when Phil asked if I would provide a weekly supplement of ratings to a few backers and bookmakers who wanted the most up-to-date form. I said, rather shortly, that if anyone wanted my ratings on a private basis it would cost them £100 a week and that would be for me. Phil dropped the subject.

'I decided it was best for me to move on. I was feeling in a rut, and becoming anxious to get out into the real world of horseracing before I was too old. I told Phil that I would see *Timeform* through to the end of the season. He said I was very unwise to leave; that the books were with the accountants and that the prospects for the future were wonderful. With the developments he had in mind, I could look forward to great things. No, I said. I saw my future elsewhere. The directorships and shareholdings that were proposed never came to pass. My share of the profits for 1948 and 1949 arrived many months after I left. Phil sent me a cheque for £80. Maybe he was mathematically correct in his calculation but my self-respect would not have allowed me to send such a derisory amount for services which were earning him fame and fortune.'

Whitford and his wife Julie left Timeform and Halifax in November 1949. He turned down an offer to work for William Hill and instead became racing manager to Jack Gerber, who was about to embark on a most successful and profitable spell of ownership which reached an early peak with the brilliant filly Bebe Grande. In 1971 Whitford became *The Sporting Life*'s Flat-race handicapper; he left the *Life* and England for health reasons at the end of the 1984 season and continues to live in retirement in Mallorca.

From 1950 onwards everything connected with *Timeform* was published from Halifax, as the company grew into a small 'family' firm with Bull its paternal head. From The Hollins it expanded into premises in Halifax itself, where packing, distribution, subscriptions and secretarial work were carried out by a small team of girls, while the men worked on the comments, handicapping and timefigure assessments. Bull was regarded with a mixture of fear and respect.

He was at times very generous—handing out bottles of wine or extra cash to the girls who worked late to pack and send out his publications; organising staff parties; pressing a salary increase though the accounts of the moment might not have seemed to justify it. He once advanced, at a moment's notice, the equivalent of four months' salary to an employee, on the assurance it would be paid back within two weeks. When one of his horses won, a flag would be raised over The Hollins, and drinks provided for the staff. He occasionally joined in out-of-work activities, once—and only once—turning out on the left wing (naturally) for the Timeform football team in the local works league. In the Fifties he arranged an office betting syndicate, in which members took shares up to £100 and participated in his own bets. It ran at a profit, but resulted in the departure of one member of staff who was tempted to cream off an extra percentage. Bull made up the deficit from his own pocket.

Derek Adams, who spent 40 years with the firm, says: 'Phil Bull was the greatest asset Timeform ever had. He had an unmistakable air of authority, he gave the company clout. He set great store on the way *Timeform* should be presented and came down heavily on anyone not meeting his demanding standards. He was not backward in exercising his right to the last word, and often to the first one, and all those in between. "Slow to chide and swift to bless" are not words which spring readily to mind when singing his praises.'

At other times Bull appeared aloof, failing to remember the name of an employee, though he might have been there for a number of years. He would call people Brother, so that he did not have to bring to mind a name, something he regarded as unimportant. Women in the office were sometimes called Sweetie, or Beautiful, for the same reason. He had an unfortunate habit of occasionally criticising staff, sometimes senior members, in front of other people.

The truncated form of *Racehorses of 1948* continued for four years. *Racehorses of 1952* was the first to feature again essays on the best horses; it was also the first from which timefigures were dropped, leaving ratings to stand alone. Fastest performances for various categories were published from *Racehorses of 1952* to *1959* inclusive, and a full list of timefigures featured in the volumes for 1956 to 1960 inclusive, but any mention of timefigures was missing from 1961 until a separate publication was produced to cover the 1976 Flat season.

As Timeform and its publications expanded, Bull took increasingly less part in their day-to-day production, leaving that responsibility to his staff, of whom Reg Griffin emerged, after joining the company in November 1957, as his closest confidante, and Arthur Shaw became the senior writer.

On 27 April 1955 Bull wrote to an associate in New York:

My not having had anything to do with the work on *Racehorses of 1954* was partly due to ill health, and partly to a desire to let my staff have a crack on their own, so as to find out whether I could safely leave them to their own resources next winter, thereby allowing me to take a trip abroad. I'm happy to say that the result reassures me.

Despite loosing himself from much day-to-day involvement in the business, Bull still seemed bedevilled by lack of time. Replying to Alec Tew, a subscriber, on 16 June 1958 he wrote:

The time-lag in the appearance of timefigures in the issues of *Timeform* is entirely my responsibility. The fact is that I do not allow anyone else to calculate these timefigures but myself, and I have, as you will appreciate, a great deal on my plate, so that I am just occasionally unable to keep up with things.

However, he was more than keen to keep his staff occupied. In the early months of 1958, after the *Racehorses* annual had been compiled and since National Hunt racing was of no concern to him, Bull devised a set of eleven examination papers, each carrying 100 marks, for his handicappers, comment writers and male clerical staff. One example from each section provides a flavour of the intensity of the test:

Rules of Racing: Explain clearly the fundamental difference between a photograph taken by the photo-finish camera and one taken by an ordinary camera (or cine camera).

Owners, Trainers and Jockeys: Comment very briefly upon any five of the trainers named below, with respect to their skill in training, the placing and management of their horses or any other matters which you think characterise them or the stables over which they preside—C. C. Boyd-Rochfort, E. Davey, G. Todd, N. Bertie, S. W. H. Ingham, J. L. Jarvis, C. J. Couch, V. H. J. Smyth.

Races and Racecourses: Draw diagrams of any two of the following tracks, marking and identifying the winning posts, starting gates and also the gradients (rise, fall or level) from the point of view of a horse racing the correct way of the course: Sandown Park, Newmarket (excluding the Summer Course), Ayr, Goodwood, Epsom, Lingfield Park.

The Horse: Discuss briefly one or other of these topics—either the points to which one should pay attention when examining a yearling with a view to purchase, or the process of 'breaking' a yearling, stating what you regard as the fundamental rule to be observed throughout.

Past Form: Give the first, second and third in any two classic races run prior to 1940, and the first, second, third and fourth in another classic race run prior to 1946.

Current Form: Head up five columns with the names of the five English classics, in the order in which they are run, and enter in each column the names of the first three horses in each race in 1957, followed by the names of the owner and trainer of the winner, and the jockey who rode it.

Breeding (Theory): Explain very briefly the genetic mechanism of heredity, and define (a) chromosome, (b) gene, (c) dominant gene, (d) recessive gene.

Handicapping: Comment briefly upon each of the following statements, stating whether you consider them true or false, and giving your reasons—(a) Two-year-olds are more consistent than older horses; (b) The bigger the field, the bigger the certainty; (c) A good big 'un will always beat a good little 'un; (d) Two-year-olds concede weight better than do their elders; (e) At the weights there is nothing between them, but Crepello has that extra touch of class which should decide matters in his favour; (f) It is easier to handicap sprinters than stayers.

Race Times: (a) Define 'standard times'; state for what purpose they are used and why they are to be preferred to record times or simple average times, for this purpose; (b) Given accurate times for all distances on a particular track over a period of, say, twenty years, say how you would proceed to derive from them a set of standard times for the course.

Betting: (a) Explain carefully the misconception in the popular view of the so-called 'law of averages'; (b) From a normal pack of 52 playing cards, well shuffled, five players, one after the other, each draw and retain a card. None of these five cards is a heart. You are the sixth player to draw a card. Are your prospects of drawing a heart greater than were those of the first player to draw, or less, or precisely the same? And why? (c) A true and perfectly normal coin is fairly tossed five times and each time comes down heads. Is the chance of throwing tails at the sixth toss greater than it was at the first toss, or less, or precisely the same? And why?

The Commentaries: Using only 1957 *Raceform* or *Racing Up-to-Date* (specify which), and no other source of information, write note-form comments for inclusion in *Racehorses of 1957* on each of the following horses—Seabiri, Schoolroom, Judicature, Retrial, Brioche.

> Bull marked the papers as thoroughly as if he were back at school, adding in red ink comments such as 'Read the question!' for those who had misinterpreted a point. The exercise was not repeated; Timeform soon began to produce a Black Book for National Hunt racing during the winter—with no assistance from Bull—but the questionnaire was modified and retained for use when interviewing for new members of the editorial staff.
>
> Bull's plan to turn The Portway Press into a limited company was first formulated towards the end of 1948. It was to have a nominal capital of £5,000 (around £90,000 in today's terms), of which, Bull told his printer Bob Charman in a letter dated 20 January 1949:

I propose to retain 52 per cent. The remainder I propose to dispose of as gifts in the following proportions: 20 per cent to Nell [his common-law wife Eleanor Oxley], ten per cent to yourself, ten per cent to [Dick] Whitford, eight per cent to Billie [Richardson, one of his oldest friends, who arranged Bull's advertising]. The Board of Directors, if you agree, will consist of myself as Governing Director, yourself, Whitford and Billie. There will be no directors' fees. Whitford will receive £800 per annum and will be under contract with the company. Billie will not be under contract and will receive no remuneration but he will give his services as hitherto, and you, I hope, will be prepared to look after the business side, distribution, etc, in a similar manner.

> Charman replied almost immediately, saying that from a business point of view he would not consider the proposition at all, but that he would agree to it from a friendly standpoint. This perturbed Bull, and on 30 January 1949 he wrote to Charman:

I have become progressively less happy about the proposed Portway Press company. When I reflect [on your reply] I perceive that it has the effect of keeping me permanently in your debt. If my proposition is satisfactory to you only because we are on friendly terms with one another, it is entirely unsatisfactory from my point of view, because it leaves the position much as it was before. I cannot go on with it on these terms.

> Charman was shaken by Bull's response. 'You must be overtired and worried to the point of distraction,' he wrote in a letter dated 3 February 1949, 'and if I have added to your problems by loosely-worded opinions, I am sorry.' Charman went on to describe Bull's idea as the 'gesture of a very warm-hearted and generous benefactor who is in the act of bestowing gifts all round,' and suggested minor amendments in the payment of directors' fees in order to satisfy the Tax Inspector.
> In May 1949 Bull informed the advertising manager of the *Sporting Chronicle* that 'The Portway Press is to be formed into a limited company on 1 January next'. It was incorporated on 2 February 1950, and the agreement authorising the sale of Portway Press to Portway Press Ltd was signed on 30 December 1950. Incidentally, the firm of solicitors which handled the details was Carter, Bentley and Gundill of Pontefract, whose present senior partner Norman Gundill is also clerk of the course and manager at Pontefract racecourse, which each year runs a race in memory of Phil Bull at a meeting sponsored by Timeform.
> In a letter to HM Inspector of Taxes in Halifax, dated 5 January 1951, Bull pointed out that the share capital issued in Portway Press Ltd was 5,000 £1 shares; 4,999 were held by Phil Bull, and one by Wendy Cynthia Bull. The suggestion of early 1949 to involve Nell Oxley, Whitford, Charman and Richardson had gone by the board. In the meantime, Whitford had left the firm, Bull and Miss Oxley had split up, and on 4 November 1949 Bull had married his assistant Wendy Carter.
> Bull explained his reasons for the turn of events in a letter to Charman dated 21 January 1950:

I have always been intending to tell you why I could not go on with the proposed scheme formulated last year, but I have found myself shirking doing so, mainly I suppose for the reason that I have a feeling I have not treated you altogether properly in the matter. This time last year I was not in an emotionally happy state and could not properly give my mind to anything, but I think the real reason why the intended scheme petered out was because I felt that it had not received the unqualified approval I had anticipated. People seemed to be pulling in opposite directions, and ... well, you know, I'm a guy who can't get along unless he's boss of his own little midden, I'm afraid. Anyhow, I've gone ahead. Wendy has a nominal holding, and

I have the rest, so there's no-one to push me around where I don't want to go.

Portway Press continued to grow through the Fifties, from 20 staff in 1955 to 37 by the end of the decade, and the leased premises in the centre of Halifax became too small. At one time the company also used two other sets of offices in the town. But in the summer of 1959 the company paid £5,700 to Halifax Corporation for a freehold site of about half an acre, with the intention of putting up a new building for use when the main office lease ran out early in 1962. The plan to build larger premises than were immediately required was scrapped when a potential tenant withdrew. A two-storey building was erected at a cost of £50,000, and from 1962 Timeform staff were under one roof for the first time since the pioneering years at The Hollins.

The first change of shareholding came when Bull divorced his wife Wendy in June 1963. He married again four years later but by then the one floating share had gone to another working director, Brian Paxton-White, who had married Bull's niece and joined the company in 1961. When Paxton-White left in the Seventies to start an employment agency, his single share was handed over to Bull's sister May. Earlier, in order to reduce his tax liabilities Bull had allotted 20 per cent of his shares to Reg Griffin, who was obliged to take a salary increase and pay over what was left after tax in return. The arrangement lasted for a couple of years before Bull decided to draw up a document to say that in the event of anything happening to him, there would be no call on Griffin. In effect, Bull had made a gift of the shares to Griffin, who had become managing director to Bull's governing director.

As Dick Whitford had noted in the late Forties, Bull's personal finances were sometimes precarious. Keeping his band of racehorses and mares was expensive; running a large house the same. In 1972 he borrowed £100,000 from his bank, remortgaging The Hollins to finance the racing and breeding operation. For the next several years he had the notion to transfer The Hollins to Portway Press, to safeguard its upkeep. Bull took solicitors' advice; they in turn talked to Counsel, who raised a number of problems, and nothing happened, except that in February 1979 Bull, on behalf of Portway Press, agreed to pay bills to various agencies 'for the time and work already done on the project'.

At various times, depending on whether Bull's cash flow was proving difficult or he was simply worried about the future for himself and Timeform, he would consider reshaping the company. Rumours also surfaced periodically that he was about to sell.

Reg Griffin saw all the moods: 'Virtually from the moment I first met Phil he would say, "I must get my things settled." And he would come up with hare-brained schemes for people to take a financial interest in Timeform. I'd ask, What's in it for them? but he wouldn't have a proper answer. Another time he'd say, "What would you think about selling Timeform?" I didn't know who he could sell it to, so he'd say, "I'm sure there are people interested, Robert Sangster for instance." He might even have approached Robert at one time.

'I was always keen to make sure the people in the company were safeguarded, because if it wasn't for them, there would be no company. At one time we tried to set up an employees' share scheme, and Phil went along with it. The documentation was done and we'd arranged for the solicitors to come to the office, but half an hour before they were due to arrive, Phil rang up and told me to cancel the appointment. "I'm not signing," he said. There was no real explanation, other than that he wanted to keep his options open from his own point of view. He didn't know what would happen if anything went wrong with his financial affairs and he didn't have the company to fall back on.'

Bull continued to turn over in his mind various ideas; he still did nothing beyond consulting professionals, he still worried. He confided in Vincent O'Brien, in a letter dated 14 April 1986:

The years are beginning to tell on me, and I am no longer on top of things to the degree that I used to be. It is not loss of *memory*, but loss of *recall* when recall should be automatic: consequently I frequently find myself overlooking things I shouldn't overlook.

In strict confidence, my major concern, and it is a very troublesome one, is the future of Timeform. Some years ago I gave Reg [Griffin] 20 per cent of the shares—I own the other 80 per cent—and the problem is that, if I were to die in this situation, the impact of taxation would be such as might put the Company in difficulties, and certainly make things difficult for my dependants.

In an effort to solve this problem I have called in the best firm of solicitors and accountants I can identify, and the proposal under consideration is to float a public company on the Unlisted Stock Market. But I am not altogether happy with this solution, and I think I can see an alternative. Timeform is a very profitable little company, with a turnover of £2 million and a pre-tax profit in each of the last three years of close on a quarter of a million.

Of course Reg is fully aware of the problem and the preliminary steps I have taken. He knows also that his interests are my uppermost concern, for I am very much appreciative of the fact that, although I created Timeform, much of the success of the Company and the continuance of its unimpeachable reputation for integrity (which is of vital importance) is due to his management. So I'm anxious, if at all possible, for a solution to be found which will ensure Reg's continuance as Managing Director.

I am a very bad businessman—largely for the reason that I have, all my life, been a creative thinker of a person, concerned with the pursuit of ideas, and little concern for making money, over and above what would provide me with a comfortable meal-ticket through life. We none of us ever enjoy more than our expenses through life; and the acquisition of wealth has never been an objective of mine. That, as I say, has made me a bad businessman, who has never laid plans to defeat taxation.

In context, Vincent, you are manifestly not only the outstanding master of your profession, but also highly successful in capitalising your skills, and in maximising the investments of your owners to a degree that no trainer has ever before achieved.

You know racing inside out (as I do); you know the wealthy people in racing (as I hardly do); you know me and you know Reg: so you see why, before I accept the purely financial solution put up by my solicitor-accountant experts, of floating Timeform as a public company with a USM quotation, I'd like to talk to you. I think I have an alternative resource which does not involve turning Timeform into a public company but which will ensure the continuance of Timeform, after my death, owned by people who value its independence and integrity, and who would wish Reg to remain in managerial control as long as he wishes to exercise it.

> Bull's 'alternative resource' failed to materialise, as did an entry to the USM. But he still pondered the subject, to the extent he appeared to have persuaded himself there was public demand for a solution. Writing to a correspondent in Dubai on 23 February 1988, he gave the impression of having fallen prey to his imagination:

As you may well imagine I've had many inquiries from racing people with interests in the City, wishing to buy the Company, or to be given the opportunity of floating it as a public company with a quotation on the Unlisted Security Market. So far I've turned them all away. But as I'm approaching 78 years of age I suppose I'll now have to give serious consideration to their blandishments. I hold 80 per cent of the shares (Reg Griffin has the other 20 per cent, which I gave him some twenty years ago, and which he has certainly earned). Reg is a tower of strength, has been virtually running the Company for a long time and is good for another twenty years at it, by which time I'll be long dead. I suppose the Arabs would be favourite, if they entered the Timeform Take-over Stakes—as they are with everything else in racing with the exception of the Jockey Club! They won't succeed in taking them over.

Bull's regard for Reg Griffin had mended well. During 1976, when Bull was working closely with a more recent graduate of mathematics (MSc with Distinction), John Whitley, to produce Timeform Computer Timefigures, the relationship became strained. There was friction between Griffin and Whitley, and Bull probably sensed it. The result was that, without the knowledge of managing director Griffin, governing director Bull sent a hand-written note to the company secretary. Dated 7 January 1977, it said:

Please make the following entry in the Minute Book and let me have it for signature when I'm in the office this afternoon: 'I appoint myself Joint Managing Director of the Company with Reginald F. Griffin, the appointment to take effect from 10 January 1977.'

Griffin could not understand what had brought on the decision. 'I had been in his office, and he was looking out of the window, his cigar between his teeth, and he said, "There are some people around here who think I no longer exist. Well, they're wrong." The easiest thing would have been to ask if that included me, but that would have been an open invitation for him to go on at length, so I purposely avoided answering. The upshot was that I got the note about his becoming joint managing director.

'He was a great one for writing notes; he was a coward, couldn't talk directly to people, or have a row with them. His oral capabilities would probably have let him down, where his written ones wouldn't. With the written word he could choose every one, change what he wanted.'

Griffin pondered his position over the weekend, and on the Monday, when the new appointment was to take effect, he carried on as normal. 'The first day came and went, then the second and the third, then a month, and nothing,' Griffin recalls. 'He never mentioned it, and neither did I.' But Bull did mention it, in a letter to a former employee, Paul Casson, who was living in America. Dated 31 January 1977, Bull commented:

Reg and I are in a strained relationship at the moment. He's been getting too big for his boots and I've been pulling him up. Exactly what the result will be I don't know. We shall see.

Bull waited three years to see the result, and then, just as quickly as he had made his original decision, he told Griffin he was to resume as sole managing director. 'I hadn't taken him up on the matter, and that's what beat him,' Griffin believes. 'I don't think he knew how to deal with it. Unless he thought the consequences were such that it would cause a rift that might have been irreparable. If I was not so committed to Timeform, it might have done.'

Griffin's commitment to Timeform and its staff was tested to the limit following Bull's death in June 1989. A major problem arose over his estate, since a will signed in 1985 appeared to have been superseded by one signed after the start of his final illness, following a stroke in August 1988. Griffin was aware of the contents of the 1985 will, since he was an executor, but knew nothing of the existence of a later version. The most recent will favoured Bull's sister May a great deal more than the earlier one by giving her 60 per cent of the estate—including Timeform—with 10 per cent to his son Ray and 5 per cent to his grandchildren. Jennifer Dawson, his last companion, received nothing under it.

Griffin took up the issue with his solicitors. 'I knew Phil well enough to know that his wishes were to safeguard the continuity of the company and the jobs of the people working in it,' he explains. 'This wouldn't have been the case if I hadn't challenged the last will. In the end a Deed of Variation was agreed, so that his son Ray received 28 per cent, his daughter Anne's two children 12 per cent each, and the other 48 per cent was split equally between such as his sisters May and Connie, his niece June Paxton-White, and Jennifer Dawson.

'As far as Timeform was concerned, the Deed of Variance split either side of Phil's family into smaller units, and neither side could agree with the other. They had 4,000 shares between them but there was never any chance of their getting together to sell outside; they simply couldn't agree among themselves. So when we came round to looking at an Employees Share Option Purchase Scheme for the company, I wrote to the shareholders and told them that I expected them to participate, just as I was doing, by selling some of their shares. I was putting in 50 per cent, and I expected them to do the same. They did. So we had sufficient shares to start the employee scheme in 1993. Within time the scheme will own the whole company, and the security which Phil had been looking for will have been achieved.'

V ERY few reviewers of the *Best Horses* series took Phil Bull to task. John Loder, writing in *The Field* in 1945, was an exception: 'I am not the least bit interested in Mr Bull's betting transactions, successful or otherwise. And if this book [*Best Horses of 1944*] is conceived by its author simply as a means of subtle advertisement for the Temple Racetime Analysis I have ceased to be interested in the publication. But if Mr Bull really has no ulterior motive in publishing this book, beyond filling an obvious gap in our annual racing literature, then I advise him, in another year, to confine his comments more strictly to the horses and let us have nothing about his own gambling activities, to which the reaction of most readers will in any case be either contemptuous or else envious. And I advise him, too, to have a little better regard for the dignity of his phrasing and not to get quite so heated. It may indeed be that, making all necessary adjustments and correlations, to work out the precise mathematical equivalent of a racetime is, as he says, "a hell of a difficult business"; but why say so in so many words and, at the same time, impress upon us what a frightfully clever chap he is.'

Loder concluded by commending *Best Horses* to his readers, saying he had been stern, even harsh, in his criticism because he wanted the series to prosper. 'Mr Bull is a gifted writer. The book is very readable. But it can still be that, even after Mr Bull has purged from his writing the more obvious tricks of demagogy— particularly that one of pretending that everyone who disagrees with him is either a lunatic or else an unlettered ignoramus. The tricks of the demagogue, though they may bring quick returns, never establish anything that endures.'

Bull's work did endure, and *Best Horses* was greeted with lavish praise by newspaper reviewers up and down the land. Even its much delayed publication was accepted graciously; 'better late than never' seemed to be the reaction.

Though Bull gave up writing for *Best Horses* after the edition covering 1947, for many years it was generally assumed that he was still responsible for some input. He put the record straight—in private, if not in public—when in a letter dated 25 March 1981, he replied to Vincent O'Brien's observations on *Racehorses of 1980*:

It is a remarkable book, and a tribute to the quality and talent of the editorial staff who produce it every year. I can claim no credit myself (I haven't written a word in *Racehorses* for over 20 years), except that I laid down the pattern and standards thirty years ago, and also provided the staff with those *Best Horses* books I wrote in the 1940s on which to model their thinking and their writing. That was a big thing. A kind of tutorial for them. And what has followed from it is just a consequence of careful selection of people on the basis of two things only: intelligence and personal quality. I am neither joking nor boasting when I say that we have at Timeform thinkers and writers of outstanding ability, probably the best there are in racing, and they are all of them, at the same time, splendid people in terms of personality and character.

One of those writers, Derek Adams, had 40 years on which to base his opinion, before he retired from Timeform in 1994. He says: 'As a writer, Phil Bull was outstandingly the best on racehorses, and allied subjects generally, I have ever read. He wrote for the punter, and possessed a fluent, uncomplicated (if verbose) style. He took great pains to express himself as precisely as his command of the English language would permit, and displayed an enthusiasm for horses that was infectious. It was a sad day when he ceased writing about racehorses.

'For all that, he was not a writer with a natural talent. He had a capacity for hard work, but his production rate left a lot to be desired. If you had charged Arthur Shaw, Timeform's editor in the 1950s and 1960s, and Phil Bull with the task of writing a 1,000-word essay on a horse, Arthur Shaw would have had the job finished while Phil Bull was still thinking about it.'

Bull's expressive writing on racehorses was evident early in the *Best Horses* series. His essay on the two-year-old Dante in *Best Horses of 1944* was both pertinent and persuasive. The following are extracts:

I have to say right away that I regard Dante as head and shoulders above his contemporaries. With due respect to Mr Fawcett, and apologies also if necessary, I regard the way in which Dante has been weighted with the other colts at the head of the Free Handicap as preposterous. They are all of them much too close to him. Mr Fawcett is a competent and very experienced handicapper: I am not. The probability is, therefore, that he is right, and I am wrong. I merely state my opinion, and add that it is one which I hold very firmly. I must invite the reader to make whatever allowance he considers necessary for the possibility that, as a Yorkshireman, my view of the horse may be coloured by a certain amount of Northern pride. I don't think it is, mind you. As a matter of fact I think the boot is very much on the other foot. It is the Southern racegoers who have consistently refused to face the facts about Dante. 'A Northern horse beat High Peak? Bah!' they said, in derision, before the Coventry Stakes. Dante treated High Peak as though he were a plater. 'Yes,' they agreed, recovering from the shock, 'Dante is a good horse. But wait until he has to deal with Tornadic colt over six furlongs in the Middle Park!' Dante experienced no difficulty in disposing of him too. Yet they're still reluctant to believe their own eyes, and now, as I write, they're talking Court Martial. He, of course, is their last hope. Well, we shall see!

Dante's time performances last season establish him as a brilliant two-year-old. My racefigure records cover only a few years, but I am convinced he is the fastest two-year-old that has been seen for a very long time.

This is the point where someone is sure to jump in with the idiotic observation that Dante is too fast to stay. They are people who habitually trot out meaningless catchphrases of this sort. And when subsequent events prove them wrong they invariably fall back on that stupid remark about the exception which proves the rule. As a two-year-old the unbeaten Bahram was too fast to stay, and the unbeaten Nearco must also have been too fast to stay, and so must have been all the other supreme champions who were also brilliant as two-year-olds. These of course are the exceptions which prove the rule. Big Game, Myrobella, etc, etc, represent normality. It is all nonsense. Any two-year-old which outclasses its contemporaries is 'too fast' by comparison with them. If it is bred to stay it usually does so, and if it isn't it usually doesn't. Dante, of course, won't stay. That has already been decided. Nearco has yet to sire a stayer, so until he does so every Nearco colt is *ipso facto* a sprinter—might get a mile, but no further. Nobody is interested in analysing the mares with which he has been mated, and his having had only two crops of three-year-olds to represent him is not a matter of consequence. The fact that from a five-furlong mare he got Nasrullah, who stayed well enough to run a close third in the Derby, is not regarded as relevant; nor is Nearco's own stamina considered of much importance. That is how it appears to be from what I have read on the vexed question of Dante's stamina during the past winter. However, *I* think it *probable* that Dante *will* stay.

Dante's action is not the long, effortless, sweeping action of the dyed-in-the-wool stayer. There is more life in it than that. On the other hand it is not the sharp and brilliant action of the sprinter. He has a long stride, but it is also a very lively and powerful stride which fits in well with my idea of him as a speedy middle-distance type. I wouldn't say he is the best mover I have seen, but he is certainly one of the most powerful movers. I have seen it stated that Dante will beat himself in the Derby by his headstrong, tearaway attitude to the business of racing and that he will run himself to a standstill in much the same way as Big Game is supposed to have done in the Derby. My observation does not confirm this. I saw all Dante's races last year and only in his second one did he run in that manner. In his other races though he displayed a natural keenness and he seemed to me quite amenable to restraint. I have already mentioned that I thought him inclined to run lazily towards the end of the Middle Park Stakes, and I am positive he did so against Glamourous at Stockton. Nevett had to wake him up at the distance. I might agree that perhaps he is inclined to pull when upsides and settle down when in front, but I shouldn't think Matt Peacock and Nevett will have much trouble in teaching him to settle down behind and I am certainly not disposed to accept the suggestion that he will run himself to a standstill.

Temperamentally Dante is a lively and sometimes a playful customer. When he walked round in the parade ring last season he usually had a lad on his back. He has put this lad on the floor more than once, and he has also treated Nevett with similar disrespect at Middleham, though he stood by and waited for him to get up again afterwards. I have also seen him back away when asked to go into the ring or into his stall to be saddled. I daresay this will bring Nasrullah's name flitting into the mind of the reader. But lots of horses do this sort of thing occasionally without there being any of that stubborn mulishness in them which was Nasrullah's undoing. Nasrullah, of course, was much more temperamental as a three-year-old than he was as a two-year-old, but it would be foolish indeed to suppose that Dante's outlook on life will deteriorate in the same way merely because he also is by Nearco. I have never seen him do anything whatever to suggest there was any vice in him, and apart from those divergences from a straight line on the first two occasions when he was off the bit, his racing behaviour has been exemplary. He has a measure of high spirit and vitality by no means undesirable in a racehorse. In appearance he is a medium-sized, compact, dark brown colt. He was particularly well developed as a two-year-old, very muscular, and with very full and powerful quarters.

Well, finally, how shall we sum up his prospects this year? He has disposed of all the opposition he has encountered without any real effort. He is unbeaten, and I submit that his record as a two-year-old is, considering the restricted opportunities provided by wartime racing, as good as that of either Orwell, Colombo or Bahram. He has recorded two remarkable time performances which leave no doubt whatever that he is a brilliant and very speedy animal; and such evidence as is available suggests that he will stay well enough to get the Derby distance. It is not possible for any horse to have higher credentials than these. His mature and rather 'set' appearance last year has led to the suggestion that he may not make as much progress as some of the other colts next year. He doesn't need to. There were some exceptionally fine fillies last year, but none of the colts came within hail of Dante.

Sir Eric Ohlson has expressed a doubt to me whether the severer winters experienced in the North, and particularly at Middleham, might not lead to his Southern opponents having a considerable advantage over him in fitness on Two Thousand day. He has pointed out how often top-class horses from Middleham have met and defeated classic winners in the second half of the season after having themselves failed in the classics. But none of the horses to which he refers was anywhere near Dante's class, and Matt Peacock's horses have always won their fair share of races in the spring. The winter so far has been as bad in the North as it could possibly be. Gallops have been waterlogged for two months, and as I write they are now covered, and have been covered for the past fortnight, with six to twelve inches of snow. But provided Matt can give him some sort of a preparation Dante has too much in hand, to my way of thinking, for me to be disturbed by the prospect that there may be fitter horses in the field for the Two Thousand. I expect him to win the Two Thousand as decisively as he did the Coventry and the Middle Park. The Derby depends on whether he proves to have the stamina for the job. The probability is that he will. There are, of course, if's and but's in everything connected with racing. Dante may lose his form, he may break down, or he may go the way of Nasrullah. Such happenings are always on the cards. But as he is a thoroughly sound and healthy horse there is no reason why these prospects should exercise the mind any more where Dante is concerned than where any other horse is concerned. The prospect that exercises my mind at the moment is whether Dante will prove to be one of the best horses of the century. We shall see.

Dante was beaten less than half a length by Court Martial in the Two Thousand Guineas (fortune was less than favourable to him) but he won the Derby in the style Bull expected.

When it came to exploding myths and misconceptions—as he perceived them—Bull was at his most strident in the case of breeding, and breeding theories. His essay on Cambyses in *Best Horses of 1947* was an example he himself held up in later years.

The sire of Cambyses was Khosro (Sir Cosmo–Straight Sequence), and the dam Mizzenette (Silvern–Orby Lass). The names mean less nowadays than they did nearly 50 years ago, but the sentiments remain as fresh as ever, as Phil Bull follows up the earlier observations of his fellow writer Quintin Gilbey:

One point arises out of Mr Gilbey's remarks, which, as it is material to Cambyses' future as a stallion, I cannot allow to pass without comment: the suggestion that it is impossible to understand where Cambyses' sire Khosro got his stamina from. Mr Gilbey tells me he is not in the least 'touchy', and he has invited me, if I think anything he has written is nonsense, not to be afraid to say so. So here goes!

To me, the answer to the question as to where Khosro got his stamina from is perfectly simple. He got it from the same place that other horses get their stamina. He just inherited it, and there is no mystery about it whatever, except in the minds of those who think about heredity in terms of 'blood'. Among the various breeding systems to be found in current literature on the thoroughbred are the *family system*, the *sanguinary system* and the *fisherman's system*. The first deals in 'tap roots', the second in 'blood' and the third in 'lines', and their adherents all think in the same damnfool way. Sir Cosmo, they say, is by The Boss, by Orby; this, of course, is sprinting blood (to use the sanguinary terminology), or a sprinting line (to use the piscatorial terminology), and so, *ipso facto*, all horses by Sir Cosmo must necessarily be sprinters, unless they are flukes, freaks of nature or exceptions which prove the rule, etc. Similarly, Straight Sequence is by Stratford, whose stock is known for its speed, precocity and lack of stoutness, and she also must therefore be tarred with this brush. And there you have it: Khosro, by Sir Cosmo out of a mare by Stratford—a pedigree with sprinting 'written all over it'!

Now I quite admit that the *probability* with a horse by Sir Cosmo out of a mare by Stratford is that it will be a sprinter, just as the probability with a horse by Owen Tudor out of a mare by Sansovino is that it will be a stayer. But it is a probability and nothing more. It is *probable*, for example, that the result of mating the bay stallion Big Game with the bay mare Sun Chariot will be a bay foal; but, since the stallion and the mare both carry recessive chesnut genes, on the average one foal in four will be chesnut. It is improbable in the degree of 1:3 that any particular foal will be chesnut, but if it should turn out to be so, it is not a fluke or a freak of nature; it is simply an ordinary consequence of the Mendelian nature of heredity. The same, in principle, applies to stamina. The only difference is that, unlike coat colour, stamina is not a simple attribute, but a compound one, embracing a number of factors, skeletal, myological, nervous, vascular, respiratory, etc, each controlled by its own particular gene-pair. Some of the factors are dominant, like greyness (absence of pigmentation) in coat colour, and some recessive, like chesnut coat colour; and each factor (gene) is capable of being passed on from parent to offspring independently, in some degree, of the other factors. Stamina, therefore, is not inherited 'en lump', as it were, nor is it inherited as a portion of a homogeneous quality possessed by the parent. It is an integration of a number of distinct and unrelated inherited units. This, incidentally, is a fundamental point about heredity. If heredity were a sort of 'mixing' of the characters of the sire and the dam, as the 'blood' and 'line' people talk as if it were, all thoroughbreds would by this time be practically indistinguishable one from another, and so would all human beings. Winston Churchill would be indistinguishable from Aneurin Bevan, and Lord Rosebery from Jack Jarvis. The whole purpose, the supreme function, of the genetic mechanism of heredity is to preserve, in the species, a continuing variety from generation to generation.

In the light of this, let us now return to Khosro, and begin by getting our facts straight. First of all, his sire Sir Cosmo was *not* a pure sprinter. As a two-year-old Sir Cosmo was beaten a short head over 7 furlongs in the Tattersall Sale Stakes; as a three-year-old he won all his three races, two over 1 mile and one over 7 furlongs; as a four-year-old he won over 6 furlongs and ran unplaced over 5, 7 and 10½ furlongs. It is perfectly true that he was pre-eminently a speedy horse, and that his stock, in the main, take after him in this respect; but let us not empty the baby out with the bath water; let's stick to the facts: Sir Cosmo won twice over 8 furlongs, and twice over 7 furlongs, and he has also sired several horses who have stayed fairly well. He is not therefore a horse of the same type as Gold Bridge. He definitely carries *some* 'genes' for stamina, inherited, no doubt, from his dam, Ayn Hali.

With Straight Sequence, the matter is clearer still. There is no question whatever about her stamina, for she won over 1½ miles as a three-year-old. It is true that it was an apprentice race and she had only a 'postage stamp' on her back, but if you examine her career as a three-year-old you will find that her trainer, Frank Butters, started her off in March in 7 and 8 furlong races, later ran her over 1¼ miles and finally three times over 1½ miles. It is obvious what Mr Butters thought about her distance potentialities, is it not? Anyhow, let's stick to the facts: Straight Sequence gained her only success as a three-year-old over 1½ miles. Furthermore, it is not difficult to see where Straight Sequence got *her* stamina from: she got it, presumably, from the St Leger winner Swynford, through her sire Stratford, who won over 8 and 9 furlongs and also carried top weight, 8–10, into third place in a field of 13 for the Newbury Autumn Handicap (1½ miles) when he was a three-year-old. Never mind about Stratford's being a sire whose stock is chiefly noted for speed and precocity: it is a fact that he himself had inherited from Swynford *some* of the genes conducing to stamina. That the characteristics corresponding to these genes are only infrequently to be observed in his offspring merely implies that such stamina genes as he did possess were mostly recessives. Thus the facts are that Sir Cosmo and Straight Sequence *both* possessed *some* of the genes which produce stamina: and both demonstrated some measure of stamina on the racecourse.

Now, Mr Gilbey, what of Khosro? I put it to you: here is a horse by a sire who won twice over 8 furlongs, out of a mare who won over 12 furlongs—is this an animal whose pedigree has 'sprinting written all over it'? And is Khosro's proven ability to stay a mile or a mile and a half still so very surprising as to make him appear almost as much a freak of nature as if he had been born with two tails? Surely not.

The whole trouble about this business arises simply out of the pernicious habit of looking at pedigrees and treating one or two particular 'lines' as if they were continuities *in fact* in the same way that they are continuities *on paper*. They are *not* continuities. Khosro is *not* to be regarded merely as an extension of the Orby–The Boss–Sir Cosmo 'line'. It is preposterous to talk about a 'line of blood' and think about it as representing a continuing attribute present in all members of that line except such as are freaks of nature or exceptions that prove the rule. I wish the word 'blood' was barred from all writings on the thoroughbred, for there will never be any clear thinking about breeding until it is. All horses are full of blood; their own blood, manufactured by themselves, not one single drop of it received from either of their parents. Its purpose is to feed the cells of the living organism. It has nothing to do with heredity. Horses have not 'sprinting blood' or 'staying blood' in their veins, they've got *blood*: the sprinting or the staying is in the horse itself, the whole horse, in the various characteristics inherited from its sire and dam.

I know somebody is sure to chip in here with the remark that people don't really mean these phrases, 'staying blood' and so forth, in a literal sense; that it is just a matter of terminology; and that all

I'm doing is quibbling about words. It is *not* just a quibble about words. When people take a word which means one thing, and use it to mean something else in a different connection, they frequently treat it (unconsciously) in its new connection as though it possessed some of the properties attributable to it in its original meaning. That is what happens with the words 'blood' and 'line'. Blood is a liquid which one can mix with other liquids in various proportions; and the characteristic of a line is that it is continuous. Hence the idea of a mating as a 'blending' of one line of blood with another, and the feeling that the offspring ought in some way to be a blend, or mixture, of what are supposed to be the salient characteristics of the blood lines selected—a conception totally at variance with reality.

Returning to Khosro again, if he is not to be regarded merely as an extension of the Orby line, neither is he to be regarded merely as the result of crossing Sir Cosmo with a Stratford mare—a phrase which implies that all Stratford mares are much of a muchness. Khosro is a horse in his own right, different from any other horse that was ever foaled; he's not just one of a bunch all bearing the same tag. It is wrong to regard a pedigree as stamped by, or characterised by, a particular pattern in it. Every individual in one generation of a pedigree is potentially of the same importance to the student of the pedigree as every other individual in that generation. To see only a couple of 'lines' forming a familiar pattern, and expect the product of the mating to conform to that pattern, is to ignore the possibilities presented by the rest of the pedigree. Every mating presents an astronomical number of different possibilities in the offspring, and our business as pedigree students begins and ends with an attempt to envisage the more probable of these possibilities. After that we must turn to the horse himself to tell us, by his conformation, his action and his racecourse performances, which of the many possibilities presented by his pedigree has, in fact, actually materialised in him. Let us therefore pass the 'blood' over to the veterinary surgeon, fling the 'lines' back to the fisherman, and begin to talk and think about heredity in the racehorse in terms of genetics. We're in the twentieth century, not the seventeenth. And if we don't understand the rudiments of Mendelian heredity we have no right to be talking or writing about pedigrees at all.

Once the struggle of producing *Best Horses* in time for the appropriate season had beaten him, Bull handed over respons- ibility to his staff and returned to using *The Sporting Life* as the major outlet for his personal views. His letters to the Editor were headed, in capitals and underlined: For publication in its entirety or not at all.

Bull was not prepared totally to lay his words and opinions before the vagaries of journalistic practice. He explained his fears in a letter to George Wigg dated 12 February 1976: 'The press I got from the speech I made at the Race-In at Sandown last Sunday was stupid and inadequate. They pick out, and paraphrase to their own purposes, what they think are the things that have impact, taking them out of context and misrepresenting them.' More often than not, Bull got his way.

He was a long-time writer to *The Sporting Life*. One of his first letters was dated 7 June 1939, from his home at 11 Veronica Road, London SW17. Submitted under his pseudonym of William K. Temple, it concerned his specialist subject, timing:

Your correspondent, Mr John Crystal, suggests that 'timing' in this country can have little or no value, and it can only be of service in countries where there is, throughout the racing season: (a) Uniformity of surface soils, (b) Uniformity of climatic conditions, (c) Uniformity of track conformations. May I be permitted to deal with his remarks?

UNIFORMITY OF SURFACES

Throughout your correspondent's letter runs the naive assumption that the Time Test involves direct comparison of the times recorded. If this were the case it is perfectly clear that not merely uniformity of soil, but uniformity of everything else would be essential. But such is not the case. No Time Test enthusiast would dream of making direct comparisons whether the times were recorded on the same kind of surface soil or not. It may be perfectly true that the racetracks of Australia, South Africa, California and Mexico exhibit the same sandy surface characteristics; but what of it?

The surface soils of the two Newmarket tracks are identical, but no Time Test enthusiast would compare, on that account, a time over the Bunbury Mile with one over the Rowley Mile. If the surface soils over the whole of Great Britain were suddenly and miraculously to be rendered uniform the task of the Time Test practitioner would remain unaltered. The fact is that the question of surface soil is bound up with all the many and much more serious questions which face the expert, and is capable of solution as and when they are solved.

UNIFORMITY OF CLIMATE

The extreme variation of climatic conditions under which racing takes place in this country certainly presents the Time Test student with his greatest problem. But it is not an insoluble one. The student is concerned not with the actual conditions themselves on any particular day, but with their effect on the times registered on that day. It is quite possible to obtain a measure of this effect by a mathematical analysis of the times of the six races.

If the climatic conditions in England were absolutely unaltered throughout the year there would, of course, be no problem, and times registered at Newmarket in April could be directly compared with those registered at Newmarket in October, without the necessity of any mathematical analysis at all. Mr Crystal suggests that in Australia, South Africa, etc, such is in fact the case. I respectfully beg leave to doubt it. Is there no rain whatever in the countries mentioned? No wind? No variations in temperature? I cannot imagine that Mr Crystal wishes to assert anything more than a *rough* uniformity in climatic conditions. But 'rough uniformity' may mean a difference of several seconds in the 'fastness' of a track, and that would be as sufficient to invalidate direct comparisons over there, as it is over here.

The question of horses being trained throughout their lives under uniform atmospheric conditions seems to me a matter of no importance. I do not for a moment suggest that training conditions are of little consequence to the trainer—far from it, but I do suggest that provided a horse can be produced at the post perfectly fit, it is the conditions on that particular track on that particular day which determine the time registered, not the conditions under which the horse is trained. In 1933 Mr Lambton is said to have 'clocked' Dorigen to have an excellent chance of winning the Lincolnshire. Subsequently the Lincoln track was deluged to such an extent that Monday's racing had to be abandoned. Nevertheless Dorigen slammed her Lincolnshire field in spite of having been trained on entirely different going.

UNIFORMITY OF TRACK

Mr Crystal's third contention is that the extreme variety of curves and gradients which characterises our racecourses 'must shatter all hopes built on Time Tests'. This statement betrays again the same disturbing misconception of Time Test technique. If Time Test enthusiasts were in the habit of making *direct comparisons* between the times returned on our various tracks Mr Crystal's point would have force. But I cannot imagine that these people exist anywhere other than in Mr Crystal's imagination. To compare times returned over the Ascot 5 furlongs with those for the Epsom 5 furlongs seems to me to be too preposterous to merit discussion. Surely it is well enough known that the actual time registered over a certain track must be compared with the Standard Time for that track before it can be compared with a time on another track.

Further, to suggest because the racetracks in Australia, South Africa, etc, are symmetrically laid down, with wide, sweeping bends, that direct time comparisons can be made between them also seems to me unwarrantable. It is not surprising that a number of trainers in these countries mentioned set little value by the results obtained. Nothing less than an absolute identity of track (an impossibility) would justify direct comparison. Nor is the fact that they are nearly all 'dead flat' of any value. Doncaster, York and Newbury are nearly 'dead flat', but 60 seconds for 5 furlongs on each of these tracks represents three very different time performances.

With due respect to Mr Crystal, I cannot help feeling that he is greatly mistaken in his ideas of how the Time Test is applied in this country.

The Racing Week, Timeform's short-lived weekly magazine, gave Bull a personally-tailored outlet, at least for the 12 editions to which he contributed the Editorial. His opposition to a Tote monopoly was argued in the issue dated 30 May 1964:

Now let us examine the proposition that racing in England would benefit from a Tote monopoly. There is a campaign going on for it. The Stewards of the Jockey Club have declared themselves in favour. Racecourse executives look eagerly in that direction, and the Thoroughbred Breeders' Association would no doubt vote in favour. Possibly that moribund body the Racehorse Owners Association might vote against it if its members could be roused from the stupor induced by the annual dinner, which seems to be its principal *raison d'etre*. The bookmakers, the intended victims of the exercise, are too busy competing for business one against another to organise effective defence and counter attack. As for the punters, out of whose pockets ultimately comes the wherewithal to support the whole racing edifice, they have no organisation and no spokesman.

Now I am very much concerned to resist this threat of a Tote monopoly because I think it would be bad for the punters and bad for racing in general. The argument for a Tote monopoly is that by channelling all betting into one pool you make it a simple matter to abstract whatever percentage you think you can safely take without killing the goose that lays the golden egg. The idea of those who advocate this policy is that the 'percentage' should be 'put back into racing' as they express it, by which they mean paid over to owners (and indirectly to breeders also) in the form of increased prize money, or handed over to racecourse executives to enable them to build new stands and improve racecourse amenities generally.

This naturally appeals greatly to racecourse executives. They see in it the answer to all their problems: imposing new stands and better amenities will lead, so they think, to bigger crowds. Well of course everyone wishes to see improved racecourses and better amenities for the public: but it can be achieved without doing away with bookmakers, and is being so achieved right now.

My view is that racecourse executives, even from the narrow point of view of their own self-interest, are mistaken. Doing away with bookmakers will not make racing more attractive and lead to bigger crowds. It would have the reverse effect. Anyone who has experience of racing in France and America knows that racing over here is vastly more interesting. And the major reason for this is simply that in France and America there is only one 'circus', one fount of interest, the actual race itself, whereas in England there are two circuses, two founts of interest, the race and *the market on the race*. Nobody should underestimate the importance of the latter.

The race itself lasts, on average, some ninety seconds: the market on the race lasts for a quarter of an hour and is full of interest. The fluctuations in the prices, the competitive betting by individual bookmakers striving to attract business, makes it a highly colourful and fascinating part of the racing scene. It has for the ordinary racegoer an entertainment value no less than that of the race itself. He can move around in the market, see the odds available and go shopping for the best prices. In short, the racegoer is not merely a spectator, he is a *participator* in the activity.

Tote indication boards are no substitute for a betting market. And walking up to a Tote window to bet without knowing what price you are taking is no substitute for active shopping in Tattersalls. That is why racegoers accustomed to racing in England find racing in France or America unutterably dull by comparison. I'm with them in this, even though my interest is perhaps more centred in the horses rather than in the betting

Among the journalists who advocate a Tote monopoly is Mr John Lawrence, who weighed in a fortnight ago with an article in the *Sunday Telegraph* on what he referred to as 'the strange phenomenon of ante-post betting', in which he suggested that this was nothing more than a gigantic confidence trick organised by the bookmakers for their own benefit. Mr Lawrence writes entertainingly and sensibly when he's talking about horses, but the views he expresses in this article on ante-post betting are so naive as to make one doubt whether he knows anything about the subject at all.

I haven't the space to deal in detail with all the confusion of thought in his argument, but here is a sample: after stating that of the 18 winners of the Derby since the war only one, Crepello (6/4) has started at a shorter price than 5/1, he goes on to say that it is 'his honest opinion that ..... no horse, however gilt-edged his credentials, *can ever be better than a 5/1 shot on the day'*. In the very next sentence he then, with astonishing lack of logic, contradicts this foolish assertion by an admission that 'Crepello *was* of course'. All I can say is that if Mr Lawrence really thinks no horse can be less than a 5/1 chance for the Derby on the day of the race I shall be happy to give him an opportunity of backing up his view with hard cash. He can ring me up at the Mayfair Hotel next Wednesday morning and I'll be pleased to take 4/1 Santa Claus if he cares to lay it.

As for his proposition that ante-post betting is nothing more than a gigantic confidence trick organised by the bookmakers for their own benefit, I suggest he takes a look at figures in William Hill's ante-post book on the Derby which we reproduce in this number of *The Racing Week*. Mr Hill said at the Saints and Sinners Derby lunch he would gladly give anyone £30,000 to take over the book. I shouldn't like to accept the offer. Far from being a bookmakers' confidence trick, ante-post betting is one of the most vitalising things about British racing, a source of enormous interest and publicity, without which racing would be very much the poorer.

And racing would be very much the worse for a Tote monopoly. You won't get more people to go racing by doing away with bookmakers. The reason why racing attracts big crowds in America is that there is no off-course betting over there; and the reason why they get big crowds in France is that admission charges are low and the big meetings are centred in the metropolitan area of Paris and held on Saturdays *and Sundays*.

We can have lower admission charges, bigger stands and better amenities over here without doing away with bookmakers and losing half the fun of the game, if Lord Harding disposes his levy with proper appreciation of the priorities. Increased prize money for owners—and I am an owner myself—should not be the first priority.

Although the Stewards of the Jockey Club came out last year in favour of a Tote monopoly I very much doubt whether they have behind them a majority of the members of the Jockey Club. Certainly there is not unanimous support for it among members. Lord Rosebery doesn't agree: neither does Lord Crathorne. I only wish they would make themselves more articulate about it. As for the bookmakers, it is time they got themselves properly organised. By concerted action they could easily demonstrate to racecourse executives how much of the actual entertainment they provide.

If, for example, they were to boycott the Goodwood meeting next July, and all of them go and bet at Redcar instead, it would, I imagine, be a salutory lesson to Mr Hubbard (clerk of the course at Goodwood, and advocate of a Tote monopoly). Like the celebrated Old Mother Hubbard in the nursery rhyme, he would find, I've no doubt, that his cupboard was bare. I don't advocate the boycott: I merely draw the attention of the bookmakers to the strength of their position.

> John Lawrence (later John Oaksey) was singled out above for criticism. He was spared the same public treatment five years later, on the topic of coupling horses from the same stable for betting purposes, when Bull put his thoughts in a personal letter dated 4 August 1969. As well as giving the future Lord Oaksey a pat on the back for his comments about pace, Bull also made him a job offer:

On your advocacy in the *Sunday Telegraph* of the 'stable entry' system—the coupling of horses from the same stable for betting purposes—I must challenge your statement that there is no very obvious argument against it. There is most certainly a very obvious and cogent argument against it.

If two horses Red Devil and American Twit, both trained in the same stable, run in the same race, coupling these two horses for betting purposes robs every punter of the right to back the one without backing the other.

I fancy the 7/1 chance Red Devil, and not the 13/8 chance American Twit. Why should I be denied the opportunity of backing Red Devil at 7/1, and compelled to take evens the two coupled? And if I fancy American Twit at 13/8 and don't want to back Red Devil, why should I be compelled to take evens the pair instead of 13/8 the one I fancy?

Any punter who backs the 13/8 favourite American Twit and leaves out the 7/1 Red Devil has only himself to blame if the longer-priced one wins. Nobody prevented his exercising his option to back both horses if he so wished. Nobody was twisting his arm.

To be compelled to couple the two horses is an intolerable invasion of a backer's freedom, for no purpose except to assuage the feelings of losing punters who fail to exercise their options.

I know what I'm talking about on this subject, both as an owner and as a backer. A few years ago I ran two horses in the same race at Redcar: Metellus, who was one of the favourites, and Dorabella, who was running for the first time and whose merit was quite unknown to me or anyone else. I backed Metellus to win me £6,000, and I didn't have a shilling on Dorabella. Both horses ran on their merits and the upshot was that in a driving finish the 33/1 chance Dorabella beat Metellus by a short-head. In consequence I lost a substantial sum on the race. But so what? Whose fault was it? Did anyone stop me having a saver on Dorabella if I had felt so inclined? So why should I be aggrieved, or feel that the authorities should protect me from the consequences of my own folly by altering the custom and denying punters who backed Dorabella the right to 33/1 to their money?

I recall another occasion on which the late John Hetherton and myself ran horses in the same race, both trained by the late Captain Elsey. John Hetherton's was favourite, and my horse was a 6 or 8 to one chance. I felt sure I'd beat John Hetherton's horse. He felt sure he'd beat mine. Why on earth should John or I have been denied the opportunity of betting on our own horses, just to mollify those punters who backed the wrong one, when they could, had they wished, have backed both of them?

You say there is no very obvious argument against denying punters a choice by compulsory coupling of horses in the same stable? Come off it, John! You can't have thought the matter out.

I find it astonishing that you, of all people, should be openly advocating that owners should be allowed to run non-triers in order to assist, as pacemakers, horses which *are* triers, and proposing that punters should be protected against those occasions when the pacemaker beats the intended.

You've got things upside down. The rules are correct as they stand. What *is* important is to see that the rules are complied with, and that stewards should make full use of the camera patrol record to see that they are.

On the matter of pace and strategy in long-distance races I am entirely with you. You hit a nail on the head when you say that 'in every slowly run race there is at least one jockey whose tactics are right'—the jockey whose mount has the best turn of foot. I would add the corollary that there must be at least one jockey whose tactics are stupid!

I don't know whether you were at Chester when Philoctetes [Bull's horse] won the Greenall Whitley. The riders of the five other runners (Lexicon's carpeted jockey apart) virtually presented

Philoctetes with the race. They allowed him to set up a lead of 25 lengths in the first half-mile, without Peter Robinson's having any desire or making any effort to do so. He never had Philoctetes out of an ordinary swinging gallop, and it was simply that the other jockeys pulled up. They just hacked along regardless. Whether they thought the loose horse was taking Peter along faster than he wished to go I don't know. What I do know is that in all my racing experience I have never seen such an example of monumental stupidity on the part of supposedly competent jockeys as was exemplified by this event. The race was virtually already won over a mile from home, yet none of the losing jocks realised it. Indeed they made no effort to get in touch with Philoctetes until five furlongs out. Unbelievable!

The reluctance of jockeys riding solid one-paced stayers to take charge and set a decent gallop when nobody else will go along and do it for them is to be explained only in terms of lack of intelligence.

Every jockey riding behind can see more of what is going on than the jockey who is in front. No doubt that makes them feel safer. No doubt, also, the matter of wind resistance is of some moment, though I think this is generally greatly exaggerated. But neither of these considerations, nor any other, is of importance comparable to the strategic demands imposed by consideration of the resources of speed and stamina possessed by the various horses in the contest.

The suggestion that slowly-run races 'could and should be prevented by a time-limit—a minimum requirement outside which the contest would be declared null and void'—is nonsense. The minimum requirement on heavy ground would have to be vastly different from the minimum requirement on firm going. These things are matters of degree. Who, apart from myself, would be competent to decide what should be the minimum acceptable time? And how should even I myself decide where to draw the line? The idea is ludicrous.

I am in entire agreement with you that those who dislike slowly-run races should keep their scorn for the beaten jockeys, and not for the races themselves.

May I say, John, how much I admire your lively writing, and, in general, the sharpness of your thinking about things. If I were to resuscitate *The Racing Week* in a new and much more ambitious format (as I may well do), there is no-one whose contributions I would more earnestly desire than yours.

In July 1971, following an unexpected request for help from a charity organiser in Sheffield, Timeform started its annual charity race meeting in aid of Cancer Relief. The first was at Doncaster—the rest have been at York—and the sunny Saturday afternoon fixture, attended by The Queen, attracted 'a pathetic attendance of a mere 13,720 people'. These were Phil Bull's words in a letter to *The Sporting Life*, dated 9 August 1971, in which he put the blame squarely on television:

It has been obvious for many years, of course, that television has completely changed the entertainment patterns, indeed the whole social and behavioural patterns of society. The process is accelerating, and where racing is concerned the consequences are becomingly increasingly serious. Especially is this so of Saturday racing.

Sitting at home, with his feet up and a drink in his hand, a man has presented to him 'on the box' every Saturday afternoon no less than 10 races, in close-up all the way, with pre-race reviews of the runners cribbed from *Timeform Race Cards* and *The Sporting Life*, betting information, post-race re-runs, interviews with jockeys and trainers and other racing notabilities, and with all sorts of other sporting events thrown in as well. All he needs is a telephone at his elbow or a betting shop on the corner.

Why should he stir? Why contemplate a train or coach trip, or getting out the car, taking the wife and kids, driving 50 miles, parking and paying admission charges all to get a partial view of something he can see far better on the TV screen in his own parlour? Is it surprising, in these circumstances, that racecourse attendances on Saturday afternoons are being seriously affected?

Furthermore, the TV networks are getting their sports programmes on the cheap. They pay peppercorn fees for top racing. What do you think the BBC offered us for the TV rights at Doncaster? A derisory £716.50! What we actually accepted from the rival ITV network I ought not to say, I suppose, but it was, in my view, but a small fraction of what it was worth to them.

The truth of the matter is that the TV authorities have sport, and racing in particular, over a barrel. They know full well the value to any sport of TV publicity, and they trade unashamedly upon it.

Racing involves a mere 10 minutes of actual contest, is virtually dead for viewing purposes when the results are known, and must therefore be shown live or not at all. Inevitably it gets a raw deal.

I doubt if there is much that can be done about it. I question the wisdom of permitting 10 races to be televised every Saturday afternoon. But certainly we have to reconcile ourselves to the consequences of the new patterns of entertainment that the advent of TV imposes and learn to live with them.

Much the most important of these consequences is the unpalatable but inescapable fact that racing can no longer be financed from the pockets of those who pass through the turnstiles. There aren't enough of them. It can be kept viable only by tapping the pockets of those who pass through the betting shops. Hence the Levy Board, of course.

Bull's letter drew a response. Not all the reaction took his side; some, he thought, even missed the point, especially the BBC's head of outside broadcasts Peter Dimmock. So a follow-up was penned on 31 August, and the subject of the influence of television, in general and on racing, was developed:

Peter Dimmock and several other of your correspondents seem to be under a misapprehension regarding my attitude to televised racing. I am *not* anti-TV: I am *not* anti-TV-racing. Quite the contrary. But I have noted a few of the facts of life. One of them is that the television has dramatically changed the entertainment patterns of society.

Of course I know that other things have changed people's behaviour patterns too: the motor car substantially; and, where racing and betting is concerned, the advent of betting shops. But the most fundamental and far reaching change is that consequent upon television. In pre-TV times all of us had to go out to get our entertainment. So big crowds at outdoor sporting events were common. Racing, football and cricket were all viable from turnstile takings, without subsidy. Theatres and Cinemas were flourishing.

The growth of TV over the last two decades has changed all this. A wealth of entertainment, sport and drama, and a fantastic variety of other attractions are now available from that little box in every man's home, every hour of his leisure time. He needn't step over his threshold. He has the world on his hearthrug. Those who wish to 'spectate', do it, in ever growing numbers, from the armchair. The result is that theatres and cinemas are closed down, turned into bingo halls or struggling along half empty; cricket grounds are devoid of spectators (except on Sundays) and racecourses, with crowds 25 per cent of what they once were, are no longer viable without subsidy. Soccer survives, standing on its own feet by virtue of a large element of youthful partisan club supporters—the kind of thing that racing cannot claim.

This change in the social scene, in the entertainment pattern, is irreversible. No use deploring it, or trying to fight against it. Nor *do* I deplore it.

Television brings to people a view of superlative excellence in all fields that they could never have had in pre-TV days: superlative football (World Cup in Mexico); superlative tennis (Wimbledon); superlative drama and comedy (better than anything I used to see on the London stage in the 1930s); social documentaries etc—none of which was available to the vast majority of people before. This isn't something to be sorry about.

Make no mistake about it, the cheapest thing anyone can buy these days, by far the best value for money anyone can get anywhere, is a television set and a television licence. For a few pounds a year a man and his family can have, delivered through 'the box', a wealth of news, information, instruction and entertainment, day in day out, that would astonish us if we weren't so accustomed to it. I certainly don't deplore it. It's just about the best thing that's happened this century.

Nor, to get back to racing, would I wish to deny to TV viewers a good coverage of live racing. For one thing, they're entitled to it, and for another thing I know darn well that racing can't do without TV.

When I said that the disappointing attendance at Doncaster on Timeform Cancer Relief day was to be explained by one word—television—I meant just exactly what I have said above. I did NOT wish to imply that it was because the meeting was televised. All I said on that score was that I questioned the wisdom of permitting ten races to be televised every Saturday afternoon.

For Peter Dimmock's sake let's have this clear. Eight races (including four at Doncaster) were televised that day. If *none* had been televised I don't believe it would have made 1,500 difference to the attendance. Of course it would have made *some* difference, but nothing in comparison with what the *general* competition of sporting television on Saturday afternoon makes.

My quarrel with Television where Racing is concerned is simple. I know, and Peter Dimmock knows, that no sport can afford to shun television. 'It is our experience', says Peter, 'that racing, in common with many sports, needs the regular shop window of television . . . Furthermore, television helps racecourses to obtain sponsors for some of their major races.'

Those are his own words! That's it exactly! A virtual admission that because of the need of *many sports* for television shop window display, and the wish of sponsors for TV coverage, he is able to buy programmes for what I call peppercorn fees.

Peter is doubtless an exceptional negotiator in this sphere. I daresay he secures many outside TV broadcasts of sporting promotions on terms highly advantageous to the BBC. It is his business to negotiate to the best advantage.

I am concerned on the other hand with the consequences for racing. What bothers me is that racecourses have their backs to the wall. I should like to see the TV authorities buying the best programmes available *for what they are worth in entertainment value*, not, if I may say so, taking advantage of advertising considerations to depress contract terms. The fact that individual sports are in weak bargaining positions hardly justifies the TV authorities in 'squeezing' them.

Peter Dimmock seeks to correct my 'unfair' contention that television fees are derisory by saying that both ITV and BBC contribute a very sizeable sum each year to racing, and the long-term contract fees . . . . . are now substantial. Very sizeable? Substantial? These terms are relative and therefore virtually meaningless.

Actually the only thing I said was derisory was the £716.50 offered by the BBC for the TV rights at Doncaster. But certainly I do suspect that *all* TV fees for racing are more or less derisory.

Peter accuses me of over-simplifying matters and using television as a rather too convenient 'Aunt Sally'. He hopes that Sir Randle Feilden, Lord Wigg, the Duke of Norfolk, the Racecourse Association and others who have the long-term interest of this great sport very much at heart and work tirelessly to this end (note the flattery!)—he hopes they will not pay too much attention to my blaming television.

I trust he does not mean to imply that I too do not have 'the long-term interest of this great sport very much at heart'. Let me assure him that in this respect the Duke of Norfolk has nothing on me. We differ only on fundamentals.

Nor, may I assure Peter, do I over simplify things. On the contrary, I am very conscious of the complexity of everything. I know, for example, that what is the racecourse's loss is the viewer's gain. If Mr Dimmock gets the racing TV programmes for BBC very cheaply and all other outdoor sport similarly, this is reflected in a TV licence fee lower than would otherwise be possible. As I said in my article, I doubt if there is much racing can do about it, except learn to live with it.

Learning to live with change was not always Bull's idea of a good thing; putting muddled thinkers straight was. The arrival of centralised handicapping gave him such an opportunity, when Julian Simcock was taken to task in a letter to his *Sporting Life* editor, dated 26 November 1971. Again the missive was headed, For Publication In Its Entirety Or Not At All. The following is the letter, almost in its entirety:

Julian Simcock's observations upon the Jockey Club's plan to replace from 1973 the personal handicap of individual handicappers by a single centralised handicap are comical.

'In the past,' he writes, 'there have been considerable differences in the ratings of individual horses by the Jockey Club handicappers. These gaps, which have occasionally been far too wide, should', he says, 'disappear completely with the introduction of the new system.'

Should? They *will*. If there is to be only one handicap, how can there be any discrepancies in the handicapping of horses? One central handicap means one definitive assessment. A single handicap can't differ from itself.

But Julian's really comical observation is that 'the leniency shown by Jockey Club handicappers to some horses will disappear completely in 1973'.

What leads him to this conclusion? Will the new central handicap be so perfect that no horses will ever be leniently handicapped, or severely handicapped? Does he suppose that the pooling of individual handicappers' views will result in perfect handicapping? Or does he think there's something magical about the use of a computer for handicapping print-out.

It's a load of cobblers. Timeform has been running a single centralised handicap for over twenty years. Our handicappers, who run it, are expert. There are none better. But we're frequently wrong about horses. We frequently give horses ratings that are too low or too high, assessing them too leniently or too severely. This is in the nature of things. There's no escape from it. Handicapping horses is a matter of skill—it is no more than an expression of opinion. It can never be otherwise. Perfection is unattainable.

Furthermore, the heading of Julian Simcock's column 'Computer to frame "central" handicap,' is nonsense. The computer won't frame the handicap: it will merely co-ordinate the handicappers' opinions that are fed into it, and print out a result according to the way it is programmed. How sensible and realistic the result will be will depend upon the skill of the handicappers involved and the adequacy of the programming.

I suspect that Mr Simcock, like many other people, credits computers with a capacity for judgement which no computer possesses.

Where judgement is concerned—the capacity to weigh all sorts of considerations and arrive at rational conclusions—the human brain is immeasurably superior to any computer, and always will be.

Computers have been programmed to play chess. But they wouldn't have a cat in hell's chance of beating Boris Spassky or Bobby Fischer in a game over the board.

So too with racing. Handicapping involves interpreting results and the running of individual horses. This interpretation turns upon understanding and appreciating the effect of differences in distance, going, the fitness of horses, the way in which they are ridden, luck in running, whether they tried or whether they didn't, and a host of other things—all completely outside the capacity of a computer to assess or make judgements upon. So, where handicapping is concerned, you can just forget the computer. I have ten brains in my office, any one of which would wipe the floor with a computer when it comes to this sort of thing.

No! Let's understand things. What the Jockey Club is really proposing to do is to replace the fallible handicaps of various individual handicappers with a *single* equally fallible central handicap, very much like the universal handicap we have employed with Timeform Ratings over the last twenty-odd years.

It will be a handicap with imperfections, sometimes incorporating serious misjudgements. This is inevitable and inescapable. Julian Simcock's idea that a central handicap will do away with 'lenient' handicapping of individual horses is nonsense. It won't.

One of Phil Bull's rare excursions into regular print outside *The Sporting Life* or his own painstakingly produced reports came through the columns of *Books and Bookmen*, a monthly literary review magazine for which he contributed articles during the 1970s, commenting on books dealing with horseracing and betting. The shallow nature of some of these volumes provided Bull with the signal to attack targets which he felt fell short of his standards.

Tim Fitzgeorge-Parker, author of *Steeplechase Jockeys: The Great Ones* (Pelham, 1971), took the full force of comparison with one of Bull's *Best Horses'* collaborators:

It might be supposed from its title that this book is to National Hunt Racing what Quintin Gilbey's *Champions All* is to Flat Racing. Regrettably it falls far short of this. The winter jumping game has gained much in popularity in recent years, largely in consequence of its superiority as a spectacle on television, but it is still the poor relation of the Flat, and Tim Fitzgeorge-Parker's book is very much a poor relation of Quinney Gilbey's. It is not merely that it is slighter, less than half as long and covers a shorter period, but it concerns itself little with the horses, lacks Gilbey's sharp critical observations and lively comment on the racing scene, and is nothing like so racily written.

Tim Fitzgeorge-Parker has plenty of anecdotes to tell, and generally he relates them well. Occasionally he lapses into the journalese of the tabloid newspaper with a phrase like 'the Aintree voodoo struck again,' or when he refers to Terry Biddlecombe as having '*literally* lifted French Excuse past the post'—a strong jockey, forsooth!

The author is, in fact, much too prone to use words for effect, without proper regard for their meaning. Consider, for example, the following sentence about Terry Biddlecombe's style in the saddle; 'He rides unnecessarily short. Those long, powerful legs deserve longer stirrup leathers. Nevertheless he sits so lightly on a horse with such a patently firm independent seat, that this idiosyncracy is obviously no handicap to him.' This is simply loose emotive writing. Long legs may *need* long leathers, but how do they come to *deserve* them? What is a *patently independent* seat, firm or otherwise? And how come riding short is an *idiosyncracy*? Riding short is common enough all over the world. There's nothing idiosyncratic about it.

Mr Fitzgeorge-Parker likes to dramatise and sensationalise the sport and to do so in a way that displays him as a knight in shining armour, of unimpeachable integrity. For several years when his charger was in the then Rothermere stables of the *Daily Mail* he had sallied forth on any racing crusade that promised good espousement and maximum publicity. His favourite dragon was the bookmaker, whose fiery betting breath was racing's bane. It is so sad for Mr Fitzgeorge-Parker that the real racing world is somewhat different from his fantasy.

There was harsher criticism to come on the subject of style when Bull examined *Lester Piggott Champion Jockey* (Arthur Barker, 1972), by Ivor N. Bailey:

If you have the slightest respect for the English language, or any real feeling for the use of words, the attempt to read this book will be an ordeal indeed. And a painful one if, in addition, you happen to be familiar with the horse-racing scene or acquainted with Lester Piggott. I hesitate to contemplate how excruciating Lester himself would find the reading of it.

The author, Ivor Bailey, is determined to write purple prose. He scorns to say something in one simple word if he can wrap it up in a dozen. Thus, neither Steve Donoghue nor Lester Piggott were merely born: Steve 'first saw the light of day', and Lester, 'a master of the art of hairline manoeuvring, timed his own advent into the world with devastating precision'. Lester is 'the grain of magic that fell out of the sky on 5 November 1935'.

Mr Bailey loves the extravagant phrase and the grandiloquent metaphor. Human interest stories about Piggott, he tells us, are 'as thick as tea-leaves in a clairvoyant's cup'; Lester's triumphs in 1960 were 'as thickly strewn around him as the confetti that greeted him after his wedding'; Piggott and Lewis 'are locked in a life and death struggle for the title'; Piggott is 'as resilient as a cork in a force-ten gale'; he is a man who 'was straining nerves that had virtually ceased to exist to prove a point that possessed no validity except in his own dedicated obsession'; he 'makes his own headlines in a hell-bent rush through life to certain triumph'.

Comparing Lester with Jimmy Lindley, Mr Bailey gives us this charming metaphorical observation: 'the odd bit of stardust that alights on a man's head to lift him above the ruck of ordinary humanity defies rational analysis'. And a few lines earlier, speaking of Jimmy Lindley's varying success over the years, he puts it that 'the graph oscillates—but for some, despite undoubted talent, unlimited courage and unstinted effort, the needle never seems to flicker to flash point'. A nice mixture of oscillation, needle, flicker and flash!

Mr Bailey's book is also enlivened for the philologically minded reader with a rich lacing of Malapropisms: footfalls for footsteps, eternity for posterity, allocates for accords, efficient for sufficient, precipitous for precipitate, exaltation for exultation, testimonial for testimony, and so on.

Mr Bailey enjoys repeated use of such phrases as 'hell and high-water' and 'hell-bent', and he's particularly taken with super-natural ideas, of God, the Gods, fate, the fates, and destiny. Lester, for example, is 'the darling of the gods', and 'the gods were in their right place in the high heavens keeping a benign vigil over Lester's star'; Sir Gordon Richards is god-like; and Noel Murless presides with god-like efficiency over an equine assembly-line at Warren Place.

'Note how odd', says our author, 'are the workings of destiny, and how everything seems to conspire to favour the chances of those loved by the Gods'. Piggott was 'marked down by destiny to inherit the mantle of the great Sir Gordon Richards'. Piggott, 'by some divine instinct handed out by the gods, always sensed that he was fated for the top'. 'Fate seems to sit on Piggott's shoulder'. 'In three crowded months in 1968 the champion experienced varying oscillations of the needle of fate', and 'the fates, though quite impartial in their design, were working for Piggott in full force.'

I like the idea of impartial Fates working for Piggott in full force! Like impartial Justice in South Africa! But I wonder how kindly Lester will take to the idea that his success is to be attributed not to his own brains and work and skill, but to the beneficent machinations of the gods, fate and destiny! What a load of crap it all is, isn't it?

This is not only a badly written book, it's a thoroughly unsatisfactory and inadequate book in every way. I do not propose to discuss the ideas in it, such as they are, because in general they are as absurd and as ill-expressed as the writing is pretentious.

Harry Carr is quoted as having said of Lester Piggott that 'For my money, he's the best rider who ever got up on a horse anywhere any time'. This, in my view, is probably not far from the truth. But as to the reasons *why*, as to the *nature* of Lester's skill and effectiveness, and the real factors that go to make him what he is as a rider, Ivor Bailey has practically nothing to say. As a biography the book is romantic tripe: as an appraisal of Lester himself as man and rider it doesn't even get to first base.

> Bull's longest contribution to *Books and Bookmen* appeared in April 1973. His assessment of Dr Otto Newman's *Gambling: Hazard and Reward* (Athlone Press) glowed with praise, and concluded with the recommendation, 'His book is probably the first serious and dispassionate study of the subject published in this country. As such, it is a valuable and instructive piece of work.' The specifics behind Bull's observations on an investigation of the sociological and economic aspects of gambling in Britain in 1967/8 are dated, but the generalisations typified by these extracts remain largely relevant:

The view that betting and gaming in England is a major industry involving inordinate manpower and the wasteful expenditure of a fantastic amount of money that can ill be afforded is widely held.

Only a few months ago in a television programme a well-known interviewer prefaced a question to me with the assertion that we, as a nation, spend twice as much on gambling as we spend on education. The truth is quite different. And there is no longer any need for anyone to guess at it. Since gambling became subject to taxation precise figures have become available, and these are published annually by the Government Statistical Service. In point of fact, the public spends on gambling less than one-eighth of what is spent on education. The TV interviewer was therefore not merely wrong, he was wrong by a factor of sixteen.

How do such extraordinary misconceptions arise? No doubt the sustained propaganda of the anti-gambling lobby has much to do with it: but an important contributory factor is undoubtedly the all too common failure to make the elementary distinction between gambling 'turnover' and gambling 'expenditure'—between the totality of what backers stake, and the totality of what they lose. Attention was drawn to this by a Royal Commission over twenty years ago, but long afterwards the Churches Council on Gambling, and other commentators, continued to speak of betting turnover as if it represented money actually *spent* on betting. In 1967 gamblers staked, in various ways, a total of £1,497 million, of which they lost £268.3 million (17.9 per cent); in 1968 the turnover was £1,436 million, and the gamblers lost, or spent, if you prefer the word, £277.2 million (19.3 per cent), of which, it may be noted, £96.4 million went to the Exchequer by way of taxation, whence it was, of course, redistributed to the benefit of the public in general.

It may be thought, perhaps, that £270 million a year is still a pretty fantastic amount to spend on gambling. It is equivalent to no more than a mere 9p a week per head of the population, or 22½p weekly for every employed adult—actually less than the cost of a packet of cigarettes. For every £1 spent on gambling in 1967, £1.40 was spent on books, newspapers and magazines, £5.60 on tobacco and £5.90 on alcoholic drink. And, one might add, about 70p on hairdressing, manicure and beauticare!

Gambling in 1967 accounted, in fact, for no more than 1.1 per cent of total personal expenditure (in 1971 the figure was just over 1 per cent). Dr Newman comments that such a level of expenditure on gambling is 'relatively modest and not by any means inordinate'. He observes also that, far from being an industry making excessive demands upon national manpower, gambling actually employs no more than 0.25 per cent of the total labour force, and he concludes that 'by even the more rigorous standards, gambling cannot be considered as constituting any other than the most minor problem in present-day Britain'.

Of course, there will always be a body of opinion which holds that all forms of gambling are no more than a waste of people's time and resources. To me this is a mistaken, not to say self-righteous, point of view. Gambling is clearly enjoyed as an entertainment and relaxation, and one is entitled to take one's entertainment in whatever form it pleases one, provided only that no-one else suffers in the process. You may regard it as deplorable that people could be so bankrupt of mental resources and devoid of cultural aspiration as to spend their time backing horses, or playing roulette or bingo. That is your privilege. It would be *their* privilege to take a poor view of the fact that society sees fit to tax these modest entertainments, on the one hand, but on the other hand to subsidise the ballet, the opera and the National Theatre, which the socially fortunate, better educated, wealthier, and more cultured members of society profess so much to love but are unable or unwilling to make viable out of their own pockets. The one form of entertainment and relaxation is as valid as the other, culture notwithstanding. In my view to scorn the pleasures of the 'uncultured' is a form of intellectual snobbery deserving of contempt.

Originally betting shops were envisaged simply as places where bets could be placed. The draft legislation included a clause making it an offence to 'loiter' in a betting shop, but that clause, which would never have been enforceable, was discarded in committee. The result has been that betting shops have developed into something quite different from purely 'operative' institutions like post offices, which it was originally intended they should be. Instead, they have acquired the character of 'regulative' institutions: community centres, fulfilling many functions and filling various social needs. In this process every betting shop tends to develop its own distinctive individuality, its community of 'regulars' being a unique social microcosm whose nature depends upon the catchment area from which its punters come, the occupations and industries indigenous to the locality, the personality of the proprietor or manager, and many other factors.

It is a pastime rather than an addiction, indulged on a modest scale, and obsessive only with an insignificant minority. There is a strong association between social deprivation and disposition to gamble, and for the majority of working men gambling makes sense. It is not merely that gambling provides a working man with his one hope of big material reward, and temporary escape from the everyday monotony of life; it provides him also with the thrill of participitation in events, and the illusion of belonging and being part of a real activity, which is denied to him in the larger world outside. When he makes a bet on a horse, he is involved beforehand in detailed study of all sorts of calculations and assessments of imponderables, and the need for judgement and decision making, none of which he has the opportunity of experiencing in the world of real life.

Deny to a man the education and opportunity to realise his capabilities in the real world, as our present socio-economic system does to so many, and who shall think it right also to rob him of the opportunity to enjoy the competences and confidences and excellences of his capacities in the fantasy world of betting on the horses or the dogs in his local betting shop, with the mirror of success and failure that it holds in miniature to life outside? Who would seek to deny him the personal involvement with others in his betting shop, the exchange of views, communication and conflict; opportunity for self-display in skill and argument; achievement exemplified in the backing of a winner? Or the pleasures of being a member of a community calling in different situations for humour, fortitude, tolerance, anger, nonchalance, or sympathy and kindliness?

The subject of gambling provided Bull with an opportunity to fire off a correction to *New Society*, though its correspondent would not be the only commentator to tumble across the turnover tripwire. In a letter dated 17 May 1974, Bull wrote:

In your Report on Gambling you state that 'more money is spent on gambling than on smoking or running a motor car'. This is ludicrous nonsense.

The *Blue Book of National Income and Expenditure 1973*, published by the Government Statistical Service, gives in Table 22 the following figures for consumer expenditure in 1972: Alcoholic Drink £2,948m; Tobacco £1,808m; Running costs of motor vehicles £2,147m; Betting and Gaming £397m.

In your article the first three figures, for drink, smoking and running motor cars, are quoted correctly, but for some reason best known to yourselves you choose to ignore the correct figure for Betting and Gaming, £397 million, and substitute a figure of £2,350 million for gambling *turnover*.

Is your writer so ignorant of his subject that he thinks turnover is equivalent to money spent? Does he imagine that all bets made are losing bets? In fact over four-fifths of all money bet is returned to the bettors. The money actually *spent* on gambling is, as stated in the

Blue Book: £397 million in 1972, of which £168 million went to the Exchequer in taxation.

Of total expenditure in 1972 (£39,263 million) Food accounted for 19 per cent, Alcoholic drink 7½ per cent, Tobacco 4½ per cent, Running costs of Motor Vehicles 5½ per cent. Gambling accounted for 1 per cent.

This is a very different picture from the one painted by your writer, who would no doubt be surprised to learn that people spend more on newspapers and magazines (£477 million in 1972) than they do on gambling.

The Churches Council on Gambling has for long sought to make out that Gambling is a major social cancer. It is nothing of the kind. It is a legitimate source of pleasure and entertainment for millions of people, and what they actually spend on it amounts to less than 40p a week per head of the adult population.

Misrepresentation of the facts by quoting betting 'turnover' as though it were money actually spent (lost) by people is to be expected of the Churches Council on Gambling. It is sad to find a publication of the stature of *New Society* misrepresenting things in exactly the same way.

As a breeder of racehorses, and a successful one at that, Phil Bull might have been expected to favour the payment of bonuses for those breeders whose produce won certain races. Not a bit of it. Bull had a wider view, and expressed it in a letter to the former Jockey Club senior steward Sir Randle Feilden, one of the few such officials for whom Bull had any time as an administrator. Writing on 20 January 1975, in response to Feilden's request to examine a paper on breeders' bonuses, Bull took the opportunity to expand his views:

I have never been favourably disposed towards Breeders' bonuses on the Flat. The breeder is engaged in a commercial enterprise. He gets his price when he sells his product. The argument that if a horse sold for a paltry sum subsequently wins the Derby the breeder is entitled to harbour a resentment at not receiving a financial cut from the owner's windfall, has never carried weight with me.

A few years ago I sold for close on £30,000 a Sir Ivor yearling which subsequently was hard pressed to win a piddling little race worth a few hundred pounds, and was never heard of again. Did I have a moral obligation to pay back to the unfortunate purchaser some of the £30,000 as compensation for the disappointment occasioned by his having made such a bad and expensive purchase? He thought I had!

A few years previously the same man had bought for £3,000 a horse that won the Irish Derby and was syndicated for £350,000 or some such figure. I asked him had he given the breeder a share in the horse or a nomination to the horse. No. He'd given one to the trainer but not to the breeder. Very well, I told him, you cannot have it both ways. If fortune smiles on you as an owner and you do not share it with the breeder, you may not, when fortune frowns on you, expect the breeder to share your misfortune by alleviating it.

As I've said, I regard the willing seller of a yearling as receiving the market price for his product. I would make two further observations. First, that there is a finite amount available in prize money, and that if you give some of it to the breeder of a horse, you must necessarily do so at the expense of the owner. Second, I believe that whether you do so or you don't is a purely arbitrary decision of no real consequence.

If you are short of owners that would be an argument against giving a percentage to breeders: and if you are short of horses, that would be an argument for encouraging breeders by giving them a cut of prize money. But, in truth, the simple economics of supply and demand would deal with the matter anyway. Horses in short supply means higher sale prices: owners in short supply means lower sale prices. A self-adjusting feed-back situation!

Look, Gerry, so far as I can think it out, this breeders' bonus question is totally irrelevant to the real problem. Racing is an entertainments business: two classes of people put money into it in return for the entertainment they get out of it: owners, motivated mostly by vanity and social pleasures; and punters, motivated by hopeful pursuit of profit or the mere pleasurable exercise of playing one's judgement against other people's—the little battle for success. Apart from these two classes, all other people take money *out* of racing—the Jockey Club, Weatherbys, trainers, jockeys, racecourse executives, paid employees of one kind and another, bookmakers, publishers of racing periodicals like Timeform, etc, etc.

That is the input-output equation where racing is concerned. At least it used to be. Nowadays there has been added to the output side a massive new claimant, the Treasury, society at large, currently taking 80 or 90 million pounds a year out of the game from the pockets of punters; and owners, for that matter.

Breeders' bonuses? A triviality. The real problem is that £90 million, and how to divert a respectable proportion of that back into racing: how to lobby, persuade, cajole, the Chancellor into a recognition that if he doesn't moderate his rapacity he may well kill the goose that lays him his £90 million egg.

Doubtless this is an unpropitious time to be tackling an unsympathetic Chancellor about it. But it has to be done, and it has to be done with belief and determination sustained until the point is won.

Let me make another point. It is the experience of Chancellors that taxation of tobacco and alcohol can be increased steadily year after year without killing these geese. Raise the tax on a packet of cigarettes or a bottle of whisky, and though it may have the momentary effect of curtailing consumption, it is merely temporary. In the long run it makes little difference; people smoke and drink as much as they did before. But this is not, and cannot be, the case where the betting tax is concerned.

When a man buys a drink or a smoke he buys a real thing, a pint of beer or a packet of cigarettes, to the drinking and smoking of which he is addicted. But there's a real article involved. Increasing the duty increases the price, and there may be some who will become non-smokers or teetotallers because they can't afford to be otherwise. But the satisfactions of drinking or smoking are such, and the addictions so strong, that they will be few.

It isn't so with betting. There is *no* article, *no* real thing that is being bought and sold. What is being sold to a punter who makes a bet is the *prospect of profit*. This doesn't apply of course to football-pool punters or those who play the Tiercé in France, donkeys pursuing the carrot of the windfall fortune prize. But it certainly applies to half the backers who frequent betting shops in England, and to 90 per cent of those who bet with bookmakers on English racecourses. The *prospect of profit*: that's what you sell to a potential backer. And it is of paramount importance, if punters are to continue to bet, that the tax on betting should not be raised to the point where punters recognise that any prospect of profit has been removed.

You cannot expect people like Denis Healey or Harold Lever [Cabinet members in the Labour Government], who have probably never had a bet in their lives, to understand this. Some years ago the Treasury was collecting many millions from Fixed Odds betting in football. Lobbying by the Pools Proprietors persuaded Reggie Maudling to slap a $33^1/_3$ per cent tax on Fixed Odds, so as to bring it in line with the taxation of pool betting. Result? What anyone who had any knowledge of the matter could have told Maudling, the death of Fixed Odds football betting, and the total loss to the Treasury of the revenue he'd been getting from it.

When I look back over the years I've been engaged in racing, the starkest fact I see is the complete failure of the Jockey Club to recognise the realities of the game they controlled and the implications of environmental and sociological changes upon it. For so long racing had been the perquisite of a leisured aristocracy, and its entertainment value for the masses was taken for granted. It was enough. It supported the game. It was indeed viable in these terms. Then, along came television, with cheap entertainment brought into everyman's home. Land values rose, racecourse attendances fell, and racing on the old terms was no longer viable. So we got the Levy, and shored it up with that.

But where, along the line, has the Jockey Club ever shown itself in *front* of the play? Never. The Benson Report [1968 Inquiry into Racing] is written throughout in terms of owners and breeders. Not once in the whole report is the word entertainment mentioned. Nowhere is the Sport's dependence upon its audience, upon the punter, acknowledged and the right inferences drawn. Is it surprising, in these circumstances, that the Treasury gets in first to milk the game of 90 million, with a miserable 8 million via the Levy for racing? The Jockey Club failed in its responsibility. You were the first person to come along who knew the score, and you were too late on the scene.

What is the position now? Where the Jockey Club is concerned, a vacuum. It was a bad day for racing when you retired, and a bad day when George Wigg left the Levy Board. There was vitality then: now there's vacuum in Portman Square. The one bright element is now, strangely enough, in Weatherbys. The old Dickensian image is out. Thanks to Simon and Charles Weatherby, and [George] Morrison. They're in the modern technological world. But where is the Jockey Club?

Just let me give you an example. Last year I sought permission of the Jockey Club to hold a Sunday Saints and Sinners Race Meeting. We applied for the fixture. It was turned down. And d'you know what the reason was that Lord Leverhulme put in his letter? That to agree to a Sunday fixture would be *to create a precedent*! As if the creating of a precedent was beyond contemplation.

When starting stalls were introduced, that created a precedent. When overnight declarations were instituted, another precedent. How can there ever be any change without the creation of a precedent? What does it matter whether a precedent is created? What matters, is surely whether the precedent is or is not *desirable*.

We want racecourses to be viable. We want people to go racing. They work (virtually) a five-day week. The days they have available to go racing are Saturdays and Sundays. So why don't we give 'em racing on the days they're free to attend—Saturdays and Sundays. Religious objections? Nonsense. People are religious in France, but they race every Sunday. So why not us?

Of course I know what the law is about it. I know that betting shops can't open on Sundays and all the rest of it. But so what? Is Sunday racing desirable or not? Racing is an entertainment, and one must present it when people are able to enjoy it—Saturdays and Sundays—not when they're at work.

The point is this: that had the Jockey Club given permission to us to have a Sunday fixture, that would have been *a foot in the door*! There would have been no off-course betting, and the Levy wouldn't have benefited: but we'd have breached the established pattern—the first step to Sunday racing, which has got to come sooner or later, whether you view it with misgivings or not.

Twenty-five years have passed since Bull penned that letter. Feilden and Bull are dead; the Jockey Club put its foot in the door in 1992 with the first Sunday race meetings without betting, and following a change in the betting laws, the British Horseracing Board has been able to sanction a series of 12 Sunday race dates with on- and off-course betting in 1995.

The Sporting Life, Thursday, November 30, 1961 7

PHIL BULL'S BLOODSTOCK
Next Week's Part-Dispersal Sale

The Yearlings

The last occasion on which Hollins-bred yearlings were submitted at public auction was at the October Sales in 1955. The six yearlings then submitted subsequently won 32 races worth nearly £30,000. They were: **Diopides** (3 races, £1,406); John O'Gaunt Stakes), **Eudaemon** (7 races, £13,039); Gimcrack and Champagne Stakes), **Haydn** (12 races in U.S.A. worth over £8,000), **Oranfilus** (2 races, £447), **Anodem** (2 races, £3,131; Great Nursery Foal Stakes) and **Orycida** (6 races, £3,302; Thirsk Classic Trial Stakes).

How did they sell? The two fillies Anodem and Orycida did not make their reserves: Diopides, Eudaemon and Oranilus made 1,000 guineas each and Haydn 800 guineas. Bought for a mere 3,800 guineas, these four colts more than paid for the purchasers 24 races worth nearly £35,000.

Here, with Phil Bull's candid comments, are the five Hollins yearlings and one unbroken two-year-old, to be sent up next Monday.

XENOCLES b.c. Nearula—Desdemona (Dante)

ORONTAS b.c. Tenerani—Orienne (Sol Oriens)

ZURYCIDA b.f. Zucchero—Orycida (Alycidon)

TAMETTA b.f. Tantieme—Carteretta (Chanteur II)

ORLICA b.f. Hill Gail—Orarca (Arctic Prince)

Unbroken T-Y-O

ANAXIMANDER b.g. Zucchero—Desdemona (Dante)

The Foals

The four foals to be sold are a bay colt by **Zucchero—Loris** (Court Martial), a bay filly by **Figaro—Iavena** (Hill Gail); **Hysineta**, a chestnut filly by **Hill Gail—Ocarienne** (Ocarina); and a bay filly by **Zucchero—Dynamene** (My Babu).

The Vendor Explains

THIS sale of the majority of my bloodstock is no weeding-out affair. It's a sad business forced upon me by pressure of economic facts. What with training fees, travelling costs, keep of stud animals, stallion fees and so on, to maintain 54 horses means an annual bill of close on £50,000. I can't afford it.

I do not breed for sale, but purely to race my own stock, as a hobby, for pleasure. My horses have run, in the past, with conspicuous success, and have enjoyed more than four times the national expectation; but the level of stake money in this country is far too low for me to continue to indulge my hobby on such a scale. Hence this sale, involving 29 of my 54 horses. Except for three or four with which I am disappointed, I sell them all with regret, particularly the mares and yearlings.

NEWMARKET DECEMBER SALES

TEN ATTRACTIVE YOUNG MARES COVERED BY TOP CLASS STALLIONS
OFFERED WITHOUT RESERVE

ANNE OF HOLLINS (1956) b.m. Tudor Minstrel—Anne of Essex (Panorama)

NANERL (1957) ch.m. My Babu—Naretta (Nasrullah)

GUERNAMENE (1956) b.m. Guernant—Dynamene (My Babu)

LORIA (1957) ch.m. Court Martial—Andorra (Panorama)

ISMENE (1957) ch.m. Hill Gail—Dynamene (My Babu)

DJERETTA (1949) b.m. Diebel—Candida (Stardust)

CARTERETTA (1951) ch.m. Chanteur II—Chart Room (Blue Peter)

TOURINTA (1950) ch.m. Tourbillon—Queen Eleanor (Stardust)

MELUSINA (1956) b.m. My Babu—Queen Eleanor (Stardust)

OCARIENNE (1956) ch.m. Ocarina—Orienne (Sol Oriens)

Horses in Training

PARIDEL 6 ch.h. Pardal—Tourinta (Tourbillon)

ARISTARCHUS 4 b.c. Hill Gail—Black Chiffon (Blue Peter)

ERATOSTHENES 4 b.c. Guernant—Lady Electra (Fairway)

TORULLO 4 b.c. Nearula—Tourinta (Tourbillon)

ZANEXUS 3 b.c. Zucchero—Anne of Essex (Panorama)

PATROCLUS 2 b.c. Guernant—Dieretta (Diebel)

THUCYDIDES 3 b.c. Hill Gail—Orycida (Alycidon)

VELMINA 2 b.f. Vimy—Queen Eleanor (Stardust)

TO DISSOLVE A PARTNERSHIP

NEGRESCO II 4 b.c. Sica Boy—Folle Nuit (Astrophel)

THE HOLLINS STUD

Although its first produce did not appear on the racecourse until 1948, Phil Bull's stud has already gained a world-wide reputation. Siring high-class stock in various countries are Hollins-bred stallions like Anamnestes (England), Diopides and Eudaemon (Eire), Beethoven (Jamaica), Candaules (Chile), Duerdilo (Turkey), Orbaneja (Brazil), Eubolides (U.S.A.) and Orgoglio (Australia). Now, for the first time, are offered at public auction ten first-class Hollins mares, eight of them daughters or grand-daughters of those four phenomenal foundation mares Anne of Essex, Candida, Queen Eleanor and Orienne, who all figure prominently on the page at the foot of the page, on the right. A very

have produced 26 individual winners of 108 races value £115,000.

To the end of 1960, 62 Hollins-bred runners (89 per cent. winners) have won 138 races under Jockey Club Rules. The 110 year-starters have earned £120,000 win money, as compared with an average of £28,000—an Average Earnings Index of 4.26. Hollins-bred horses have won 4.26 times the national average. The most successful British stallion in recent times (with over 100 year-starters) is Hyperion. His stock, over the years, have won 3.87 times the expectation. Hollins horses have been more successful, on an average, than Hyperion horses!

Average Earnings Index 4.26

---

1 'No weeding-out affair'
The Sporting Life—November 1961
Full-page spread

T OWARDS the back of *Racehorses of 1954* there appeared a four-page display advertising Bloodstock For Sale. The lead-in announced: Mr Phil Bull, whose Hollins Stud has bred the winners, in the past four seasons, of 43 races under Jockey Club Rules to the value of £32,576, proposes to reduce his bloodstock holding by 25 per cent to 33 per cent.

There followed a comprehensive list of Bull's broodmares and horses in training, with details of their racing and stud records, plus the younger stock. Inquiries regarding the purchase of any horses on the list were invited. Similar advertisements appeared in most subsequent annuals until the practice was discontinued in 1978, by which time Bull's breeding operation had been wound down considerably as a result of spiralling costs. Every year the whole of the stock was genuinely on offer; not just the potential stallions or the broodmares.

Bull sold Romulus (winner of the Sussex Stakes and Queen Elizabeth II Stakes), the best racehorse he bred, as a foal; and Eudaemon (Gimcrack Stakes and Champagne Stakes), Tubalcain (Ascot Stakes, Queen Alexandra Stakes and Goodwood Stakes), Orosio (Cesarewitch) and Tonito Pitti (Grand Prix de Bordeaux) as yearlings. But the majority of the home-breds carried his colours, and they made a significant contribution to his success as an owner.

The Hollins Stud was founded by Bull in 1947 with four mares—Lady Electra, Candida, Orienne and Anne of Essex. The stud did not exist as a tangible entity; it was the corporate name for Bull's breeding operation, which involved boarding mares and rearing foals at John Coggan's Home Stud near Salisbury in Wiltshire, William Hill's Sezincote Stud at Moreton-in-Marsh in Gloucestershire managed by Norman Lonsdale, and in Ireland, Tim Roger's Airlie Stud and Jackie and Liam Ward's Ashleigh Stud.

By the end of 1954 the Hollins Stud had become well established. The 43 races mentioned in the advertisement included the Champagne Stakes and the Victoria Cup won by Orgoglio (by Nasrullah out of Orienne) and the Chesham Stakes and Richmond Stakes won by Eubulides (My Babu–Candida). The broodmare band had expanded to eleven; there were twelve horses in training with Charlie Elsey at Malton, and six yearlings following on. And the stud continued to flourish. 'Bloodstock Available' in *Racehorses of 1964* ran to nineteen pages, the most space it ever occupied: 'Mr Phil Bull, whose Hollins Stud has bred the winners in the past fifteen seasons of 196½ races under Jockey Club Rules to the value of £170,091, welcomes inquiries ...' etcetera. When the advertisement appeared for the last time, in

Racehorses of 1977, it listed five horses in training, two yearlings, and six mares, three of whom were due to foal.

As early as 1956 the emergent breeding operation had one of its fillies placed in a classic, when Arietta (Tudor Minstrel–Anne of Essex) came third to her stable-companion Honeylight in the One Thousand Guineas. Thanks largely to Eudaemon, who was sold for only 1,000 guineas to Mrs Elsie Foster, Bull finished fifth in the breeders' table that year, ahead of some of the sport's best-known names, the Stanley Estate & Stud, Astor Studs, Marcel Boussac, Dorothy Paget and Lord Rosebery among them. In 1957 he finished equally highly placed in the owners' table, behind The Queen, Sir Victor Sassoon, Lionel Holliday and Jim Joel, and was sixth in the breeders' table. This owed much to the exploits of the two-year-old colts Pheidippides (Court Martial–Queen Eleanor) and Guersillus (Guersant–Cantarilla), the four-year-old colt Dionisio (My Babu–Candida) and the four-year-old filly Orinthia (Ocarina–Orienne). Pheidippides won the Gimcrack with a performance that earned him 9st 1lb in the Free Handicap, while the less precocious Guersillus, who went on to run fifth in the Derby and won the Gordon Stakes and City and Suburban Handicap, received 8st 2lb.

These were the days when top-class horses and those verging on top class could routinely be seen running in handicaps at the main meetings. Dionisio, rated just below top class by *Timeform* at 126, won two of the big betting races in 1957, the Victoria Cup and the Wokingham, then was sold for £10,000 as a stallion to the Baroda Stud. Orinthia, in her last season before retirement, won the Great Jubilee Handicap and the Manchester Cup under the 5lb-claiming apprentice Greville Starkey. Bull was a great advocate of using a good apprentice in handicaps, especially over longer distances, and he put up another 5lb-claimer, Pat Eddery, when Philoctetes won the Northumberland Plate in 1970.

Arietta was retired as a three-year-old in 1956. She was to make an immediate impact in the paddocks. Bull was able to afford, for the time being, to stick to his policy of breeding from the best stallions and had her covered in the first year by the Derby and St Leger winner Never Say Die, the next by the great Ribot in Italy. The first mating produced a good horse in Sostenuto, the second an even better one in Romulus. Both were aptly named, particularly Sostenuto, as Bull turned with great pleasure to things classical—musical or antiquarian—for inspiration for his horses' names.

Sostenuto never really fulfilled his potential. He split a pastern early on at both two and three years, and ran only three times over that period. He won all three starts but circumstances prevented his meeting opposition that might have tested him fully. In *Racehorses of 1962*, Arthur Shaw wrote: 'If Sostenuto's four-year-old career could be fairly described in terms appropriate to a musical composition, it might be said that the exposition was long-winded and disappointing, the development a notable example of harmonic progression, and the coda dashing and brilliant.' The coda was well worth the wait. At York in August Sostenuto ran right away from the Ebor field in the last furlong and a half, winning very easily indeed by eight lengths from Cracksman. The winning rider was Don Morris, Bull's third retained jockey after Edgar Britt and Edward Hide. Bull provided Morris with his first winning ride—Beethoven at Pontefract in 1955—and many more before his death in a car crash on the York–Malton road in 1966 at the age of 28.

Bull sold Romulus as a foal for 19,000 guineas—at the time equal to the record auction price in Britain for a foal—to Charles Engelhard, the American industrialist who later won the Triple Crown with Nijinsky and other St Legers with Indiana and, in successive years, the brothers Ribocco and Ribero. Romulus beat all except Privy Councillor in the Guineas in 1962. He was one of seven fallers in Larkspur's Derby, but miling was his game and by the end of the season he could fairly be considered the best in Europe. As well as the Sussex Stakes and Queen Elizabeth II Stakes he won the Greenham Stakes and Hungerford Stakes at Newbury and the Prix du Moulin de Longchamp. *Timeform* rated him at 129. After a four-year-old career that proved a sad anticlimax, he was syndicated and stood in Britain until exported to Japan in 1969. Incidentally, his son Petty Officer won the Timeform Gold Cup at Redcar three years running.

The Sixties added at least four more names to the list of notable Hollins-breds: the colts Mozart (Alycidon–Candida), Dion (Guersant–Anadem, out of Anne of Essex), Philoctetes (Never Say Die–Orinthia) and Charicles (Bleep-Bleep–Candida). Mozart did well in the United States as a four-year-old in 1961, winning the Wilwyn Handicap at Laurel and the Kelly-Olympic Handicap at Atlantic City; he had received 8st in the Free Handicap after racing in Britain as a two-year-old for Bull. Mozart's half-brother Charicles, foaled when the mare was twenty-two, won the Wokingham in 1968, while Dion and Philoctetes were useful staying handicappers, Philoctetes the better-class one. More of Philoctetes elsewhere!

By contrast the Seventies and Eighties were lean times for the stud, though Aureoletta (Aureole–Tartarelle, out of Orarca, out of Orienne) finished third to Mysterious in the 1973 Oaks, and little Fiordiligi (Tudor Melody–Dorabella, out of Anne of Essex) raised hopes that she might also become a classic filly when she won the Sweet Solera Stakes and finished a close second in the May Hill Stakes in 1977, only to fail to train on. Fiordiligi achieved some distinction afterwards as the dam of one of Bull's last winners, the quite useful sprinter Ho Mi Chinh, and she was also the dam of possibly the last winner he bred, Marionella, who carried the colours of his friend Dick Warden when successful at Beverley and Pontefract in 1988.

The staying hurdler Angelo Salvini (Relko–Sweet Sauce) was probably the last good horse to come out of the stud. Bull lost little time in selling him to Jim Joel once the gelding's Flat-racing career was over. Bull had not the slightest interest in jump racing. For him, winter had long been the time to prepare *Best Horses* and *Racehorses*, to cope with being unable to get out of The Hollins because of snow, and—with no apparent enthusiasm at times—to go on holiday abroad. *Chasers & Hurdlers*, the companion National Hunt annual to *Racehorses*, did not make its first appearance until 1976, and then only at the suggestion of other Timeform staff. Yet, curiously, Bull had a runner over hurdles in 1957. This was Souvrillus, trained by Bill Dutton, who ran four times from January to March that year. Eighteen months later Bull sold Souvrillus for £1,250 to an owner with Atty Corbett, and in the letter confirming the sale he explained: 'You need take no notice of his failures over the sticks. I only jumped him in an effort to get him to settle down, because at that time he was particularly headstrong. In making him settle down, the jockey dropped him so far out of the races as to destroy any chance the horse had of winning, despite which the horse ran well, especially at Wetherby.' Within a month of Corbett's taking over Souvrillus he won a novices' hurdle, but Bull maintained his lack of interest in this branch of racing.

Bull was a buyer as well as a seller, and on an appreciable scale. He acquired Khaled's half-sister Lady Electra, who became known popularly as the 'Idol of the North'. The story of Lady Electra's purchase is told in the chapter on William Hill.

Lady Electra was a prolific winner, including of a wartime Substitute Lincolnshire Handicap, and a high-class racemare for Bull. None of the fillies brought into the stud from 'outside' made the same impact as the quartet there from the start, although some won races and bred winners for Bull. One such purchase in the Seventies, Hypatia, whom he let go to France before she had a foal on the ground, turned up after Bull's death as the grandam of Sheikh Mohammed's good sprinter-miler Lycius. Another, the

French One Thousand Guineas and Oaks third Sweet Sauce, bred him the 1979 Chesterfield Cup winner Philodantes.

The best colt Bull owned that he did not breed himself was Negresco, whom he bought after his third outing as a three-year-old in 1960. Bull saw him run a fast-finishing third to Angers in the Prix Hocquart at Longchamp, and persuaded William Hill to put up the money for an equal 37.5 per cent stake, with Francois Dupre retaining the remaining 25 per cent. Next time out, still trained by Francois Mathet, Negresco made all the running in the Grand Prix du Printemps at Saint-Cloud. But for his next appearance Mathet's very young jockey Yves Saint-Martin received a ticking off in *Racehorses* that year for riding an ill-judged race in the Grand Prix de Paris, where Negresco made up an enormous amount of ground in the last two furlongs to snatch fourth behind Charlottesville. Negresco had the final race of his career in Britain, finishing third in the Doncaster Cup in 1961. In December that year Negresco was sold at auction for 1,200 guineas—'a tiny sum by comparison with what they'd paid for him' one of Bull's aides recalled—and he went to Poland as a stallion.

In 1961 Bull purchased a Grey Sovereign colt foal for 2,700 guineas. He made up into a big, powerful individual with an enormous stride, and under the name of Lanark he showed some very smart form, despite being dogged by injury. Lanark was sent to Vincent O'Brien in Ireland to be trained for the Guineas after finishing second in the Gimcrack for Bill Elsey. He looked right on course when he beat a useful field in his trial, the Athboy Stakes at Phoenix Park, but a fractured sesamoid intervened. Potentially he was one of the best horses to carry Bull's colours; he was also the only one trained by Vincent O'Brien.

THE first horse that Phil Bull owned did not run in his name. Iceland was bought, having already been named, for 35 guineas from an executors' draft at the Newmarket yearling sales in October 1941. She ran as a two-year-old for Miss Eleanor Mary Oxley, Bull's mistress. Bull had been separated from his first wife Doris, whom he married in 1935, for at least three years; he was still teaching in London and operating the Temple Racetime Analysis under the pseudonym William K. Temple, two factors which precluded him from using his own name under which to race horses. But the thrill of Iceland's winning first time out was no less diminished. On 25 April 1942, starting 9/4 favourite in a five-furlong, 15-runner fillies' plate worth £123 to the winner, she won by a neck in a field of debutantes at Pontefract, Bull's local track. Bull described it as a 'fairy tale start'. Iceland was trained at Malton by Cecil Ray, who had made the original purchase on Bull's behalf. They first met when Ray was training at Epsom and Bull was living in Putney, South London. Ray moved North to train at Grove Cottage Stables, which was convenient when Bull himself returned to Yorkshire in 1945. Iceland ran a further eight times as a two-year-old and won again at Pontefract in August, but she was weighted out of her later races and was sold at the end of the season.

A hand-written letter from Miss Oxley to Weatherbys, dated 5 December 1942, asked for a statement of her account to be forwarded to her accommodation address in west London. It explained: 'It is improbable that I shall be able to race again until after the war.' Miss Oxley did not race again under her own name, but Phil Bull did, almost immediately, and there was no disguising one of the chief influences in the naming of his earliest horses.

Bull bought the readymade filly who became known as Lady Electra in July 1942, persuading William Hill to stump up a loan of £1,000 towards her purchase price of 3,500 guineas. Two months later, and shortly before Eleanor Oxley gave birth to Bull's daughter Anne, he paid 525 guineas through the Irish bloodstock agency of Kerr & Co. for a yearling filly by Panorama. Bull called her Anne of Essex.

Neither ran in Bull's name at first, though. The Jockey Club was concerned about his supplying racing information to the public and originally declined to grant him registration as an owner. Both Anne of Essex and Lady Electra were placed in the ownership of Billie Richardson, one of Bull's oldest friends, with the result that at the end of the 1943 season W. Richardson featured in seventeenth place in the owners' list in Britain, with two horses having won six races worth a total of £1,436. Lady Electra won five times, including in the Substitute Lincolnshire Handicap at Pontefract, and Anne of Essex once. Richardson's racing colours have a familiar ring to them—cerise, white circle back and front, cerise cap. In 1944 Bull was accepted as a registered owner and was listed with the self-same colours as Richardson, which remained with him throughout.

Anne of Essex, trained by Cecil Ray, won first time out at Stockton, starting second favourite, but never won again. Then came two further indications of Bull's affection for Miss Oxley—Eleanor Mary, a Panorama filly like Anne of Essex, who cost 750 guineas and won as a three-year-old; and Queen Eleanor, whom Bull bought privately for 1,250 guineas. Queen Eleanor was beaten on her Catterick debut when favourite but made handsome amends next time, winning by five lengths at Pontefract, where she won again three weeks later. That year, 1945, Bull also had Orienne running for him. Bought for 210 guineas at the Newmarket yearling sales, Orienne was beaten into second on her racecourse debut, when favourite for the Pontefract race previously won by Iceland, but she won next time at Catterick, and the following year won a handicap at Ayr.

The Jockey Club stewards had cleared Bull to own horses in November 1943, but there was another hitch in the autumn of 1945, when he received a letter from the Jockey Club Office in Newmarket, informing him: 'After the end of this season, so long as you are connected with the business of "Temple", the stewards will not be prepared to give any trainer permission to train your horses. Should, however, you sever all connection with the business of "Temple", there will be no objection to a licensed trainer training your horses. The stewards will naturally require adequate proof that your connection with the business of "Temple" has been completely severed.' It took Bull until the early weeks of 1946 to convince the Jockey Club this was the case. But another problem was just around the corner.

Cecil Ray, Bull's trainer, had his licence withdrawn in 1946, after one of his horses was found to have been doped in a race at York. At that time Jockey Club justice insisted that the trainer should be summarily warned off. Ray died within a few years, a broken man. Bull was appalled at the Jockey Club's treatment of Ray and sought to have his name cleared and the policy changed. He had some success, but it came too late for Ray. Bull believed the stress of the case was a contributory factor in Ray's death.

Writing to Ray's son, also Cecil, who lived in Johannesburg, on 10 June 1952, Bull said:

Trainers are still losing their licences as in the past, but there are signs of a slightly more reasonable attitude on the part of the Jockey Club, and they have started a security scheme for the protection of racecourse stables and the exclusion from these stables of all persons other than the lads in charge of the horses. Even owners cannot visit their own horses unless accompanied by the trainer.

No stigma now attaches to your father's name so far as the Jockey Club goes. After your father's death I sent all the papers to the Jockey Club (after preliminary correspondence with them) and although they did nothing more than acknowledge and return the papers, their attitude to myself has changed markedly, so I know that they have accepted the evidence in the documents.

It appears from your letter that you are not aware just how conclusively these documents did in fact pin the job on one of the lads in your father's stable, but you can take it from me that the evidence was perfectly conclusive. If you are ever over here, you can inspect the documents, but your father entrusted them to me, and I do not propose to let them out of my keeping.

> Thirty years later, Bull confided to Alex Bird that Cecil Ray, shortly before he died, asked Bull to promise that one day he would expose the whole story. Recalling the case in a letter to Bird dated 10 November 1982, Bull wrote:

The investigations I myself conducted into the actions and movements of Ray's lads at York (the day the horse ran) pointed to the culprit, though proof was lacking.

After the Stewards had held their farcical inquiry, Cecil Ray engaged a private inquiry agent. His inquiries took a long time, but he eventually came up with the truth, which confirmed the suspicions raised by my own inquiries.

Ray was employing solicitors, and it was they who dealt with the Jockey Club. I think I have all the papers filed away, but I have neither the time nor the inclination to go through them.

My recollection is that Ray's solicitors were successful in compelling the Jockey Club to withdraw the 'warning-off' notice. Cecil Ray was free to go racing. But, of course, he'd lost his licence and his livelihood.

> The papers to which Bull referred in correspondence with both Ray's son and Bird have never come to light. Whether they were returned to Bull's care is open to question, despite his assurances, and it may be that he was merely using this ploy to smooth the feelings of Ray's son following his father's death. But Bull did not forget the case, making oblique reference to it in his submission to the Royal Commission on Gambling, published in January 1977:

The Jockey Club maintained only one real sanction to deal with serious breaches of its rules—the Alice in Wonderland off-with-his-head sentence—'warning off' *sine die*: the fact that the severity of such a sentence prohibited its use except very rarely was a standing encouragement to would-be wrongdoers to 'chance it'.

To make such a sanction even minimally effective the Jockey Club was obliged to find victims of whom to make examples. This it did by gestapo and Star Chamber methods—identifying its victims among the expendable lesser fry, never among those who trained or rode for members of the Establishment.

With the victims caught, the so-called inquiries that followed were conducted as courts martial, though without benefit of advocacy on behalf of the 'accused'. The verdicts were a formality, pronounced in military style and published in words calculated to take away not merely a man's livelihood but his good name as well. In this way the then stewards, to my knowledge, destroyed the lives of three trainers completely innocent of anything but notional negligence, of which the stewards themselves were guilty every day of the week.

Nor, thanks to a deplorable ruling by Lord Justice Goddard which would not stand up today, could the victims find redress in the courts. The integrity of the Jockey Club in the 1940s was somewhat below that of the bookmakers whom they barred from many members' enclosures.

One of the three trainers to whom Bull referred was Cecil Ray; he made the revelation in a letter to the Jockey Club senior steward Lord Howard de Walden, dated 4 February 1977, in which he enclosed, in confidence, a copy of the submission, 'partly because you have been very kind to me, and because I have much respect for you and am aware of your lifelong committment to racing'. Bull went on to discuss Ray's case:

One of his horses had been doped. I well remember his telling me on the 'phone of his having received a summons to 15 Cavendish Square [the Jockey Club office]. I remember his bewilderment. I remember telling him that this was no inquiry, and that he was about to be warned off. I well remember my own efforts to find the villain responsible for the doping; how I interrogated his head lad, his travelling head lad and every stable boy who had been to York the day the horse ran there.

I remember taking them all to York for a reconstruction, having them go through all their movements, recalling what they did and who they spoke to. I remember catching one of them out in a deliberate lie (and he, indeed, subsequently turned out to have been one of the two people involved).

I remember attending the farcical charade that passed for an inquiry, and the way Cecil Ray and I were treated. I remember Cecil's distress. I remember the notice in the Calendar. I remember the subsequent business with solicitors and counsel, and the engagement of a private inquiry agent who finally got to the bottom of it, much too late. I remember how the loss of his licence affected Cecil Ray, how it took all the life out of him. I remember going to see him at Epsom when he was dying, and his extracting a promise from me that I would write it all up and clear his name. I never did. I have box files full of documents about Cecil Ray's case and those of Jim Russell and two other victims. But this is the first I've ever written about any of it.

I remember, too, in what ways and for how long I too was a victim—guilty by association—and the serious consequences for me, but for which my whole life would undoubtedly have been far different. My horses would have been trained by Noel Murless in the late 1940s. He dare not take them. It took years for me to become a member of the club stands at Newmarket, Epsom and Goodwood. It was Lord Rosebery (one of the three Jockey Club Stewards who had warned Ray off) who got me made a member at Newmarket; but even his sponsorship failed at Epsom. I was a pariah.

When Ray lost his licence, Bull sent his horses, including Orienne, to be trained for the 1946 season by Norman Scobie, who was stationed in the racecourse stables at Doncaster. In the middle of the year Bull moved his horses again, to Michael Everitt at Middleham, but the pair did not really get on and within a couple of years, apart from a brief association with Willie Stephenson, Bull's horses were with Charlie Elsey at Malton. In 1951 they included Anamnestes, Elsey's first winner for Bull, and Orgoglio, who won the Champagne Stakes. 'My real success as an owner began when Captain Elsey began to train for me,' Bull wrote in his autobiographical notes. 'They had a great rapport,' Reg Griffin recalls.

Charlie Elsey retired at the end of 1960 and handed over to his son Bill. Bull kept his horses at Highfield Stables, but there was never the same feeling between owner and trainer and Bull spent the rest of his life in racing looking for a replacement for the Captain. At the end of the 1965 season Bull broke his association with the Elseys. His prospective classic colt Lanark went to Vincent O'Brien and the rest were split between Albert Cooper in Malton and Teddy Lambton in Newmarket. Reg Griffin recalls: 'As a paddock observer Phil always admired the way Albert Cooper's horses looked and were turned out, and the plan was that about eight horses, including four of William Hill's which were suited to the Northern scene, would go to him, and the rest to Teddy Lambton, whom he'd known for a long time, though Phil didn't approve of his long record of drinking rather heavily.'

The fact that Peter Robinson was Lambton's stable jockey also influenced Bull. Robinson [father of the current jockey Philip Robinson] had been a very close friend of Griffin for some time, and was a regular visitor to The Hollins when he stayed in Halifax for major Northern meetings. Bull was aware of Robinson's reputation—'He was a bit of a villain when it came to riding Lambton's horses,' Griffin says, 'because he used to do what he wanted with them, just as he'd done with Lord Rosebery's horses at Jack Jarvis', when he was getting them ready with a run before the Scottish circuit.' But Bull made it plain to Robinson he would have no 'jockey's games' played on his horses.

Robinson was not retained by Bull, unlike Edgar Britt, Edward Hide and Don Morris at the Elsey stable. Bull had a particular regard for the Australian Britt, whom he credited with 'introducing and establishing the short-stirrup riding style in this country, not Lester Piggott'. When their retainer ended in 1957, Bull wrote to Britt on 11 December:

I wish you to understand that my taking this step stems more from future considerations than present ones. No owner has had his horses better ridden than mine have been in the past eight years. You have ridden many brilliant races for me, and much of the success my horses have had has been due to your handling of them.

Bull hoped Britt would continue to ride for him 'when occasion arises', and they remained very good friends, but the retainer went to Edward Hide because Bull could no longer guarantee having first choice of Britt for his and William Hill's horses, whom he managed. The same later applied to Hide, and Bull took a retainer on Don Morris in 1963. In letters dated 17 and 29 October 1962, Bull put the position to Hide, who in between wrote to say, 'It would be a blow to be virtually sacked for no apparent reason':

In present circumstances you have choice of mounts whenever the stable runs two or more horses in a race; and on certain occasions, when there are several meetings on the same day, the choice as to where you will ride is also yours.

This arrangement no longer suits me. With 23 horses to manage I feel I need the services of a jockey whom I can direct to ride what I wish him to ride.

I hope you won't take this as implying any criticism of yourself, or that you have lost my confidence. That isn't so. I propose to continue to participate in your stable retainer, and shall endeavour to make riding plans for my horses that fit in as far as possible with general stable arrangements.

As things have been in 1962, the decisions as to what you will ride and where you will ride lie with you. Not with me. You make these decisions to suit yourself. If you wish to ride (or Bill [Elsey] wants you to ride) in an important race at Sandown or Goodwood or Ascot, when I need you at Pontefract, you do so. I don't blame you. It's in your interests to do so. But it's not in my interests and it doesn't suit me.

When Teddy Lambton's financial troubles forced him to hand in his training licence halfway through the 1969 season, Peter Robinson gave up riding and took over the stable. There was never any question that Robinson would train long term for Bull. On the one hand Bull was fearful that Robinson would not always run his horses on their merits, says Reg Griffin; and on the other Robinson feared that Bull's reputation as a gambler would prevent his being granted a permanent licence—a remarkable turn of events in view of Robinson's own reputation! Even though Bull always insisted his horses were run 'straight', the latter point had cropped up before. Noel Murless, for whom Bull had the highest regard, felt unable to train for him in Newmarket. Sam Hall had not been keen to take Bull's horses, when he left the Elsey stable, for the same reason. And Sam Armstrong had to turn down William Hill's horses because he was told the Jockey Club would not countenance a bookmaker having horses trained in Newmarket. Subsequently they did, however, allow Hill's horses to run in his wife Ivy's name, and they were based at Newmarket, with Bruce Hobbs.

On Lambton's departure from training, in 1970 Bull sent three horses, including Philoctetes, to Staff Ingham at Epsom, a filly to Sally Hall and the three-year-old Diaz to Tommy Fairhurst at Middleham. Described by Griffin as 'a thoroughly bad horse who never won a race,' Diaz was sold at the end of 1970 for 640 guineas. It was a case of how the mighty had fallen, for Bull spent considerable time trying to persuade Sir Ivor's owner Raymond Guest to take an interest in Diaz as a two-year-old in exchange for a share in the Derby winner. 'Can you fault him?' Bull asked in a letter to Guest, dated 7 May 1969, enclosing a photograph of the colt as a yearling. 'I can't. For over twenty years I've had all my horses photographed every year. The most charming individual was Pheidippides. Orgoglio, Arietta and Sostenuto were fine yearlings too. So also Diaz.' Bull went on:

You ask me what I think Diaz is worth. That's a question almost impossible to answer. People pay, in my opinion, ridiculous prices for horses these days. As you know, £25,000 is not reckoned out of the way for a well-bred high-class individual. Yet we both know that, statistically speaking, no young horse whose merit has not been demonstrated on the racecourse can be worth £5,000. Even for the most exclusively selected yearlings the 'break-even' figure would be much less than that. So the objective answer to your question is that neither Diaz nor any other untried two-year-old is worth £25,000. The subjective answer is that I would be reluctant to sell him for that figure. I'm like you. I seek to have the superlative horse; to win the Derby. A small owner-breeder like myself does not get many prospective Classic winners. But when one does come up with what looks like the right article, a person like myself has to be really in need of the money to pass up the grand gamble by selling the horse. So to hell with objectivity!

That's what this business of breeding and owning horses is all about. I'm not a wealthy man. I have to pay my way as I go along. But I'm a gambler and I prefer to temper boldness with prudence rather than the other way round.

I'm persuaded that Diaz is my best Classic prospect since Orgoglio, Arietta, Guersillus and Sostenuto. To a large extent this is other people's doing. The horse is a fine individual and a lovely mover with a perfect temperament. I know these things at first hand. But, of course, the same may be said of many, many horses, year after year, who never make the classic grade.

> Diaz never made any grade, never mind the classics, and Bull continued to seek his elusive classic winner. He also kept up the search for another Charlie Elsey. Barry Hills perhaps came the nearest to both, training Aureoletta to finish third in the Oaks, but he was followed by Mick Easterby and then Peter Easterby, and finally Clive Brittain, who was sent Ho Mi Chinh because it was thought his equine swimming pool would help the horse's knees, which were injured when he came down on the road.
>
> Bull knew whom he would have liked to take Elsey's place, but Lanark, in 1965, was the only horse that Vincent O'Brien—born on the same day, 9 April, as Bull—ever trained for him. Bull was anxious for O'Brien to take the yearling filly Relza (by Relko out of Lady Electra's daughter Berganza) but the Irish trainer delayed seeing her, and on 19 December 1968 (the year of Sir Ivor) Bull wrote:

I wish you were to train her. This, however, is not feasible now, so I'm afraid we must send her elsewhere. And so, if Relza runs second or third in the Oaks, instead of winning it, I shall lay it at your door! I say this with immense good humour of course. However purple any filly's pedigree or perfect its conformation, it is always 20/1 against its being good enough to run in the Oaks let alone win.

> Relza was sent to Staff Ingham, along with the Never Say Die colt called Diaz, whom O'Brien had also declined, but more pointedly! On 21 January 1969, Bull lamented again that O'Brien was not to train either:

I have more regard for you as a trainer than for anyone else in the British Isles, and, furthermore, we speak the same language. Racingwise. You know me and I know you, and we understand one-another. Staff is all right. He's a good trainer. But I don't know him. He's a bit of a 'loner', you know, and I haven't yet been able to make real contact with him. But that's beside the point.

You and I talk the same language. If you trained in England, I'd want you to have all my horses. As it is, and since I race for the fun of the thing, I must have most of my horses trained over here if I am to see them run. But where potential Classic horses are concerned it's a different matter altogether. You can have your pick of those any time. I want you to train 'em. Or leave the picking to me: rely on me to send you what I think have the Classic potential. There's no problem about this. If they're not up to Classic standard, when you've had a chance to try them out, they can easily come back, and should do so, to take their chances over here.

I try to breed horses only on 'Classic' lines (by and large). They're foaled. They're yearlings. Some you can wash out right away at sight. Others are doubtful. A few are impressive and excite anticipation, or have no faults and might be Classic material. OK, you take your pick, or let me take mine.

But, and this is the point, Vincent, you know as well as I know, that the difference between success and failure in this game, between winning a Classic and running second, third or fourth is minimal, a few pounds, and, if you're with me, you know damn well that this is in the trainer's hands. You, as a trainer, are, like Mathet and Pollet in France, 7lb in front of the ordinary good trainer. I know this, and have known it for years. It's nothing new to me. Charlie Elsey was like you in some respects. I know the value of this training flair and genius. It is, to an owner, the difference between success and near-misses. Jim Joel has found it out. Think how long he persevered, for loyalty's sake, with Ted Leader. He's talked to me about it.

So understand me: I know you and appreciate you—better perhaps than nine out of ten of your owners. And you know me. I've not been at this game for fun for a year or two. I've been in it for 30 years and I know what it's about. I also know damn well that I'll get nowhere with people like Teddy Lambton (nice, well-meaning and friendly guy that he is!). I'm being frank with you, and to the point. I know what I wish to do. I've 20 years (at best) to live, and I would value your assistance to achieve, in racing, what I wish to achieve in the years that remain. I need you to train my top horses—not the others.

> Relza ran once as a two-year-old for Ingham, before joining the unraced Diaz in the North the following year. Relza, trained by Sally Hall, showed above average ability and won three races, but she was two stones off classic standard. Diaz was even farther behind. And O'Brien came no nearer training another Lanark for Bull, though the pressure went on, as in a letter dated 10 July 1973:

Training, as I have always said, is the critical factor. I'm very happy with Barry Hills. I regard him as one of the very best trainers over here, and he is a most acceptable and agreeable person. But whenever I have any potentially Classic animals among my yearlings—horses which would not be out of place among the imposing American-bred population at Ballydoyle—I'll ask you to look 'em over in the hope that something may take your fancy enough to make you wish to train it! My expectation of life (on pedigree) is about another 22 years. So you've 20 years in which to train me a Classic winner! We should be able to manage it, don't you think?

> Bull's classic aspirations had been triggered as a youngster. In a review of Quintin Gilbey's *Champions All* for *Books and Bookmen* Bull wrote:

When I was a schoolboy in my teens, the solitary photograph that hung above my bed was not of my latest girlfriend, or of my parents, or of Wilfrid Rhodes or Walter Lindrum; it was a photograph of a racehorse, Colorado, winner of the Two Thousand Guineas of 1926. He was a bonny little horse, the apple of my adolescent eye. I was his fan. When a big, slashing, headstrong horse Coronach beat him in the Derby, I wouldn't believe the result; and when, the following year, my little favourite twice trounced Coronach, making the score three–one in his favour, I was like a dog with two tails.

The records say that Lord Derby owned Colorado. Not to me he didn't. In my schoolboy mind I owned that horse, even though I was mostly stuck at a desk with Latin grammar when I might have been watching him win his races, which, could hardly have been of less benefit to me than the Latin proved to be.

His highest ambition went unfulfilled. In a letter to Lady Beaverbrook, dated 5 July 1976, he wrote:

You're better off than I am. You've won a Classic and I've been trying for 30 years without success. Arietta ran third for me in the One Thousand and Aureoletta in the Oaks. Guersillus was beaten two short heads for third place in a bad Derby. That's the closest I've got, though I might have won a Two Thousand with Lanark if he hadn't split a pastern a few days before the race, and perhaps a Derby with Sostenuto, who did the same thing in May, when ante-post favourite.

Bull's bloodstock interests were steadily reducing; he told Lady Beaverbrook: 'Unfortunately, being a relatively poor man, I frequently have to sell my best prospects in order to stay in the game at all.' Much later, in a letter dated 25 March 1981, he told Vincent O'Brien:

I fear my personal involvement in breeding and owning racehorses is now but a shadow of what it once was. I can't any longer afford to play in the top league and I've no intention of playing in the third division: so I've only one horse in training and a couple of broodmares. I've also a fine yearling, a colt, which regretfully I'll have to send up at the Houghton Sales.

Selling stock was nothing new to Bull. He sold Eudaemon for 1,000 guineas as a yearling in 1955, and wrote to a friend in New York in September 1956: 'I still have his dam Queen Electra and if anyone offered me $42,000 for her, I should accept it, and if you were the intermediary, the odd $2,000 would be yours.'

Incidentally, Bull later repaid at least some of the money he received for Eudaemon when his owner Mrs Foster fell on hard times. Her name appeared on the Forfeit List, and Bull instructed Weatherbys to charge the amount owing to his account, though he ordered them not to tell her or anybody else who had paid.

Pheidippides was offered to a Maryland stud owner for $60,000 shortly after his win in the 1957 Gimcrack Stakes, and to an Australian agent in Sydney for £20,000 the following February. By June Pheidippides had lost his classic tag, and Bull was offering him to inquiring British agents at £10,000. In September he was sold to the Ballykisteen Stud in Ireland.

With a business that offered no income during winter, a betting operation which on average made good money but could be unpredictable, and a growing band of horses, Bull was always vulnerable to offers. Whether he regarded them as hostile or not depended on circumstance. At the end of 1962 he sold the good mares Arietta and Anadem, and the potential stallion Sostenuto for a combined total of £96,000, a little over £1 million in today's terms.

Reg Griffin recalls: 'Phil took everything with equanimity, including his betting. If he won £5,000 a day, he would get into the car, light up a cigar and within about two miles he'd be asleep. The next day, if he'd lost £5,000, the same thing would happen.

'Dealing with horses, he knew the risk when he was selling. He was a reluctant seller, because he knew that if he could come up with a good stallion, he would hit the jackpot. Unfortunately, either the money ran out or he ran out before he achieved it.

'He was regarded by the Inland Revenue as a "hobby breeder", which meant that everything he had bred or trained came out of his own pocket. He chose to keep it that way and take the chance on coming up with a top horse. He described his racing operation as doing it on a shoestring.'

Once the money for a sale had gone through, Bull regarded the matter closed, whatever the future may hold. His fatalistic view of subsequent events was not always reciprocated. Early in 1961 he sold the twice-raced three-year-old colt Idamante for £4,000 to an owner in John Benstead's Epsom stable. After an uneventful outing at Epsom's April meeting, Idamante refused to start in a race at the Derby meeting, and Reg Griffin recalls that Benstead spoke to Bull at the races on behalf of the owner. Bull assured him that Idamante had never given trouble whilst in his ownership and suggested the owner and his agents should check with Charlie Elsey. The answer came back from Malton that nothing serious had been amiss, but connections pressed Bull about whether he would refund some of the purchase price in view of their disappointment. After the Derby meeting the colt bolted on the way to the start at Royal Ascot and again refused to start. Bull responded by sending a cheque for £3,999 19s 11d. 'They can have the horse for a penny, to show my contempt,' he told Griffin. The story goes that when the owner met Bull, he thanked him for the kind gesture. 'You've missed the point, brother,' Bull replied. 'It wasn't intended to be anything of the sort, it was to show my contempt!'

One of the more controversial events concerning Bull arose indirectly, as a result of his association with William Hill. As well as looking after his own horses Bull managed Hill's racing interests, along with those of the bookmaking firm's director Lionel Barber and two Jamaica-based friends, Harry Dayes and Frank Watson. Hill moved a number of horses to Charlie Elsey when he saw the success Bull was having with the stable. Among the first was a filly, Cantelo, who won all her five races as a two-year-old in 1958, ending with the Royal Lodge Stakes.

Bull managed her three-year-old career with a view to the classics, and after winning the Cheshire Oaks she finished second to Petite Etoile in the Oaks. Cantelo then won the Ribblesdale Stakes and finished fourth in the King George VI and Queen Elizabeth Stakes, before being aimed at the St Leger. First she ran in the Park Hill Stakes, three days before the classic. Discussing events at Doncaster with Geoffrey Hamlyn for his proposed biography of William Hill, Bull said:

Teddy Hide didn't ride one of the best races in the Park Hill Stakes. He came round the turn with the leaders and went to the front soon afterwards. Looking round, he saw he had the beating of the animal that was close up with him, and thought the race was more or less won three furlongs out. So instead of making the most of the animal's stamina, and sending her about her business, he sat with a nice little lead, thinking he would go on and win comfortably. But there was an animal of Murless' in the field called Collyria, who came along with a wet sail in the last furlong and beat her.

There's no question Cantelo should have won. I was in doubt whether it was worth running her in the St Leger, but we discussed it and Billy Hill said, 'Let her take her chance.'

I didn't give her much chance of beating the colts in the Leger, but Teddy Hide did exactly what he ought to have done in the Park Hill Stakes. As soon as they got round the turn he sent the mare about her business for all she was worth, and she established a lead. They couldn't get to her, and she won. When they came to the unsaddling enclosure, there was a demonstration, from the people who didn't understand these things. To them, here was an animal that belonged to a bookmaker, who had got beaten when it was a short price at 9/4 on in the Park Hill Stakes, and had won the St Leger at 100/7. All they could see was a stroke. But you couldn't persuade Billy Hill to have a shilling on a horse.

After the Park Hill, there had been plenty of people telling Billy that Teddy Hide had ridden a bad race, and Teddy was very riled. So Teddy Hide, thinking to make his point with Billy Hill when he got off after the Leger, said to him: 'Well there you are, if I'd given the horse a hard race on Wednesday, it wouldn't have won today.' A journalist overheard this and it was reported in the Press, which made the situation worse.

The facts are that first of all Billy Hill would have given a lot of money to win the Park Hill Stakes, with a mare that's only been beaten twice in her life. The Leger is three days ahead, it's got to be won, and a bird in the hand is worth two in the bush. And Billy has no interest in betting.

I bet on her in the Park Hill Stakes. I thought she was a good thing. But when the Leger came along, my bet as Billy's manager was a place-only bet.

The only other thing to add is that after Cantelo had won the Leger, Charlie Elsey told me: 'You know I knew this animal would improve after the Park Hill. The ground has been so hard I've been frightened to work her on it. The race she had in the Park Hill was just what she needed to put her one hundred per cent.' He said he was glad she ran in the Park Hill because if she hadn't, she might not have won the Leger.

Not so controversial, but more than a little perplexing at times was Bull's choice of names for his horses. Identities ranged from Greek history (Thucydides, Aristophanes) to Greek philosophy (Anaximander), from Roman poetry (Ovid) to Italian poetry (Sannazaro), from classical music (Haydn, Beethoven, Mozart and Ravel) to plain mischief. Sometimes it was not possible to tell whether Bull was having a joke. In his foreword to *The Wit of the Turf* (Leslie Frewin, 1972), Bull wrote:

I've often been taken to task for giving my horses un-pronounceable Greek names. Absolute rubbish! They always roll nicely off the tongue. It wasn't my fault if the bookmakers referred to Empedocles as Empty Bottles, and to Anamnestes as Ham And Egg Teas. Once, after Lord Rosebery had made some crack at my expense, I was able to crack back at him by explaining that my horse Aristarchus was not, as generally supposed, named after the famous Greek astronomer who first measured the size of the earth. It was in fact named after Lord Rosebery getting out of his bath—'arry-starkers!

133

The story—like Bull's tale of his father's experience with Doricles—is almost certainly apocryphal, but its telling, and acceptance, would appeal to his barely concealed, but always publicly denied, delight at being noticed. There was, however, a real person behind two of his last horses—Angelo Salvini, named after the head waiter at the George Hotel in Huddersfield, who would work at The Hollins when Bull had house parties; and Ho Mi Chinh, a virtual malapropism which started out as serious intent. The details were encapsulated in a letter, dated 1 February 1984, to Hamish Alexander at Weatherbys:

Your letter of 26 January explaining that I am debarred from naming my colt by Homing out of Fiordiligi HO CHI MINH for the reason that 'it is Jockey Club policy to tread warily when there is any risk of causing ill feeling' and it is felt 'that Ho Chi Minh's influence and following is still strong enough to warrant such caution', fascinates me.

I note that the name HENRY KISSINGER was accepted for registration for a horse currently racing. Dr Kissinger's deep involvement in the bombing and defoliation of Cambodia and Laos (with which countries America was not at war), contrary to American law, and his complicity in the concealment of this from the American public, is well known and well documented. It angered not only the Cambodians who suffered the devastation of their country but also a significant minority of Americans who objected very strongly to what was done.

That Kissinger's 'influence and following' is still strong is attested by the report recently furnished by him to the President of the United States advocating a substantial increase in American finance for the repressive Right-wing governments of El Salvador and Honduras, and this again is the cause of much 'ill feeling' in Nicaragua and among Americans who resent the policies being pursued by the Reagan administration in Central America.

Am I to take it that this 'ill feeling' and the continuing influence of Dr Kissinger would not have permitted the use of the name 'Henry Kissinger' for a racehorse in this country, had the Jockey Club been aware of the above facts? It seems to me an outrageous position.

Similarly, the proposition that because Ho Chi Minh's influence and following is still strong, and that there may be people around who continue to harbour ill feelings towards him many years after his death, seems to me even more outrageous and ludicrous.

However, as you tell me that this is Jockey Club policy, and as it is your ruling that I may not therefore register the name HO CHI

MINH for my colt by Homing out of Fiordiligi, I request that you register for it the name HO MI CHINH.

Ho Mi Chinh was the last of Bull's horses in training to go through a sale ring, when trainer Nigel Tinkler bought the five-year-old for 2,400 guineas at Newmarket on 26 October 1987. Ho Mi Chinh's 13-year-old dam Fiordiligi and her seven-year-old daughter Nonabella were sold at the same venue—for 8,000 guineas and 4,300 guineas respectively—on 1 December 1988, and the Hollins Stud and stable was no more. Bull died a little over six months later.

Bull's distaste for breeding theories, 'bloodlines' and 'nicks' was total, and regularly documented. He preferred the maxim of breeding the best to the best and hoping for the best, following up with the best care for the produce and the best training for the racecourse, with the classics his chief aim.

He outlined his breeding philosophy during part of a patient and courteous correspondence with a small stud owner, Arthur Tew, which went on for at least four years. On 2 September 1957 Bull wrote:

The idea that you can breed decent animals by using twenty-guinea stallions is wide of the mark. There is really only one rule for success in breeding good horses and that is to breed from the best mares you can afford, to send them to the best stallions you can get, regardless of expense, and to rear the stock with a view to giving them the maximum possible chance of development, again entirely regardless of expense. You cannot breed good horses on the cheap.

It may be very enjoyable to watch your foals skipping and gambolling in the snow as happy as so many jack-rabbits. If you are satisfied with that enjoyment, well and good. But if you are hoping to breed good-class horses you will have to think not about the happiness with which the foals gambol in the snow, but about rearing the foals to be well grown, well muscled individuals with all the physical advantages you can give them.

On the tail-female debate Bull was even moved to disagree with a member of his own staff, when following publication of a letter by Miles Napier in *The Sporting Life*, he replied, on 6 October 1975:

That the writer of the 1971 [*Racehorses*] article on Brigadier Gerard thought it worthwhile to trace the horse's ancestry back to

135

Pretty Polly doubtless reflects his belief that such things are of interest to readers. I daresay they are. But include me out. So far as I am concerned Pretty Polly is merely one of thirty-two individuals in the fifth generation of Brigadier Gerard's pedigree.

Does Mr Napier know who his own great-great-great-grand-mother was, in female line? If so, how much of his own wit, wisdom, skill and personality does he attribute to her influence? Why her, to exclusion of the other fifteen? Similarly with regard to Pretty Polly and the other fifteen grannies in Brigadier Gerard's fifth generation.

A month later, this time in response to Alan Yuill Walker in the same newspaper, Bull returned to the theme, with a personal invitation:

I suspect that Mr Walker feels that I deny, in some way, the importance of the contribution to the breed made by such mares as Mumtaz Mahal, Black Ray and Pretty Polly. Not at all. I don't deny it in any way. There is nothing surprising about the eminence of these mares as tail-female progenitors.

Mumtaz Mahal and Pretty Polly were outstanding racecourse performers. That presupposes exceptional genetic endowment. Neither could pass on more than half their genetic content to any of their daughters. But, of course, half a classic package is vastly superior to half a plating package. And the mating of Mumtaz and Polly with high-class stallions vouchsafed to their daughters genetic endowments qualitatively way above average. Statistically there is a further fifty per cent loss of Mumtaz and Polly genes in the grand-daughter generation, and further 'dilutions' at each succeeding generation. But the family of a Mumtaz Mahal or a Pretty Polly kicks off at a high level.

With Black Ray the case is rather different. She gained no distinction on the racecourse. Her distinction was exceptional fecundity. She had nineteen consecutive foals, of which ten were fillies. Her chances of becoming the ancestress of good animals were therefore two and a half times the normal, purely because of the size of her family.

Perhaps I might add that I have a filly foal by Amber Rama out of Relza, who is a daughter of Berganza, out of Lady Electra, out of Eclair, out of Black Ray. The statistical probability is that no more than one thirty-second of my Amber Rama filly's genes derive from Black Ray. Do I face this fact, accept the genetic reality, and assess the probable merit of the foal in terms of Amber Rama (Timeform rating

133) and Relza (rated 91)? Or do I kid myself that the foal is blessed with Black Ray magic?

Should any breeder or bloodstock agent with any exaggerated reverence for Black Ray wish to buy two mares and a filly foal tracing to her, will he kindly get in touch with me? I shall price them realistically. He can have the magic for nothing.

On the question of stallions, Bull made his point early, on 26 January 1952, in a letter to Baron Henry de Gelsey, saying:

I don't like the practice of getting nominations only for specific mares. I have, on occasions, been compelled to do so in the past, when I particularly wanted a certain stallion, and I did it with Ocarina. But as a general procedure I object to it, because it puts an irksome restriction on my freedom of choice when I come, later on, to decide all the matings. I like to do this mating business 'in one', at the end of the season, when I know precisely what possibilities are open to me.

On one occasion when this question of naming a mare arose, I told the stallion owner I very much wanted a nomination to his horse, but that if I was to have one it must be allotted to me on the basis of the general quality of the mares in my stud, and that the choice of the particular mare must be left to me, to decide in the usual way at the usual time. He could then approve the mare or not, at the proper time. I sent him a list of my mares, and he fell into line with the suggestion.

Bull might have decided his mating plans 'in one' at that time, but in the Sixties and Seventies it was a different story. Reg Griffin recalls: 'Phil loved playing the mating game, which started in about July and went through until perhaps the day before the covering season started. He had the names of all the stallions and all the mares written on neatly-cut cards, and would switch them around at his leisure, going through the various permutations until he thought he was spot on. He'd carry these around in his black briefcase, and if we travelled on the train, he'd bring them out, spread them on the table and start again.'

While Bull was breeding his mares to middle-distance stallions, aiming for classic success, the rest of the bloodstock world was beginning to march to a different tune, with a greater emphasis on speed and American-based sires. 'Speed wasn't regarded as of any great importance by a lot of private breeders,' Griffin points out, 'but suddenly the world changed around these people. Phil was one of them, but I don't think it ever dawned on him until it was perhaps too late.'

Bull saw the light in time to write to Jim Joel, in a letter dated 23 September 1971:

For too many years now I have been breeding from stayers— such horses as Never Say Die, Exbury, Right Royal, Worden, Charlottesville, Relko, Aureole and so on, to the virtual exclusion of sprinters. It has been a mistake. The racing pattern does not cater adequately for horses bred for stamina—it caters for them very inadequately indeed. I've always been aware of this, of course, and have frequently protested about it. But I've persisted in the folly of not trimming my breeding policy to the prevailing wind. However, not any more.

I've decided to breed for the racing that is, not for the racing that ought to be. I can't afford that luxury any longer. This is quite a turn-round in policy for me. Overdue!

Two years later Bull's holding of stallion shares had reached 17. He explained in a letter to Vincent O'Brien dated 10 July 1973:

Any breeder aiming at Classic success must seek nominations to the top American horses. But I can't afford to buy nominations in America. I must have shares. That's the only economically viable procedure. For far too many years I've been taking nominations to such as Crepello, Right Royal, Charlottesville, Herbager and Ragusa, etc, at great expense and with little success. I've now drawn the line at that. Henceforth I don't buy the top-priced nominations. If I can't get the share, I don't use the horse. The change of policy is about to pay off. I have acquired shares in good stallions, including Brigadier Gerard, Zeddaan, Welsh Pageant, Amber Rama, Connaught, Right Tack, Relko, etc., so I'm now self-supporting as far as stallions go, and with Thatch and Roberto to add to the list, and good mares to send to them, it can only be a matter of time before I come up with some good classic material.

When one gets to 63 years of age, there may not be all that much time left, but at any rate I'm bred to longevity on both sides of the pedigree! So there may be time yet.

There was not, and in the next fifteen years, before the stud was finally wound down, Aureoletta remained his last placing in a classic. And around her there remains a mystery.

Among owners and breeders, no subject connected with *Timeform* has caused greater concern than the rating a horse achieves and the description of its ability level in the *Black Book* comment. On the latter point Bull himself wrote to Leolin McClean on 30 September 1980:

Yes, it is a shame that some horses are of no account, bad or useless. I've had a few myself so described in Timeform. I didn't take it personally to heart. They say that a man will generally take anything derogatory you may say about his wife, but not about his horse. As you say, the horse's merit is expressed by the rating, so why put it into words? It's a point which I have made myself. But there's neither insult nor harm in it.

The bigger insult, it seems, is the allocation of a lower *Timeform* rating figure than the owner thinks his horse deserves. That remains the subject of most frequent questioning, but Bull always championed his company's integrity and impartiality, and on occasion even had to admit defeat at the hands of his staff.

In a letter to Vincent O'Brien, dated 12 March 1973, he grudgingly conceded:

I've just been taken severely to task by Dr John Stollmeyer of Trinidad over the relative ratings of Sir Ivor, Nijinsky, Roberto and Brigadier Gerard. Frankly, I think Stollmeyer is right. I know Brigadier Gerard doesn't really stay beyond a mile, and I recognise the excellence of his performances over a mile when the ground was on top, but I think my handicappers' view is extravagant. I am unhappy about it. I took it up with Reg [Griffin], seeking his support in the hope that he would approve a modification of Brigadier Gerard's rating. But he didn't support me or give his approval, so I refrained from interfering. I still don't like it. It's a bit of a bugger, isn't it, when a chap in Trinidad writes to you in exactly the terms you think yourself, and you still feel compelled to permit something to go through with which you disagree.

Perhaps it was a measure of Bull's mellowing, for it would be hard to imagine similar compliance happening in his heyday. Yet he may still have been able to exert a degree of pressure over ratings, especially, it would seem, over Aureoletta. Bull made a singularly rare appearance as a writer for *Racehorses* with the 1973 essay on his filly; it falls way below the standard of his Forties writing. Even more intriguing is a comparison between the ratings for the top middle-distance three-year-old fillies of 1973 as they appeared in the final issue of that year's *Timeform* weekly issue and *Racehorses*.

139

The general level of *Timeform* ratings rises through the season and is adjusted downwards in time for *Racehorses*. Thus six fillies in Aureoletta's bracket were lowered by between 5lb and 7lb in the few months between publication of the last *Black Book* and *Racehorses*; another was reassessed with a 10lb fall. By contrast, Aureoletta stayed exactly the same, being rated 118 in each case. The inspiration of something less than impartiality appears to have been at work.

W HEN a bookmaker closes a winning account, he can usually expect a response from the aggrieved party. It would not normally be the kind which starts a thirty-year business association and friendship. That, however, seems to have been the case with Phil Bull and William Hill, though there are conflicting stories of how the initial contact came about.

It happened in 1940. According to the manuscript of an unpublished biography of the bookmaker William Hill, which journalist Geoffrey Hamlyn submitted to Bull in 1965: 'For some time Hill had been perplexed by a fairly large number of winning accounts which normally would not be showing a profit. He made some very thorough investigations, and soon found the common denominator. They were all following a system devised by one William K. Temple, BSc, which necessitated following a series of horses in their various engagements and backing them at Tote odds. Examining the system at some length, Hill found (or thought he had found) that the only reason they showed a profit over a prolonged run was that occasionally one of the horses won at a fantastic Tote dividend of 80/1 or 90/1. Hill thought the quickest way of stopping this was to refuse all these clients to bet at Tote odds, and to accept Starting Price only. This was done.' Hill was unaware that William K. Temple was really Phil Bull, using a *nom de plume* to cover his employment in schoolteaching, but he was soon to find out.

Bull's recollection was that Hill was closing winning betting accounts among subscribers to the Temple Racetime Analysis, a weekly list of horses he recommended backing at level stakes based on their time performances. Hamlyn quoted Bull saying that he rang William Hill in protest, saying that 'bookmakers ought to be prepared to pay winning punters as well as accepting money from losing ones, and that it was quite unethical to do this sort of thing'.

Whatever the exact nature of the original phone call, it led to Bull's being invited to visit William Hill in his Park Lane, London office. Hill's description to his would-be biographer Hamlyn was of 'a man of about 30, with flaming red hair and a beard of similar colour, in a cheap sports jacket and a pair of flannel trousers several inches too short for him'. It seemed as if it might be a short conversation, but it lasted for several hours, as, according to Hamlyn, 'Bull produced yards of statistics on foolscap and graph paper, proving conclusively that his clients would have been winners equally at SP as at Tote odds, but not by as much. The graphs were all in different colours, giving the times of horses, their performances on hard or soft going, etc, allowances for the wind, and so on'.

That was 1940; the conversation went on until William Hill's death on 16 October 1971, for shortly after the initial meeting, Bull joined Hill's office as personal assistant and general factotum in the business. Bull had gradually begun to lose interest in the profession of teaching, for which, he once noted, he was always intended—'I was educated to be a teacher, in other words given no alternative, no guidance that other careers were open to me'. Racing was beginning to take up more and more of his time.

As well as working in the Park Lane office, arranging Hill's advertising and discussing ante-post prices, Bull went racing with Hill to the restricted number of courses open during the war. Bull also advised Hill on bloodstock, was with him when he bought his first stud at Whitsbury, and managed his horses in training when they went to be trained by Charlie Elsey in the North. Bull helped in other ways, as he explained in a letter to the American trainer Albert Winick, dated 25 October 1971, nine days after Hill's death:

You don't really know, you can't know, of course, what a real hole in my life Billy Hill's departure leaves. It's over thirty years since I first walked into his office. The friendship was immediate and real—a two-way exchange of affection and help and advice and ideas and assistance.

I bought him Kong and sent her to Nearco and Nasrullah, breeding him Nimbus and Grey Sovereign, when I managed his breeding activities in the early days. Later I managed his horses in training when we won the Gimcrack with Be Careful and the St Leger with Cantelo (which I named for him after the famous soprano April Cantelo) and a host of other races.

Everything I did with him and for him turned up trumps. Even this last year. I promoted a race meeting at Doncaster, with seven big stakes races, one of which was sponsored by Bill. Who do you think won his race?—The Queen! And Bill had the pleasure of being invited to tea with her.

In the early days, when he was setting up his business in Park Lane, I was the one who engaged his staff for him, did his advertising, went racing with him and gave him the race analyses on which he used to bet.

In a way, you know, he was my chick. I had a proprietory feeling towards him. Then, of course, he grew too big for me. Too harsh, too severe, too demanding, and I had to opt out of working for him in order to preserve my own individuality and play my own hand in my own way. He wanted me to accept a share in his business. But I couldn't because I dare not sacrifice my independence.

He respected me for that too, you know, Al. And as a result, our relationship never soured. I was his closest friend for thirty years. When he was in trouble emotionally, in danger of losing his relationship with Sheila [Baker], I rescued him, and fixed it up again between them.

On the other side he was always *in loco parentis* to me. If I wanted advice or help in deciding things racing-wise or breeding-wise, it was to him I turned for it. And always he was there in the wings for me waiting for me to fluff my lines and there to help. If I'd ever run on the rocks financially, he'd have been there to throw me the lifebelt. I never had to call for it. But it is a comfort, you know, to go through life knowing that always there's someone behind you like Bill, who cares for you and will be at hand to rescue you if you run into difficulties.

Now, with his death, that's all come to an end. It is indeed the end of an era for me. I have lost my staunchest friend of longest standing. Fortunately I have others more recently acquired and am not alone. And I'm a pretty strong character in my own right, well able to stand up to life and make the best of it, and help others along the way as I go. But the loss of Bill is real to me.

It throws me back on my heels, on my own resources, with others to support and help and succour, and no-one on whom I myself can fall back, or to whom I can call for help. So it is, and always must be, as we grow older and our friends fall by the wayside: all part of the adventure and the sadness of living!

In some ways Bill was a most unsatisfactory person: especially in his personal relationships and in his attitude to women (which was deplorable in the extreme): but in other ways he was a great guy—basically kindly and considerate and full of concern for people; and a person of real integrity and fundamental honesty. I'll miss him a great deal more than I can tell you.

Shortly they're going to hold a Memorial Service to Bill at one of London's big churches. I'm an atheist. I detest Christianity and all religions. But I'm going to have to deliver the address in tribute to my friend. It is proper. No-one could do it as I will. I assure you that every person who attends that service will leave the place the better, the stronger and the wiser for what I shall say.

Bull kept to his word when William Hill's memorial service was arranged for 12 November 1971. His address was warm but

143

not one-sided; there are some references to character which Bull himself appeared anxious to emulate—'honour and integrity, impatient of incompetence, forthright in the expression of his views'—but there are also giveaways to Bull's own faults—'a perfectionist who could be a demanding taskmaster, sometimes too quick to criticise and blame, and all too slow to praise or compliment':

William Hill was my firm friend for over thirty years. Of his career as a bookmaker I shall say little. William began at the bottom of his profession, rapidly rose to the top, and lifted the whole profession with him as he went. He took from bookmaking the check suit and gold watch-chain image and gave it a new respectability and integrity. He became the greatest bookmaker of all time, both on the racecourse and off, with a centralised SP organisation on a national scale such as had not been seen before. It will not happen again. William's death is the end of an era. There will be none like him again.

William also made his mark upon the Turf itself. Cantelo, Nimbus and Grey Sovereign were products of his studs: these and the stallions he imported—Chanteur, Ballymoss, Sica Boy, Celtic Ash, Taj Dewan and Gyr—will have big influence upon the British thoroughbred for many years to come.

I wish to speak to you, however, not of William Hill the bookmaker or the breeder, but of William Hill the man. I will not pretend that he was any paragon. To those who worked with him he was a perfectionist who could be a demanding taskmaster, sometimes too quick to criticise and blame, and all too slow to praise or compliment. He was flawed in other ways too. Which of us is not? But William was a man whose qualities of character far outweighed his failings and his disabilities. Best of all, he had a real concern for justice and the welfare of people. Not theoretically, in the mind, but practically.

During the war his cashier at Hill House embezzled over £20,000, and was sent to prison for twelve months. Bill immediately provided the man's wife with a job. I was instructed to find a school for her two young sons. In the middle of the Flat season we spent three days inspecting a school evacuated to Blaenau Ffestiniog in North Wales. Bill then arranged for the education of the boys and also made a substantial donation to the school funds.

That experience gave me a regard for William Hill that nothing could ever destroy. For a man to accept a financial responsibility is easy; for a man voluntarily to accept a moral responsibility that is not his, is another matter: but for a man to disregard the demands of his own pressing affairs and go to such trouble to help the dependants of someone who has just done him an injury, is an education in ethics.

This was but one of the many actions in the life of William Hill. He was a man scornful in his contempt for snobbery, impatient of incompetence, rough and uncompromising in his judgements, and forthright in the expression of his views. He was a man of honour and integrity. He could be a very charming and considerate host. There will be few of us here who have not frequently enjoyed his hospitality: few who have not received some kindness at his hands or been helped by him in one way or another.

The most important thing in life is not success in one's affairs but personal relationships. Friendships. We are lucky, indeed, if, in a lifetime, we make two or three real lasting friendships that are proof against all adversity and all vicissitudes. That was how it was between William and me. There were times when what he said or what he proposed to do I could not countenance. No doubt he felt the same of me. But our respect for each other always bore the strain. And if my ship had ever run upon the rocks, he'd have been right there to throw the lifebelt to me.

To very many people William's death will have brought a real sense of personal loss. That is its own tribute to him. My own personal loss is very real indeed. Most of the important events in the last thirty years of his life I shared. It seems I stood beside him most of the way along the road—from the time I went with him to buy Whitsbury, till three weeks ago when they lowered his body into the grave in the churchyard there.

> Bull's reference to being thrown a lifebelt by William Hill actually happened at the 1942 Newmarket July Sales when Bull paid 3,500 guineas for an unnamed maiden three-year-old filly, by Fairway out of Eclair. She was part of a draft owned by the American store magnate Marshall Field, and four lots after the twelve-year-old mare Eclair had been sold to the Aga Khan for 3,500 guineas, her daughter went for the same money to Cecil Ray, the Epsom trainer, bidding on Bull's behalf. Bull had seen the Eclair filly as a two-year-old, noted how well she walked, and thought to himself, 'If only I could own an animal like that'.
> Bull's comments to Geoffrey Hamlyn pick up the story:

I had been doing pretty well backing horses and had a bit of money. I had about £2,500 all told, and I thought I had a very good chance of getting it for that. So I went to the auction with Cecil Ray, my trainer, and I told him to go up to £2,500 to buy the filly.

Cecil went up to £2,500, then somebody else bid two-six. Cecil looked at me and I said, go on. The person who was bidding against me was the Aly Khan. The upshot was that I actually went to 3,500 guineas, and it was knocked down to me, with the Aly Khan the underbidder. Now I didn't have £3,500 in cash at all—all I had was £2,500. I had property—I owned a house and what not—but I didn't have the money to pay.

So immediately after the auction I walked down the road from the sales paddocks to the telephone and I rang up William Hill and said to him on the phone—Bill I've bought an animal and I can't pay for it, will you lend me a thousand quid? So far as I remember he said to me, 'I think you're an idiot, I think you're not right in your head, but I'll lend you the thousand quid'. So I was able to buy the mare.

It was named Lady Electra, and won me ten races including the Substitute Lincolnshire Handicap at Pontefract. She was a very good mare, no argument about it. She has been a relative failure at stud—she bred five or six winners but all winners of egg and spoon races, no winners of any consequence—but she also bred Queen Electra, by Big Game, the dam of Eudaemon.

I don't remember exactly the date when William Hill bought Whitsbury, but I do remember going down with him and we walked round the place, and as far as I remember he had to pay £60,000 for it. Bill had given me authority to buy him mares to form a stud, and I went to the auction at Newmarket and bought him a mare named Kong, a grey mare who had won the Wokingham Stakes in 1939, for 710 guineas. Kong became the dam of Nimbus, who won the Two Thousand Guineas and the Derby, and also the dam of Grey Sovereign.

There is a story attached to the breeding of Nimbus. Bill bought a couple of shares in a syndicate that started in Nearco, owned by Martin Benson, and I had the job of arranging the mating of the mares.

I decided to send Kong to Nearco, and Bill came to me and said that Martin Benson thought she was not good enough. I said this was ridiculous, and went down to Benson's place, the Beech House Stud, with Bill. Benson didn't know a great deal about the business of breeding horses, and was being guided by a man called Stafford Smith, who would put on the table all sorts of charts and beautiful colours showing all the various blood lines, and talked in a very erudite way about mating animals with a view to blending the blood lines and so forth. But he and Benson didn't really have any idea of the peculiarities of breeding horses, and were only concerned with pedigrees.

I said, 'Look Bill, you own a share in Nearco; it isn't up to Benson to tell you what mare you are going to send to Nearco, you have the right to send what mare you like. In my view this is the right mare to send to the horse'. So he insisted with Benson, Kong went to Nearco, and the result was Nimbus.

> The story of William Hill's loan, which bought Lady Electra and indirectly set in motion Bull's reputation as one of the most successful racehorse owners in the North of England, was well accepted. Bull himself was anxious to show there was another side to his relationship with William Hill. He pointed it out in a letter, dated 10 July 1973, to Sam Burns, managing director of the company which carried on after Hill's death:

If he lent me £1,000 to help pay for Lady Electra in 1942, there was an occasion when he was in Park Lane when I lent him £5,000 or £6,000 to tide him over with the pay-out when the bank wouldn't accomodate him any further.

He was always a far better judge of other people's characters than I was, and his advice saved me from making many mistakes. But I had to teach him how to write letters and deal with lots of other things where his lack of formal education was a handicap. We complimented [sic] one another in many ways, especially where the breeding and racing of his horses was concerned.

His racing successes were gained when I managed his horses (Be Careful, Cantelo, etc) and Charlie Elsey trained them. And if I had been more concerned with making a fortune and less with living a pleasant and agreeable life, I might now be sitting in your chair, Sam. He offered me £10,000 a year, a directorship and a 20 per cent interest in the business if I would give up my own Timeform interests and join up with him. But he was too demanding a guy to work for and I valued my freedom too much. I turned his offer down and told him why.

In recent years we enjoyed one another's company, exchanged ideas and argument, and I enjoyed his hospitality on many occasions. One service I was able to do for him. He'd behaved badly towards Sheila, and she'd left him and was about to shack up with another guy. He was knocked out by it. I dropped everything, found Sheila, talked to her, gave William a salutory dressing down and sorted it out for them. But frequently it was the other way round and he helped me see sense when I was off beam.

So you see, Sam, when William died there was a bloody great hole in my life. And, of course, there still is. I no longer have anyone to turn to if need should arise—no-one, to fall back upon. I felt, indeed, like a boy who has lost his father, even though it had sometimes been me who had been the father and he the boy.

'OUR primary intention was to promote something of real and lasting value to racing.' So said Phil Bull at the Timeform Gold Cup Inauguration Dinner in Doncaster's Mansion House on 20 October 1961, the night before the first running of Europe's richest two-year-old race of the time. Bull even credited his righthand man Reg Griffin with 'the original suggestion for this particular race', though later he was more than happy to take the written word of others that it was his invention.

Griffin recalls that the seed was sown as Bull drove him, sister May and mother Dolly back to Halifax from the races at Doncaster in October 1959. Bull had paid his customary, after-racing social visit to the racecourse office of Albert Cammidge, chairman of the Labour-run Doncaster Race Committee, and announced he was going to sponsor five races the following year, Timeform putting up £1,000 in prize-money and the racecourse executive matching the contribution for each.

In the car Griffin raised the subject of sponsorship with Bull, and suggested that five races worth £2,000 each would be wasteful, since such races were commonplace. 'Why don't you put the £5,000 together, get the racecourse executive to put in £5,000, and make it a big race?' Griffin asked. Bull's only observation was that if that became the case, he did not want a handicap; he suggested it should be for two-year-olds. Back in the office the following day, Griffin examined the Doncaster programme and identified a suitable vehicle, a two-year-old event over the round mile, to which he applied the conditions for a £10,000 race and ensured that entry closed when the horses were yearlings. 'That sounds wonderful,' said Bull, and Cammidge and his Race Committee agreed.

In 1960 the October Stakes, with five runners, was worth £2,109 to the winner; in 1961, its successor, the Timeform Two-Years-Old Gold Cup, with thirteen runners, was worth £21,893 to the winner. The official title of the race did not please Bull. It is 'ungrammatical and too much of a mouthful', he told his eve-of-race guests in 1961. But he was happy to have achieved his purpose, which he said had been summed up in a nutshell by John Lawrence in the *Sunday Telegraph*: 'The express aim and object of the Timeform Gold Cup is to give a really worthwhile opportunity to high-class two-year-olds bred to stay.' Bull confirmed the point in his speech:

That indeed is our aim. The fact is that none of the long-established two-year-old races provides such an opportunity. In 1960 there was only one solitary two-year-old race run beyond six furlongs with more than £1,000 added money. The important traditional races—the Gimcrack, the Champagne, the National Stakes, the Imperial Stakes, the Cheveley Park and Middle Park—are all five- or six-furlong races.

After the end of June it is exceedingly difficult for a staying-bred horse to beat a sprint-bred youngster over five or six furlongs. All these important traditional two-year-old events can be won with pure sprinters, and they are. With more and more sprinters being bred, it is increasingly difficult to win a top two-year-old race with a potential classic horse. So what can a trainer do with such a horse? He may as well forget about it till it's a three-year-old.

Surely it is high time somebody put on at least one really valuable race for staying-bred horses of classic potential. The Timeform Gold Cup is our contribution. No purely sprint-bred horse will win the Timeform Gold Cup.

Of course there were criticisms when the race was announced. Wasn't it too late in the season? Wouldn't all the best horses be already put away for the winter? Why run it over a round mile when a good straight mile was available? And anyhow, wouldn't it be better to make it seven furlongs? Why not make it a handicap, that would be sure to draw a big field? It is easy to answer these questions.

Seven furlongs would be pandering to speed again. A handicap would fill the field with second raters, discourage the running of fine classic horses. A round mile is preferable to a straight one because it provides a better education for a potential stayer, who will have to race round turns the following year, and be taught to settle down in a bunch of horses.

The only really valid question is whether the race comes too late in the season. I myself would, I think, prefer it a week or two earlier—if only because that would decrease the likelihood of heavy going. But I hardly think it is a serious point. The Grand Criterium in France is only a week earlier, and it is frequently decided on heavy going, but it is invariably won by a very high-class horse who takes no harm from it, trains on well, and proves his merit again as a three-year-old.

The suggestion has been made that the Timeform Gold Cup should be transferred to the St Leger meeting, and replace the Champagne Stakes, which has suffered in recent years from competition with the York Gimcrack Stakes a fortnight earlier. I can't agree to this. The proper place in the calendar for this race is not earlier than the first week in October. So far as the Champagne Stakes goes, it would be well, if I may make a suggestion, to increase the distance to seven furlongs.

> In an annotation to his copy of the speech, Bull wrote: 'a speech which, though it didn't come up to my own standard of an after-dinner speech, went down very well (much better than expected) and brought congratulations from many journalists and others, who would hardly have proffered them merely out of courtesy.' It had one significant effect. In 1962 the Champagne Stakes was run over seven furlongs for the first time.
>
> Though Bull referred in his speech to the Timeform Gold Cup being expected to attract potential classic horses, it was certainly not his intention to stage a classic trial for two-year-olds. The erroneous impression was clearly picked up by at least one journalist—and has been repeated down the years—since Bull was stung into action on the day after the 1962 race. His letter to the editor of *The Sporting Life*, dated 21 October, read:

The remarks of your contributor Warren Hill about the Timeform Gold Cup are arrant nonsense.

The race was not, I repeat, NOT designed with the aim of providing a good guide to the following year's classics. That it will in the long run provide a better guide to the classics than six-furlong races such as the Gimcrack, Champagne and Middle Park Stakes is self-evident to anyone who thinks logically about racing. But this fact is quite incidental, and of little importance. The purpose of the race is to provide a worthwhile opportunity for high-class two-year-olds bred to stay to race for a valuable stake over a distance commensurate with their stamina.

Before the promotion of the Timeform Gold Cup, high-class staying youngsters didn't have any such opportunity. The National Stakes, the big two-year-old races at Ascot and Goodwood, the Gimcrack, the Champagne, the Imperial Stakes and the rest of the valuable two-year-old events were all run at five or six furlongs. At such distances staying-bred youngsters are at a grave disadvantage with the sprint-bred Abernants, Whistlers, Grey Sovereigns and Golden Clouds.

In 1960, with the solitary exception of the Royal Lodge Stakes, there wasn't a single two-year-old event beyond six furlongs with more than £1,000 added. The whole two-year-old racing programme was so heavily weighted in favour of the sprint-bred horses as to make the racing of a good-class staying-bred youngster hardly worthwhile. It is still far too heavily weighted in that direction. The

Jockey Club recognises this. Their alteration of Rule 64 was a step in the right direction, but it needs practical implementation in the establishment of new, valuable and worthwhile two-year-old races over seven furlongs and one mile. The Timeform Gold Cup is one such race. That's why I sponsored it. And it is to be valued, like all other races, *as a race*, not as something to provide resourceless and thought-lazy journalists with guidance as to what might win next year's classic races. Time enough to decide what the best three-year-olds are when they *are* three-year-olds.

For Warren Hill to criticise the 1961 Timeform Gold Cup because the first three, Miralgo, Escort and Prince Poppa haven't won a race this year is silly. The first three in last year's Gimcrack Stakes haven't any of them won a race this year. Gustav and Sovereign Lord, first and second in last year's Middle Park Stakes, haven't won a race this year either. So what? How does Warren Hill account for this? Were these races too severe? Have they left their mark? Were they run too late in the year? What rubbish!

Miralgo, the 1961 Timeform winner, was beaten a short-head by Hethersett in the Voltigeur and ran third in the St Leger. Prince Poppa ran third in the Two Thousand. To describe such horses as 'not having trained on' is to use words with complete disregard for their meanings.

Romulus, Hethersett and Larkspur were fourth, fifth and close-up seventh in the 1961 Timeform Gold Cup. Romulus has proved himself the best miler of 1962, Larkspur won the Derby and Hethersett the Leger. What can one say of the quality of the thinking of a journalist who tries to explain this away by suggesting that maybe they didn't suffer any ill effects from the race because it's not likely they were pushed out to the limit. Was there ever a clearer example of rationalising the facts to suit one's prejudices?

The plain fact of the matter is that no two-year-old race in recent years has attracted a better field than did the 1961 Timeform Gold Cup. The horses that ran in it have this year won 13 races worth £98,658, including the Derby, the St Leger, the Queen Elizabeth II Stakes and the Queen's Vase. I haven't the time and can't be bothered to go through the records to see if there is any other two-year-old race with a better record in this respect. But I feel quite safe in challenging Warren Hill to find one.

As for Warren Hill's final statement that it is probably too early to pass judgement on the Timeform Gold Cup, and his feeling that a hard race so late in the season can do nothing but harm to a potential classic horse—hasn't he heard of the Grand Criterium? And of Right

Royal V, Never Too Late, Bella Paola and all the other top French two-year-olds of recent years that won or were narrowly beaten in the French equivalent of the Timeform Gold Cup, and went on to outstanding classic successes the following year?

Too severe a test? Too late in the year? Does Warren Hill have to have the evidence hit him between the eyes before he can see it?

> The reference to Rule 64 related to a change introduced in 1962 which advanced the start of six-furlong two-year-old races from 1 September to 1 July, and allowed seven-furlong and one-mile races for two-year-olds from 1 September.
>
> The 1962 running of the Timeform Gold Cup was won in brilliant style by the filly Noblesse, who beat another Irish-trained runner, Partholon, by an easy three lengths, with Star Moss three quarters of a length away third, and the rest at least six lengths behind. The following year Noblesse won the Oaks by a street length; Partholon won the Ebor Handicap, and Star Moss finished second in the St Leger on an interrupted preparation.
>
> In 1963 the Timeform Gold Cup produced controversy, when Scissors—owned by the sponsoring company's good friend Anne Biddle—finished a neck first past the post but was relegated to second behind Lionel Holliday's Pushful for interference. All Saved was a length and a half away third; Palm fourth, Soderini fifth, and Phil Bull's Metellus last of the ten runners.
>
> Although *Racehorses of 1963* commented at length on the relegation of Scissors in favour of Pushful, Bull kept his own counsel until he spoke at the St Leger Dinner the following September. He used the occasion, and the example, to make a plea that was to become familiar over the next 25 years:

One of the most surprising decisions to come out of the Stewards' room in recent years was the disqualification of Scissors after last year's Timeform Gold Cup. As my company sponsor the race I thought it proper at the time not to enter the controversy which blew up over the affair. I made no comment. But I'd like to make a comment now, because an important principle is involved.

There is no argument that Scissors contravened the rules. His rider [Liam Ward] barged his way out from the rails and bumped the horse on his right. But there is equally no argument that this did not in any way interfere with Pushful; and there's also no argument that Scissors won on merit.

What Scissors and his jockey did I have seen happen time and time again on the racecourse. You see comparable cases every week, without disqualification following, and without disciplinary action against the offending jockey. That is what incensed most of the journalists who wrote about it afterwards.

For myself, I think that the fault lies with the Rules of Racing. As they stand, they are conducive to this sort of inconsistency of action by local stewards. The Rules say that for bumping, crossing, and so forth, a horse is liable to be disqualified. But they give no guidance to local stewards on what actually merits disqualification. And they make no distinction between interference which affects the result of the race, and interference which does not affect the result. I think they should.

I think the Rules should state explicitly that no horse shall be disqualified (or have his placing altered) on account of any act of his jockey unless in the opinion of the stewards the result was affected thereby.

Infringements by jockeys which don't affect the result of the race call not for disqualification, but for salutary disciplinary action against the jockey: suspension or fine, as may be appropriate. To inflict a massive injustice on the owner, by depriving him of a stake won on merit, is no way to discipline the rider for an infringement of the Rules which does not affect the result. I beg the stewards of the Jockey Club to review this aspect of the Rules.

> Bull continued to beg the regulatory body to alter the emphasis of the interference rules for the next 25 years, till the day he died. Some changes were made, bit by bit, but the major thrust to which Bull returned time and again, in private or official capacity, remains untouched.
>
> In the meantime, Pushful finished second in the following year's Lingfield Derby Trial and Con Brio, the biggest sufferer from Scissors' meandering, won the Brighton equivalent, while Soderini was third in the St Leger. Metellus won small races at Newcastle, Carlisle and Ayr.
>
> In 1964 the eleven-runner Timeform Gold Cup was won by another Irish-trained runner, Hardicanute, who came from last to first in the Doncaster straight to win by a neck from Leonardo, with Brave Knight third, Nentego fourth and Never A Fear fifth. The following year Hardicanute's career was ruined by two bouts of the cough; Brave Knight won the King George V Stakes at Royal Ascot, and Never A Fear started favourite for the Oaks but was well beaten. By this time, though, the Timeform Gold Cup was no more.
>
> Explaining his reasons for starting the race, and finishing Timeform's association, Bull wrote in a letter to the journalist Geoffrey Gilbey, dated 18 November 1964:

You are, of course, quite right in thinking that the advertising value in sponsoring a race is not great, even when the race is a near-classic and gets as much publicity as the Timeform Gold Cup.

When you reflect that the £5,000 we put up for the race every year would pay for a 6-inch double column advert twice a week in the sporting press throughout the year, from which there would be hard cash returns, you'll see that this must be so. But I knew this when I first proposed the race. Although the publicity which would be forthcoming for Timeform was welcome, I never supposed it would be worth £5,000 a year, or anything like it.

My reason for sponsoring the race was a recognition that the programme of two-year-old racing was urgently in need of such an event, and the desire to demonstrate how successful it would be.

At the time, £5,000 a year was neither here nor there to my company, so I didn't mind giving it (half of it would have gone to the tax man, anyway). However, now that my original purpose has been served, I see no reason why I should carry on just for the fun of the thing, to subsidise a race which is so obviously of such value and importance in the pattern of two-year-old racing. Surely it should be the business of the new Turf Board to see to this and of the Levy Board to finance it.

The Timeform Gold Cup has in four years established itself as the major two-year-old classic. If anyone has any idea that the Middle Park Stakes holds this title, let them look at the horses that ran in the Middle Park this year and see how they're bred. Could anyone conceivably imagine any of the four runners being in the field for next year's Derby or St Leger or King George VI and Queen Elizabeth Stakes, let alone winning one of these races?

The fact that the Timeform Gold Cup has in four years achieved this position (despite the noticeable coldness of the Jockey Club towards it), demonstrates how much such a race was needed.

But in my view races of this consequence and character in the overall pattern of racing should not be left to the caprice of a sponsor, who may abandon his sponsorship at any time. They should be part of the permanent framework of the racing season, for which the Jockey Club should have made itself responsible years ago.

Now, at long last, we have the Turf Board appointed to do this very job. So now is the right time for me to discontinue sponsoring the race and hand it over, ready-made, to the Turf Board and the Levy Board. If they take it, the £20,000 I've put into establishing the race will have been well spent. If they don't, they should be ashamed of themselves.

Of course it will need a new title. How about the Harding Gold Cup, or the Levy Board Gold Cup, or the Turf Board Gold Cup, or the Miralgo Stakes?

The race became none of these; nor did it necessarily capture the imagination of the new Turf Board. Its future was, indeed, 'left to the caprice of a sponsor'. *The Observer*, whose racing correspondent was Bull's great supporter Richard Baerlein, took over in 1965, and its sponsorship has since been followed by that of the William Hill Organization, which gave it the Americanized title of Futurity, and the *Racing Post*, which appended the word Trophy.

The race has continued to attract some of the criticism to which Bull referred in his 1961 speech, but it remains the most valuable two-year-old staying race in the British calendar, and truly can be said to have fulfilled Bull's ambition to 'promote something of real and lasting value to racing'.

The Timeform Charity Day, held once at Doncaster in July 1971 and annually in June at York since, has similarly carved a niche in the Flat racing season. It owed little to Bull other than his blessing, for when the Doncaster racecourse manager Noel Nettleship passed on to him a letter from the regional organiser for the National Society for Cancer Relief, Mrs Irene Hunt, he directed it immediately to Reg Griffin.

Mrs Hunt, who lived in Sheffield, knew nothing about racing but she was aware that Ascot had staged a race meeting in aid of her charity and believed the North could do it as well, if not better. Griffin took up the challenge—on the proviso that no-one interfered—and having secured sponsorship for all seven races, totalling £60,000, he produced the richest one-day programme ever staged in Britain. It was also the first time the Jockey Club had granted a fixture on the application of a commercial firm, and the first at which every event was broadcast on national radio.

The trump card for the promotion—for which Bull can take credit—was the appearance of the Queen, who was invited to pay her first visit to the course for 15 years and to use the Royal Box facility in a new grandstand opened two years previously. She accepted, and watched her colt Charlton—named after the footballing brothers—win the featured William Hill Gold Trophy.

Though the crowd was disappointing, below 14,000, and the number of runners, 40, unattractive, the precedent was set.

The following year, 1972, the Jockey Club refused to grant an extra fixture, telling Timeform it must find an existing prog-ramme. The meeting was moved to a Saturday at York in mid-

June. Bull continued to have little to do with the considerable organisation of the event, but he enjoyed the race meeting, and basked in the reflected glory of the eve-of-race dinner, which was supported by the Duchess of Kent. Bull quickly came to address the Duchess as My dear Katharine in letters. He was quite taken aback when, during her illness, he sent flowers with the message, 'Get well soon, Phil', but received no acknowledgement.

WHEN Phil Bull left off writing for his *Best Horses* series with the much-delayed 1947 edition, his published work was largely restricted to letters and occasional articles submitted to the racing press—*The Sporting Life* and *Sporting Chronicle*—and reports on various issues, such as the massive tome he prepared for the Rothschild Royal Commission on Gambling in January 1977.

Bull was not a natural writer; he usually needed several scrupulous attempts to produce the text he required. Yet the end-product was invariably worth waiting for.

One of the most prolific sources of Bull's material was *The Racing Week*, a slim, pocket-sized volume which he launched in March 1964 and killed off three years later. *The Racing Week* was Timeform's first venture into a magazine style, offering selections for Saturday races, informed comment on the previous week's events, and a unique, but later much-copied, interview with a trainer about his horses. It also gave Bull the opportunity to state his views in public regularly, for he contributed the Week's Editorial for the first twelve weeks.

Arthur Shaw, a brilliant writer whom Bull had recruited in 1953 to contribute many of the longer essays in the *Racehorses* series, had left to renew his teaching career in 1963. In September 1964 Shaw was persuaded to return, and he took over the *Racing Week* editorial immediately. Bull occasionally wrote articles and his speech at the St Leger Dinner in 1964 was printed in full, but his subsequent contribution to the magazine was to answer readers' letters.

At first Bull was full of enthusiasm for his new role; Your Questions Answered appeared weekly, and he would reply at length on a variety of topics. But the feature disappeared between September 1964 and April 1965, before coming back with renewed vigour during the summer. Thereafter, until the magazine folded, Bull's input was patchy, and during the last year of publication his contribution amounted to a tribute following the death of his retained jockey Don Morris, a reply to a reader's inquiry, and a published letter explaining why the magazine was being halted:

With much regret I have to break the news to you that *The Racing Week* is to cease publication, in its present form, with next week's volume, No. 156, on Saturday 4 March.

I feel sad about this because it has been a splendid magazine, lively and varied, and well worth anyone's half-a-crown a week. Different people will miss it for different reasons. Some, of course, will miss the coded selections, which have shown a level-stake profit on the Flat in each of the last three years. What I shall miss most of all will be the regular weekly interviews in which leading trainers expressed in their own words their views of the horses in their stables and talked frankly of their prospects for the future. This was something new in racing journalism.

Not only do I feel sad about the demise of *The Racing Week*, I feel a sense of defeat too. But one has to bow to the economics of things. The cost of printing and distribution is such these days that no magazine or newspaper can exist without substantial revenue from advertising. I suppose it was here that we made our mistake: we never set out to make *The Racing Week* a vehicle for large-scale advertising. Pity!

However, it's an ill wind that blows nobody any good. The loss of *The Racing Week* will mean that certain innovations and improvements can be incorporated in *Timeform* and the *Timeform Race Cards*. I think I may promise you also a new book or two I've had in mind for some time.

A good Flat Season to you.

Bull blamed lack of advertising for the death of *The Racing Week*. Since none had been actively sought, this was an easy excuse. The failure to extend the scope of circulation beyond subscription and a handful of newsagents who already stocked Timeform products was a bigger contributory factor. Bull was unwilling to pass on trade commission to the wholesalers; it was a poor reflection on his business sense. It may also have been a reflection on his inability to see a project through to its proper conclusion.

Devotees of *The Racing Week* still look back on the magazine with affection. As archive material, it has no better recommendation than being the source of Phil Bull's published opinions on a number of subjects. The following is a sample of replies which remain pertinent, or illustrate Bull's unwillingness to turn a blind eye to poor phrasing or a misconceived idea.

Question. To my mind the most significant information concerning a horse is its weight and size. I am convinced that both these factors greatly determine the inherent capabilities of a horse. Perhaps you would oblige me by commenting on this?

Weight and size in the thoroughbred are, to *some* extent, correlated with merit. *On average*, small horses are less good than big horses: and well-made horses are better than light-framed, lightly-built horses. But note the qualification *on average*. They say that a good big 'un will always beat a good little 'un. This is nonsense. A good big 'un will only beat a good little 'un if it is good enough! You have only to think of Hyperion or Exbury. The truth is that size and weight are only two of *many* factors affecting the merit of a racehorse. Action, freedom of movement, muscular power, respiration, zest and courage, and a host of other matters are also material.

Question. What should one look for as the horses parade?

This is a big question that would need a long article to answer properly. Briefly, you should look, in the paddock, for evidence of a horse's fitness and well-being: backward and unfit horses usually betray their lack of condition by carrying too much belly and by a general 'slackness' of appearance: some horses are naturally round-barrelled and rather gross, and this may fox you occasionally, especially with sprinters. The muscles of a fit horse stand out clearly and are not concealed by a subcutaneous layer of fat. A lean and skinny appearance may denote either an underfed or overtrained animal, and a horse that walks round in disinterested fashion with its head on the ground may be tired and dispirited. Look for one that is bright in its coat, carries itself alertly and walks with freedom and purpose: an occasional jump or kick shows that it is 'full of itself'.

Question. At some courses, such as Chester, the draw is of considerable importance, and knowledge of it would affect a punter's calculations. What then is the objection to publishing the draw with the overnight declarations?

None at all. It should be done. At present the draw for places is conducted by the Clerk of the Scales on the course. It could just as easily be done in Messrs Weatherbys' office the previous day. An alteration in the Rules of Racing would be necessary, of course, and since the draw is of considerable importance on some courses, there is an obvious reason for the draw to be made by a highly responsible person in the presence of others. In France and USA the positions in the draw are printed on the race card. So they should be over here, and in the morning papers too.

Note: Overnight declaration of the draw was introduced, but not for several years.

Question. Is it not time the Jockey Club took action against trainers when their jockeys ride overweight?

There are lots of points here. First of all the weights should be raised all round. Underfed and stunted youngsters are less common in these days of the welfare state than they used to be. The average weight of jockeys is higher today than it used to be 40 or 50 years ago. The Jockey Club has tinkered with the implications of this instead of dealing with it properly. They made provision in the rules for raising the weights in handicaps after the final acceptance stage if the highest weighted acceptor had been originally allotted less than 9–0. They should have made it 9–7 instead of 9–0. And if they had thought seriously about the matter they would also have drawn up regulations designed to prevent unintelligent Clerks of Course from framing the weights in condition races at a level so low as to make it difficult for trainers to find competent jockeys to ride. I have in mind particularly maiden races for three-year-olds and upwards.

Of course, if they did this you'd have objections from the lightweight jockeys who would argue that this was taking the bread out of their mouths. But racing isn't run, and shouldn't be run, with the interests of lightweight jockeys as an important consideration.

With your main contention I am in entire agreement. There should be a rule prohibiting carrying of more than a specified amount of overweight. I should fix it at 3lb at the most.

Question. How long is it possible for a trainer to keep a horse in peak condition?

A peak is a peak, not a plateau, so your question is badly phrased. A good trainer begins by building up the physique of a horse, and then proceeds to get him fit without rushing the process. After that he should be able to keep the horse in a general state of fitness over long periods. But a rest is beneficial to a horse, just as it is to you and me. Top-class trainers do the former and don't forget the latter, judging matters according to the programme envisaged for the horse, but always proceeding from the horse to the programme and not the other way round.

Question. How does one start to study breeding?

This is a devastatingly ingenuous question. How do you begin to study anything? Well, in the ordinary way you read up the subject, commencing with the simpler introductory books and proceeding to the more detailed, comprehensive and technical treatises. Unfortunately, where the breeding of thoroughbreds is concerned there is practically nothing in print that is worth reading. The few books that have been written on the subject have, in my view, as much relation to the realities of the matter as Astrology has to Astronomy. The weekly Press Columns by 'breeding experts' are in the same category —much erudition, tap-roots, inbreeding, out-crossing, sire-lines, prepotency, etc., overlaid with a top-dressing of genetics, mostly misunderstood. It is a world of fantasy.

Heredity in the thoroughbred racehorse is no different from heredity in any other animal. So your first study, if you really wish to understand things, is genetics. It's a tough subject. But there is no escape if you are serious about it. Get a primer on simple genetics and make yourself familiar with its fundamental concepts. Then think about horses, interpreting their performances and racing characteristics in relation to those of their sires and dams, in terms of the understanding you have gained from reading genetics, always remembering that heredity is only half the story: environment being the other half—nurture, training, riding, etc.

One word of warning: don't confine your attention to good horses: bad horses merit equal attention: your study should, in fact, embrace a large number of horses selected at random. Dealing only in good horses—the top 1%—is precisely what leads our learned commentators on breeding up the garden path. Nine-tenths of breeding fallacies originated thus.

> *Question. What have you to say about the running of your horse Idomeneo, which finished last of four when 2/1 on at Pontefract on 9 July, and then won at 3/1 at Catterick a fortnight later. Shouldn't this be a case for a stewards' inquiry?*

Idomeneo is a horse with a temperamental quirk. You may have read what I said in an early number of *The Racing Week* about the sour and dispirited way Idomeneo ran last year and how Joe Sime described him as a 'pig of a horse'. I had thought that the long rest we gave him after July 1963 and the tender way in which we had had him ridden this year might have cured him completely. Certainly Idomeneo ran with commendable zest in his first four races this year. But he didn't at Pontefract. When he drew up to the leader three furlongs out he looked certain to win, but Another Phoenix came up on his outside just before the turn and squeezed him. According to the jockey, Idomeneo resented this, dropped his bit and refused to race from that point. At Catterick my instructions to Don Morris were to take any steps necessary in the race to see that this didn't happen again. He succeeded in doing this and the horse ran a genuine race and won.

If it will remove from your mind any suspicion that there may have been some funny business, I can tell you that I have a standing order with each of two bookmakers to put me £200 each way on all my horses in training (with the exception of two two-year-olds which haven't yet run) every time they run. Unfortunately I thought Idomeneo so good a thing at Pontefract that, in addition to the standing bets, I had another £800 on him on the course. But when he ran at Catterick I merely had the two standing bets. Such is racing.

However, I agree with you entirely that the difference in running should have been inquired into. It is not sufficient that there is an answer. It is not sufficient that the Stewards should know what the answer is. No matter who owns the horse concerned, blatantly obvious discrepancies in running should always be investigated and the full explanation published in the *Racing Calendar*—not merely a recorded minute that the explanation has been 'noted' or 'accepted'. It is in the interests of the good conduct of Racing, not only that justice should be administered impartially, but that it should also manifestly be seen by everybody so to be administered.

Question. What optical dimensions do you find most suitable in binoculars used for racing purposes?

Most people who go racing seem to be quite satisfied with a magnification x 8, but for myself I think this is too low. Years ago I used to use binoculars with a magnification x 18. The pair I now use have a magnification x 15. One objection to a very high magnification is the difficulty of holding the binoculars steady so that the image does not waver. I have never experienced any difficulty in this respect. I would not recommend you to buy a pair of binoculars for racing with a magnification of less than x 12.

The diameter of the object lens should always be as large as you can get it. Especially with a high-powered pair of binoculars, for otherwise the field of view will be restricted—not less than 50mm or 60mm, I should say.

Question. What have you to say about the losing run?

The first thing I have to say is that you must not regard this as due to the intervention of some supernatural malevolent force determined to stand in the way of your success. It's not due to your being an unlucky person.

Losing runs are inevitable. Everyone experiences them at some time or another, but they are simply part of the overall statistical pattern of events, and one must learn to accept them with equanimity. Nobody knows when a winning or a losing run will start or when it will stop. So there's nothing you can do about it except continue to select your bets with the care and attention you should always employ.

Question. You say that one should bet only when the odds available about the horse you think will win are longer than they should be. But how does one decide when this is the case?

I should have to write a book on the subject to give you a proper answer to this question. But broadly it is a matter of knowledge, experience and judgement. You have a number of horses in a race, and you assess their respective chances, taking everything into account—the merit of each horse, its racing character, whether it will be suited by the distance of the race, the state of the going or the track conformation. Our publication *Timeform* is designed to give you just this information for every horse, so far as it can be discovered. Jockeyship and recent evidence of fitness are other things that should be taken into account.

When you have thoroughly weighed up the race, you may express your view of the probable result by 'pricing up' the various runners, just as a bookmaker does on the racecourse. These prices you can then compare with the actual prices offered by the bookmakers (or forecast in the press). Then if the horse you really fancy is actually offered by the bookmakers at much longer odds than you priced it yourself, you have a bet. The point is that you shouldn't *always* back your fancy: only when the odds are favourable.

Suppose for example that you fancied Coronado in the last race at Doncaster on 24 March this year. You are inclined to back the horse; you think it is the one with the best chance of winning. But there are 39 runners, none of which has yet raced this season; and it's a sprint race in which luck in running may well play a part. Taking these things into account, you figure that although Coronado is entitled to be favourite, his odds should certainly not be less than 4/1.

On the course at Doncaster, however, Coronado opens at 3/1 and is backed down to 13/8. *You* can't back him at these odds if your opinion is that he should be at least a 4/1 chance. So even though you fancy the horse, you restrain yourself from betting. This is the kind of restraint and judgement you have to employ, if you are seriously intending to make your betting pay in the long run.

Question. Can you please give me some advice on race reading so as to obtain the benefits of watching a race through binoculars?

Well, the first thing you have to do is to learn the 'colours' before the race, so that you can identify every horse instantaneously. Secondly you have to know the horses, their peculiarities, and how they need to be ridden to the best advantage, so as to be able to recognize when they are not ridden to the best advantage. Thirdly you have to recognize that a race is not just an academic exercise but a real contest between galloping horses on turf, round turns, with a considerable play of fortune, horses getting in one another's way, jockeys seeking to gain advantages and to impose disadvantages on others: you have to be alive to 'incidents' arising out of this, noting horses that lose ground at the start, get into trouble in running and so forth, especially if these horses are to be seen going on strongly at the finish. Finally you must note how the horses are going throughout the race, and particularly towards the end of the race: you must pay great attention to the jockeys and how they are riding, especially over the last two furlongs. Horses that are hard held, racing on the bit; horses whose jockeys don't seem to be bothering unduly—these are things to look out for. In a sentence, you have to be alive to what is happening and be capable of putting the correct interpretation upon it. This is a matter of knowledge and experience. I can't give you this. You can only acquire it as you go along.

Question. It's quoted that a few years ago you made eight per cent profit on betting turnover, but less now. I would be interested if, taking this year [1965] as an example, you broke down your betting into sections, giving us the profit or loss in each section, e.g. condition races, two-year-olds and handicaps, and giving examples of your betting.

Yes, it would be interesting. I've often promised myself I would analyse my betting in this way. But I've never done so. I guess I will some day, just for the fun of the thing. At present I have too much to do to bother about it.

Question. In your opinion what percentage of all races could be said to be 'fixed', rigged or otherwise unfairly run? Would you say that there is at least one race at each meeting that is 'fixed' in some way?

No, I certainly would not say anything of the kind. My view is that the percentage is very small indeed, probably less than one per cent. But of course these things cannot be *known*. They can only be guessed at. If, in a field of four runners, three of the jockeys ignore the fourth, permit him to establish, without effort, an unassailable lead and present him with the race, who is to say whether this was bad judgement or ill intent?

I have seen three- or four-runner races where jockeys of known competence and intelligence have ridden in such a manner as to make a 'conspiracy to lose' the only reasonable explanation. And I have not the slightest doubt that these things do go on.

There has also been talk on occasions, of a 'jockeys' ring', fixing races for betting purposes, but I have no evidence that would enable me to deny or confirm the existence of such a ring.

Since the 'fixing of a race' involves the co-operation of all the jockeys, or at any rate of all the riders of the horses that have chances, it must be obvious purely on logical grounds that the opportunity to fix a race won't occur very often. Bear in mind that jockeys have loyalties to, and receive rewards and presents from, the owners and trainers for whom they ride. Bear in mind too that the majority of jockeys, like the majority of solicitors, are as honest and straightforward as you think yourself to be.

If you think about this, you'll see that the incidence of fixed races must necessarily be low. Far lower than you have suggested. My view, as I have said, is that it is less than one per cent—less than fifty races a year.

I agree with you about there being too many non-triers. One non-trier is one too many! And you do see them. But I suspect that here too you have an exaggerated idea of the incidence of 'stopping'.

The only way to stamp it out is for the Jockey Club to make full use of a complete camera patrol covering every yard of the race, with this end in view—examining every race film in detail, and suspending or otherwise penalizing jockeys as frequently as may be necessary to enforce the rules. That would be tackling the job properly. To rely upon warning somebody off once every three or four years, as a deterrent to others, is entirely useless.

Note: full camera patrol coverage of every race is now in operation, but it took several years to be implemented.

Question. What percentage on betting turnover should one regard as a satisfactory rate of profit? If I want to make £1,000 per year, what should my stakes total during the year?

In odd years, blessed with good fortune, my own profit from betting has sometimes exceeded 20 per cent on turnover. I have also had the occasional losing season. Over the years my rate of profit has been about seven and a half per cent. I doubt if anyone could maintain a profit of over ten per cent on turnover *in the long run*. So you couldn't hope to make £1,000 a year backing horses unless your total investments exceeded £10,000 a year. £20,000 would probably be nearer the mark. Of course you wouldn't require that amount of capital: you'd be turning over the same money week after week. Don't ask me how much capital you *would* need. I couldn't answer that, for I know nothing of your skill as a punter. Most punters make a loss in the long run and would eventually exhaust any capital with which they started, however big.

> *Question. What do you think about the racing maxim, 'Never bet in handicaps'?*

I think it ridiculous. If you judge a horse to have a winning chance substantially greater than is commensurate with the odds you can bet at, then you have a worthwhile *bet*, whether the race is a handicap or a weight-for-age race. It is true, of course, that in general handicaps are more difficult to weigh up than weight-for-age races, but to deny yourself all betting in handicaps on that account is to empty the baby out with the bathwater. Hard and fast betting 'maxims' (except the criterion I have mentioned above) are undesirable—no more than mere precepts for the guidance of people who don't really understand the basic realities of betting.

> *Question. A two-year-old running his first race in a five-furlong sprint shows plenty of speed for the first three furlongs. Descriptive reports say that this horse would be more suited to an extra furlong. Please could you tell me how this conclusion is arrived at?*

Your question touches on a matter of great importance to everyone concerned with interpreting the running of horses, and assessing their distance requirements. Consider not a five-furlong race, but a mile race. A horse is up with the leaders two furlongs from the end, and then loses his place. Does the horse lack stamina, and might it be better to race him over six furlongs? Or is it that the horse lacks pace and would be better suited by a mile and a quarter or even a mile and a half? To some people it may seem paradoxical to say that either explanation is possible. But it is true. The sprinter fails to hold his place in the last two furlongs of a mile race for want of stamina: the stayer loses it through inability to quicken, when the pace is really turned on at the end. In interpreting which of these two explanations is the correct one, or the more probable one, with any particular horse, by far the best guide is the horse's breeding, and by far the worst guide is what the jockey says to the trainer when he comes in after the race. It is, I suspect, in consequence of listening to what the jockey has to say that several well-known trainers (I could name them, but I won't) persist in continuing to race staying-bred horses over inadequate distances, when a mere glance at the horse's breeding would give them the right answer. I see numerous cases every year.

I'm always on the watch for them. For if at length the trainer eventually does run the horse over a distance commensurate with its breeding, that's when you may well find a bet that represents real 'value'.

> Question. I would like to know your opinion on the best way to bet. In recent years betting haphazardly (i.e. win only, each way, yankees etc.), not level stakes, I have met with some success and I was making a profit. However, during the last six months I have completely changed my mode of betting, and tried to make a more methodical approach but with disastrous results. Should I go back to my original way of betting or carry on as I am now betting?

I'm afraid you've got the wrong angle on this, brother. Finding the right horses to bet on is far more important than worrying about how to bet on them. When you back a double you merely combine two shorter-priced contingencies to make one longer-priced contingency. There's no intrinsic advantage in it, and no disadvantage. Similarly with trebles, accumulators, yankees, etc.

Your recent lack of success is not due to your method of betting, but to betting on the wrong horses.

Where win or each-way betting is concerned the matter is different. Here there is advantage to be gained by betting each way only when the place part of the bet is value. When you bet each way in a field of nine runners, you are taking a quarter the odds that your horse will finish in the first third of the field: but when you bet each way in a field of eighteen runners, you are betting that your horse will finish in the first sixth of the field. Other things being equal, the former place bet is twice as good as the latter. So you shouldn't bet each way in big fields. There are, however, other matters to be taken into account when deciding whether to bet win only or each way. It's a fairly big question. I can't give you a comprehensive answer here. I wrote briefly on the subject in my articles in *The People* earlier this year, and at greater length some years ago in *The Mathematics of Betting*. This is unfortunately now out of print and unobtainable. But I'll be republishing the important parts of it some time in the near future.

> *Note:* In the remaining 24 years of his life Bull failed to revise or reprint *The Mathematics of Betting*, despite pleas from several people to do so. Timeform updated and printed it as part of *Betting the Timeform Way* in 1993.

> *Question. In a strong betting market, what volume of money is necessary to depress the price of the favourite at 6/4 down to 5/4?*

Your question is based upon a misconception. A shortening in the market odds offered on the racecourse about a particular horse does not depend on the *amount* of money invested on the horse, but upon the *relation* between the weight of money for that horse and the weight of money for the other horses in the race.

Ten thousand pounds invested at 6/4 (to win £15,000) wouldn't alter the horse's price if the other horses in the race are also at the same time being backed to win upwards of £15,000 apiece. On the other hand, if there is a conspicuous lack of support for the other horses in the race, then a mere few hundred pounds for the favourite might well suffice to make it harden from 6/4 to 5/4.

Much depends, too, on other factors. For example, *when* a bet is made. A bet struck immediately the first prices are put on the boards, when the market is very sensitive, is likely to have much more effect on the price than one struck later when the market is well established.

Furthermore bookmakers react not only to the size of a bet, but to the person who makes it. If an owner whose normal bet on one of his own horses is around £25 comes along and puts £100 on, the bookmaker will take a deal more notice of that £100, than he would take of a £100 bet by a man who thinks nothing of having a thousand on. Similarly, a bookmaker will take far more notice of a £100 bet from a hardened and successful professional than he would of £100 from a wealthy socialite or mug punter. There are other considerations too, but I think I have said enough to make it clear that your question is not a realistic one.

> *Question. In relation to the period of time a general freeze-up lasts, how long would you suggest one should allow after a thaw, before*

horses in general can be expected to recover their form shown before a freeze-up?

Oh dear! What a bald question! In general, you say? Well, I suppose you can't get a horse fit in less than about six weeks. So if a freeze-up is such as to keep horses completely inactive for a lengthy period that would be it—six weeks. But, of course, no freeze-up keeps all horses inactive. Most trainers manage to keep their horses moving one way or another. To tell you the truth I don't really understand what you mean by your question.

Note: The letter-writer almost certainly knew what he meant, and so would most readers, but this was Phil Bull in one of his prickly moods, giving no credit to someone who could not express his thoughts perhaps as lucidly as the man to whom he had turned for advice.

T HE small, white-haired, white-bearded figure rose from the centre seat at the top table. Wearing a bow tie and maroon smoking jacket, he was unmistakable. He put down the glass of white wine he had poured for himself, from a bottle he had taken there for himself. He unclamped an ever-present cigar from the tight, moist grasp of his lips. Phil Bull was about to speak.

The occasion was the second annual dinner of the North West Racing Club, held in an hotel on the outskirts of Preston on 5 March 1982. Bull's audience of about 100 were the members, their wives or husbands, girlfriends or boyfriends, and guests of one of Britain's foremost non-elitist racing clubs, set up to give members of the public in the sprawling north-west of England a chance to play a more active part in horseracing than they could as individuals. Bull, the main speaker, was in his element.

It was 11pm before he began his address. For ninety minutes he roamed the stage of British racing in a keynote speech which brought out the main issues of the day with a force and clarity that few could emulate. It was fit to grace a professional occasion, where serious observers of racing politics would have taken in its points, considered them carefully, and made up their own minds. Here, he lost the attention of most of his audience after 15 minutes. Try as some of them might, it was too much, too late in the day, in the wrong arena.

It was not that Bull had misjudged his audience. His speech was intended as a distillation of all he stood for, all he sought from racing. He would have used the text whatever, and whoever was ranged in front of him. Later years revealed it to be one of two equally important speeches he was to make in the last years of his life.

Bull began by explaining that the theme of his speech was to be Power, taking his text from an unguarded remark by the former senior steward of the Jockey Club, Lord Howard de Walden, that 'the name of the game is Power'.

The Jockey Club are rarely so candid. They prefer to keep such things quiet. But few people know the weight of the reality behind Lord Howard de Walden's words; few know where power in racing now resides; or how it threatens to shape the future of racing, and how it promises to affect the racing that you members of the North West Racing Club hope to enjoy. I propose to enlighten you.

The agenda and tone were set immediately. Bull went quickly through the historical scene, explaining that years ago racing was the sport of Kings and aristocrats; then it became organised for spectators, before the depression and war intervened. After the war racecourses remained viable, until television came along. Crowds fell, and the Government responded by legalising off-course betting. They set up the Levy Board and made punters foot the bill for horseracing.

So here we are. Racing today is a branch of the entertainment industry, subsidised not by direct grants from the Treasury, but by punters' money, lifted out of punters' pockets, absolutely without their consent or approval. And the power struggle today is really about who gets his hands on the punters' money, and who decides how it is spent.

The entertainment racing provides is twofold: the visual spectacle on the racecourse and on TV; and the betting, seven per cent on the racecourse and 93 per cent in the betting shops. The show is staged on the racecourse, but the entertainment is essentially in the betting. The punter is the paying customer of the racing entertainment. And all the entertainers, bar the horse, are after his money, or what is left of it when the Chancellor has taken his whack.

Don't let anyone kid you. Racing is not about improving the breed, or the supremacy of the British thoroughbred. That's a Jockey Club and Thoroughbred Breeders Association fiction. Racing is about betting.

Don't let anyone tell you that racing is an industry of national importance. It isn't. In terms of bloodstock trade earnings it is negligible. In terms of the people it employs it is relatively unimportant. Punters outnumber all other people in racing by thirty to one. To all intents and purposes the owners and the punters (including racegoers) foot the bill for the whole exercise.

> Bull had shot down what he regarded as two popular myths;
> that racing is about improving the breed, and that it is an industry
> of national importance. He was warming up to an assault on a
> bigger target, the Jockey Club.

You'd think that in a modern democratic society an entertainment industry like this, heavily subsidised at the punters' expense, should at least be controlled and administered by a body answerable to and responsible to the people involved in the industry. But this is not the case.

It is run by an undemocratic, elite, private club which is answerable to no-one, and does not even publish its accounts: the Jockey Club. It makes the rules, and allocates the racing fixtures. True, the Levy Board holds the purse strings, but the Levy Board is now firmly in the embrace of the Jockey Club.

Forty years ago the Jockey Club's power in racing was absolute —unchallengeable, even in the law courts. And it exercised power frequently in a draconian and arbitrary manner, sometimes disgracefully. Its attitude to those engaged in racing was one of 19th Century aristocratic privilege and social segregation. Its concept of discipline and observance of the Rules of Racing was a military one, applicable only to the ranks. Trainers and jockeys of horses owned by members of the Establishment could do as they pleased, provided they were not too blatant about it. They could, and some of them did.

I knew one member of the Jockey Club whose horses were 'hooked-up' on several occasions, with his full knowledge. I knew his jockey. I knew a Steward of the Club who acquiesced regularly in the careful 'readying' of his horses till the time was ripe. And I could tell you of another respected Steward, the horses in whose stable were frequently 'stopped' for betting purposes, but who was too stupid to know what was going on.

With the non-Establishment owners and trainers and their jockeys it was quite another story. The Jockey Club maintained only one real sanction to deal with serious wrongdoing, with pulling horses, or with the doping of horses—the Alice In Wonderland 'off-with-his-head' sentence, 'warning off' *sine die*. And they selected their victims always among the expendable lesser fry.

With the victims caught, the so-called inquiries that followed were conducted as courts martial, though without the benefit of advocacy on behalf of the accused. The verdicts were a formality, pronounced in military style and published in words calculated to take away not merely a man's livelihood, but his good name as well.

In this way, to my knowledge, the then Stewards of the Jockey Club destroyed the lives of three trainers completely innocent of any wrongdoing or complicity in it.

Bull named Cecil Ray, who trained for him, and Jim Russell as two of the three trainers. His contempt for what he described as the Jockey Club's abuse of power was boundless.

Let nobody talk to me about the Jockey Club's 200-year reputation for integrity and discipline. In the 1940s it stank.

Strangely enough, it was an Establishment trainer who ended the nonsense about holding the trainer responsible, and chopping off his licence if one of his horses was found to have been doped. Jack

Jarvis. One of his horses ran atrociously; no dope test was ordered, so Jack himself had it tested, and declared it to have been doped—publicly. Only an Establishment trainer would have dared. Jack Jarvis trained for Lord Rosebery.

And strangely enough it was a woman who demolished the inviolability of the Jockey Club's domestic authority. Mrs Florence Nagle, in 1966. She had been training horses for 20 years, quite openly. But the male chauvinistic Jockey Club barred women from holding a licence, so her licence had to be held by a surrogate male proxy. Mrs Nagle thought this nonsense had gone on long enough. So she took legal action. The Jockey Club capitulated and Mrs Nagle won her licence.

As with starting stalls, overnight declarations and innumerable other long-overdue changes, the Jockey Club had invariably to be pushed, dragged or chivvied to the gate.

> Since Bull had been in the forefront of campaigns for such changes, he was quick to champion a fellow spirit. Here he was about to introduce Lord Wigg, chairman of the Levy Board, a Labour politican who knew his way about Westminster and Whitehall and, one suspects, the man whom Bull might like to have been.

His first act was to relieve the Jockey Club of its control over the spending of the levy. In their view the Levy Board's function was merely to collect the levy and hand it over. Wigg's predecessor, Lord Harding, had swallowed this. But in fact it was illegal.

George Wigg was a parliamentarian. As always, he'd done his homework. He knew the provisions of the Betting & Gaming Act 1963. So when the Jockey Club told him that his function was to collect the levy, and they would handle the spending of it, he told them, in parliamentary language, to 'go and get stuffed'.

Racing was now under dual control, with the Levy Board employing the blunt instrument of financial discretion, and the Jockey Club pursuing its policies administratively and through the Rules of Racing. The two were frequently at odds. But Lord Wigg took charge in a dynamic way, and pushed things in the right direction, insisting upon fixture list criteria which would maximise the levy, and doing great work in many areas.

General Sir Randle Feilden, the Senior Steward, had the unenviable job of dragging the Jockey Club along. Between them, Lord Wigg and Gerry Feilden were responsible for the most fruitful years of change in racing history. And the real credit for it all was

Lord Wigg's. George Wigg's arrival at the Levy Board was the best thing to happen to racing in my lifetime. He saved British racing.

> Bull was well into his stride, and the history lesson was about to become even more technical as he started to explain 'some highly instructive and dexterous footwork by the slippery Portman Square mandarins'. Those members of the audience who had paid their money expecting nothing more than a meal, a few drinks and a chance to debate horseracing with their friends were about to be given a lesson in the intricacies of racing politics.
>
> They were told how the Bloodstock and Racehorse Industries Confederation (BRIC) was set up in 1974 to give those involved in racing a say in the way the sport should be conducted. They heard how the following year the Government, through the Home Office and urged on by one of the big bookmaking associations BOLA, appointed a study group to investigate setting up a Racing Consultative Council. They learned that the Jockey Club had reacted to 'these two threats to its authority' by establishing the Racing Industry Liaison Committee (RILC).

By doing this the Jockey Club sought to cut the ground from under the feet of BRIC. RILC was virtually a carbon copy of BRIC—with the essential difference that RILC had no executive power, was firmly under Jockey Club control, and was chaired by the Senior Steward. This was what occasioned Lord Howard de Walden's famous remark 'The name of the game is Power.' Only once did RILC seek to assert its collective will. Lord Howard quickly put it in its place. 'Your function is merely advisory', he said.

> Bull was a member of RILC, representing punters and racegoers. It was his first such role, after a lifetime spent snapping at the heels of the Jockey Club as a private individual. He was shortly to take up a more prominent position, as the first chairman of the Horseracing Advisory Council (HAC). This was a body developed from RILC, which Bull had said was in the grip of the Jockey Club.

The HAC, however, was to be different. It was to be independent, a company limited by guarantee with its own chairman and its own secretariat. The Levy Board would arrange with the Home Secretary for its funding and to provide it with offices. The Jockey Club would make available to its chairman one of its three seats on the Levy Board, with the approval of the Home Office, and the HAC chairman would be invited to attend the Jockey Club's monthly meetings.

In the House of Commons debate, on 29 October 1979, Willie Whitelaw, Home Secretary, welcomed the formation of the HAC. He emphasised that it was not a Government body, but that it would act as an advisory body to the Levy Board. The HAC's advisory standing with the Jockey Club was not mentioned, because the Club is a private organisation outside the Home Office's responsibility. The HAC's advisory relationship with the Jockey Club is at the discretion of the Club.

Obviously this new HAC baby was conceived by the Jockey Club, in intercourse with the Levy Board; and Willie Whitelaw was roped in as godfather to legitimatise the child. It was a political copulation, a marriage of convenience. In case some future government should take up [a suggestion to establish a British Horseracing Authority] later on, the parties to the marriage wished to be able to present themselves as a united family of three: Lord Levy Board providing the cash, Lady Jockey Club running the racing household, with a nice new healthy advisory member of the family to keep the outside racing interests busy and happy.

> Bull told how he took on the role of 'child-minder'. It did not last long.

What possessed me to accept a leading role in this charade I'm damned if I know, for I saw the realities of it clearly enough. But quite unexpectedly on 23 January 1980 I found myself the HAC's first chairman, in the enthusiastic hope that I could give the HAC some teeth and make it a force of consequence which the Jockey Club and the Levy Board would be forced to take real notice of. For the fulfilment of that hope I relied upon the power of the spoken and written word—the only power available to any advisory body. I was soon to be disillusioned. And on 1 August I resigned.

> Bull declined to go into his reasons. But he hinted at two considerable constraints.

The first concerns confidentiality. There are, of course, many occasions when insistence upon confidentiality, of communications or of what happens at a meeting, is desirable and legitimate. But except when there are good and solid reasons for that confidentiality, it is important that the public should be informed of what is going on.

But always, when power lies in the hands of a few, confidentiality becomes a weapon. They want to keep everything covered up until they can face those over whom they have authority with *faites accompli*. It is like that with both the Jockey Club and the Levy Board.

The first thing that Johnny Macdonald-Buchanan [Senior Steward] did when I became chairman of HAC was to impress on me the confidentiality of all Jockey Club papers and of everything that happened at Jockey Club meetings. Much the same thing was said to me by Tristram Ricketts [chief executive] at the Levy Board. He even mentioned the existence of the Official Secrets Act—almost as if he expected me to sign it—lest I should, by a loose word, put the security of the state at risk!

This insistence on the confidentiality of virtually everything effectively castrated me as a communicator with the Press and the public, and frustrated my hope of making the HAC a force of consequence.

The second thing that was quickly borne in upon me at the HAC was that neither the Jockey Club nor the Levy Board had any intention of accepting, or paying attention to, the HAC's advice on any matters of real moment, if they themselves didn't agree with it, however strong our case might be. On trivialities and minor matters, yes, they would seek advice; but not on matters of policy or vital issues of real consequence.

> Bull went on to outline one example of his frustration, when a paper he wrote, suggesting changes to the rules relating to in-race incidents, received widespread endorsement, went forward with HAC backing to the Jockey Club, but was rejected in a paper which he said 'was the most ridiculous farrago of abysmally stupid nonsense you ever read.'

The crunch for me, however, was the Blue Report. This was a report by a committee of inquiry, composed of the three Home Office-appointed members of the Levy Board and three members of the Jockey Club. It was unveiled by Lord Plummer, the chairman, in April 1980. The report itself contained no evidence, and was prepared without prior consultation with any racing interests. It was said to have been written by Lord Weinstock, with Major Michael Wyatt and Mr Louis Freedman at his elbows.

All three are members of the Jockey Club and owner–breeders with strings of horses in training or substantial breeding interests. So of course the report was heavily loaded in that direction. In my view it was little more than a statement of how the wealthier owner–breeders would like to see the levy redistributed to their own better advantage.

In effect, to create a scheme to hand out more punters' money to wealthy owner–breeders, and less to the little owners of modest horses: implemented, it would starve many racecourses out of business and drive many small owners of moderate horses out of the game. A typical Jockey Club elitist exercise.

Of course there was a widespread outcry against it. I wrote a memorandum for the HAC recommending that the report should be firmly and unequivocally rejected. My memorandum was approved unanimously by the HAC, and our rejection of the report communicated to the Joint Racing Board. It made no difference. Lord Plummer, an experienced political operator from his days as leader of the Greater London Council, railroaded the deplorable package through. It was implemented with minor modifications in 1981.

Need I say more about the reality of the HAC's official status as an advisory body to the Levy Board? It provides a communication channel for the flow of information. Apart from that the HAC is no more than a cosmetic charade whose existence suits both the Levy Board and the Jockey Club.

> Conceding that he had 'gone on too long, it's getting late'—it was fast approaching midnight—Bull produced one more volley at the elitist target.

Ex-public schoolboys fill 43 per cent of army commissions, 54 per cent of diplomatic posts, 60 per cent of top civil service positions, and 70 per cent of directorates of top firms. 75 per cent of Conservative MPs, 77 per cent of directors of the Bank of England, 80 per cent of judges and QCs, and over 90 per cent of Conservative Cabinet Ministers are ex-public schoolboys. All from six per cent of the population! But the Jockey Club beats the lot hands down.

When I last looked up the score, its membership was 100 per cent from the public schools, and 63 per cent were Etonians. Just to round it off, 71 per cent were commissioned officers or titled gentlemen. Of course we've had a few additions to the Club since then, including five ladies.

The point of interest is the way in which the elitist social mores of these people are reflected in the policies they impose on racing. They view racing as an owner-breeder affair, not as an entertainment. The emphasis is on heavily-endowed Pattern races and weight-for-age events; they despise handicaps. They frustrate the very purpose of handicapping by raising the minimum weight that may be carried, so as to load the scales in favour of the better horses at the expense of those at the foot of the handicap.

They are determined to channel as much money as possible to big establishment racecourses and as little as possible to the others. Prize money is so structured that the top 10 per cent of owners win over 95 per cent of it, and 70 per cent of owners don't win enough to clear the cost of entry fees.

They make no attempt to match the races they frame to the horse population available to run in them. Races for maidens regularly have to be split into several divisions; horses have to be ballotted out. Yet they persist in increasing the number of races framed for high-class horses which attract few runners.

This is done, so they say, in order to encourage 'quality'—as if you could encourage people to grow big feet by manufacturing more size 12 shoes. I won't go on. Such elitist policies are simply lunacy. I shall leave it at that.

Urging his audience not to be disturbed and to leave racing politics 'to people like me', Bull praised the evening's organisers, said he had enjoyed himself, and sat down. Mental concentration among a group of people largely unused to such depth of observation—especially so late at night—had long since waned. Yet the speech was notable, for its clarity and wide range, for its pinpoint targetting.

Two years later, in 1984, Bull was back at the North West Racing Club annual dinner. This time his subject was the punter.

It is the fashion these days to talk about the Racing Industry. The phrase is misleading. Industries normally have a saleable end-product. The coal industry has coal, and the steel industry has steel. But nobody speaks of a football or a cricket or a tennis industry. What these activities produce is entertainment. The same goes for horse racing. It's a branch of the entertainment industry.

Some people talk about the racing industry as though its end-product was the horse; as though racing was about producing high-quality horses. It's nonsense. Producing the horse is the business of the breeding industry. Motor racing isn't about making Formula One cars. That's the motor industry's business. Motor racing is about entertainment for people. So is horse racing.

The racing entertainment is twofold: the spectacle on the racecourse, also shown on television, and the betting on the races. Racing wouldn't last ten minutes on turnstile takings and what it could get from TV. Without the betting there would be no spectators, and nothing to sell to TV. The betting is the essence of the game: and less than seven per cent of it is on the racecourse: over 93 per cent is in the betting shops. That's where most of racing's customers are. And as Rothschild's Royal Commission said, 'It would be wrong to treat their way of following racing as less worthy than that of the spectators, especially when Thursday's betting-office punter may be Saturday's spectator'.

There are about three million punters. We outnumber all other people involved in racing or betting by over 30 to one. And we pay for our entertainment through the levy on our betting.

The finance for racing comes from four sources: from the TV authorities; from the sponsors, in prize-money, mostly for advertising purposes; from the punters; and from the owners, who spend an unquantifiable sum in providing the horses and racing them. All the other people involved contribute skills and services, but not money. They are 'takers-out' from racing, not 'putters-in'. Broadly speaking, it's punters and owners who foot the bill.

> Bull proceeded to examine the individual forces which affect punters, beginning with 'the most voracious taker-out, Her Majesty's Government'.

With the Betting and Gaming Act [1963] on the statute book it wasn't long before the Treasury got the scent of punters' pockets. Soon it was busy picking those pockets by means of a General Betting Duty [rising from 2.5 per cent on all bets to eight per cent off course]. It does not mean taxation at eight per cent. It's not like a price increase in the shops of 8p in the pound. The reality is quite different.

In 1982 racing punters staked £2,460 million. It's calculated that they got back 80 per cent of this in winnings and returned stakes, leaving them £492 million out of pocket. The punters did not lose that in their betting, for included is £197 million that went in betting duty to the Treasury, and £19.1 million in levy to the Levy Board. So what punters actually lost on their betting was £276 million.

They paid public taxation of 71 per cent [general betting duty] on that, and private taxation of seven per cent [to the levy]. And so the punters' betting loss of £276 million was increased by 78 per cent, to £492 million. That's the real tax you're paying, 78 per cent. So don't let anyone kid you your betting is only taxed at eight per cent.

> Bull pointed out that betting turnover was going down because punters were beginning to realise the score. And he

2   Phil Bull's formative years took him (above) from childhood, with an early dramatic role, through Hemsworth Grammar School, to graduation from Leeds University. Below, he figured on the front row (second from left) of the university chess club.

3   One of Phil Bull's longest-standing associations was with the bookmaker
William Hill (left). Bull managed Hill's horses when they were trained in the North,
among them the filly Cantelo. In 1959 she silenced a large part of the large crowd at
Doncaster (below) by winning the St Leger, only three days after being beaten
at odds-on in the Park Hill Stakes.

4   Phil Bull became one of the most successful owner-breeders in the North, thanks to an association with the Malton trainer Charlie Elsey (right). Bull would watch his horses work on the gallops, meticulously recording their performances, as well as having them photographed (below).

SP Malton.   March 16th
    First Gallop

        Orinthia   7-4   E Hide
        Sonrullas   7-4   J Capen
        Dionisio   7-13 E Britt

            1½ (comf)   1

5 Three jockeys were retained during Phil Bull's
heyday as an owner—Edgar Britt, seen below (right)
with his successor Edward Hide,
and, above, Don Morris.

6   As a racehorse breeder, Phil Bull was always open to offers for his bloodstock.
Eudaemon, seen below winning the Gimcrack Stakes at York in 1956, was one of the
earliest big-race successes he sold. Above, Bull joins Eudaemon's owner
Mrs Elsie Foster and trainer Charlie Elsey at the Gimcrack Dinner.

7   Phil Bull founded his Hollins Stud in 1947. The first big-race winner he bred was
Orgoglio, seen being led in after beating Olympic in the Champagne Stakes at
Doncaster in 1951. Orgoglio went on to win the Victoria Cup
at Hurst Park as a four-year-old.

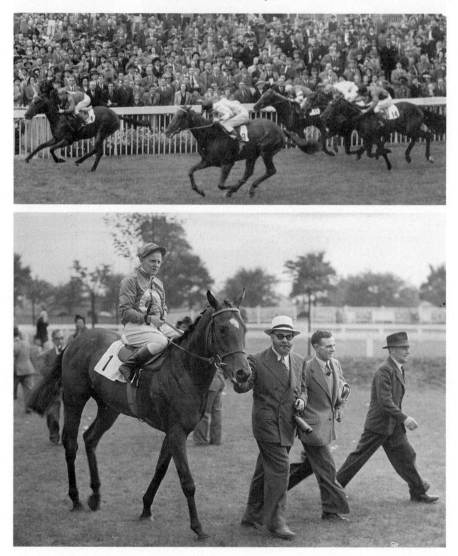

8   Success as a racehorse owner brought Phil Bull the tangible reward of an impressive array of trophies. Among the first was the prize won by Pheidippides in the Gimcrack Stakes at York in 1957. Pheidippides, ridden by Doug Smith, is seen winning from Pinched and The Queen's colt Pall Mall, and being greeted in the winner's enclosure by Bull and trainer Charlie Elsey (second right).

9–10 Over the years from 1942 Phil Bull became a familiar figure on British
racecourses, whether presenting trophies for Timeform-sponsored races, taking centre
stage as an owner, or marking his card from a spot around the parade ring
as he prepared to take on the bookmakers.

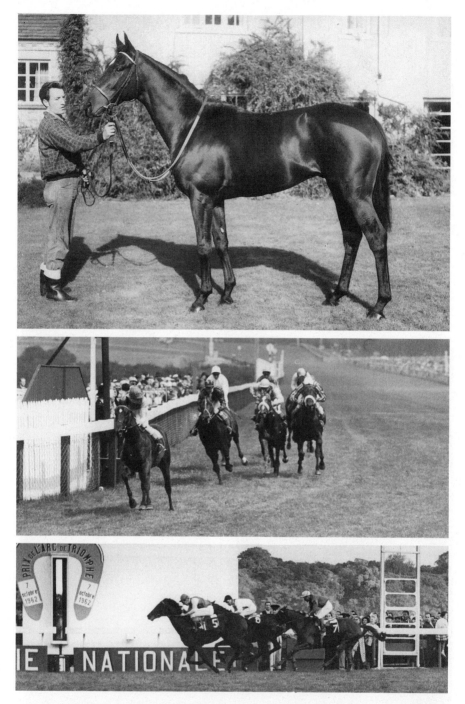

11   In order to finance his operation as a racehorse breeder Phil Bull was at various times forced to sell his produce. The best horse he bred, and sold, was Romulus, pictured (top) as a two-year-old in 1961. The following year Romulus, carrying Charles Engelhard's colours, was Europe's leading miler. Among his five wins in 1962 were (centre) the Sussex Stakes, in which he beat Cipriani, Songedor and Nereus (right), and (bottom) the Prix du Moulin de Longchamp, which he won comfortably from Sturdy Man and Prince Altana.

12 Though Phil Bull had horses placed in two classics—Arietta and Aureoletta—the ultimate success eluded him. Potentially one of his best horses was Sostenuto, who was twice struck by injury at crucial times. He still pulled off one of Bull's biggest successes, when in 1962—the year of Romulus—he raced away from a strong field, led at a margin of eight lengths by Cracksman (hooped sleeves), in the Ebor Handicap at York. Bull could afford to look pleased in the winner's enclosure; he had backed Sostenuto to win £4,000.

13   The Timeform Gold Cup was a masterstroke of innovation, as Europe's richest
staying race for two-year-olds, while the annual Timeform Charity Day meeting has
become the biggest fund-raiser of the year for Cancer Relief. Phil Bull is pictured (top)
in 1961 presenting the first Timeform Gold Cup to Gerry Oldham, after his colt Miralgo
had beaten Escort and Prince Poppa. Below, Bull beams in delight as The Queen,
accompanied by her racing manager Lord Porchester (left) and the Lord Lieutenant of
South Yorkshire, attends the first Timeform charity meeting in 1971, at Doncaster.
Among those behind the principal party are, from the left, William Hill, Brookie Brooks,
Tom Forrest, Tim Thompson, Ron Magee and Reg Griffin.

14   Phil Bull's regard for George Wigg (right) as chairman of the Levy Board,
and his pleasure in the success of Sir Ivor, owned by Raymond Guest (centre),
are well documented. Bull was not so pleased that Guest declined to take up an offer
to buy his home-bred colt Diaz (below) as a yearling in exchange for a share in Sir Ivor.
The racing career of Diaz proved that Guest was well out of the deal.

15 Though generally serious and straight-talking, Phil Bull had a softer, humorous
side to his character. He is pictured playing Popeye, and adopting unusual headgear.
Women played a major part in his life, and, below, he joins two strong female
influences—his mother Dolly and sister May (second left),
who sit alongside May's daughter June (left).

16   Riches won from betting on horses furnished Phil Bull
with a lavish lifestyle once he had returned to Yorkshire
after the war and bought The Hollins (top)
on the outskirts of Halifax.

17   Phil Bull's last appearance in public was to attend
the William Hill Golden Spurs Awards lunch in London in March 1989, when deputy
chairman Len Cowburn presented him with a trophy for lifetime achievement in racing.
Bull's famous racing colours had already been carried to success for the last time,
by Ho Mi Chinh—seen winning at Newcastle as a two-year-old—
at Doncaster in May 1986.

rounded on the Government for its ambivalent attitude towards betting.

If you pitch the tax so high that it's obvious to the punter he has no chance, or make him lose his money too quickly for the game to be enjoyable, he will either give it up altogether, or seek some way of betting without tax.

Not only does the betting-shop punter get a raw deal from the Government, so does racing generally. Of the money lifted from punters' pockets in duty and levy, 91.2 per cent went into Government coffers, and only 8.8 per cent to the Levy Board for horse racing. The last time I looked at betting in America and France, racing's slice of plunder was 41 per cent in the States and 21 per cent in France. In Britain it is 8.8 per cent.

If you want to know how the British Government loves its £200 million contributor, visit a betting shop. The law doesn't allow a proprietor to tell you where his shop is. He isn't permitted to advertise. He can't display betting concessions or ante-post odds in his shop window.

When they were legalising betting shops, the Christian moralists got in on the act. Betting is sinful, so they did their best to give a betting shop the status of a brothel—without its internal comforts or attractions.

Step inside the door and you'll be lucky if you can find a chair to sit on, or a table. Strictly speaking they shouldn't be there. And no music, no entertainment, no refreshment of any kind, no radio or television. The place has to be as bare and uninviting as possible, so as to ensure that you will go into it only if you feel you have to, and will get out of it as soon as you can. You won't be allowed there after 6.30pm. And not at any times on Sundays. You have the churches to thank for all this. So much for our vaunted British freedoms! And so much for the Government's concern for punters and their interests.

This was 1984, remember. Bull moved on to the Levy Board, the statutory body which assesses, collects and spends the levy which bookmakers raise by way of deductions from punters' winnings.

The punter has no standing in all this, and he's not represented on the Levy Board. When the Act was passed, the levy was to be a payment by bookmakers out of their profits. There was no thought of punters being involved. But nowadays the bookmakers collect it and hand it over to the Board, and every penny is paid by the punters.

The weakness of the punters is that they have no national organisation. This doesn't mean that punters should be denied representation on any body concerned with the governance of racing. In Orwellian terms, sheep are entitled to have a say in their shearing. What it does mean is that the sheep are defenceless when the wolves fall upon them.

> Bull began to detail where the punters' money had gone, showing that the Levy Board had collected over £164 million between 1961 and 1982. It had produced a total surplus for spending of £138 million, and had gradually increased the proportion given to prize-money from 54 per cent over the first thirteen years to 72 per cent in 1979 and 1980. He pointed his finger at the culprit.

This was a direct result of the Levy Board's capture by the Jockey Club, and of the Board's acceptance of Jockey Club policies. Prize-money support was transferred from the minor racecourses which needed it most, to the major racecourses that needed it least, and it was channelled into the so-called quality races, preferably Pattern races and weight-for-age events. The policy also lowered the prize-money and increased the entry fees for the smaller races.

In short, it was designed to hand over more of the punter's money to the wealthy owner–breeders with high-class horses, and less of it to the little owners trying to win modest races at unfashionable meetings. To him that hath much shall the Levy Board be generous with punters' money: to him that hath little shall the Jockey Club vouchsafe the guaranteed sweepstake, the surcharge and the bigger entry fee.

The hard truth is that because of its excessive concern with prize-money the Levy Board has not discharged its responsibilities in other directions. For example, there is no comprehensive coverage of racing by film or video-patrol camera. The RTS/Omega photo-finish timing camera is first-class technical equipment but is in use on only 15 of the 36 Flat racecourses.

And what about the pretence of keeping punters informed of betting and market changes? Newmarket with its thermometer system that conveys practically nothing; and Doncaster and other courses with odds-boards being gropingly sorted and slowly inserted into outdated structures. This kind of service to the customer is a joke.

But, Bull was pleased to say, there was a light on the horizon, following the appointment of Sir Ian Trethowan as chairman of the Levy Board and publication of his first policy statement. It recognised that racing is an entertainment business—'a breath of fresh air', said Bull. Not so Jockey Club policy, 'in particular its preoccupation with Pattern races and others framed for top horses'.

The Jockey Club frequently defends its policies in this area by saying they are designed to encourage quality and reward merit. To me this phrase makes absolutely no sense.

Presumably 'to encourage quality' means to encourage breeders to breed better quality horses, better-class horses; in short, better horses. But isn't this exactly what all breeders have been trying to do ever since the days of St Simon? They need no encouragement.

If you doubled the prize-money in all races tomorrow, it could have no effect whatever on the quality of the horses running in them. Of course, to increase prize-money selectively, raising the value of a particular race, will attract better horses to run in it. But that's not 'encouraging quality'. It's redirecting the existing quality.

As to the second objective, does anyone seriously suggest that racing could be run on the simple principle of rewarding merit? Only weight-for-age events without penalties or allowances do that. With their exception, all racing is ordered not on the principle of rewarding merit, but of penalising merit, in the interests of making the events more competitive, making them better spectacles and better mediums for betting, more interesting and better entertainment.

Talk about encouraging quality and rewarding merit is meaningless. Apparently it still needs hammering into Establishment heads that racing is about providing entertainment for people, not paying homage to quality. Everyone enjoys the presence in racing of high-quality horses. Everyone likes to see the Shergars and the Nijinskys. They're the stars the game throws up occasionally. They add to the entertainment, that is all.

Pattern races were born out of a French objection. The idea was born that races should be classified, and penalties and allowances should be based on the classification of the races won, and not on their value. Now it has become something vastly different. The whole exercise is run in the interests of breeders. As far as conveying any indication of a horse's real merit, it is virtually meaningless.

But the most serious consequence of the Pattern set-up is its rigidity, the way it is solidifying the overall structure of racing in its existing mould. Nothing can be allowed to interfere with it.

Bull said he had seen the effects at first hand, when a request to run a £100,000 race at the Timeform Charity meeting was turned down because of Jockey Club objections based on its clashing with existing Pattern races.

No competition with existing Pattern races is permissible. Why on earth not? Isn't racing itself all about competition? Why must existing races be so protected? If the cooks can't stand the heat, they should get out of the kitchen. Why keep on telling us that racing must help itself: that managers and clerks of the course should show initiative, drive and imagination, and so on; if such initiatives are to be frustrated and denied.

It reminds me of Lord Derby's objection to the Ebor's having a £10,000 prize, on the grounds that it could be won by an ill-bred horse at the foot of the handicap, and this would distort the Winning Sires list. As if the purpose of racing was not to provide entertainment, but to furnish an acceptable Sire's list.

I am in no way opposed to having well-endowed Group 1 weight-for-age races for high-class horses. They make splendid, highly competitive events of great interest to everyone, punters included, betting-wise and racing-wise. And there's a good argument for having a rationally planned structure of such events. But no such structure ought to be regarded as sacrosanct, or advanced as a reason for ruling out an imaginative addition to it, especially if the innovator is introducing new sponsorship money and has found a suitable slot for his race.

And so Bull turned to the topic which concerned him most at this time, Rule 153, the part of racing's legislation 'which really betrays the Jockey Club's total disregard for the interests of punters', he said.

This is to do with the interference caused by jockeys in the course of a race, and what stewards are permitted to do about it afterwards: whether disciplinary action is called for by a jockey's actions, and whether the result of the race is to be altered or not.

The effect of the rule is quite clear. A carelessly or improperly ridden horse that interferes with another horse has to be disqualified to last place, or placed behind the horse it interfered with. There is no 'may be' about it. It doesn't matter whether the horse won by a short head or ten lengths; it doesn't matter whether the interference affected the result of the race or not; and it doesn't matter whether the horse interfered with had any chance at the time, or where it finished, or how far it was beaten. The rule gives the stewards no option.

The injustice that flows from this is obvious. The rider alone commits the offence; but it is not only the rider who has to suffer a penalty. Three totally innocent parties are also penalised: the owner and trainer of the disqualified winner (or placed horse), and the punters who backed it (unless they happen to be betting first past the post).

The indifference of the Jockey Club is really amazing. They are not in the least interested in justice, only in discipline. In 1979 and 1980 I submitted papers on Rule 153. The answer I got from the Jockey Club's Disciplinary Committee was compounded of misrepresentation, evasiveness, refusal to address the issues, and either plain ignorance of their own rules or shameless mendacity.

Lord Manton's first words on the subject when he became senior steward [1982] were, 'Every other country has the same rule as we do, so it seems universally accepted that it is the best rule.' The Jockey Club nailed its own collective ignorance to the mast in the same way, making the same assertion, in writing to the Horseracing Advisory Council, the same year. This, despite the fact that I had already shown on several occasions that the assertion was false.

Other countries do not have the same rule. I know of no country that makes disqualification mandatory for careless or improper riding, as it is here. How does anyone account for the Jockey Club's refusal to face the fact, and its repeated assertion to the contrary? Is it really ignorance, or what?

Bull declined to answer his own questions, and moved on to his closing point—about bookmakers—in another long political session which had tried the patience of the majority of North West Racing Club members present.

He had washed his hands of the Rule 153 business, he said. That was not quite true. He continued to make his point about inequality as often and as forcefully as he could for the next few years; he encouraged others to keep the issue of so-called injustice to the fore. Gradually a degree of change in Jockey Club thinking was introduced, and eventually it became no longer mandatory for a carelessly ridden horse to be disqualified. For more serious offences there was little indication the Jockey Club was inclined to take up Bull's plea for separation of rider and horse.

His two speeches to the North West Racing Club were remarkable on several counts—not least that he should use the occasion of such a social gathering to delve so deeply into the politics of the game. He majored on racing being an entertainment, but bored the majority of his audience in the process!

By this time in his life, though, his stage had become limited, especially once he left behind the Horseracing Advisory Council in 1980. The racing trade press—*The Sporting Life* and soon-to-fold *Sporting Chronicle*—was still open, but composing his thoughts was more and more time-consuming; he made no contribution to his Timeform publications. Only this platform gave him room to expand and he did not miss the opportunity.

Looking back over the two speeches, racing has moved on apace in less than 15 years. Many of Bull's points have been taken up, in part if not in whole. The Jockey Club's all-embracing power has gone; the British Horseracing Board has brought a degree of democracy to decision making. The emphasis on entertainment has been taken up—in policy statements at least—by the BHB and the Levy Board. The Government has relented a little on general betting duty, including removing it from on-course betting. The Home Office has paved the way for betting shops to compete on the same promotional terms as other High Street retail outlets; televised racing comes in every day, from almost every meeting, and betting shops are open in the summer evenings—and on certain Sundays.

Punters still have no strong national organisation; Rule 153 remains short of Bull's ideal, and he would probably argue that the programming of races is not nearly flexible enough. He would argue, but would he listen to counter-arguments? It's doubtful.

F EW written or filmed features about Phil Bull were received with unreserved enthusiasm by the subject. Kenneth Harris's BBC television interview and Hugh McIlvanney's profile in the April 1975 issue of *Pacemaker* were notable exceptions. Harris became a friend; McIlvanney was rewarded with a complimentary reference in a letter dated 17 March 1975, after Bull had seen a pre-publication proof:

I envy you your journalistic skills. I've read several of your pieces recently, all done within a week or two. And I think of your coming to spend a few hours with me—far, far too short a time to do more than scratch the surface, I would have thought; and then I see what you produce from it, and the skill with which you put it together and made it interesting and readable. I wouldn't have a hope of doing such a thing myself.

Perhaps not, but Bull's unusual rash of modesty would hardly have extended to disagreeing with McIlvanney's opening paragraph: 'If the most dramatic figure in British racing since the Second World War has been Lester Piggott, surely the most lastingly influential has been Phil Bull. By force of personality and intellect he has done more than even the most progressive of his contemporaries to bring a stubbornly anachronistic sporting industry face to face with the realities of its current situation.'

Bull might have argued over the word 'industry', but the rest fitted neatly as an independent commentary to the notes he made in 1969 under the heading Own Impact On Racing Scene:

At a time when it was hazardous to criticise Establishment, did so. Demolished breeding superstitions. 1) Did great deal to educate racing public to realities of racing [six years later McIlvanney used almost the same form of words]; 2) Devised new and original method of assessing and recording merit of horses—ratings 140–40; 3) Gimcrack speech: starting stalls, overnight declarations, cine record of races, display of photo-finish strips and distances from photo, advocated centralisation of racing and abolition of sellers; 4) Alteration of Rules (Rule 64b); 5) Timeform Gold Cup.

That Bull decided to reverse his first two points after making an original draft may be of no consequence, and his lack of recognition for the part played by Dick Whitford in the creation of *Timeform* ratings is wholly consistent with his later writing and interviews. But there can be no doubt that his single biggest original contribution to racing was the promotion of this unique opinion of the relative merit of racehorses, from the same generation or from different eras. It became internationally recognised, and was eventually mirrored by the Jockey Club in its handicapping method. The International Classifications endorsed by the European Pattern Committee came to use the same rating scale of 0–140.

Bull's opinion of Timeform's publications was expressed in his introduction to a 40th anniversary brochure in 1988:

Though they are of value to owners, breeders, trainers, jockeys and everyone professionally engaged in racing, not forgetting, of course, journalists and TV commentators, every single one of our publications was designed by me in the first place, not for any of these people, but specifically for punters. I designed them, in fact, to meet my own requirements as a punter: to provide, for every horse, all the facts and information that experience has taught me were required for successful betting: and to present them as clearly and concisely as possible. That policy continues. It's the Timeform touchstone. For forty years I've never made a bet without it.

The last sentence might have contained an element of promotional licence—betting £2,000 (unsuccessfully) on the strength of a gallops report from trainer Barry Hills was not the 'value' approach he used in his heyday—but towards the end of forty years he was perhaps entitled to overlook an exception or two.

Bull's close association with betting and his appreciation of the punter's position was paramount. The McIlvanney profile quoted him:

What is so sad and so alarming regarding the future of racing is the refusal to admit the obvious, that the vital audience for the sport is no longer on the course but in the betting shops, and that it is absolutely wrong to go on claiming that the interests of owners and breeders are synonymous. This is, above all, an entertainment industry, and it is the audience that matters.

If private owners ceased to exist that need not mean the end of racing. The Levy Board could own horses; commercial companies could own them; groups of people could own them. The alternatives are numerous enough.

Those people in the betting shops must be looked after and given the consideration they deserve as the ones who can guarantee the future of racing. Their facilities should be improved. There should be

TV in the shops, for instance. The Jockey Club should re-orientate its thinking in favour of the punters, and there should be a relaxation of the controls applied to the ownership of horses so that firms can run them in their own names, working men's clubs can own them, and so on. There must be a liberal and progressive attitude to this.

> This was an owner–breeder speaking, in 1975—before commercial companies, syndicates and working men's clubs were allowed to become part of the regular racehorse-owning population; before televisions were allowed on the customer's side of the counter, and before Satellite Information Services began beaming the huge majority of British races into betting shops.
>
> Bull consistently nailed his ideas on the Jockey Club door. His frustration was frequently evident, as in a letter to George Wigg, dated 24 November 1969, beginning with his attempts to get action at Newmarket by way of letters to *The Sporting Life*:

It is exactly thirteen months since I drew Randle Feilden's attention to the stupid calibration of the paddock odds board at Newmarket. He promised he'd do something about it immediately. He did absolutely nothing. Hence my use of the sledge-hammer on this occasion. Now we'll get action!

It's eighteen months since I asked Randle Feilden [Jockey Club senior steward] to get a white line painted across the front of the starting stalls to assist people trying to time races. He promised to see to it. Six months afterwards he said Racecourse Technical Services 'thought it impracticable'! You can't believe it? It's true. I was dumbfounded—literally—and had to walk away without comment.

Do you recall my lengthy letter to *The Sporting Life* some two or three months ago regarding penalties in handicaps? A few days ago I had a 'phone call from Jakie Astor. Apparently he has been requested by the Turf Board to report to them on the subject, and he wants me to furnish him with a memorandum about it.

It's a lark, isn't it? I tell 'em what's wrong. They stir in their slumbers. Appoint one of their members to report on the matter. And he comes back to me to ask me to tell 'em again. Even more comical, when you know the undercurrents! Jakie says, when he phones: do you want me to write to you on my own letterhead, personally, or should I do it officially, through Weatherbys? It took a second for me to see the importance of this. But I saw it. He wanted to know whether it was possible to pick my brains with or without acknowledgement!

So I said: 'Look Jakie: It's immaterial to me. Write it on lavatory paper if you like. I'll be happy to tell you what I think. Tell me what you want to know and I'll answer to the best of my ability. Just tell me your terms of reference.' So he says: 'Yes, well all right, I think I'll get David Weatherby to write to you about it.' Weatherby's letter arrived yesterday.

This business is amusing, you know. People running racing who don't think, don't understand and can't do the job, looking for outside help, preferably without having to acknowledge it. But this actually is progress! Twenty years ago they wouldn't even have acknowledged a problem. Ten years ago they'd have looked at it and done nothing. Now they're leaning over backwards to try and do the right thing, if only someone will tell 'em what is the right thing to do!

> Never short of suggestions, Bull continued to advance them for over thirty years. On 22 January 1986 he wrote to the latest Jockey Club senior steward, Lord Fairhaven:

As you said at York, change is very much in the air for racing— it's at a modal point in its life as a major entertainment, as it was when George Wigg and Randle Feilden had to deal with the implications of legalised off-course betting and the Levy. The big factor is, of course, television.

TV brings entertainment directly into the home. People no longer have to go out for this entertainment. So all on-site entertainments have lost their customers. All of 'em: the sports and the arts. It is not the televising of racing that takes people off the racecourses: it is the availability of TV entertainment generally. In the past the Jockey Club and the racecourses have felt that TV exposure of racing was robbing them of racegoers. Not true at all. In fact, those on-site entertainments that suffer least from the advent of TV entertainment are those that get the most television exposure. It is vital that racing should get as much TV coverage as possible, not merely because this builds up sponsorship, but because it is advertising for racing and creates and increases interest in it.

The soccer authorities have made the same mistake: fighting the TV people for bigger fees, instead of thanking their lucky stars for TV exposure. It hasn't taken them long to feel the draught from their mistaken policies. And they're now struggling to get back to the prime position they held before.

Racing is in a far stronger position than football. Why? Because of betting. They bet on football—but only purely as a lottery, the Pools. We may thank Reggie Maudling for killing fixed-odds betting, so that the only serious betting now available to the public is on horseracing.

Make no mistake, for the public racing is not about breeding but about betting. The Jockey Club and the Thoroughbred Breeders Association may try to persuade people that racing is about breeding top-class horses and the winning of Pattern races. All that's very fine for the Sheikhs and the Sangsters. But they don't make the turnstiles tick on the racecourses—they don't pay for admission.

True, the Shergars and the Oh So Sharps, the Slip Anchors and the Pebbles draw the crowds when they run: but how often do they run? What draws people to racecourses, and to the betting shops, is the betting. Like it or not, betting is the lifeblood of racing, and this is something that the Jockey Club is only slowly and reluctantly learning. A proper understanding of it will result in changes in the Rules of Racing and a new attitude towards the structure of racing programmes offered to the public.

I don't say this gleefully. Quite the contrary. For myself I'm concerned with the top horses and always have been, with weight-for-age races rather than handicaps. But my concerns are irrelevant. Racing is about betting, and if it is to be presented for maximum entertainment of the public, it is this aspect of it that has to receive attention, not the interests of the owners and breeders, which, heretofore, have had prior attention.

> The previous month Bull had approached Lord Fairhaven personally, after hearing him deliver a speech at the Gimcrack Dinner on York racecourse. He told him it was the best he had heard there by any member of the Jockey Club. In his letter he explained: 'It was not a light-hearted compliment after an exceptionally good dinner, but a serious value judgement.' Bull knew all about Gimcrack Dinner speeches: he had been listening to them for over thirty years, and the one he himself made in 1957 has been held up as the prime example of his forward thinking. It was not, however, the first in which he outlined far-reaching proposals for the sport. He had already paved the way when proposing the toast to the Doncaster Corporation Race Committee at the St Leger Dinner in the Mansion House in September 1955.
>
> Concentrating first on the course where the final classic of the season was due to be run, he said much the most important improvement needed was a new grandstand:

I believe Doncaster is the only racecourse in the country where the paying customers in Tattersalls have no covered stand accommodation, so that in wet weather all they can do to get out of the rain is to crowd into the bars and alleyways, from where they can't see anything of the racing.

There is always good racing at the St Leger meeting. But I should like to see it cater more exclusively for the best-class horses. Four selling races are out of place at the Leger meeting. One is enough.

Next I should like to see a race-timing camera used at Doncaster. Races are now electrically timed at Newmarket, Ascot, Birmingham and Redcar, and York will also be in line next year. I can assure you there is a great deal of interest in race times. Even the meanest dog-tracks have their races electrically timed.

Finally, I should like to see the current ring prices of all the runners in each race prominently displayed in the paddock, as at York and elsewhere. People cannot be in two places at once, looking at the horses in the parade ring, and watching the betting. And the more information you give people about their sport, the more you heighten their interest in it. I see no reason why the current market odds should not be announced over the public address system every couple of minutes or so.

> Forty years distant, some of the observations make quaint reading: covered stands, timing on a major course, prominent display of odds are all taken for granted. But not in 1955. Patrons of the Tattersalls enclosure at Doncaster had to wait until 1970 and Nijinsky's St Leger before they had a roof over their heads; a comprehensive, up-to-the-minute odds board did not appear until digital technology came on the scene around 1990. Leger meeting selling races disappeared altogether about the same time.
>
> Moving on to the wider scene in his speech, Bull said there were many other changes and improvements he would like to talk about, but they were outside his province and, in any case, he did not expect to see most until he was 'out racing on the Elysian fields in company with Lord George Bentinck, Admiral Rous, John Gully, Lt-Gen Anthony St Leger and company, watching Meld and Acropolis take on Eclipse, Voltigeur and The Flying Dutchman in a Celestial St Leger'. He prefaced most of his targets with the word 'celestial':

I expect to see a racecourse with one finishing post which will be in front of the stands, not two furlongs down the track. I expect the draw to be given for each race with the entries in Messrs Weatherbys' Calendar, and overnight declarations in the Press. I expect to see all the runners arrive in the parade ring before their owners. I expect to see a starter who always gets the whole field off in line, not merely three quarters of it. I expect to see judges who always confirm their decisions by reference to the photographs, which are displayed for all to see after every race. All races will be timed, and the time recorded by every horse that ran published against its name in the Calendar. And if there are objections to be made, I shall expect them to be made by the stewards, not by the owners; and the objections to be decided according to a standard interpretation of clear and unambiguous rules.

> Forty years ago Bull was expecting a lot; today most features are commonplace, and common sense. Times have changed, but slowly. Strangely enough, when Bull made his Gimcrack Dinner speech a little over two years later, he admitted: 'It seems I'm expected to explode a few fireworks. I'm sorry to disappoint anyone, but this speech comes about ten years too late for me: ten years in which the Jockey Club has pinched most of the crackers I might have let off.' He highlighted some of the changes:

The photo-finish has been introduced, so I can no longer complain that the horse that finishes first doesn't always get the verdict. That used to happen more frequently than most people suppose.

Electrical timing equipment is being installed on more courses. The doping menace seems now to have been disposed of—not by the wicked barbarity of imposing warning-off sentences upon innocent trainers, but by the simple expedient of locking the stable door, setting up an efficient racecourse stables security system.

Then there's the watering of courses, which was so frequently a one-sided affair. It has always seemed idiotic to employ a first-class handicapper to ensure that all the horses have equal chances, and then to allow Mr Clerk of the Course to come along with his watering can and give those drawn on the far side a 21lb advantage over those on the stand side, or vice versa. That, I hope, has been brought to an end by the Jockey Club's instruction that courses are to be watered only with a view to promoting the growth of herbage, and not with a view to altering the going.

Quite recently we have heard the death knell of Produce Races and Foal Stakes. I wish selling races were going with them. They are a pointless anachronism with several highly undesirable features.

The past ten years have also seen vast improvements made in the amenities on some racecourses. This was vividly brought home to me when I went to Hurst Park in October for the first time since

1939. I hardly knew the place—the rebuilt stands, replanned paddock, attractive surroundings and everything bright with new paint.

> Bull probably over-estimated the effect of the watering instruction, and even he could not have forecast that Hurst Park would stage its final meeting in 1962, exactly five years after the visit to which he referred. Despite his opening observation, he did take the opportunity to look into the future:

We still have with us the odd course where the management hasn't fallen for these new-fangled ideas of bringing racing up to date; where hardly a pot of paint has been spilled; where flower beds are unknown; where the early running in long-distance races still takes place out of sight of the stands, and some of them finish a furlong or two down the track, as they did in the days when it was customary for the spectators to canter down on their hacks.

What further changes would I like to see in the next ten years? My experience of racing abroad is not extensive, but it is sufficient to show me that in some respects we are woefully behind the times.

Take, for example the starting of races. Only those who have seen the starts effected in America can appreciate how bad our starting is by comparison. In the States it is the rare exception for there to be more than a length between first and last as they leave the gate.

I didn't find the starting quite so good in Venezuela as in the States, though they use the same [Puett] starting gate. But what did impress me there was the cine-record which is made of every race for the benefit of the stewards. Eighteen minutes after the winner had passed the post I was shown a complete slow-motion cine-record of the race from start to finish; every yard of the race photographed from two angles, and every movement of every horse and jockey available for detailed inspection, in forward motion, in reverse, or as a still photograph. No arguments in the objection room in Venezuela! The stewards don't call the jockeys in to ask them what happened: they call 'em in to show 'em what happened.

A third respect in which we are woefully behind the times is in this matter of overnight declarations. I know I won't get many thanks from other owners and trainers for saying this, but the advantages greatly outweigh the disadvantages. To have an accurate list of runners in the Press every morning would benefit everyone. Overnight declarations, efficiently organised, would also mean racecards printed with runners, jockeys and the draw. It would do away with number boards and number-board staff, and lengthy announcement of runners. Incidentally, if and when overnight declarations are introduced, I hope the Jockey Club will do it boldly and not in a tentative, half-hearted manner.

Other suggestions I should like to make are minor ones. I'd like to see a change in the rule which demands that a disqualified horse shall be placed last. I'd like to see more use made of the public address system—as, for example, in the periodic announcing of current market odds. Boards displaying current market odds are excellent if they supply up-to-the-second information, as at York. The one in the paddock at Newmarket is ludicrously inefficient. The prices displayed invariably bear no relation whatever to the actual ones in the ring: 100/8 chances at 5/2; 6/4 chances at 10/1. It's just a joke.

I should like to see more use made of the photo-finish strip, a valuable record of the finish of every race. Let it be obligatory upon the judge to inspect the photograph after every race. By all means let him announce the first three as they pass the post if he wishes. But let it be his duty always to see that his verdict is confirmed by the photograph. And let the distances between the placed horses be taken in every case from the photograph. Then we shall no longer see distances of five lengths returned as three-parts of a length, and half a length as three lengths. I saw both these things happen on the same afternoon in consecutive races. Making sense out of the form book is difficult enough without the complication of false distances. The photograph is there, so let us have accurate distances between the first six horses.

These things are important. When a man goes to the races to see Crepello, only to find him a non-runner, he feels cheated; when he sees his fancy shown at 10/1 in the paddock and finds it 3/1 in the ring, he feels annoyed; when he sees the horse he's backed left four or five lengths, quite unnecessarily, he's angry; when he hears a verdict of four lengths announced when it's plain that one length would be nearer the mark, he's disgusted. Is it surprising if he goes home depressed, and wearily informs the wife that he's through with racing: that the game's crooked, the starters are in league with the bookmakers, the judges are blind and the stewards incompetent? None of these things is true, but there are occasions when a man might be excused for thinking they were. Some of the suggestions I have made turn on the question of finance. I don't propose to discuss this, except to mention that I am in agreement with the view that the SP bookmakers who derive their livelihood from racing should do something to support it. Most of them would be happy to do so. But to obtain revenue from this source on a national scale needs legislation which we are unlikely to get. In the circumstances, let us welcome the sponsoring of races and refrain from looking gift horses in the mouth.

> This was 1957. Starting stalls were used in Britain for the first time on 8 July 1965, at Newmarket. The camera patrol began its first full year of operation in 1961, with 120 days' racing on seventeen courses; it now operates on all courses. Overnight declaration of runners came first, then the draw and then the jockey; but it took until the early 1990s for the package to be completed. It is no longer mandatory for a disqualified horse to be placed last, but there are exceptions that Bull would not accept, which come in a subsequent chapter under Unfinished Business. Public announcement of current odds has been improved, and displays are more visible; use of the photo-finish strip has been extended. And legislation was indeed introduced so that SP bookmakers could support racing financially, though it came out of the punter's pocket by way of a Levy.
> Incidentally, Bull's Gimcrack Dinner speech came in the middle of a remarkable hat-trick for him. He bred and sold as a foal the 1956 Gimcrack Stakes winner Eudaemon; he bred and owned the 1957 winner Pheidippides, and he managed on behalf of William Hill the racing career of the 1958 winner Be Careful.
> Bull put the blame for most of the inefficiency squarely on the aristocratic shoulders of the Jockey Club. He spoke to this general theme when invited to propose the toast, The Sport of Kings, at the St Leger Dinner in 1964, beginning with a comment that 'by far the most popular sport of kings seems to have been the one enjoyed in the bed-chamber' and moving to his modern target:

History relates that no more affable monarch ever cast his leg over a mistress's garden wall than the celebrated Charles II. Addressing an audience and striking a kingly attitude, he said impressively, 'I am, I hope, a father of my people.' And a voice from the back called out, 'Of a good many of 'em, at any rate!' Charles II was easily the most successful sire of those days. With a high fertility rate. Many of our present-day aristocrats owe their existence and their titles to his nocturnal prowess.

As far as I can see this is the only country left where there are any kings and queens still available to go racing. We have the best racing in the world. Not in every respect. But in general. And when I look at the singular manner in which it is run, I think it's a miracle.

The game is controlled by a hereditary aristocracy: it is administered by an old stud-book family whose origins are shrouded in the mists of histories and the cobwebbed darknesses of Cavendish Square [Jockey Club office headquarters]. The horses are handicapped by ex-army and naval officers. Some of them use *Timeform*: the others appear to be using nautical almanacs. The races are started by majors and colonels with the aid of a Heath Robinson contraption entirely unsuitable for the job, and now abandoned by almost every country in the world. And the meetings are supervised by stewards drawn from the ranks of the local gentry, with a fund of racing wisdom and experience acquired in the hunting field and on the grouse moor.

I grouse occasionally myself, about one thing or another: but I don't hunt. So I haven't yet been called upon to act as a steward. But I did have one narrow escape last year. One of the executives at a Northern meeting came up to me before racing. 'Lord So-and-So hasn't arrived, would you please deputise for him as a steward?' Good heavens, I thought. Are my talents, integrity, racing knowledge and experience suddenly to receive official recognition? The official quickly disposed of such a preposterous idea. 'We've looked everywhere,' he said, 'for someone to stand in, and you're the only chap we can see around who has any dignity. There's a poor attendance today.'

I swear that I had never suspected it. It must have been the umbrella I was carrying that misled him. Fortunately the missing steward turned up soon afterwards, and a full complement of dignity was available for the adjudication of any objection.

By the time Bull came to speak at the St Leger Dinner in 1971, for what proved to be the last time in the surroundings of the Mansion House, he was able to report progress on many of the topics he had raised over the previous sixteen years. He began by asking guests to remember 'what things were like twenty-five years ago':

The Jockey Club ran racing with great dignity and condescension. No criticism was acknowledged; no suggestions accepted, and no answers ever given. There was no dialogue and no discussion. Journalists thought twice before they wrote, lest they put their Press passes at risk.

Weatherbys were straight out of Dickens. They weren't available on the telephone: you had to have a chit from St Peter to get an audience: and you had to be a member of the Establishment to be received with courtesy. Otherwise you were put severely in your place by some underling clerk or other.

It's quite different now. Weatherbys are up to date: approachable and courteous. The Jockey Club no longer plays God. It accepts criticism; is quite prepared to discuss, and to modify its policies accordingly. This change in the climate of racing has been revolutionary.

There's been a similar change in the conduct of racing. Thirteen years ago I was advocating in my Gimcrack speech the need for starting stalls, overnight declarations, the camera patrol, for fuller use of the photo-finish strip, and so on. All these changes and many others have been made. Racing is vastly the better for them. Better conducted, straighter and cleaner all round. Only a few years ago it was possible to make a lot of money simply by betting on horses you'd seen hooked-up in races—strangled. We used to find six or eight cases every year. Nowadays such things are so rare as to be virtually non-existent.

> For significantly altering the climate and conduct of racing, Bull praised the Jockey Club senior steward Sir Randle Feilden. For putting racing on a firmer footing through the Betting Levy Board, he singled out George Wigg:

The person who has been mostly responsible for effecting the revolutionary changes is Sir Randle Feilden. In the seven years since he became senior steward in 1965 he has done a tremendous job. All of us owe him a substantial debt.

Lord Wigg has done a magnificent job since he took charge at the Levy Board. He got his priorities right. His first concern was to maximise the Levy—to get as much for racing as possible. In doing this he won the respect and co-operation of the bookmakers. That in itself was a feat! His second concern was to distribute the money to the best possible advantage of racing. This is where he came into conflict with the Jockey Club. The Jockey Club isn't altogether happy with Lord Wigg's disposals. Their viewpoints differ. The essence of the difference is that the Jockey Club tends to view racing from the interests of breeding and the thoroughbred: Lord Wigg views it more from the betting and entertainment angle. Broadly speaking I believe Lord Wigg is right. But there's much to be said on both sides. There's a great deal of thinking to be done on fixtures, race programmes, races and prize-money, if the right answers are to be found, from the betting and from the breeding point of view. I want to see the thinking done, and the answers found. I think the different viewpoints might then be reconciled.

Allowing for the changes that had come, and were still coming, Bull produced two topics he wished to advance for the general welfare of the sport—Sunday racing, and a reduction of the on-course betting tax:

Why shouldn't we race on Sundays? People are at work on weekdays. They can't go racing then, unless they absent themselves from work. The Government and industry deplore absenteeism. Well why not give people the opportunity to enjoy their sport when they're not working—on Sundays?

This has nothing to do with religion. France is a religious country. But Frenchmen race on Sundays. All their big races are run on Sundays.

As things are here, the law says you can't bet on Sundays, and you can't charge admission to a racecourse on Sundays. This is stupidity. Things are either right or wrong in themselves: not according to the day of the week.

To bring about a change in the law is a formidable undertaking. But we're shortly to join the Common Market. The Government is going to have to make a lot of changes in the law to bring us into line with our European partners. Now is the time for the Turf authorities to plan lobbying the Government to get these stupid laws amended.

Right now [the Chancellor] is collecting between fifty and sixty million from punters, via the betting tax. It's a penal tax. Five or six per cent on turnover is massive in terms of its consequences for the punter. To all intents and purposes it makes it virtually impossible for him to bet with any prospect of profit in the long run.

Nine-tenths of the fifty or sixty million the Chancellor gets comes from SP betting in betting shops. This whole edifice stands on the on-course market. It is important that this should be strong and healthy. It isn't, and it's getting weaker. As it does so, it becomes increasingly liable to manipulation by the big betting-shop organisations. It is too much to hope that the general rate of tax might be lowered. But racecourse attendances are dwindling. Mr Barber [the Chancellor] should be grateful to racing for what he's getting, and do something in return. He should abolish the on-course tax, or cut it by a half at the very least. It would be a shot in the arm for racing.

More than fifteen years, and several Chancellors of the Exchequer, later, the on-course betting tax was scrapped from 30

March 1987. The Jockey Club had taken up the cause, and with other sections of racing it lobbied Parliament. It eventually did the same in pursuit of Sunday racing with betting, but early attempts at forcing legislative changes were poorly handled in Westminster and success took longer. Though three Sunday meetings were put on without a bookmaker service, it was not until 7 May 1995—nearly six years after Bull's death—that the first fixtures with on- and off-course betting were staged.

With Sunday racing and a reduction of on-course betting tax still unresolved when Lord Rothschild's Royal Commission on Gambling was gathered together, Bull included both items in his *magnum opus*—a veritable *tour de force*—a private submission which ran to 370 paragraphs and approximately 40,000 words. It was dated January 1977 and represented an accumulation of the various strands of thought he had outlined since 1955, with up-to-date information culled from his own research. In certain instances, statistical details were published for the first time, such as the real tax paid by punters, the impact of a twenty per cent deduction from betting stakes, and examples, for all percentage take-outs from bets from twelve per cent to thirty per cent, of the number of times a punter could bet and re-bet from capital of £1,000 before it was extinguished.

Gambling on horseracing was the root of the submission, but the administration of the sport, and that part of the betting industry on which it fed and depended, provided the branches on which Bull hung his thoughts, reflections and observations. His foreword explained he had sought "not so much to make detailed and specific recommendations, as to throw light on the scene in a way that will, I hope, assist the Commission in making its own judgement as to what changes are desirable and practicable". It did not take a Sherlock Holmes to uncover the clues to Bull's ideas for change.

Explaining the role of the various sections in racing, he noted those who 'put in' and those who 'took out'. He was against breeders' prizes, and the 'arbitrary proposition' that it would be reasonable for an owner's expectation of his return to equate with his basic training fees. He highlighted the failure of the Tote to compete with bookmakers in race-by-race betting, other than as a bookmaker, and also to create a special niche in pool betting. He saw the 'moralist's thumbprint' on betting-office regulations, and said there was no good reason for not allowing shops to open beyond 6.30pm or on Sundays. On the control and administration of racing, he exploded the myth of 'the Jockey Club's integrity': he exposed the inadequacies of the Jockey Club-inspired Racing Industries Liason Committee: and he disapproved of the principle of the Levy Board's being 'a body with statutory authority to conduct selective taxation of one section of the community for the benefit of another, outside the normal fiscal system'.

Having started his submission with a claim that he had not sought to make detailed and specific recommendations, his closing twenty-six paragraphs did exactly that, beginning with the bones of his advice:

The time is ripe for the dichotomies of Levy Board and Jockey Club, Bloodstock and Racehorse Industries Confederation (BRIC) and Racing Industries Liason Committee (RILC) to be ended, and racing brought under the control of a single statutory authority. The need for it is pressing and obvious.

Her Majesty's Government should enact the replacement of the Horserace Betting Levy Board by a corporate body to be known as The British Racing Board, charged with the control and administration of horseracing, and vested with all the powers and authorities presently exercised by the Levy Board and the Jockey Club.

The Racing Board should be a body of no more than seven or eight members; and since racing is a national entertainment financed in part from public money, it is desirable that its composition should have an inbuilt balance between the members representing racing interests and the Government appointees who may be said to guard the public interest.

It should be possible for anyone involved in racing to find his way to a seat on the British Racing Board, but he should be able to reach that seat only by way of eminence achieved on some racing body. The interests that the various bodies represent differ in importance, so there are priorities to be taken into account. This calls for a democratic elective structure, embracing all properly constituted racing bodies and associations, which would give effect to such priorities.

Below the British Racing Board, Bull proposed a two-tier structure, with a British Racing Council (BRAC) as the upper tier, and a Racing Employees & Trades Association (RETA) as the lower. RETA would elect one representative to serve on BRAC; three members of BRAC would sit on the British Racing Board, which would determine the bodies to be represented on BRAC. Bull's view of the BRAC set-up was to have elected or nominated representatives from the Racehorse Owners Association, Racecourse Association, Thoroughbred Breeders Association, National Trainers Federation, Jockeys Association, Licensed Officials

Association, Bookmakers Committee, Horserace Totalisator Board, Horserace Writers Association, Racegoers Club and the newly-created Racing Employees & Trades Association.

The new body, RETA, he said, was 'intended to be the voice of people employed in racing and of trades ancillary to racing, such as bloodstock agencies, auctioneers, insurance brokers and shipping agents, the various racecourse staffs associations, the National Farriers Association, the head lads, stable lads, stud grooms and stud employees associations, the Society of Master Saddlers, and so forth'.

Bull went on to define the British Racing Board more precisely:

It should consist of a chairman and six other members, of whom
a) the chairman and two other members should be appointed by the Secretary of State for the Home Office, and be persons the Secretary of State is satisfied have no interests connected with horseracing which might hinder them from discharging their functions as members of the Board in an impartial manner;
b) one member should be appointed by the Secretary of State or by the Minister for Sport who should be a person with wide experience and knowledge of racing;
c) three members should be elected by and from the members of the British Racing Council, and should include the Council's chairman for the time being and the chairman for the time being of the Racehorse Owners Association.

That the Racehorse Owners Association should have a seat on the Board as of right required no justification, Bull said:

Owners contribute substantially to financing the promotion of racing—more than do punters. There are no other major contributors to racing's finance, and owners are therefore fully entitled to representation on the governing body.

Not so the racecourses, he explained. What they put into promoting race meetings, including the provision of prize-money, was recovered from racegoers in admission fees or from punters via Levy Board support or Commentary fees, plus television fees and money put up by race sponsors. Bookmakers and the Tote did not warrant representation either. Financially they did not contribute to the promotion since every penny they handled came out of punters' pockets. The fact they were represented on the Levy Board was the result of their powerful Parliamentary lobby and the Government of the day's failure to recognise the realities of the situation when the Betting Levy Act of 1961 was devised. The only way the Bookmakers Committee or the Tote Board could find its way on to the British Racing Board would be through the election of its representative on the British Racing Council.

Bull's failure to provide a seat on the British Racing Board for the Jockey Club was deliberate:

It is inappropriate, and contrary to the principles implicit in the constitution of such a National Board, that any private club, whatever its traditions, history or background, should have as a club any right to participation in the control of racing. That its members may have an expertise born of experience is irrelevant. The place for the utilisation of that is elsewhere.

It has been suggested that a new Racing Board might be set up in such a way as to leave the Jockey Club with authority over the Rules of Racing and disciplinary matters. This is completely unacceptable. It would create an intolerable situation, far worse than that which now obtains between the Levy Board and the Jockey Club, in which policies decided upon by the Racing Board could be frustrated by rules made by the Jockey Club.

The British Racing Board must have complete authority. Any body to which it might delegate responsibility, for rules or anything else, must be required to give effect to the Racing Board's directives.

There might be a role for the stewards of the Jockey Club, Bull suggested, through the day-to-day running of racing. However, he added that it was hardly likely that, shorn of the power to which they were accustomed, they would want to carry on as executive stewards answerable to the Racing Board. On the other hand there was a part for Weatherbys to play, by continuing as racing's secretariat. Bull summed up:

I suggest that the functions presently performed by the ten part-time stewards of the Jockey Club be put in the hands of a director-general and such number of full-time British Racing Stewards as may be necessary, probably four. All five appointments should carry substantial salaries.

There is no reason to suppose that Messrs Weatherbys would not be happy to serve a new British Racing Board. In sharp contrast to what it used to be, Weatherbys is now one of the most efficient and up-to-date organisations around. Without Weatherbys racing would come to a full stop—and Weatherbys would have nowhere to go. The ancient office of Keeper of the Match Book must not be lost to the nation!

> Bull, who circulated about two hundred copies of the submission, including to the Press, knew full well his views would not be universally accepted. He admitted as much to the Commission chairman Lord Rothschild when delivering a personal copy with a letter dated 31 January 1977, saying: 'If, by some of the things I've said, I lose a few friends, it will be sad, but I won't lose the ones I value.' He expanded on his feelings in a letter dated 15 February 1977, responding to Jockey Club member Jim Philipps' 'kind and appreciative remarks' about the submission:

Much of what I've written won't make me popular. But when you're past 60 that hardly matters. What does matter to me is how I've said things. I write with excess of enthusiasm and exuberance, and sometimes I feel on reading it afterwards that I'm too aggressive, didactic and careless of the feelings of others, and wish I'd put things in a gentler way. I don't wish to look in the mirror and find myself seeing George Wigg's face.

On the other hand, there are things that have to be said that are bound to upset someone, however you say them. I can well imagine some members of the Jockey Club who have done a great deal of hard work for racing, and done it well, and are as earnest as I am myself, feeling aggrieved by some things I have written about the Club. I take no pleasure in that, I assure you. Quite the contrary.

Fortunately there's balm for my discomfort in letters I've had from Gerry Feilden, Lord Howard de Walden and other members of the Club, and in yours. Thank you.

> Bull seemed to be more irked, in the short term, by the fact he was not sent a copy of the Commission's report as soon as it was published. Discussing in a telephone conversation with the Labour MP Denis Howell its publication, and failure to press for evening and Sunday opening of betting offices, Bull said:

Let me tell you. I haven't got a bloody copy. I'm furious. Rothschild has not sent me a copy. I didn't even get an invitation to the press conference. I'm furious about it. All the knowledge I've got is what I've seen in the bloody newspapers. I've got to get it through the Stationery Office, and that might take three weeks.

Howell promised to send Bull a copy of the report. His fury abated, only to be inflamed again in December 1977, when the Jockey Club decided unilaterally that it would consider setting up a new racing authority. This, it said, would take over the statutory powers of the Levy Board, with a chairman and two independent members appointed by the Home Secretary, one of whom would represent those who earned their living from racing and the other would become chairman of the Racing Industry Liaison Committee. Two members would be appointed by the Jockey Club, and other representatives would come from various organisations, including the Tote and the Bookmakers Committee, but there was no punters' representative.

Bull went back on the attack, and he read out to Ossie Fletcher, editor of *The Sporting Life*, a letter he asked to be published the next day:

The Jockey Club knows that the Royal Commission is highly unlikely to recommend that control of racing should continue in the hands of the Jockey Club as presently constituted, so it has now decided to do an Ian Smith: it seeks to erect a new facade behind which it can not only hang on to its executive power but also acquire the financial power presently held by the Levy Board. The Jockey Club views racing exclusively as an affair of owners and breeders; it is totally unconcerned with racing as a national entertainment or with racegoers and punters, except as a source of revenue from which to subsidise what it calls the Racing Industry.

The Jockey Club would dearly love to be able to get its hand in the punter's pocket and do what it likes with the loot; the Levy Board stands in its way, hence the continuing friction between the Club and the Board, and the Jockey Club's desire to get rid of the Levy Board. The new authority it proposes would be stacked with Jockey Club-orientated members; its public accountability through the minority of government appointees would be a laughable fiction.

With power in the hands of a new authority constituted as proposed by the Jockey Club, nothing could save the racing public from predatory plundering by racing's vested interests. Fortunately the Royal Commission is unlikely to be hoodwinked by these proposals. Systems of private taxation like the betting levy are quite wrong in principle: it is doubly wrong that the potential beneficiaries of such taxation should control its imposition.

Bull was right. The Government soon made it known that neither it nor any successor, of whatever party, would countenance an authority, as suggested by the Jockey Club, taking over the Levy Board. But change remained in the air. The Jockey Club did establish a new advisory body to represent various sections of the racing industry, and Bull became the first chairman of the Horseracing Advisory Council!

Ten years later, under the senior stewardship of Lord Hartington, the Jockey Club went farther, much farther, and set about establishing a new authority, which formally began its existence as the British Horseracing Board in June 1993, with Hartington as chairman and the HAC subsumed into a standing committee known as the Industry Committee. Democracy came to the selection process for membership of the BHB, and among its original aims were to take over the Tote and the distributive functions of the Levy Board.

However, the BHB and its constituent committee and responsibilities are not Bull's idea for a British Racing Board. Time alone will tell how far it moves towards, or away from, the Bull model. In the meantime, the Jockey Club occupies a back seat, though certainly not quite so far back as the Bull vehicle envisaged.

ONE of the most common mistakes which journalists, and not a few horseracing insiders, made about Phil Bull was to suggest that he should have been allowed to join the Jockey Club. Even George Wigg, chairman of the Levy Board and one of Bull's closest allies, was persuaded by the argument, writing on 8 October 1976 that 'They should have elected you as a member of the Jockey Club a long time ago, and put you on the Racing Industry Liaison Committee as a Jockey Club representative.' Some observers went further and hinted that secretly Bull would have enjoyed such election. Not a bit of it. Bull loathed the Jockey Club as an institution, though not all its members personally.

Bull was not a club man—as he pointed out in a letter dated 9 March 1957 to an acquaintance who had introduced him to his club in New York: 'I greatly enjoyed being shown round. I am not a club man myself, but I recognise a well-appointed and well-run club when I see one.'

And he was certainly not a Jockey Club man—as he made plain to Ossie Fletcher, editor of *The Sporting Life*, in a letter dated 15 March 1983:

I wish you'd keep your estimable journalists in order, and give them some instruction on the nature of the Jockey Club.

John McCririck's column carried an assertion that 'my continued exclusion from the Jockey Club angers Jack Logan, John McCririck and every intelligent racegoer except the understanding sage himself.'

This is nonsense. What on earth leads Mr McCririck to believe that wisdom or sagacity have ever been regarded as qualifying anyone for membership of the Club?

The Jockey Club is an elite, private, establishment body. The essential qualifications for membership are social and financial, not intellectual, and not at all to do with competence, experience or achievement in racing. Over 200 years of tradition sustains this social exclusiveness and nothing is going to change it if the Jockey Club can help it.

Jack Logan and John McCririck do well to campaign for a different power structure in racing, but would they please desist from arguing that I should be elected to the Club. So long as I still have something to say about racing I shall value my freedom and independence as a writer and critic. I am 73 years of age. I'll be dead soon enough, and I have no desire to be prematurely buried in Portman Square.

Bull's objections to the Jockey Club were earlier detailed in his submission to the Royal Commission on Gambling (January 1977), but not everyone had got the message, as was obvious from a letter to Tony Stafford, as editor of *The Racehorse*, dated 23 February 1977. It commented on views expressed by the newspaper's pro-Jockey Club correspondent Roger Mortimer, and also made a point about Bull's own feelings towards inclusion:

Perhaps I should spell it out in words of one syllable, for Mortimer's benefit, exactly what I do object to. I object to racing's being run by a private club whose membership is confined to that six per cent of the population educated at public schools as the Jockey Club's membership is.

Does that mean I object to people with public school educations? Of course it doesn't. I should object just as strongly to racing's being run by a Masonic club, or any other club the membership of which was limited by social exclusiveness or any considerations other than racing considerations.

Membership of the Jockey Club is presently confined to ex-public schoolboys. That excludes 94 per cent of racing people, among whom there are many with first-class racing knowledge and experience. I object to their exclusion. I think it disgraceful. And so do several Jockey Club friends of mine.

Mr Mortimer says that I would like to see the Jockey Club go. Rubbish. What I'd like to see is the Jockey Club constitute itself in a proper manner, making itself truly representative of racing brains, not social class. Then it *would* have a claim to run racing. As presently constituted it has no claim. And if it insists on maintaining its present exclusiveness, it *will* go.

No doubt Mr Mortimer would like to interpret this in personal terms, and insinuate that I have a personal interest. Let me tell him I have no such interest. I'm 66 years of age and on my way out. The Jockey Club needs younger men than me; people of zest and enthusiasm, who see racing as what it is, an entertainment for people, who understand it and want to make it good. I could name half-a-dozen such people off the top of my head, without having to think.

They don't include people like Mr Mortimer, who presume to criticise a serious and objective submission without having read it, who don't deal with a single argument put forward in it, and end up lying about it.

Despite his understandable stance against Jockey Club membership, Bull did get involved in committee work, though he displayed an ambivalent attitude which finally and spectacularly resulted in his turning his back on corporate decision-making. Why he ever got involved with the Horseracing Advisory Council at all is a question he himself asked. But that came later.

Ten years before the HAC was invented Bull expressed his feelings to Quintin Gilbey. His letter, dated 25 April 1969, began:

The fact that I can't lick boots or toe the Establishment line has meant that I had to choose between getting myself in the Establishment's bad books, with the consequent discomforts that this would have entailed, or enjoying my racing and owning horses and being *persona grata*. I am sorry to say that although I haven't always kept my mouth shut, on balance I have opted for pleasure and enjoyment, rather than fighting the battle.

Bull was clearly understating his role, though whether it was done deliberately is not obvious. He had taken up the fight on several occasions, though a previous, bitter experience, recounted to George Wigg six months after his letter to Gilbey, might explain the apparent conflict between opinion and action. On 2 October 1969 Bull wrote:

A few years ago I was a member of Lord Porchester's committee (Thoroughbred Breeders Association) on the Pattern of Races. It was a frustrating experience. Porchester [now Lord Carnarvon] had a bee in his bonnet—a very small bee, but one that he was determined to pursue.

The wider implications of our terms of reference were ignored. I tried to draw attention to this and to make my points, but without success. Discouraged, I acquiesced, and have never forgiven myself for being a signatory to a report that was altogether inadequate and quite unsatisfactory.

I should have produced a minority report, embracing the whole field within our terms of reference, which would have made the majority report look silly. Unfortunately I allowed my discouragement to take command, let things go by default, and thereby missed my opportunity.

There are times when an earnest person—however conscious of the need for compromise in committee work, however anxious to give service and not rock the boat—should opt out and insist on the publication of his views. This was one. But I was inexperienced and did not see it.

The minority report I should have produced would really have been something. The result that Porchester and [Jakie] Astor and [John] Hislop produced, and I put my name to, having failed to carry them with me, was almost puerile. I left that battlefield defeated and discouraged. It annoys me in retrospect: the aces were in my hand and I did not play them, because (to mix a metaphor) I did not want to rock the boat! It won't happen again.

> Bull's attitude towards the Racehorse Owners Association also displayed signs of contradiction, at worst, or a healthy change of mind at best. When, after his Philoctetes had won at Redcar in July 1969, he received a pro-forma seeking his membership of the ROA, he replied that he had 'lost all interest in the ROA many years ago when it drew its own teeth at the behest of the Jockey Club and resigned itself to becoming little more than an annual wining and dining get-together'.
>
> Frank Beale, the association secretary, tried again, saying that the ROA had 'moved quite a long way since the early days' to which Bull had referred. Beale concluded: 'You are just the sort of person I would like to see on the Council; we should then never be short of ideas and our meetings would never be dull.'
>
> Bull was as susceptible to flattery as the next man and enjoyed living up to the various images portrayed of him, but he was not to be persuaded. His response asked how far the ROA had come since the early days and wondered if a change had been made in the constitution 'since the modification of its articles at the insistence of the Jockey Club'. Beale replied enclosing a copy of the Articles of Association, to which Bull came back, on 1 September 1969, with a five-page letter which began, 'At the risk of burdening you with more correspondence . . .' There followed an elaborate explanation of Bull's refusal to join the ROA, which began with his early experiences and ended with his current position:

There have been many occasions in my life when I have found my own self-interest in conflict with conviction as to what is desirable for the common good. Some of these conflicts, I regret to say, have been resolved on the side of self-interest.

For example, quite early in my serious involvement with racing, as an owner, breeder and commentator on the game, I found myself highly critical of the manner in which the Jockey Club and Weatherbys ran the show. I thought it not merely deplorable, but in some ways positively disgraceful. At first I was militant about it: determined to say what I thought. But I very soon found that, not merely did this make me *persona non grata* with the 'powers that were', but actually put at risk my whole life in racing.

In those days, when you needed a chit from St Peter to have audience with Francis Weatherby, and when disciplinary action by the Jockey Club was peremptory, devious, arbitrary, and not open to question or debate, when journalists (and newspapers), fearing for their Press passes, had to be careful what they said, and when one's career in racing was actually at risk if one was not approved of by the Establishment, a man had to think twice before dipping his pen in the vitriol.

I thought twice. I loved racing. I wanted to own horses and breed them. I wanted, as all people do, to be 'accepted'. I wanted to feel at ease on the racecourse, to enjoy the game and make a career in it. So I trimmed my sails to the prevailing wind.

Self-interest won. My love of the game, my desire to make my career in it, and to enjoy my racing, triumphed over my public duty in the interests of justice and fairness. I opted for comfortable self-interest and the common good.

Was I right or wrong? I'm in no doubt. I was absolutely and completely wrong. I failed for want of courage. And have never ceased to regret it. There have been other occasions too, not to do with racing, when considerations of self-interest have led me not to do what should have been done.

Believe me, I deplore them all. I am essentially a logical person with a high regard not only for the rights of the individual but also for his responsibilities to society. I take these things seriously, and my failures to put my own personal interests in their place and restrain them in the knowledge that they take no priority over the interests of others, my failures to act in what rational thought tells me just and fair and to the common good—these things make me retrospectively dissatisfied with myself.

I've told you all this at some length because I want you to understand the reasons for my reluctance to join the Owners Association. It is simply once more the conflict between self-interest and what I think is 'right'.

I am not a rich man. But I have eight horses in training and it is obviously greatly to my advantage that stake money should be increased, and the charges on owners (entry fees, etc) reduced. This, in essence, is what the Owners Association seeks to bring about, and what it mostly concerns itself with. That's fair enough. An Association of Owners may be expected to pursue the interests of its members.

But, you know, I simply cannot accept the proposition that owners need, or should have, the support of money from the punters via the Levy Board, or that such a subsidy is for the good of racing in general.

Racing is in trouble at the moment. But the trouble is not lack of owners. We have more owners now than ever before, owners prepared to pay vastly higher prices at the yearling sales than ever before. We have more breeders than ever before, breeding more horses than ever before. Does this suggest that owners and breeders need to be subsidised? Surely not.

Owning horses is not an obligation, or a privilege: it is a pleasure—a pleasure for the rich man. Nobody compels him to own horses, nobody twists his arm. He doesn't do it altruistically in order to support the Sport of Kings or improve the breed. He does it for pleasure—because it gives him satisfaction. And there is no more justification for the public's being called upon to subsidise his owning horses than there would be for calling upon the public to subsidise a man's keeping three mistresses or a yacht in the Mediterranean.

Racing has never been short of owners, or horses, or people prepared to breed them. It certainly is not so at the present time. What it *is* short of is racegoers, whose payments at the turnstiles make racecourses viable—punters, who go racing not chiefly to see the horses, but to bet on them. I think it quite wrong that money should be taken out of the pockets of the punters, via the bookmakers and the Levy Board, and used to increase stake money so as to subsidise owners and breeders.

Mind you, I know there are other considerations. I can see a case for using Levy Board money to sponsor prestige races and keep their value in line with those of other countries. I appreciate also that if the punters' pockets *are* to be picked, it is well that as much as possible of the pickings should come back into racing rather than go into the coffers of the Chancellor of the Exchequer.

There are many other matters which if I were a member of the Association I would wish to advocate in the interests of owners: overall racecourse admission, car parking, alterations to rules, the pattern of races and their conditions, training fees, jockeys' presents, etc etc,—but so long as the Association concerns itself chiefly with prize money, I feel I should be more of a liability to you than an asset.

> That seemed to be the end of it. But within less than a year
> Beale was acknowledging his 'great and unexpected pleasure' in

welcoming Bull as a member of the ROA, and by 1974 he was a fully active member of its Council. From regarding himself as a liability, he had decided to fight the fight from within—and that within a year of confessing, in a letter dated 10 May 1973 to George Wigg: 'I'm not really bothered about the racing any more. It's not really worth the expenditure of intellectual energy I have available in the limited time that is left to me.'

Not unexpectedly, Bull was sometimes in a minority on the ROA council. On the topic of evidence to the Royal Commission on Gambling, he received the nearest thing to a private rebuke from chairman David Sieff, who wrote: 'I was a little concerned at your comment that the ROA seemed to be heading in the wrong direction or possibly that I was leading them astray.' To which Bull replied, in a letter dated 18 March 1977:

Be clear about it. I don't criticise anyone. The Council is a committee and its views and policies are necessarily a consensus of differing opinions. It is up to me as a member of the Council to play my part in formulating the concensus by expressing my views; and if I fail to carry the Council with me, that's too bad. The same applies to everyone else. Individuals must either acquiesce in the policies adopted by the majority, or, if they feel too strongly about it, get off the Council.

Naturally I am sorry to see the Council endorsing the ridiculous attitudes and policies embodied in Submissions to the Royal Commission, but having done my best in a mild sort of way when these things came up for discussion, and failed, there's no more to be said.

Consensus, when Bull's views went unachieved, he could take, it appeared; but compromise was another matter. That led to another letter to David Sieff, dated 24 September 1979, explaining why Bull had surrendered his place in the owners' team trying to work out a new Training Agreement with the National Trainers Federation. Bull wrote:

I had two reasons for withdrawing from the negotiating committee: first, I was so put out by the way things have been conducted so far that I didn't trust myself to keep my equanimity with Jeremy Richardson [for the NTF], which is no frame of mind for a negotiator; and second, I am not by nature a compromiser, and therefore, I think, not equipped to be a negotiator.

My strength, I believe, lies in a capacity to identify a problem, pare it down to its essentials, think it through logically and come up with rational and convincing answers, where these are available. I'm not arrogant enough to think my answers are necessarily right, because I think them to be so. But I don't take kindly to the sort of obstructionism that refuses to look at the argument.

> Far from 'not really being bothered about racing', as in the comment to George Wigg, Bull had taken on another responsibility by this time. Yet, as with the ROA, he at first declined to become the Racegoers Club's nominee on the Racing Industry Liaison Committee (RILC), which was cobbled together by the Jockey Club—faced with threats to its authority from the setting up of a widely representative body known as the Bloodstock and Racehorse Industries Confederation (BRIC) and the establishment by the Home Office of a study group to investigate a Racing Consultative Council, an advisory body independent of the Jockey Club.
>
> In May 1976 the Jockey Club hurriedly announced that it was winding up its Racing Policy Committee and its Joint Associations Liaison Committee to replace them with RILC, which had no executive power and was chaired by the Jockey Club senior steward. In late-September 1976 Bull was approached by Tony Fairbairn, chairman of the Racegoers Club, to be its RILC representative. Bull said No thanks:

It is kind of you to assure me that I would be acceptable in that capacity to the Senior Steward, though I cannot for the life of me see why the representative of the Racegoers Club should have to be acceptable to the Senior Steward, or to anyone else other than the members of your Club itself. That you should mention this to me rather betrays the set-up, doesn't it?

Anyway, I'm afraid you must count me out. I'm not the right guy for the job. The Racegoers Club has no pretentions [sic] to represent the interests of punters as a whole, and I have better things to do than punch the air in a powerless advisory body whose advice the Stewards have no intention of taking unless it suits their book. RILC is nothing more than a smoke screen defence against BRIC—a pretense [sic] of enlarging its base and democratising itself.

I must continue to argue my case in the press. It won't influence the Jockey Club or its Stewards, of course, but it has some effect on public opinion. And Her Majesty's ministers *can* read, you know.

> Within less than a fortnight Bull had been persuaded to join RILC in the Racegoers Club seat! He went into it commenting in a letter to George Wigg, dated 9 October 1976:

You know as well as I know that the Racing Industry Liaison Committee is just a cosmetic exercise—a smokescreen put up by the Jockey Club to defend itself from the threat to its position which it thought might be presented by BRIC: another pretence of broadening its base to provide an illusion of democratic responsibility.

However, there's possibly half a chance the Jockey Club may have created something it can't control. As a voice for the punter (I can't be any more than that) I'll be in a minority of one, and I go along just for the ride, to liven things up and see what happens.

Cosmetic exercise and smokescreen: words which were soon to surface in another arena where Bull played a major part, if only fleetingly. It was the Horseracing Advisory Council, to which Bull became firstly a representative of the Racegoers Club, secondly its temporary chairman, thirdly its first permanent part-time chairman, and fourthly its first casualty—all within the space of seven months. The period began with hope and ended, metaphorically, in tears. Many of the reasons can be seen from Bull's previous involvement in racing 'government', but only hindsight proved the points.

While RILC was finding its feet, Lord Rothschild's Royal Commission on Gambling deliberated. Its report was published in July 1978, with among its major recommendations the establishment of a British Horseracing Authority, which would be a voluntary organisation with an independent chairman, ten to twelve strong and representative of the racing industry. It should take over the Levy Board's functions except assessing and collecting the Levy, and should eventually own all British racecourses. Within two months it was acknowledged in Westminster that the main aim was unacceptable, since no government—Tory or Labour—would agree to public funds being spent by other than an authority accountable to Parliament.

The Jockey Club, which had taken fright at the original suggestion and set up a working party under Michael Wyatt to examine a new British Horseracing Authority, responded by widening its brief and suggesting an independent consultative or advisory body, representing all the major racing interests, with its independent chairman taking one of the Jockey Club seats on the Levy Board.

At this stage, in July 1979, there was no place for the racegoer or punter on the new body; the Racegoers Club nomination on RILC would have disappeared. Bull was furious about what he regarded as a vital omission—as well as another example of the Jockey Club's lack of regard for a major funder of the sport. In a phone conversation with Richard Baerlein in July 1979, he railed:

I'm horrified by a body which has got the Masters of Foxhounds Association on it, bloodstock agents, Transport and General Workers Union, Master Valets Association, and not a single representative of the effing punter, who foots the bill. I told them at the last meeting of RILC, 'Do you suppose these people aren't concerned with racing? They're the customers'.

Bull feared that the Jockey Club was angling to hang on to its control. 'The control of racing should be drawn from the people involved in it, including the punters, since they provide the finance,' he told Baerlein. 'I'm concerned that it shall not fall into the public schoolboys' lobby to run the whole show again. I want this blown apart in the Press. I don't want it behind closed doors at RILC, the Jockey Club or the Levy Board. I want it blown into a public debate.' Baerlein knew what was expected of him.

Later in July, Wyatt stepped aside and the Jockey Club withdrew from the working party. It was reassembled under the RCA chairman Brookie Brooks and when it produced a draft report in September, to be submitted to the Jockey Club and Levy Board for approval, Bull's pleadings had paid off. In *The Sporting Life*, John McCririck was able to reveal—because Bull had primed him with a copy of the proposal—that a two-tier advisory committee would include a punters' representative. Over the phone the day before its publication, McCririck read and checked his copy with Bull, and assured his informant that his identity would be lost among the news. 'I don't think anybody knows,' McCririck said. 'I think we're safe there.' To which Bull replied: 'It's not a case of whether you're safe, it's whether I'm safe.'

Both were safe, and when in December 1979 the first representatives were elected to the general council and executive committee of the Horseracing Advisory Council, the Racegoers Club pipped the commercial Daily Mirror Punters Club to provide a nominee. Bull was their man. He was also nominated to a four-man sub-committee charged with finding an independent chairman, who would sit on the Levy Board and attend Jockey Club stewards' meetings. Bull proved to be that man also.

When Bull addressed the North West Racing Club in 1982, he recalled the events of two years previously: 'Quite unexpectedly on 23 January 1980 I found myself the HAC's first chairman, with reluctance and on a temporary basis at first, and then on a permanent basis.'

Judged on the evidence of telephone conversations which Bull taped in his office or home, the words 'quite unexpectedly', 'found myself' and 'reluctance' have a curiously hollow ring. It might not have been Bull's intention to become chairman when

216

he, Bob McCreery, Michael Pope and Tony Villar first set out to find a candidate, but it was the case as soon he was appointed to the temporary position on 23 January.

Bull's lack of faith in the HAC composition was apparent even before the outset. Shortly before Christmas 1979 he stirred the thoughts of Sir David Llewellyn—columnist Jack Logan of *The Sporting Life*—in a late-night phone call:

This is a nugatory exercise because it doesn't have any powers, and the people who have been nominated on the executive council are a right shower. It appals me. I thought the sensible thing was to opt out and simply say the whole thing is a stupid, cosmetic exercise. Then, I thought, these things are really what you make 'em, we'll give it a run and see what I can do with it. If I can make it stand up, I'll give it a bash. But there's a load of dead weight on the general council. There are a number who've got no vision about things other than the confines of their own little sphere. Then the executive committee is too big, and too many of them have no real understanding of the reality.

Bull ran through the names being suggested as chairman —Edward Cazalet, the barrister: 'The usual Etonian public school background, represents the Jockey Club, totally unsuited, unsatisfactory person for the job, and he won't be able to give the time to it.' Bernard Penfold, manager of Sha Tin racecourse in Hong Kong: 'Brookie Brooks is insistent he's an extremely good guy, but he has a military background, the way the Jockey Club have run their whole disciplinary affairs in the past, I don't like it.' And Charles Frank, a vet: 'As far as I understand he's bone from the neck upwards, totally unsuitable, a man of no standing.' Despite his reservations, Bull leaned towards Penfold—'The big advantage is that he's external to the show. He seems to be the only runner as far as I'm concerned.'—but he knew who would have been his choice. 'John Sanderson, a fellow of considerable intelligence, who knows the score about the whole game. But he's not a runner. He'll get a fantastic salary from the York Race Committee, and he is very happy in his job. And does a magnificent job.'

Bull also raised a more fundamental matter which concerned him about the new body:

The Jockey Club were absolutely horrified when they were told that no government, of whatever complexion, would countenance a body running racing which was not accountable for the public money that it received. So they immediately thought they must do something that will enable the Government to set up a controlling body for racing which will incorporate this new body, which represents the industry as a whole. So the purpose of doing away with RILC and setting up the Horseracing Advisory Council is to be able to turn round to the Government after a year, eighteen months or two years and say, Look, this has functioned very well; these people give us good advice and we work on it; now give us the whole thing in one body and give us control of it. That's what the ultimate aim is.

By the middle of January 1980, Bull was reviewing his opinion of Bernard Penfold, having met and talked to him in London. In a phone call to John Sanderson, Bull sought more information but concluded that Penfold 'gave the impression we really ought not to be asking him these questions, and it suggests he's not likely to take kindly to the council's directives. He's perfectly capable of saying, 'This is ridiculous, you can stuff your job, I'm going home to Southampton'.

There were, however, few alternatives. Bull explained to Sanderson that the sub-committee had seen Michael Opperman—'who doesn't measure up at all'—and Douglas Bunn, 'who runs Hickstead'. Bunn had impressed over lunch, but, Bull said, 'We were inclined to appoint him, but there seems to be considerable antagonism towards him, and a good deal of derogatory smoke in the air'. Perhaps it was because Bunn was said to be 'very difficult, an abrasive customer who would not get on very well with anybody, least of all with the Jockey Club'. Bull did not know, and he conceded to Sanderson: 'We're now in the situation where we don't have anybody to appoint if we don't appoint Douglas Bunn.'

As the HAC executive committee meeting on 23 January 1980 loomed, rumour had it that a temporary chairman had been found—Phil Bull himself. But when Graham Rock, the *Sporting Chronicle* journalist, and former Timeform employee, rang to ask whether Bull could either confirm or deny the report, he was met with the reply: 'I don't know anything about it myself . . . nothing that I can tell you.'

Bull did know something about it, but on this occasion felt unable to help the Press. It quickly emerged, and Richard Baerlein was the first person Bull rang:

Because of all the work that has got to be done in the next two months, the executive committee asked me if I would take on the temporary job of chairman. I've accepted. Now this—and I'm speaking absolutely confidentially—is precisely the job I ought to have. I shouldn't be sitting on that bloody selection committee. I should be a candidate. The precise job I ought to have in racing is this one. So it's up to you.

Once again Baerlein was being put in no doubt about his role. 'It's up to you,' Bull repeated. 'I can't do it because I'm on the selection committee, that's put me in an awkward spot. I would be quite prepared to give up the other things that I do, just to concentrate on this. I'd take a flat in London and get to work on it. You're the only one I've told. Be discreet.'

It was only minutes before Bull relayed the news to another trusted friend, Sir David Llewellyn. He rattled off some of the names of the candidates the sub-committee had looked at— Edward Cazalet: 'A dead duck from the start'; Bernard Penfold: 'Treated it as somewhat demeaning that anybody should be interviewing him'; Douglas Bunn: 'Came over very forcefully, very much clued up, an intelligent fellow, but there was a whispering campaign against him'; Michael Opperman: 'Applied for the job having seen the discussion in *The Sporting Life* but not equipped for the job'; Charles Frank: 'A nice guy, pleasant, but really isn't big enough for the job.' Then came the important part, that the executive committee had unanimously asked Bull to take on the job temporarily.

Llewellyn was about to get the Baerlein treatment. 'After some hesitation I accepted it,' Bull said. 'I ought not to have hesitated, because this job is exactly up my street. It's the precise job I'm equipped for. But how long it'll last, I can't tell you. It's sure to last until the middle of April [when Penfold might be available] because we have nobody else to see.'

Llewellyn picked up Bull's drift much more quickly, saying: 'I'm sure you're the right person; it never occurred to me that this is how it would end.' Whatever Bull said two years later, it had definitely occurred to him, though he pointed out his dilemma: 'I'm on the selection committee; I can't put myself up. Somebody has got to move. Be discreet, boy.'

Bull's final call that night was to Tom Kelly, editor of the *Sporting Chronicle*, who pondered on the temporary nature of the job. Bull suggested it was a line he should pursue, adding: "I'm inhibited from pursuing it, unless I get a lead from somewhere. Any initiative has to come from the outside, it can't come from me."

With such precise advice coming from Bull's direction, it seems odd that in reply to a letter of congratulation from the Levy Board chairman Sir Desmond Plummer he should feel compelled to say: 'Take no notice of what Dick Baerlein reported me as having said. He always gets things half right, and presents the wrong half.' Of more subsequent interest is to note Bull's reply to Plummer's welcome aboard—'I hope I don't fall overboard.'

Appointment to the HAC chairmanship appeared to revitalise Bull, who had several times referred in letters to his tiredness, his waning interest in racing, his realisation that time was moving on. Only age was on his mind as, in a letter dated 5 February 1980, he replied to congratulations from John Macdonald-Buchanan, the Jockey Club senior steward:

I am now an old man, a mere month or so from life's supposed normal span. Perhaps I should by now be tired of the pursuit of these racing purposes. I'm not. Indeed I'm wrapped up in them as fervently as ever I was. But I'm aware of the apparent intractability of some of racing's problems; and I have learned to know the pace of change. I was an iconoclast; I am now a polemicist; and I shall sit in your councils wearing that gown, and seeking diplomatically and unabrasively to propound rational solutions to the problems.

On 13 February Bull accepted the permanent position as chairman of the HAC. On 1 July he wrote to Sir Desmond Plummer and John Macdonald-Buchanan tendering his resignation. His term ended on 31 July, and the following day he was succeeded by Bernard Penfold.

From the outset Bull knew he was in for a rough ride—he admitted as much in those words to Gerald Dawson, one of his executive committee members, in a letter dated 18 February 1980, adding: 'All I ask of members of the executive committee is that they should not pursue sectional interests but should examine every proposition from the point of view of the overall welfare of racing.'

Within six weeks Bull felt moved to write to Dawson again, in the light of events following presentation of his paper on Objections:

Let me spell it out to you. The business of the Executive of the HAC is to get its priorities right and think in terms of the overall welfare of racing. You cannot make changes in anything without some people benefit from the changes and other people are adversely affected.

If a change in the Rules of Racing is proposed which involves a change in disciplinary procedures where jockeys are concerned, which they may think is anti-them, naturally they are going to resist it. They're concerned only with how it affects them. But racing is not run for jockeys. It's run for everybody. For the public. And people who sit on the executive committee are not supposed to pursue sectional interests. They're supposed to look at the overall picture.

There are two things I'm not going to stand for. If the HAC is going to be effective, it has got to be positive, and the fact that there may be minorities and dissentients from the resolutions of the executive committee is not going to be allowed to reduce it to impotence.

The second thing concerns the papers I myself write. They are not free of error. But they happen to be what I think. If I seek the endorsement of the executive committee, then I get it or I don't get it, and I may be prepared to amend or modify my papers in some degree to get that endorsement. But nobody is going to tell me what I may write or publish under my own name without the endorsement of the HAC. I submit to no censorship.

I wish to make the HAC an effective body. I wish it to be co-operative. I intend to be co-operative myself. I've spelled it out in my review of aims and objectives. But I am not prepared to play around with platitudes to suit everybody. The HAC has to be a dynamic force in racing. You're part of it. If you find you can't go along with my thinking, that's just too bad for me. But please understand the wide perspective of the whole thing. By all means kick me up the bum when you think I'm wrong, but bear in mind the realities I've spelled out in my paper on the Aims & Objectives.

I've been in this game as long as you have, or longer. I know it from the inside as owner, breeder, punter, writer, journalist, publisher and so on. I know the Rules of Racing as well as you do, and I know the Jockey Club and the Levy Board and the rest of the racing political scene.

I seek your support. I have a bloody difficult job to do, and the biggest problem is to weld the various sectional interests in racing into an effective voice of what they call the racing industry.

At around the same time unrest loomed from other quarters of the HAC, following publication in the racing Press of Bull's papers on Rule 153 and the Aims & Objectives of the HAC, before the General Council had debated them. Breeders Bob McCreery and Michael Wates were particularly incensed. Bull's reply to McCreery ran to nearly four pages, admitting that the 'release of the two papers to the Press, as it was done, was a great mistake', but defending his right to send out a personally prepared paper, as in the case of the Rule 153 report. The other paper, he said, had been produced at short notice, and in hindsight it was a mistake to send it to the Press—'But I didn't have hindsight.' Rounding off a letter written at length 'because I value your support and advice', Bull set out his stall:

Please don't misunderstand me. I am only the Chairman of the HAC. Power in the HAC resides not with me but with the General Council, and I have no wish to usurp the Council's prerogatives. I am the Council's democratic prisoner—quite properly so. It is my function to give effect to what the Council decides. But it is also expected of me to point a direction and give a lead. I regard that as important. Indeed it's the only aspect of the job that makes it personally in any degree rewarding. I assure you I don't mind being on the losing side of an argument, or being defeated on a vote. That's democracy. But if it should come about that the broad direction I point and the general leadership I give are not to the liking of the Council, that'll be the end of my chairmanship.

In the event, the force of elements outside the HAC bent Bull's frustration beyond breaking point. Shortly after he resigned, in a phone call to John Biggs, director general of the Racehorse Owners Association, Bull lamented:

I can't get away from the fact that this is essentially a cosmetic exercise; that's what it's intended to be, and anything that's done by the Jockey Club is going to be a sop to keep it in being for their purposes. It's made far worse by the fact that the general council and the executive committee want to gag me. They haven't the confidence in me to allow me to speak out about these things. I'm not allowed to print things, to publish things, except with their approval. I don't say that's wrong, but it is castrating me and preventing me from doing my best service to racing.

The last straw was the Blue Report, published in April 1980, in which officials of the Jockey Club and Levy Board proposed a new prize-money scheme where the emphasis for spending Levy Board contributions was directed more towards the better races and the bigger racecourses. The HAC, given seven weeks to comment on a study which had taken a year to compile, rejected the report and asked for its recommendations to be delayed. The amalgam of Jockey Club and Levy Board which made up the Joint Racing Board ignored the request.

Bull's one published reason for resigning was that he lived too far away from London and the job required a high degree of personal liaison with members and executives of the various racing bodies who were mainly based in the capital. 'There are also other reasons that I do not think it necessary to go into now which have weighed with me in coming to this decision,' he added in his formal resignation letter of 1 July.

He promised Sir Desmond Plummer and John Macdonald-Buchanan he would not go further into his explanation before his term ended on 31 July, and he kept to his word, in public.

'The whole set-up is little worse than a charade, which did not occasion me any surprise,' he told George Wigg in a letter dated 6 July, after Wigg had sent a message of understanding which contained the observation, 'I am one of the few who have got an idea of what you have been through because they did the same to me.'

By 27 July Bull felt able to expand, as he did in a letter to the MP Sir Timothy Kitson:

True though it is that trying to establish and run a new organisation in London from a domicile in Halifax has its drawbacks, and that this, as I said, was *one* of the reasons for my resignation, it was, in fact, the diplomatic reason that turneth aside a probing Press, with a view to not embarrassing the Levy Board, the Jockey Club or the HAC itself.

The truth of the matter is that the HAC is badly constructed, and is really no more than a cosmetic charade that suits the Jockey Club and the Levy Board, until such time as Willie Whitelaw can find parliamentary time to legislate on the Rothschild Report.

Neither the Levy Board nor the Jockey Club treats it seriously or has the slightest intention of paying attention to its advice when that advice is contrary to pre-established policies. They will seek the HAC's advice on such trivialities as excessive use of the whip, or whether tubed horses should be allowed to race, and so forth; but on an important matter such as a change in the Rules relating to objections, recommended not only by the HAC but by the ROA and the Racegoers Club, the Jockey Club doesn't want to know.

And in the matter of the Blue Report or the 1981 Prize Money scheme both Turf authorities completely ignore the HAC's rejection of these things, and the whole racing industry's rejection of them, simply because their minds were made up and closed long before either the HAC or its constituent bodies were consulted.

The 'industry', if that is what one wishes to call it, has no more real say now than it had twelve months ago when the Jockey Club ran its own RILC cosmetic job. That is exactly how it is, and that is the reason why I have resigned. I won't be a party to such a pretence.

Whether General Penfold will acquiesce in this situation I don't know. I guess he will. But Generals Eisenhower, Montgomery and Paton rolled into one wouldn't be able to change it.

Bull delayed going into greater detail in public about the background to his resignation for nearly two years, until in March 1982 he made the first of two keynote speeches to the North West Racing Club. There, he went on at length. But what he felt had been summed up in a sentence in a letter to Vincent O'Brien, dated 25 March 1981:

You don't need to ask me why I opted out of [HAC] after four months: my time—what few years remain to me—is too valuable to me to be wasted on idiots who can't think and don't want to know about anything that doesn't suit them.

Bull's committee work was over. On becoming chairman of the HAC he had given up his nomination on behalf of the Racegoers Club and relinquished his position on the Racehorse Owners Association Council. The Owners wanted him back after his resignation, but he declined, replying, on 13 August 1980: 'In the circumstances I think it would be as well if I opted out of racing politics—at least for the time being.'

He had pondered walking away completely. 'I'm tempted to leave the arena altogether,' he confided in a letter to racehorse owner Marcos Lemos shortly after his resignation, then quickly added: 'But I don't think that will happen.' And to George Wigg he wrote: 'I have a number of things I still wish to do, and I have no intention of frittering away the little time I have on meaningless charades and cosmetic exercises. I intend to say the things I have to say before I'm too ga-ga to say 'em effectively. And I'm not talking only about racing.'

Bull did continue to have his say, occasionally, but his brush with one of the sport's highest ruling bodies had been a sorry experience. However, he remained a member of the Racegoers Club Committee until August 1986, when he tendered his resignation with the observation:

I have never taken an active part in Club activities. My concern has always been a political one: to protect and further the interests of racing's customers, the punters and the racegoers, who through the Levy and the turnstiles provide the finance without which racing could not continue.

As the representative of the Racegoers Club on RILC when the HAC was being born, I was a midwife who insisted that punters and racegoers should have representation. I had to fight to get it, against the argument of Major [Michael] Wyatt and others, that a club of racegoers could not be regarded as a constituency entitled to appoint a representative on an advisory council.

It has always been a club of racegoers: it has never made itself the voice of punters. And I, the member of the Committee best equipped to do something about it, am regretfully conscious of having failed to tackle the job.

At seventy-six years of age, it is time I made way for someone with the zest and sense of purpose that the passing years have eroded in me.

Incidentally, Bull was succeeded as the Racegoers Club's nominee on the HAC by Dick Whitford, who had worked with Bull shortly after the war and without whom Timeform ratings would not have been devised. And Whitford was succeeded by Reg Griffin, Bull's longtime assistant and confidante, and Timeform managing director.

W HENEVER Phil Bull addressed the fundamentals of horseracing, he did so through the eyes of a punter. No ordinary punter, maybe, but he nevertheless kept the needs of the average backer uppermost. As a racehorse owner he expected to pay for his pleasure, in the same way that a man should expect to pay for his golf, he would say. As a racehorse breeder he expected to spend and to receive the market price for his produce, and no more. But as a punter he wanted to be recognised as a provider, a 'putter-in'. He expected others to appreciate the fact.

His view of racing as an entertainment has surfaced in many of the comments already quoted. They were brought together in a lengthy letter to the editor of *The Sporting Life*, dated 15 June 1978, which took as its starting point remarks made a few days previously by the Levy Board chairman Sir Desmond Plummer:

Racing is no longer a private cricket match for owners and breeders, an exercise whose primary purpose is to determine which horses are best worth breeding from. That's what it used to be in the good old days of the big owner-breeder establishments, when the promotion of race meetings was viable on turnstile takings. Those days have gone by.

The advent of television, bringing entertainment of all kinds (World Cup, Wimbledon, superlative dramatic productions and all the rest of it) directly into the home, together with high taxation, has killed racing as an owner-breeder sport. It is no longer viable in those terms.

It is now essentially an entertainment for people. The entertainment lies in the betting, and 93 per cent of it is in the betting shops, not on the racecourse. Deplore that as much as you like, but it is a fact. Racing depends now for its survival not upon the Aga Khans, Lord Derbys, Solly Joels and their owner-breeder establishments of the 1920s: it depends upon its revenue from betting, upon the Levy. In short, the punter.

Is the Jockey Club aware of this? Well, the realities have certainly been brought to its notice. But in fact it continues to perform as though nothing had changed in the last fifty years. Sure it wants to grab as much as it can from the punter, pressing Sir Desmond for more and more from the Levy. But does it look at racing from the betting point of view, or structure racing with a view to maximising its betting appeal? It does not.

It has its Pattern Race Committee and its Race Planning Committee: it has its Wyatt Report upon how best to assist the breeding industry, and its Sumner Report upon how to encourage the breeding of steeplechasers. All these things are concerned with breeders, breeding high-class horses and providing races for them. But where is its Betting Committee? Its Racing as Entertainment Committee? Its reports upon Service to the Punter and Racegoer, or upon Maximisation of Racing's Revenue from Betting? They don't exist.

This is not a matter of no consequence. It is vital to the future welfare of racing. If the Jockey Club were really aware of its responsibilities, and discharging them, it would be campaigning for Sunday racing wholeheartedly, not paying lip service to the idea; it would be concerning itself with amenities in betting shops; with service given to punters; and it would be structuring its racing programme not from a breeding point of view but also from a betting and an entertainment point of view.

Let me take this last point only, as an example of the Jockey Club's failure to get its priorities right in the light of the changed circumstances in which racing finds itself. Sir Desmond Plummer spoke of the need to revamp the racing programme. He's dead right. The structure of the programme of races throughout the season is traditional, virtually the same as it was in my youth, with minor modifications, mostly initiated by sponsors.

What the Jockey Club and its Race Planning and Pattern Race Committees do is to titivate things and put restrictions on sponsors in respect of prize monies permitted, so as to preserve these traditional patterns and solidify them. To make matters worse, in pursuit of equine elitism it emasculates big handicaps by quite unnecessarily restricting the weight range in the interest of favouring the high-class horses. This destruction of the betting potential of such races is ludicrous, for a handicap is a handicap, presumed to equalise the chances of the horses concerned.

> Behind one of Bull's suggestions for the Jockey Club—a restructuring of the programme to provide a major betting event every Saturday—was the 'advent of municipal lotteries and the prospect of national lotteries', which he said was 'a threat to racing's income's from the betting levy'. Seventeen years on, his theory on the latter point is about to be tested. Then, he explained his reasoning and his solution:

There are millions of people who are pure gamblers. They play the football pools, or take tickets in lotteries, in pursuit of the big prize or dividend. To them betting 'value' is irrelevant. If racing doesn't cater for these people, their gambling propensities will be lost to racing.

Does the example of Joe McGrath's Irish Sweepstake mean nothing to the Jockey Club? Joe McGrath knew very well that a lottery tied to a racing event had an appeal that a pure lottery lacked. He capitalised on that, and the Irish Hospitals benefited accordingly. The Jockey Club should think in these terms. It should have in mind, too, the French Tierce.

What is required specifically is this:

1. A restructuring of the racing programme to provide, every Saturday (in the absence of Sunday racing) a major betting event such as the Grand National, Lincolnshire Handicap, Cesarewitch, Cambridgeshire, Ayr Gold Cup—mostly handicaps, but not excluding a major weight-for-age event or a classic such as the Derby.

2. The conditions as regards entry, forfeit, declaration of runners and penalty for withdrawal, should be such as to make these races media for ante-post betting (to capitalise on the publicity attendant thereon), and also to provide as solid a list of runners as possible, sufficient to enable a big weekly pool exercise to be run on them.

3. The running of a 1-to-6 forecast on such races every week, under the aegis of the Tote, would attract betting duty at only 7.5 per cent. But it would be essential if it is to be a major event on a national scale (which is what is required) to solicit the co-operation of the TV authorities, and also, so as to secure the maximum catchment for bets, the co-operation of all bookmakers and their betting shops. The co-operation of bookmakers could be obtained by payment of an attractive commission.

> Bull went on to address the matters of security and advertising, and warned against repeating the 'stupidity' of at least one previous Tote promotion with 'little ideas such as the running of a Roll-Up on a selling race at Catterick on Eclipse day'. He concluded:

I do not assert, in making these suggestions, that this is the only way to tackle the matter. What I do assert is that the Jockey Club should regard these things as its business: that it should cease looking at the structure of racing only from a breeding point of view, and should start giving serious attention to the betting on which the viability of racing so much depends.

I suggest that it should embrace the betting and entertainment view of racing, and put the weight of its authority behind a Committee appointed to inquire into the betting aspects of its race programmes. If it does not do so it is neglecting its duty to racing.

It took time, but the Jockey Club moved gradually towards the 'entertainment' theory, and its stewards and officials came to realise it was necessary to take account of the needs of the betting industry. The British Horseracing Board, with no tradition behind and a clean sheet in front, took up the principle from the start. It is committed to taking account of the interests of racegoers and punters, but, with no bookmaker on the board, it remains to be seen whether it will fulfil any of the intentions Bull set out for the Jockey Club.

On behalf of the Racehorse Owners Association, Bull conducted his own inquiries into 'factors affecting the volume of betting on individual races'. Carried out for periods of Flat racing in 1973 and 1974, they followed the lines of the advice he gave the Jockey Club in his *Sporting Life* letter of June 1978, and used confidential information supplied by the bookmaker William Hill. From the first, Bull deduced:

The volume of betting attracted by an event is a function not of the quantity but of the quality of the runners—or, more precisely, of the amount of publicity and public interest associated with the event and the runners contesting it.

From the second, which was more comprehensive in the collection of data but covered a shorter period, he concluded:

Handicaps are emphatically not the punter's favourite betting medium. Punters of all betting habits are least attracted by sellers and most attracted by weight-for-age and condition races, with handicaps in between. The amount of betting generated by a race is virtually independent of the number of runners.

While the statistics were factual, interpreting the evidence, Bull said, was 'a matter of opinion: so we must beware of seizing upon superficial interpretations which fit our preconceived notions, or offer support for arguments that suit our purposes'. For those reasons he urged owners—tempted by the 'particularly strong correlation between the value of a race and the amount of money bet on it'—to look elsewhere for reasons to support the proposition that the Levy Board should contribute more towards prize-money:

The volume of betting on a race isn't due to the size of the prize-money; it isn't the size of the prize that attracts the betting. The amount of betting on a race is a function of public interest in the event, which itself is a function of prestige and publicity and the quality of horses contesting the event. Of course you can't attract the best horses and win prestige and publicity for a race without endowing it with substantial prize-money. But what is substantial is a relative matter. It's the differentials in prize-money, not its absolute level, that determine things. Doubling the prize-money for all races across the board would be nice for owners, trainers, jockeys and others, and would reduce the export drain on our best thoroughbreds; but it wouldn't have the slightest effect upon the volume of betting.

More money is bet in weight-for-age and condition races than is bet on handicaps. I daresay this will please [those who] feel it confirms them in their policy regarding Pattern races, from which handicaps are entirely excluded. In truth it should do nothing of the kind.

That more money is bet on weight-for-age races than on handicaps is merely a consequence of the fact that we so order our racing that the most valuable events, framed to attract the very best horses of classic quality, and which receive the greatest Press and media publicity, are all weight-for-age races. This is not so in other countries. The biggest betting bonanza in Australia is on the Melbourne Cup, a handicap, which attracts a crowd of 100,000 to the race track. If we ordered our racing on the American pattern, with handicaps massively endowed with prize-money, the betting picture would be quite a different one.

Bull's 1974–75 reports on betting factors were pioneering documents. The idea was taken up several years later by the Levy Board, which established a Betting Patterns Working Party, including representatives of the major bookmaking organisations and the Tote, as well as the Jockey Club/BHB, to study indexed figures provided by the major bookmakers and the Tote. The absolute, but commercially sensitive, details from which Bull worked are not yet made available to the Levy Board group.

Reference to a major weekly betting race, using the Tote and asking punters to forecast the first six finishers, had formed part of Bull's submission to an inquiry into the Tote by the Select Committee on Nationalised Industries. In a further submission, dated 26 January 1977, following a Tote paper delivered to Lord Rothschild's Royal Commission on Gambling, Bull warned against the intentions of the Tote following a £2 million on-course computer project:

The proposals put forward are altogether bolder and more aggressive than was envisaged. They involve nothing less than a complete take-over by the Tote of all off-course betting. Any pretence of justifying the Tote's existence in terms of its original purpose—the provision of an alternative form of betting to bookmaker betting, the profits from which were to provide finance for racing—has been abandoned in recognition that punters are not interested in totalisator betting, and that the Tote in its totalisator capacity cannot even pay its own expenses, let alone provide finance for racing. Having failed to deliver the goods after half a century as totalisator, with the benefit of an on-course monopoly, the Tote has gone into bookmaking, solicits an off-course monopoly and seeks statutory power to bring this about by the progressive take-over of all its bookmaking competitors. Its credentials for the job are hardly impressive.

Bull set aside 'the Tote's deplorable ethics' and outlined his objections to the proposals. They included the loss of ante-post betting, the loss of racing's trade newspapers for lack of advertising, the loss of service from the closure of 6,000 betting shops, the loss of jobs for 'some twenty to thirty thousand employees', and a potential twenty per cent loss of turnover. He concluded by examining the Tote chairman's motives:

Mr Wyatt's priority is the provision of finance for what is called the racing industry. His whole submission demonstrates this. My priority, on the other hand, is the provision of service to the punter. Betting is the punter's pleasure: he pays for it: he's quite agreeable to making a contribution to the promotion of racing: but he's not there to be fleeced on behalf of other people's 'racing industry'.

The Tote's business is to provide a service to people, not to get as much as it can out of their pockets. Its provision of finance for promoting racing is its secondary function. I suggest that Mr Wyatt should get these things in the right order. I am by no means anti-Tote, but I should like to see it tackling the job it was established to do, providing a genuine totalisator service, alternative to bookmaking, in those fields where pool betting can be expected to flourish.

Times and the Tote have moved on. Some things have changed: the Tote is able to pay its way; talk of an off-course monopoly has gone. Some things do not change, except that Mr [Woodrow] Wyatt is now Lord Wyatt of Weeford. But Bull's observations remain relevant, especially with the Government's having put Wyatt and the Tote on notice that they have until the end of March 1997 to examine the possibility of a handover to the BHB.

Progress in another area has taken some account of Bull's wishes, but not all. In 1995 there are nineteen Group 1 races for which male horses are eligible: geldings can run in twelve, but the 2,000 Guineas, Derby, St Leger, St James's Palace Stakes and three two-year-old races are still open only to colts and fillies. The number in which geldings can compete has been enlarged since Bull wrote to the editor of *The Sporting Life* on 6 March 1978, but his main thrust has yet to be met:

Racecourse performance is rightly regarded by breeders as a criterion of potential stud value. Group 1 races point the best performers. But the informativeness of the results of such races is diminished, not enhanced, by barring geldings from taking part.

Traditionalists would doubtless be outraged by the success of a gelding in the Derby. But if the best three-year-old in training is a gelding, it is well that it should be seen to be so. Even at Epsom. We may regret that such a Derby winner would not be available for stud duty: but is that a reason for denying to him the honour he merits, or to his owner the prize that goes with it?

For the entertainment they provide, the Brown Jacks, Boldboys and Kelsos are as appreciated by the public as are the Sagaros, Abernants and Nijinskys. Opening all Group races to geldings would increase the (necessarily) small number of high-class horses available to provide the entertainment in such races: it would in no way inhibit breeders from selecting the best available entire horses for breeding: nor need it disturb the devotions of worshippers at the altar of Improving the Breed.

Keeping alive, or simply bearing in mind, some of Bull's ideas is possible. Some have been ground inexorably into dust. John Biggs, the Racehorse Owners Association director general, made a series of observations on points raised by Bull in his speech to the North West Racing Club in 1982. In a letter dated 17 March Bull responded point by point before he came up with a fresh line:

There are one or two important things missing from the account in my speech of the Jockey Club's pursuit of ultimate power. One of them is its acquisition, for next door to nothing, of ownership (through Racecourse Holdings Trust) of half a dozen racecourses. Its long-term aim here is again to strengthen its position in the event that a future Government should set up a new Racing Authority.

The ownership and running of these racecourses, *per se*, is of little consequence to the Club. Its concern is its retention of power. I intend to take an early opportunity of exposing how these racecourses were acquired, and their development financed by punters' money provided by the Levy Board. Those tracks should be owned by the Levy Board, not by the Jockey Club.

Bull's promise to expose Racecourse Holdings Trust did not materialise in print. Instead, the group doubled its interest in racecourses over the next twelve years, during which time a new authority did emerge, though not through direct Government intervention. RHT's most recent—and at £30.25 million its most costly—acquisition was in 1994, when it bought the United Racecourses group, comprising Epsom, Kempton and Sandown, from the Levy Board. Far from owning racecourses, the Levy Board, under chairman Sir John Sparrow, decided it was time to get out of the business.

Bull would have been appalled by the recent growth of Racecourse Holdings Trust, which remains a wholly-owned subsidiary of the Jockey Club. But whatever he might have said, its progress would not have been halted. He would have been on safer ground with such outstanding issues as discretionary penalties, mean-rating handicaps and race timing. All occupied his thoughts, which remain worth examining.

Since *Timeform* ratings impinged heavily on the official handicapping system, Bull devoted time and energy to various aspects of this type of race. Penalties concerned him, and he pointed out the 'illogical and indefensible provisions of many handicap events' in a letter to the editor of *The Sporting Life* dated 4 August 1969:

The Ebor is an example: several relatively modest handicappers have incurred 8lb penalties (equivalent to eight lengths at one and three quarter miles) for having won races worth more than £1,500. On the other hand, Park Top, a superlative mare, of top classic standard, incurs no penalty at all for her success in the £31,100 King George VI and Queen Elizabeth Stakes, the most prestigious race of the year open to three-year-olds and upwards. This absurd situation arises because the conditions of the Ebor state that no penalty shall increase a horse's weight to more than 9st 7lb. Where is the logic behind this?

Is it an attempt to persuade high-class horses to take part in the Ebor? If so, it is highly improper and contrary to the intention implicit in the definition of a handicap. It is indeed almost tantamount to inserting in the conditions: winner of the King George VI and Queen Elizabeth Stakes to be allowed 8lb!

Or is it thought that horses on the Flat should not be asked to carry more than 9st 7lb in a big handicap. Why not? Not only is 10st the normal top-weight in handicaps these days, but I can recall innumerable high-class horses which carried burdens of over 10st in valuable handicaps, when the top-weight was normally 9st 7lb and the bottom weight 6st. Furthermore, horses are cheerfully expected to carry 12st and more over fences at distances of three miles and upwards under National Hunt Rules.

There is another matter. I see no conceivable justification for half-penalties. But if I'm wrong—if there *is* some justification that escapes me, what about the weight-for-age difference between three-year-olds and their elders? If older horses are to be given a half-penalty concession, do not equity and logic demand that the same favour be extended to three-year-olds originally handicapped at weight-for-age or over?

The whole business of penalties in handicaps is thoroughly unsatisfactory. Clerks of the course frame their handicap penalty clauses, and impose 5lb, 7lb, 10lb and 14lb penalties quite arbitrarily, according to individual caprice, and entirely without regard to considerations of distances over which the races are run.

Everyone knows that a 7lb penalty over five or six furlongs represents no more than a couple of lengths, which may easily be fortuitously gained or lost at the start or in running, whereas a 7lb penalty in a two-mile event, which represents seven lengths, is quite a different matter. If we are to have penalties in handicaps, the scale of the penalties should be inversely related to the distances of the races.

The truth of the matter is that penalties in handicaps are an anachronism. However justifiable such hit or miss adjustments may have been in the days of primitive communications and dependence upon publication of everything in the Racing Calendar, they are out of place in these days of overnight declarations and telephoned and telexed instructions.

In this country, where ante-post betting on big handicaps is such a uniquely entertaining and desirable feature of our racing, I suggest that in all handicaps: penalties be done away with; horses which win between the original allocation of the weights and seven days before running shall forthwith be rehandicapped at the discretion of the handicapper, and the reappraisals supplied by Weatherbys for immediate publication in the sporting press; horses which win less than seven days before the date of running shall not be eligible to compete.

A system of discretionary penalties was tried for a Timeform-sponsored handicap, but the Jockey Club was not impressed and allowed the idea to die. The need for day-to-day discretion on handicapping has itself faded, with speedier rehandicapping following introduction of a five-day entry system for most races—Bull produced a paper advocating a four-day entry in March 1974, incidentally—but the general principle remains worthy of note.

Discussion of mean-rating handicaps occupied Bull, the instigator, and Ken Allday, the less enthusiastic Jockey Club controller of programmes, for at least four and a half years. Bull outlined his ideas in a *Sporting Life* article in July 1976, and followed up a month later with his answers to observations raised in response. In his original article he expressed concern about the number of races in which many horses were handicapped below the minimum weight to be carried on the day, and in effect had either to carry overweight or miss the race. Bull's answer was simplicity itself, so he said: let every handicap be open to whatever horses trainers wish to enter; let the weight allotted be determined by the ratings of the horses entered, with the middle of the handicap equated with the mean of the ratings.

Bull outlined the advantages of 'mean-rating handicaps' and suggested what should be done if a very good horse was entered in a low-value handicap and was given a weight of, say, 10st 9lb:

No restrictions on what horses may enter any race are required; no top and bottom weights need be specified in the advertised conditions of any race; the weights are automatically determined by the ratings of the horses attracted by each event; the need for grading of races and the publication of ratings in the Calendar disappears; any cause of irritation to clerks of the course, sponsors or trainers is removed. I suggest that nothing be done. If the trainer or the owner feels that it is unreasonable to ask his horse to run under such a burden, the answer to the owner is that nobody is asking the horse to run, and the answer to the trainer is that he should not have entered the horse in such a modest event in the first place.

The two *Sporting Life* articles were reprinted in a paper, dated May 1980, which Bull was asked to submit to the Jockey Club. At the start of the following year he was still in correspondence with Allday, and getting nowhere, despite maintaining his topicality by using examples from the National Hunt world to back up his argument. His letter of 7 January 1981 began with an interpretation of the reasons for reservations expressed by Allday and David Swannell, the Jockey Club senior handicapper:

Mean-rating handicaps, in the terms in which I defined them, cannot favour any horses, top or bottom of the handicap. All horses carry their allotted weights. That you and Major Swannell have many reservations about the scheme, may well be. But what you cannot sustain is the statement that they favour any horses. What you really mean is that you'd like the big handicaps to be won by the better horses. You hate to see 'em won by something with a featherweight on its back. It is you, you and Major Swannell, and the Jockey Club, who seek to do favours to horses, and you're prepared to tear up the principle of handicapping in order to achieve your objective.

A handicap, by definition, cannot favour any horses. The whole function of a handicap, its declared purpose, is to equalise the chances of all runners, and, if the handicapper does his job properly, that is what it does. Jockey Club policy effectively frustrates this purpose where horses at the foot of the handicap are concerned. It does so with the deliberate intention of favouring the better-class horses, in flagrant contravention of the basic principle of handicapping.

It is not enough that the better-class horses have the Pattern races and well-endowed condition races made for them, they must needs have favours done to them also in handicaps by being protected from possible defeat by inferior horses at the foot of the handicap. The thing is a joke.

> Having dealt at length with examples from National Hunt, and the damaging effect the new system of raising the weights for handicaps at the overnight stage was likely to have on ante-post betting, Bull turned to the offer of a meeting with Allday and Swannell to hear their objections:

First of all, I remind you that you are considering mean-rating handicaps not because of any request from me, but because the Jockey Club (which seemed in ignorance that those articles were ever written) asked me to furnish information about mean handicaps. I have a concern for the welfare of racing and a desire that it should be well run; but I assure you that it is no skin off my nose if you and Major Swannell and the Jockey Club choose to persist in the present idiocies where handicaps are concerned. Having retired from the HAC, I'm simply an observer of the scene, and I have no wish to make a long journey just to be told why you and Major Swannell don't agree with me.

I doubt if there is anything I can usefully add to what I've written. But if you think there is, and if you think there are genuine questions about the answers to which I might be helpful, of course I'll come. Any time. To suit your convenience. I'm free.

There are 'technical implications which would best be discussed on site'? I don't believe it. There's nothing technical about programming a computer to deal with handicaps in the way I've suggested. It is simple and straightforward. But, if you really think there are things technical or otherwise on which you wish my advice or assistance, I'll come whenever it suits you, and I'll bring with me my own expert computer programmer to deal with computer questions that might be outside my own competence.

I wish you a happy New Year.

Allday continued to argue that the best horses would be discriminated against under mean-rating handicaps; Bull continued to say that doing favours to one or two horses at the top end of the handicap disadvantaged a great many more at the bottom end. Mean-rating handicaps have never seen the light of day, but the idea remains on the table. It sits alongside the bundle of paperwork which details Bull's last great cause.

Bull pursued the fate of disqualified horses from the Gimcrack Dinner of 1957 to his grave: his campaign produced some results but not acceptance of his fundamental principle by those in a position to change the rules. His reference in the York speech was brief: 'I'd like to see a change in the rule which demands that a disqualified horse shall be placed last.' The vast amount of paperwork he subsequently produced included letters to the Jockey Club, articles for the Press, reports for various organisations, and a betting agreement with his bookmakers, of whom all but one took up his arrangement to bet first-past-the-post.

He produced his first major paper on the subject of Rule 153, which covers what happens when a rider is found to have caused interference to another horse in a race, for the Racehorse Owners Association in January 1980. Before 1963, the stewards had no discretion in dealing with cases of interference during the running of a race; after, they had just two alternatives: if the interference was deemed to be accidental, they had the option of overruling an objection, altering the placings, or disqualifying the horse who caused the interference; or if the interference fell into any other category—careless, reckless, dangerous or improper—disqualification to last place was mandatory, 'regardless of the fact that the horse may have won or obtained its placing manifestly on merit', Bull said.

The question of merit was the kernel of Bull's argument. In his 1980 paper he explained:

Implementation by stewards of meetings of the rules as they stand frequently imposes upon them decisions that are patently unjust and unfair to owners and punters, are not understood by and frequently resented by the public, and often result in ill-conceived criticism of stewards of meetings.

Innumerable instances of the injustice of the rules as they stand could be quoted. The public is disturbed by these things, and racing press commentators are apt mistakenly to attribute them to the caprice and incompetence of local stewards. The fault lies not with local stewards but in the rules by which they are bound.

What is wrong is that the rules relating to objections and inquiries, as they stand, fail to draw the necessary sharp distinction between the disciplining of jockeys and matters relevant to assuring equity in the result of a race.

These two things are quite separate. If jockeys transgress in their riding, if they flout the rules, they should be disciplined for so doing by penalties that fall upon them, and them alone, by fines or suspensions of severity appropriate to the nature and iniquity of the offences. The penalties should not be visited upon the owners of the horses, by unjustly depriving them of prize-money.

The equity of the result is a separate matter. An objection to a horse, or an inquiry by the stewards, in respect of an incident in running, should be divorced from disciplinary measures against jockeys, and confined to consideration of the equity of result of the race. Disqualification of a winner, or a placed horse, on account of an incident in running should follow only if, in the opinion of the stewards, the incident affected the result of the race. Alteration to the placings in a race should be made only with a view to restoration of the equity of the result.

Insofar as an incident in running is attributable to culpable malpractice or breach of the rules on the part of the jockey, this is a matter calling for disciplinary or punitive measures against the jockey. That, and only that.

The confusion of these things implicit in the rules as they stand is historic. It stems from the time when the only sanction available to the Jockey Club to deal with malpractice on the part of individuals was 'warning off', and the only sanction in respect of objections was disqualification and relegation to last place.

Such black and white judgements and punitive measures are quite out of place in the modern world. We understand things better. We have the benefit of instructed stewards and stipendiaries, and the advantage of the evidence of camera monitoring of races. It is up to us to deal with things in a more sensible, just and equitable manner.

What is called for is: (a) a redrafting of the rules relating to objections and inquiries in respect of incidents occurring in the running of a race, with a view to confining them to consideration of the validity, justice and equity of the result; and (b) a formulation of rules designed to deal with undesirable or reprehensible in-race behaviour by jockeys, and the disciplinary measures that such behaviour should invoke.

> Bull sought to separate horse and rider in cases of interference; the Jockey Club considered that owner, trainer and rider should be considered as a team, not as unconnected individuals. For as long as discussion of changes to Rule 153 has gone on, the Jockey Club's disciplinary committee and its overall panel of stewards have argued that measures on the lines that Bull advocated would put safety at risk. They would lead to a win-at-all-costs approach by jockeys, whose suspensions and fines would be recompensed by grateful owners. Bull was well aware of the argument but said the fears, though understandable enough, were groundless:

The importance of safety in racing is not in question. Effective measures to deter jockeys from reckless or improper riding are necessary. What is being contended is that deterrents to such riding are already available in the rules, but are not being used, and that stronger ones can, if necessary, be written into the rules, which would place the penalties for transgressions where they belong, upon the transgressors. The proposal is not merely that disqualification to last place should be dispensed with as a disciplinary measure, but that it should be replaced by salutory and effective disciplinary measures against errant jockeys which do not, except in minor degree, involve concomitantly unjust penalisation of innocent parties. At present things are the other way round: the use of disqualification to last place as a disciplinary measure results in the major penalties falling upon the owners, while the offending jockeys get off relatively lightly.

The Jockey Club disciplinary committee considered Bull's paper at length, and turned down his recommendations. Bull described their reasoning as being 'compounded of mis-representation, evasiveness, refusal to address the issues, and either plain ignorance of their own rules or shameless mendacity'. An example from Bull's inevitable response illustrated his frustration. It dealt with the Jockey Club's avowed intent to treat all parties as a team, which argument Bull described as 'breathtaking':

When I employ a jockey to ride a horse for me, I employ him as a professional to exercise his professional skills on my behalf, for which I pay him, exactly as I employ a chauffeur to drive me or a painter to paint my house. I do not make the jockey my agent, and I am no more to be held responsible or penalised for his misdemeanours than I could be held responsible for the painter's spilling his paint on a neighbour's doorstep, or for my chauffeur's offences against the Road Traffic Acts.

The person who commits the offence is the one who should pay the penalty. Conspiracy is another matter, and a serious one, but it must be established and not assumed: and the possibility of conspiracy, with which the disciplinary committee is so obsessed, should not be used as an excuse for perpetuating rules that dispense injustice to owners and punters.

As with all matters to which he devoted time, effort and mental energy, Bull was convinced about the strength of his argument on Rule 153. He was sure that change would arise from his logic, but he was less certain about the direction it would take. A letter to John Biggs of the Racehorse Owners Association, dated 17 March 1982, highlighted his reservations:

The Jockey Club's stance is so manifestly ridiculous that they're bound to modify it. They'll certainly make changes, defensively, but I assure you they'll be half-baked and unsatisfactory. They will simply not face up to the fundamental point—the separation of matters concerning the equity of the result (alteration of placings) and the disciplining of jockeys. If they don't disassociate these things and deal with them properly, then they'll make a balls of it.

By the time Bull stood before members and guests of the North West Racing Club at their annual dinner in March 1984, his patience—never too evident over Rule 153—had worn threadbare. He told the audience:

So far as I am concerned I have washed my hands of the business. The Jockey Club is incapable of getting it right. Only when some serious consequence of Rule 153 hits it smack between the eyes will it see any light. What or when that might be, I've no idea.

It happened, the Horseracing Advisory Council argued, at Royal Ascot on 16 June 1988, when Royal Gait romped away with the Gold Cup, the easiest winner for many a year, but was disqualified on account of his jockey's careless riding. The HAC revisited the issue of Rule 153 as a result of the case, and in May 1989 it endorsed a working party's conclusion that stewards should be given the same discretion to deal with careless riding as they had in the case of accidental interference. The Jockey Club turned down the recommendation, but added to the interpretation of discretion available to stewards for accidental interference from the start of the 1990 Flat racing season.

In November 1993, more than four years after Bull's death, the British Horseracing Board took up another attempt by representatives of 'the industry' to change Rule 153. It recommended to the Jockey Club that the treatment of careless riding should be brought into line with the latest rule on accidental interference, allowing the finishing order to stand if the horse causing interference had not improved its placing in the process. The Jockey Club responded with a compromise, creating a new category of offence, irresponsible riding. More winners on merit would keep their just rewards as a result, but Bull's principle of separating horse and rider still went unrecognised. It remains the major item of unfinished business in a huge catalogue of change and influence.

A S the title sequence rolls, a silhouetted figure seated side-on to the camera leans forward to light a long cigar and then settles back in his chair. The voice-over begins and the camera pans high across green fields to settle on a large house surrounded by trees.

'This film is about a man who lives here in the hills above Halifax in West Yorkshire. He is a philosopher, mathematician and writer, who forty years ago retired from schoolteaching and began to earn his living from backing horses. In order to help him to do this more successfully he devised the most comprehensive guide to racehorses and their relative merits ever to be seen on the tracks. His understanding of the importance of the speed at which the race was run and the form of each horse prompted its title, Timeform. Originally a one-man show, it has grown over the years into an organisation which now employs over 130 people. The inventor's name, Phil Bull, has become synonymous both with racing and backing winners.'

In the meantime the viewer has entered the house and climbs a wide, sweeping staircase to the first floor landing, turning right along a narrow corridor and making for a distant, open door. At the vital words 'Phil Bull', the nature of the room is revealed. Lying beneath a layer of foaming bubbles, exposed from the chest upwards, Phil Bull is taking a bath. He has a newspaper in one hand, the cigar in the other. The camera angle, pointing down from shoulder level, makes him appear tiny and frail, his white beard dominating from the mountain of soap which preserves his decency.

The incongruous opening heralds Citizen Bull, a documentary made by Granada TV for the independent network and shown on 22 December 1982. Between footage of Bull at home at The Hollins, or striding purposefully across the racecourse enclosures at Newmarket and York, or watching racing from his box at Epsom and Doncaster, a selection of his speeches and writing is delivered by Freddie Jones, a character actor well known for his television and theatre work. As well as portraying Bull—with cigar but minus beard—at the Saints and Sinners Club annual lunch in 1976, the Gimcrack Dinner in 1957, and the St Leger Dinners of 1955 and 1964, Jones plays the three main characters in brief extracts from The Tramp Among the Tombstones. Rumbling sound effects of foreign invasion in wartime Britain are meant to heighten the play's dramatic tension; instead they obscure Bull's penetrating but deeply involved words and philosophical sentiments, as mouthed by Jones.

Around Bull's interpretations on the meanings of life and death, he expounds his thoughts and views on racing: the Jockey

Club, starting stalls and overnight declarations, Rule 153. He surprises a rails bookmakers' representative with a reference to his first-past-the-post betting agreement, an item presumably filmed before Tom Kelly, the *Sporting Chronicle* editor, wrote for the first time about Bull's scheme.

Bull's betting is featured: he narrows the six-runner Jockey Club Stakes down to three, decides none is a value bet, and then bets on two. His saver on Ardross comes up, though his race-reading, from a television screen in the Newmarket members' restaurant, provides encouragement for his bigger bet until the last half-furlong. In the Derby, he says the favourite Golden Fleece is not value; he backs Persepolis, Peacetime and Jalmood to return between £800 and £2,500 for his total stake of £900. Golden Fleece wins; Persepolis 'is given plenty to do in the straight', says Bull to camera. Everything comes right in the St Leger, and an uncharacteristic punch of the air signals that Bull has backed the winner Touching Wood; he is £5,000 better off, and his filmed credibility rises accordingly.

The exercise took from spring to autumn to compile, and involved Bull in lengthy preparation of personal notes, as well as even longer consultation with the researcher Spencer Campbell and the producer and director David Drury. Bull was sorely concerned that the result might not portray him as he would want to be portrayed; that it would give the wrong impression. Drury was made well aware of these concerns, and in a letter to Bull dated 9 November he attempted to allay the subject's fears: 'The film is progressing, in my opinion, very successfully, but as I'm sure you are aware it is a long process. I thought it wise at this point in the proceedings to drop you a line as much to put your mind at rest.

'In a conversation we had many months ago I said the film I wanted to make was a complex amalgam of life story, observation, information and polemic. Citizen Bull has fulfilled all the demands both you and I originally placed upon it when we first met last March. Firstly that there is no overt preoccupation with money, stakes and winnings etc. Secondly that the polemical themes, generally connected to the Establishment and the Jockey Club, be given a correctly balanced airing. And thirdly that attention be given to general attitudes about life and philosophy. I have laboured hard and long, endeavouring to accommodate these things, and I would like to think I have pulled the marriage off, within the exigencies of a 52-minute slot.'

Drury went on to outline the shape of the film, including footage at the Woburn stud of Henrietta Tavistock—'This is a quite remarkably charming sequence which is primarily designed to soften the audience's heart and open their eyes to a side of your character (flirtation and affection) which they have hitherto been denied access.' He ended: 'Things are still in a mild state of flux and clearly this vain attempt can only hint at the shades of meaning in the film as a whole, but I hope it at least points towards the general direction and gives you an insight into my concerns and pre-occupations.'

Bull's response came straight to the point; dated 16 November, it began: 'I'm afraid you can't put my mind at rest.' It went on:

Don't misunderstand me. I'm very well aware of your problem in making the film, within the restraints imposed upon you. I'm aware too of your earnest desire to make an artistic job of it and also to make it truthful, not only in your eyes but in mine as well, and at the same time to satisfy the requirement of TV entertainment.

At first I was moderately enthusiastic, and I always had faith in you and Spencer, for whom I had affectionate regard and in whom I had confidence. Sad to say, the enthusiasm and the confidence (though not the affection) have been in some degree eroded.

I appreciate your giving me an outline of what's in the film, but it really gets me nowhere, you know. In at least two important respects the slants that your summary implies are false—or at least that's how it seems to me.

You are intending to call me in to a viewing shortly. In what capacity? To contribute anything? Or merely to exercise my right of exclusory veto if I take exception to something? If the latter, I am not with you. So far as I know, you may have produced a lovely film with which I'll be pleased. As things are, my expectations are apprehensive. And my misgivings are not to be allayed by words.

When Citizen Bull was transmitted a little over a month later, Drury's original outline had been retained. Bull was not pleased. He said as much in a reply to Terry Mooney, manager of the Kiltale Stud in Co. Meath, dated 11 January 1983:

Thank you for your letter, which sets out your views very lucidly. I enjoyed reading them. If it is of any interest to you, I think that the TV film was a load of crap.

Bull usually afforded his correspondents an expansive reply; this was remarkably abrupt. Mr Mooney had 'been meaning to write' to Bull for some time. The TV programme gave him the inspiration, and he brought up several points: on Bull's having 'given away' the dam of Stilvi [Djerella, ex Djeretta ex Candida]—'You must have been as sick as a parrot to see the million given for her daughter recently on her way to visiting the horse you can't afford, Golden Fleece!'; on his breeding policy—'You did manage to breed some useful horses, albeit messing up their careers by bad management on occasions'; on his standing as a philosopher and playwright—'I would rate you about 7st 7lb on the handicap. In fact, I think I would have to put a mark against your name, the one that stands for unreliable'; on his admission to Henrietta Tavistock that he had never seen a mare produce a foal—'It did not surprise me, it is typical enough of the narrow perspective of your life.'

That last thought alone might have been sufficient to provoke Bull's short, sharp reply; Mr Mooney's closing advice, on Bull's search for serenity, was almost certainly the clincher. In summary he said: 'Serenity is a peace that comes from a silence in one's soul, that allows God to speak to it. The saints have achieved it. Nobody I know that studies chalk and boards ever came remotely near it. As a wise punter you have been known to have a 'saver' where you have backed a certain horse and thought it prudent to cover the bet with a wager on what seems to be the main danger. You have wagered that the outcome of death is nothing, finish, kaput! This is a bad bet. It's the worst wager you have ever made, because you have nothing to gain by it and everything to lose if you are wrong. Have a 'saver' on God—that's the best bet you'll ever make.'

Bull continued to smart over the television film. On 21 January 1983, he wrote to the artist John Bratby: 'Pray do not take too much notice of that supposed documentary on me. The portrait bears little resemblance to the original. Granada conned me into it and reneged on all the undertakings they gave me.' And to Teddie Beverley, one of the famous trio of singing sisters, he wrote: 'I didn't enjoy it all. It gives a completely false picture of me as a rags-to-riches story of an ex-schoolmaster turned successful gambler, hobnobbing with the aristocracy. For me, almost everything worthwhile was left on the cutting-room floor. As to the miscast actor Freddie Jones delivering my lines as though he were reciting seventeenth century romantic poetry, he was a disaster.'

A week later Bull was ready to be more expansive in explaining his displeasure, even though friends and associates had written in praise of the portrayal. Was Bull right and everyone else wrong? Correspondent Ray Berry congratulated him on the programme, but in a letter dated 28 January 1983 Bull begged to differ:

I feel the film, as shown, is not a matter for congratulation, and I did not enjoy it at all. I was conned by the ITV people. When I agreed to co-operate with them, I sought assurances that the subject would not be trivialised, but it would be a serious documentary. They gave me the assurances, and guarantees, and the right of veto if there was anything in it to which I objected.

They shot thirty times the requisite length of film, and almost everything worthwhile was left on the cutting room floor, and what they actually presented was an ITV rags-to-riches story of a guy who spends his life wandering round racecourses, betting in large sums, and graduates to hobnobbing with the aristocracy, livened just occasionally by odd things not quite so stupid and banal.

They did not call me in to view the rough-cut film until far too late for anything to be done about it, defending themselves with excuses about union problems. I tried to get alterations made. In particular I sought to get rid of the sequences in which I was supposed to be impersonated by the wholly miscast actor Freddie Jones, delivering quotations from my speeches and a didactic play I wrote in 1937, reciting my lines as though he were reciting Shakespearian sonnets. They gave us three days in which to re-record them. I spent a day with a film crew trying to do the impossible, then threw in the towel, washed my hands of the whole business and told them to do what they liked with the thing. I have not spoken to them since.

Of course it is of no consequence. Just one of those things one puts down to experience. Not worth bothering about or wasting a regret upon—except that I have wasted the best part of a year of my life—time I didn't have to spare. I regret that.

It wasn't the director-producer's fault. He did his best in the filming. The guy responsible was the Executive Producer, Steve Morrison, who controlled the make-up of the film but had nothing whatever to do with the shooting.

Of course I've had a postbag of letters from people who, like you, enjoyed the film, so I suppose, from a viewer's point of view, it can hardly have been as bad as I found it. But it was, to me, a travesty of what it should have been: not in the same class as the conversational documentary which Kenneth Harris did with me ten years ago.

Bull had been one subject in a series of face-to-face interviews conducted by Kenneth Harris, the political journalist and commentator. The outcome pleased Bull, though not before he had expressed his concern about an advance promotion for the programme run by the BBC. On 19 September 1972, five days before transmission, Bull wrote to Harris:

I'm astonished, and not a little angry to find that the BBC referred on Sunday night to your interview with me, as with 'Phil Bull, Gambler, who has made a million out of the horses'. Both statements are false, and if it should turn out that that is the way the programme presents me, I'm going to be incensed about it. You know well what I feel about this. Incidentally, I have received no contract from the BBC. Do they always deal with things in this manner? Programme first and contract afterwards?

Harris was quick to respond. He rattled off a telegram to The Hollins: 'Just received your perfectly justified letter. Bob Thorpe [producer] and myself as astonished and angry. That trailer unbeknownst to us. Representations have been made department concerned. Regards.' Timed twelve minutes later, a second telegram arrived, from Thorpe: 'Sincerely feel your complaint about word trailer from Presentation justified. It was done without consultation with producer. I apologise on behalf of the BBC. Can only maintain that Sunday's programme does not contain any such errors and am convinced that you will feel it is perfectly fair to you. Furthermore am amazed that you have not received the contract. It is not normal BBC policy to do it in this way, and I will certainly look into the matter as soon as possible.'

Bull was happy—as satisfied as he was with a complimentary feature which Hugh McIlvanney produced for the *Observer*, where Bull was given credit for the many facets of his character—and he and Kenneth Harris became friends. He was rarely so pleased. His disappointment at the 'slanted presentation' of the BBC2 programme Great Gambling Britain is noted in the next chapter; his reaction to an ITV feature on 28 August 1969 threatened to run it close. The theme of miner's son to gambling millions continually worried him.

In preparing for the 1969 ITV programme, he voiced early concern to producer Barry Cockcroft in a letter dated 13 May:

I have given much thought to your proposed Rough Shape for the Documentary on myself, and I am bound to say now that I think you are getting this all wrong. Your slant is wrong and your approach wrong. You must forgive me, but I must be blunt about this. You're mesmerised by this *News of the World, Daily Mirror* rags-to-riches idea:

son of miner to wealthy owner, etc. This is all right in its way—as a kick-off, if you like, and I don't mind your making a bit of a play of it. But to take this as your theme isn't doing me justice or being fair to me at all.

I am not an insignificant figure in racing, nor am I a figure whose claim to public interest is merely that he has graduated from a terrace house with an outside loo to a mansion. That's a point of interest only. I have done real and valuable things in racing. My contribution involves the following achievements.

1. I have made substantial profit from betting. This is of minor consequence but of interest to viewers.

2. I have devised and published an entirely new and original method of assessing horses—a running handicap of all horses in training—which is unique in the world, and has had an international impact. I don't think you appreciate this. But other people do, all over the world.

3. As a result of my books '*Best Horses*' of 1943 to 1947, '*Racehorses*' of 1949 to 1968, *Timeform* from 1948 to 1969 and Timeform Race Cards, I have done more to educate the racing public to the realities of racing than anyone in racing history.

4. When I won the Gimcrack, a dozen years ago, I made a speech at the Gimcrack Dinner which had far-reaching consequences for racing. If you read the speech you will know. I made sharp criticisms and many suggestions. Every one of these criticisms has been accepted and every one of the suggestions I made have been adopted. The changes in racing over the last decade have been in no small part the result of what I said.

5. I was responsible some years ago for a major alteration to the Rules of Racing. I gave evidence before Lord Rosebery's Committee and pressed a case which resulted in two-year-olds being allowed to race over six furlongs, seven furlongs and one mile much earlier in the season than previously.

6. I devised, sponsored and promoted the Timeform Gold Cup—a £20,000 race for two-year-olds over one mile in October—which became overnight the most important race for two-year-olds in the Calendar, and established this race in the face of official (Jockey Club) opposition. Nobody disputes the importance of this achievement.

7. As an owner-breeder, starting from nothing, I have bred and owned the winners of innumerable high-class races. Without question I have been the most successful Yorkshire owner-breeder of the last quarter of a century.

I am not bragging about these things. You force me to say them to convince you that you have the wrong slant. I am entitled to be billed and shown in your documentary not as a coal miner's son who hit the high spots, not as a rags-to-riches glamour boy, but as the Yorkshireman (if you like!) who has had the greatest impact on racing this century—Yorkshire's racing expert—choose your own phrase.

I object to being portrayed in the rags-to-riches image. By all means make this point if you wish, but do not bill me that way. I have plenty of entertaining and interesting things to say on my early life, life as a schoolmaster in London, on Betting, on Owning and Breeding horses, on Publishing racing books and periodicals, on Winning the Gimcrack, on establishing the Timeform Gold Cup, on identifying what is right and wrong with racing, and on life in general: on religion, on the failure of democracy, on the fallacy of freedom, on brainwashing and conditioning of people, on the population and technological explosions and the failure of governments to deal with these things, and on the very understandable and much to be desired revolt of youth all over the world.

These things don't come within your orbit in this programme? OK. But they are me, and if you're doing a documentary on me you cannot leave them out entirely.

Agreed, that I am a racing personality, and that in this context my views on life are unimportant. I don't agree with this, because I am convinced that my views on life are more important and valuable than my achievements in the racing field. No matter! Play 'em down if you wish. But I am a person of some importance in the racing world and I will not have myself portrayed from terrace back street to Members' enclosure to titillate the typical reader of *The People*, the *News of the World* or the *Daily Mirror*. It is not only not fair to me, it is not fair to yourself or your viewers. If you do it that way, you will be missing an opportunity and finishing up with a ten-a-penny, run-of-the-mill feature. That's my opinion.

I ask you to portray me as a person, whole and round, interested in life, the whole panorama of life (with views and observations that are worth hearing), who has made racing his profession, and brought to bear on it an intelligence that has made some impact on the racing scene:—not merely as a successful punter graduating from ragged pants to morning dress regalia at Epsom! I have contempt for that.

Bull could not have expressed his feelings more plainly; they were genuinely held, personal beliefs. The fact that they may serve to strengthen an outsider's view—that he held unjustifiably grand opinions of himself and his achievements—would not occur to him. And if, by chance, it did, he would dismiss it as unworthy, and untrue.

Through a summer of preparation Cockcroft stood his ground with understanding and patience. He even elicited an apology from Bull, to which Cockcroft replied: 'You have never been difficult—challenging is the word.' Bull became even more contrite, and on 22 August he wrote to Cockcroft:

Disagreement and forthright expression are all very well, but my rudeness and asperity deplorable, and make me feel ashamed and angry with myself.

I've thought a lot about this whole business on and off. You come to me, knowing nothing of me as a person and precious little of the racing scene in which I live. You have to learn as you go along, and you start with a conception of the subject (myself and racing and betting), and the way to present it, which I think is mistaken, and which all along I try to fight against. On the other hand you are an experienced producer, an expert in your field; and know your own medium, of which I am virtually as ignorant as you are of racing. I have to learn, as we go along, what you are trying to achieve and endeavour to contribute what you wish. There is, I am sure, no conflict between us, it's a conflict and a problem which is inherent in the situation.

On my side I think your original conception of the way to present me is basically wrong. You, on your side, may well think that I am merely a racing man and a gambler (though not in the ordinary sense, God bless us!) with delusions that I am really something else, trying to make you present not me, but my fantasy of myself.

This is all wrong. And most unwelcome to me. I found it embarrassing. The healthy man is merely concerned to be and to do. And to be put in the position of having to project oneself, and to defend oneself from being projected in a role that is in some ways unacceptable, I found both embarrassing and distasteful.

I shall watch the transmission, with mixed feelings no doubt, but with fair certainty that it will be from the technical and public point of view a good film.

In the event Bull conceded that the production qualities proved him right—'Technically very good and effective', he told Cockcroft in a letter shortly after transmission. But he was not totally happy:

I escaped the worst of what I feared. But was it not rather as I forecast? That everything I had to say about religion, or the American way of death, would be cut, would disappear from the sound track? Didn't I say so?

I don't blame you for it. It's the set-up. Nobody must say anything anti-Christian, anti-American or controversial, lest it might upset the viewer. Censorship. To be expected. The conformity to orthodoxy, please the customer, don't upset the Christian do-gooder, milk and water morality, the puerility of its entertainment: that's ITV to a 'T'. And that, with the commercials, is why I don't watch ITV. How much it would benefit from a Carleton Greene, or a Ned Sherrin, or a Rushton!

> Anxious that he should be portrayed in the right light—his light—on television, Bull attempted to be even more strict with the written word, and if it came from his own pen, he sought total control. An indication of his concern was contained in a letter to Ossie Fletcher, *The Sporting Life* editor, dated 8 March 1974, enclosing a confidential report he had produced, and referring to a previous article he had submitted for publication:

You know that one of your sub-editors deleted the last few lines of the article, and I had to have 'em put in a letter the next day. Caroline, good though she is, made an error in that, so that it read 'the function' instead of 'a function'.

The consequences of this little bit of sub-editorship have been: 1. A degree of misunderstanding in the article, since the last four lines were probably the most important in the whole article; 2. Correction in a letter the following day, which probably very few people noticed; 3. I've had to write long letters to George Wigg and Nick Lees to explain things and sort them out; 4. Other similar consequences for me when people comment on what I've said.

I'm making a plea. In the past I have had an understanding that *The Sporting Life* doesn't publish anything I've written—article or letter—unless in full, without the alteration of a comma.

Previously I used to specify such an embargo on each article or letter. This time I didn't. I thought it was understood. I'm not sore about this—just disappointed, and embarrassed by the repercussions.

You told me that my letter was too long. Fair enough. If it's too long, you have the option of not publishing it. But if you do—letter or article—I have to insist on publication in full. I'm not invading editorial prerogatives. I concede them. You can't publish things that are libellous, or a possible source of embarrassment to people. I try not to write such things.

But, you know, I go to great trouble to express myself with precision, and I don't want any sub-editors mucking my copy about to save a few lines of space, or because he thinks something I say is redundant or unimportant. Before anyone alters anything I write for publication, I want the proposed alteration put to me for my approval. Otherwise no publication.

I hope you won't think I am making a song and dance about nothing. Sub-editors are indispensible. I know. I've nothing against 'em. They do a good job. But please don't put me at their mercy!

> Bull's plea was heard but not, apparently, heeded to the full.
> In a letter dated 19 April 1974, he again appealed to Fletcher after
> some rearrangement of his words, and suggested a solution:

I don't have my original copy before me, so I don't know whether in these respects your sub-editor has improved on my English or not. No doubt, since you say so, he has.

I'm perfectly certain, if he were to go through the Prefaces to Bernard Shaw's plays, or through Bertrand Russell's writings, he could find good use for his blue pencil there as well. He would remove Shaw's and Russell's boobs and imprecisions and redundancies, and incorporate his own boobs; just as he has done with my copy. I do not compare the quality of my writing with that of Shaw or Russell but I am concerned with the integrity of what I write. My writing style is my own—warts and all—imperfect English as well, if you wish—and I just won't have your sub-editors, or anyone else's, 'correcting' it or 'improving' it.

You gave me an undertaking that it wouldn't happen. I rely on you to keep it. And to relieve you of the need to make sure that your knights of the blue pencil don't get out of line (that's a mixed metaphor and I'm well aware of it), anything I send you for publication will, in future, carry a printed sticker putting an embargo on alteration. Then, after you've exercised your prerogative of publishing or not publishing, perhaps your composing room will behave itself.

> Placing conditions on the publication of his own words was
> one thing; ensuring that the correct slant—his view of the
> slant—emerged when others became involved was something
> else. He still tried his hardest to set the parameters.

Ken Hurren, a freelance working for the *Daily Telegraph Magazine*, first wrote to Bull suggesting a feature on his life and times in and out of racing on 28 April 1970. The article appeared at the end of September that year, 183cm of fairly familiar prose, which began: 'Phil Bull has had more influence on the character of British racing in his time than any of your dukes and earls, which is a rare feat for a coalminer's son from Yorkshire.' But getting from start to finish was a tortuous process. It began to take shape when Bull insisted on authority over what went into the feature and how it was headlined and captioned. Hurren observed that the last word had to be with the newspaper but that every care would be taken to take account of Bull's wishes. Bull took up the issue in a letter dated 12 May 1970:

You are quite right that I've had previous experiences which make me seek protection. It is not that I've anything to hide: it is simply that I object to being made use of to project a tendentious slant with which I completely disagree, and also that I object to being portrayed merely as a chap who has made a fortune out of backing horses and so forth.

Some years ago I was the subject of a tendentious piece of reporting (as a result of an interview I gave), which decided me that I would never again lend myself to the production of an article on myself without the right to approve the finished article and the right of final veto if necessary.

A year or two afterwards another glossy magazine wanted to do a profile. I agreed. Journalist and photographer arrived. I gave 'em lunch. D'you think I could get the conversation off betting, how much I'd won, and that sort of thing? Not a bit of it. In due course they submitted the profile. It was virtually a sanctimonious anti-gambling tract, hung on me. Fortunately I had insisted on the right to approve before publication, and a right of veto if necessary. In writing. Naturally I told them they couldn't publish. They wanted to know in what way they could alter or amend the article. I told them there was no way it could be altered or amended that would make it acceptable to me—that the whole slant of the thing was false and unacceptable. I vetoed publication.

That experience confirmed to me the wisdom of protecting myself in advance.

As you know, I'm a publisher myself and a journalist of long experience. I'm well aware that any editor worth his salt is jealous of his prerogatives, freedoms and responsibilities. I know also that every competent journalist or skilful writer who takes a pride in his work resents its being hacked around by editors or sub-editors, and there'd be no joy for him in writing if he were denied the right to express his thoughts and his own personal point of view. I should be the last person to wish to interfere with these rights, freedoms and prerogatives.

Anyone is, of course, entitled to write about anyone else at any time and express whatever views and opinions he wishes, with only the laws of libel and defamation to inhibit him.

But if I am asked to co-operate with a writer, give an interview and provide other facilities, this is a different matter. I become a party to the exercise, and I am entitled to seek whatever undertakings and impose any restrictions I feel necessary as a condition of co-operating in the exercise.

I have, I assure you, not the least reason to suppose you will produce an article to which I would take exception or wish materially to alter. On the contrary, I'm sure I'll be very pleased with it.

Nevertheless, I don't want there to be any misunderstanding about this: I co-operate with you only on the clear understanding that 'the final text of the article shall be subject to my approval, and that it may not be published without my approval'. I should like to have an unequivocal assurance that this is so.

Hurren came up with an assurance and he and Bull continued to correspond on the feature through midsummer. Together they worked through a first draft and on to a rewrite which came near the finished product. From a letter Hurren wrote on 24 July 1970, two of five comments on Bull's suggested alterations illustrate the nature of the revisionary work: 'I'm sure William Hill's recollections of your "ill-fitting clothes" is faulty, so I've expunged that. I notice that you deleted the references to your mother, sisters, children and wives. So be it—except that I do feel you should let the one-line reference to the matrimonial situation stay in, if only because its omission would be more noticeable than its inclusion. To spell it right out: those who know you would know you'd censored it, and more important perhaps, those who don't know you would assume that you must be a homosexual!'

Among the many newspapers and magazines which Bull received, and sometimes read, a single exception to his principle of total control emerged. *Private Eye* could do no wrong, other than by not regularly making itself available in Bull's 'backwater of West Yorkshire', as he described his situation in a letter to the editor, Richard Ingrams, dated 15 August 1978:

I have the honour to have been maligned in your columns on four or five occasions. So far, to the best of my knowledge, you haven't managed to get a single fact right about me, except that I'm a Yorkshireman and the originator of Timeform. I don't complain about this. Bless you, I'm too long in the tooth. But I don't want to miss the occasion when you refer to me in your columns, and, by mischance or otherwise, you do manage to get something right.

The only way I can be sure of this is by placing an order for delivery by Her Majesty's mails. So that's what I'm doing. Cheque enclosed.

Forty years ago, in my innocence, I complained to the editor of a national newspaper that an item in his paper was untrue and that he knew it to be untrue. His reply was, 'What does it matter whether it is true or not, so long as it is news?'. A quarter of a century later when I reminded that editor (who was a friend of mine) of what he had said, he denied it—indeed he was affronted.

As for me, I'd rather have an intelligent liar aiming in the right direction than all the Thatchers, Levins or Whitehouses purveying their ideas of truth in the wrong direction. Hence my regard for *Private Eye*.

You have my full permission to lie about me, as heretofore, at your pleasure; and my assurance that whatever you say, you are most unlikely to induce me to indulge in litigation, or even denial.

H ORSERACING can give the impression of being a closed community, cocooned in its own thoughts, words and deeds, immune from the outside world, oblivious to what is going on around it. Phil Bull could never be accused of taking no account of other elements and influences; he thrived on them. Encouraged by his father to read widely from being very young, he had his early views fashioned by the environment of his birthplace, the Yorkshire mining village of Hemsworth, where his father Bill was involved in local Labour politics and his uncle Gabe was the MP. It was not surprising that Bull donated £500 to the Hemsworth Miners' Wives Support Group at Christmas 1984, at the height of the miners' strike.

When asked to appear in a TV documentary on his life in the late 1960s, Bull fashioned answers to his own questions, aimed at explaining his political and religious views. His notes read:

What do you regard as the most significant changes that have taken place in your lifetime?

Five highly significant things have happened in my lifetime: the Russian Revolution, which has split the world into two camps—the Capitalist world and the Communist world; the invention of the atom bomb and the H Bomb, which keeps the world poised on the brink of annihilation; the invention of the computer, which enormously increases Man's resources and control over his environment—an invention exceeding in importance that of printing; television, which has revolutionised communications and brought the world into every home; and the invention of the Pill.

How do you see the world today?

The world is in disarray. It always has been so, of course. The earth's natural resources and human energy are being wasted as never before—armies, navies and airforces, manufacture of weapons, bureaucrats administering a vast complexity of taxation and social benefits of all kinds. Democracy is not working. Parliament is in disrepute—centuries-old rules and procedures, MPs without offices or desks or secretarial assistance, indulging in puerile debate, half of 'em trying to govern and the other half trying to stop 'em. Western industrial life is so complicated that Governments are no longer in control. They are in the grip of social and economic forces they can't handle. In my youth it was argued that war would be prevented by a 'balance of power'. That turned out to be a delusion. As between the Communist world and the West today we have a 'balance of terror'. That won't work either. The one bright and hopeful sign today is the student movement. Young people are rejecting the values and institutions of their elders. They are seeding a new revolution. High time too. Let us hope it arrives before the elder statesmen start throwing the H bombs about. In the meantime one must earn a living and do what comes to one's hand. And I must busy myself in the little pond of racing.

Are you religious?

No. I'm a humanist. All religions to me are superstitious nonsense. The Christian religion is the most pernicious of the lot, for four reasons. Like all religions it is inimical to rational thought. Secondly it is a hypocritical religion. The most religious country in the world is the United States; the fifth commandment is 'Thou shalt not kill'. Yet half a million Americans are currently engaged in dropping high explosives and napalm bombs on villages in Vietnam, with priests there to make 'em feel better while they're doing it. No logic in that. Only hypocrisy, emotive conditioning and lack of concern for people. Thirdly it is a proselytising religion which feels it has a duty to impose its beliefs on others. Fourthly it is a highly reactionary force. Ever since the year 1600, when they burned Giordano Bruno at the stake for the theological heresy of stating that the earth went round the sun, the Christian Churches have resisted practically every advance of knowledge and technology and humane reform. Its attitude nowadays to sex, divorce, abortion and the Catholic attitude to the Pill are modern examples. Untold cruelty and unhappiness has been caused to people by churches acting in defence of theological dogma.

Fitting nowhere into this catalogue of answers, Bull also wrote: 'The important thing in life is to do the things that give you pleasure, and enjoy life to the full. To me there are no categorical imperatives, and no afterlife. Life is simply for living.'

And at the bottom of his typewritten notes Bull added, in his own hand, 'Personal wealth, personal extravagances—cigars, wine, fleet of racehorses.'

He might also have mentioned the castellated eminence of The Hollins, his acquaintance, through racing, with some of the wealthiest families in the land, his staying in the best hotels in the country, and his holidays (however little enjoyed) in Jamaica.

Together, they sum up the apparent contradictions of Bull's life—his strong, radical beliefs on the one hand, his acceptance of an inevitability that he could not change things on the other. And somewhere in the middle comes his despair (which he preferred to describe as despondency) and disillusion, which became increasingly evident in later life, as he carried on deep-meaning correspondence with a variety of contacts, from the Labour MP Tony Benn to the socialite Countess Bunny Esterhazy.

Bull himself would not admit to any contradictions. Indeed, he was at pains to prevent the Champagne Socialist image being given, especially when it was linked with his activities in the betting ring. Television programmes about him rarely found favour; so much so that it was surprising he co-operated—except that he enjoyed the role of showman, however much he tried to play down that side of his character. Typical of his reaction was a response to Trevor Philpotts, following his portrayal of Bull in the BBC2 programme Great Gambling Britain. Bull wrote:

I am bound to write to you not so much in protest as in disappointment, though I cannot deny the element of protest insofar as the programme concerned myself. May I say that if I had understood from the start the purport of the programme, I doubt if I would have participated. The title itself would have been enough to confirm my fears of 'slanted presentation'.

What disturbed me at the time, and increasingly afterwards, was the manner of presentation. Though I made it clear to you that I would not be portrayed in the character of a rich gambler who had made his fortune out of backing horses etc, this in fact was the way it was tackled. The statement of my gains from betting, the shots of the stately 'castle', the red Rolls-Royce and so forth. I relied on your assurances. It turned out otherwise. It was not my views and opinions upon horseracing and betting that you were concerned with, so much as portraying me as in the character I have indicated. Of course I am an experienced person and should have known better. I have only myself to blame. I cannot blame you for presenting the programme from your own viewpoint. But people who make these 'documentaries' have their responsibilities. In particular they are under an obligation not to select what they show so as to present a false picture, or pander to condemnations they know will be popular. I am bound to say that I do not think your programme escapes criticism on this score. If you show me, to make a point, you must show me whole and round and quote me when I deny your point.

It is easy to demonstrate that all gambling activities are non-productive, wasteful of human energy and trivial. I could not agree with you more on this point. If I were making a 'documentary' on religion, I should not have the slightest difficulty in showing that the same thing is true of priests and parsons. But who says that activities which are non-productive (whatever that may mean), wasteful and trivial (perjorative words prejudging the issue) are undesirable?

It may be said that compulsive gamblers ruin their own lives and those of others dependent upon them and close to them. True enough. So also of compulsive drinkers, compulsive drug takers (addicts) and of anyone who does anything 'compulsively'. All this means is that almost anything one does to excess has consequences that are bad for the individual and for society as a whole. Indeed, the word 'excess' begs the question. He who pursues financial success is applauded when he succeeds: he who does so to such a degree and with such disregard for everything else that money is his 'god' is despised. Very well. None of this disposes of the right of a person to obtain pleasure from drinking, smoking, business activities or gambling, and the unexceptionable nature of such activities, provided they do not damage or threaten the general welfare of society at large.

> Philpotts' programme had touched a nerve, and despite Bull's reasoned reply, the contradictions remained. Perhaps they were inevitable.
>
> Though Bull read widely, in later life he largely took in 'popular' writing, as could be found in the *New Scientist* or the *Guardian*. He read and admired Bertrand Russell's political works, but appears not to have seen his early-20th Century, reputation-forming works as a mathematical philosopher. He followed the American intellectual Noam Chomsky, but was unaware of his formative work in the late 1950s. 'He never read anything that was very difficult technically,' says John Whitley, who worked closely with Bull at Timeform in the 1970s. 'He was a big fish in a small pool—generally surrounded by the people involved in racing—and he never got out of it.'
>
> Nevertheless, Bull's interest and involvement in philosophy, politics and religion cannot be ignored. They consumed so much of his time, especially when he began to spend more and more of it away from the racecourse, even if he had to amend his outlook over the years. He explained in another prepared note for his 1969 TV appearance:

When I was young, I used to think that logic was all-powerful. That all you had to do to put the world to rights was to identify what was wrong, point it out, and weight of evidence and force of argument would win the day. It isn't so. People are so emotionally conditioned, so captive in the views and attitudes of the time, that they are beyond the reach of reason.

Bull outlined some of his influences and ethics in a letter dated 11 February 1970, replying to a lengthy expression of self-doubt by the horseracing author and journalist Quintin Gilbey:

I do not think I could go along with you that Bertrand Russell, Gandhi and Martin Luther King were the greatest men of the present century. Bertrand Russell certainly. Without question. But Ghandi's ludicrous ideas about sex, his domineering attitude to his wife and his deplorable treatment of his son are to be set against his social concern and political skill, and Martin Luther King's piety knocks him for me. But of course I agree with you about Churchill. He, more than anyone else, I guess, won the war, but he was essentially a fighter, a military man, the egotist supreme, with whom concern for people and understanding of society was in short supply. A Napoleon. No more.

I would take Bertrand Russell certainly. Then I'd think about Lenin, Castro, Einstein, and perhaps a 100/8 outsider Krushchev. I must have missed many other top runners. Please don't think I don't have high regard for Gandhi (I named a horse after him!) and Martin Luther King. Let's put things in perspective, brother. Remember Newton? The greatest mathematical genius that ever lived, who spent most of his life engaged on ludicrous biblical researches into genealogies and the displacement of the Ark! Mozart, was a Freemason; Beethoven, a most unsatisfactory character; and Karl Marx, neglected his family, for his ideas.

This business of deifying people, seeing them as angels or devils, is nonsense, of course. The best of us (should I say them?) is an imperfect human being. Between you and me—Bertrand Russell and concern for humanity apart—I love Mozart. But there are so many people deserving of admiration.

Pure communism has much to commend it, you say? I agree with you. Sometimes, frequently, I have described myself as a communist. I think I would still do so, for I believe in the right of each person to an equal claim on the beneficence of his environment, regardless of his colour, height, intelligence, skill, acquisitiveness, meekness, humility or other qualities or disabilities. I do not regard the fact that I am intelligent, skilful, capable of asserting superiority, as justification for my having claim to more of the good things of life than anyone else. On the contrary, I regard my intelligence and skill as a pure genetic accident, comparable with such things as red hair, short stature or early balding.

One thing hits me between the eyes: the American way of life. In the singular Americans are okay. In their mass, in their way of life, their conditioning, their beliefs, their actions as a nation, they are the equivalent of the Nazis in the 'thirties. For Jews, read Communists. To the Nazis the Jews were non-people, fit for the gas chambers: to the Americans the Communists are non-people, fit for napalm. Can *you* tell me, can *you* discern, any difference, any ethical distinction in this? I can't. My view is that the Americans will incinerate the lot of us in pursuit of their self-righteous, self-assertive Christian beliefs.

Do you think I do Christians an injustice? You cannot rule out the possibility that there may be a God. Quite right! You can't rule out the *possibility*. Could you prove to me that there are not thirteen frozen pink elephants in permanent orbit round the sun between the Earth and Mars? You can't you know. You can't rule out the possibility. You have doubts about the non-existence of God, you say, because you can't prove things one way or the other. Okay: I *give* you the thirteen frozen pink elephants. And *commend* you to a belief in them, *on the same grounds*. The reason you can believe in God, but not in the thirteen pink elephants is that when you were at prep school and at Eton, they didn't have you say prayers every morning to the thirteen pink elephants!

Come on! Get rid of this mythology. You don't believe any more than I do in virgin births, walking on waters, resurrections, ascensions to Heaven or sitting on the right hand of God in some fancy place up in the skies.

What you *do* know is that *Organised Christianity*, the Popes, Cardinals, Inquisitions and Bishops, have perpetrated in the name of Christ the most diabolical crimes imaginable; you know they're still doing it. Priests in Vietnam condoning napalm bombing. Priests blessing nuclear submarines, each carrying 16 hydrogen nuclear warhead missiles capable of delivering thousands of times the human destruction of Hiroshima.

You'll be dead soon. So will I. Do you really think there's some survival for you somewhere? Where? In what form? Up in the skies as a spirit, they used to think. You know the extent and nature of the universe: that light takes 10,000 million years to cross our own galaxy? That there are thousands and millions of such galaxies. That you are an insignificant little piece of living matter on a minor planet of a minor sun in one such galaxy. Where exactly is your Heaven, now that the up-in-the-skies-as-a-spirit idea has been abandoned. As laughable as the idea of the thirteen frozen pink elephants?

The final point is this question of Christian ethics. There are those who reject all the Christian mythology and church trimmings, but continue to call themselves Christians, because they are under the strange delusion that being a Christian is synonymous with being a good person, an ethical person. They mean well. But I object strongly to the idea that you have to be a Christian to be ethical. May not Buddhists or Hindus, or agnostics or atheists be ethical? The attempt of Christians to 'make a corner' in ethics is arrogant and impertinent nonsense. I go further. Much further. I regard the peculiarly Christian ethics as falling well below what they should be. Half of the ten commandments are stupid and the other half so impracticable as to be valueless as guides to conduct in the modern world. The Christian ethics in the field of sex and marriage are deplorable and have been responsible for immeasurable unhappiness in the Western world.

The idea—the typically Christian attitude—'do unto others as you would be done by' sounds fine on the face of it. But it isn't. The tastes and needs of others may be quite different from yours, and to do unto *them* according to *your* idea of what is good for them may well be, and often is, both arrogantly presumptive and altogether unjust.

Christian ethics are really little more than a hypocritical sham. A drug under whose influence Christians can perpetrate crimes against humanity and think themselves to be behaving ethically while they are doing it.

For Bull's definitive view about ethics and morals, and the difference between them, a letter written ten years later—23 December 1980—provided the answer. Bull told the *Observer* feature writer Brian Lapping that he had approached Lord Rothschild for a ruling on the subject:

He didn't feel able to give me an answer there and then, but said that he would give it some thought. A month or two later he wrote me saying that he had referred the question to a professor whom he described as his 'philosophy mentor'. He didn't identify the prof, but my guess is that he is one of the Oxford profs, probably Bryan Magee, who made such a balls of interviewing Noam Chomsky and Herbert Marcuse in his 1978 Men of Ideas philosophy series on TV.

Anyhow, Rothschild sent me a lengthy quotation from a letter he had received which purported to answer my question. In fact all that it did was to seek to explain the *common usages* of the two terms, morality and ethics, as though they were virtually synonymous, whose meanings depended largely upon the contexts in which they were used.

I then wrote to Rothschild saying that his mentor was not displaying his qualifications for mentorship, and that 'he hadn't even taken the string off the parcel'. Rothschild did not reply.

For me, there is a clear distinction between ethics and morality. If I could put it in a sentence it would be that: morals are nothing more than a set of rules (of behaviour) that moralists seek to impose on everyone else: ethics are concerned with seeking to arrive at rational judgements as to how people ought (desirably) to act, in the interests of the welfare of society as a whole, in the context of the ever-changing human situation.

Historically, morality has been in the hands of the priests (who were the first educators). All the various moralities are therefore closely associated with religious belief systems. Hence: the eye for an eye, tooth for a tooth, moralities so evident in Christian and Moslem societies. The absence of such beliefs in Buddhist societies; and the ideas of punishment and retribution which mar the former societies, with their proselytising policies in the interests of 'saving souls'; their certainty that they know what is best for others, and their arrogant determination to see that they get it whether they like it or not, even if it is necessary to torture them to do it. In short: *morality is ethics loused up by religious superstition.*

> Bull had long espoused atheism, and was never too old to put people right about its correctness—even those who did not doubt it, merely used a wrong word to describe Bull's disbelief in God. Such was the reason for Bull's letter (17 March 1988) to the racing journalist Jon Freeman, congratulating him lavishly on a feature article but still pointing out:

There is only one word I would quarrel with: your suggestion that I might be described as a devout atheist. Atheist certainly, and thoroughgoing, or whatever adjectival emphasis you wish to add, but surely not a word which is itself soaked in religion. A devout atheist is a contradiction in terms! If someone could show me just one piece of solid, incontrovertible evidence for the existence of any of the hundreds of deities around, my atheism would be abandoned from that moment. I am not devoted to it!

> The devotion to, or at least the acceptance of, religion among those around Bull upset him, especially in the case of his great

friend William Hill, in whom Bull appeared to see much of himself but without the capacity for clear, philosophical thinking. Discussing Hill with journalist Geoffrey Hamlyn for a subsequently unpublished manuscript dated December 1965, Bull said:

He is very much concerned for the welfare of people in the mass, his position is very much on the left, but it is, in my understanding, that of a person who knows where he belongs but doesn't really understand what the score about it is. He is perfectly able to distinguish between a Harold Macmillan and a Harold Wilson; he is very conscious that the American way of life is deplorable, and in feeling is very much on the left (he was a great admirer of Aneurin Bevan), but if you come down to the tintacks of arguing the realities of questions like freedom, and the basic problems of humanity living in mass in a modern civilisation, I don't think he has much understanding.

He is a left-wing man, his position both politically and socially is, because his upbringing from early days preconditioned him to be so. This is the case with most of us. Our positions politically and socially are not normally those we arrive at by rational thought when we are of a mature age, but they are the result of the conditionings to which we were subject when we were young.

He has given large donations to various things, like Cancer Research, and he has given a good deal of money to the church—which I think is deplorable. He is not really a religious person at all, never was. I think this began with the unfortunate suicide of his daughter. And the influence on him by Father John Byrne, who you might say has been his private parson for the last ten years.

His contributions to the local church come from a certain sort of paternalism, a wish to do something good for somebody else. I don't think it is really that he has any religious persuasions. He thinks the money he is giving is going to a really good cause.

Bearing in mind Bull's persuasions against religion, one of his more unusual correspondences was with the Dean of Westminster, Dr Edward Carpenter, which lasted for about four years, after the two met at Sandown races in July 1974. Dr Carpenter and his wife were entertained for lunch and for their first visit to a racecourse found themselves positioned next to Bull. Whether the seating plan was deliberately arranged this way is not publicly recorded! However, Bull followed up a few days later with a letter, and under separate cover sent a copy of *Racehorses of 1973* and a volume of *Best Horses*, as well as *The*

Misery of Christianity, by Dr Joachim Khal, of which Bull said: 'You won't be able to agree with it but it will certainly interest you, if only as an instance of man's disillusionment with the Christian religion.'

Bull added: 'I'm ashamed to say I haven't read any of your books. If you tell me which of your works you regard with most pride and satisfaction, I shall take immediate steps to remedy the omission.'

Dr Carpenter replied: 'I much enjoyed meeting you and exchanging ideas. We don't quite see eye-to-eye but I certainly respect your views and the integrity which I know informs them. In the realms that we were discussing there are, I admit, "no knockdown arguments": we must follow the truth as it is given us to see. I certainly find interest in *The Misery of Christianity* and hope some time to comment upon it to you. I suspect, from a cursory glance, that I may think Dr Khal grossly overstates his case.'

Within a few days Bull had written back, thanking Dr Carpenter for his letter but eager to make his point: 'As to "truth", I go along with [Karl] Popper in the view that ultimate truth is unattainable, though that must not commit us to keeping an open mind as to whether the earth is flat. Some things we "know". It is a year or two since I read Khal's book. My reflection, as I recall it, was that he only states half the case!'

Four years later, in August 1978, Bull turned on the radio halfway through a talk given by Dr Carpenter, and was moved to write again. He began:

You'll remember me, I guess. I'm the bewhiskered chap you met on Sandown racecourse a couple of years or so ago. You may remember also a proposal that you and I and Countess Esterhazy and Mrs Carpenter should get together to debate the Christian Ethic. It never came off.

Bunny Esterhazy is a rootless, quicksilver wanderer of a girl, forever unavailable when you want her, and I'm an old intellectual warrior, forever building mountains for himself to climb and loading himself up with burdens he can't carry. So it didn't come off.

The debate never did come off. Though Bull admitted he could not see eye to eye with one of the foremost figures in the British Church, he was willing to debate the issues. The same could not be said of his eventual attitude towards the Humanist movement, as represented by the British Humanist Association. In 1968 Bull wrote of his serious concerns for the future direction of the Association to the secretary of the West Riding group,

David Hersee. A year later Hersee approached Bull to ask if he would make contact with a spinster living in Halifax 'who is obviously in need of a sympathetic visitor'. Having mentioned that 'the word "sympathetic" rules out the character who wrote a couple of extremist, gabbling and insulting letters to me last year', Hersee attempted to sweeten the pill by adding, 'You could be hiding an almost human character behind those splenetic outpourings and be just the person to pay her a visit.'

Hersee had picked the wrong man, as Bull pointed out:

I do not agree with the policy currently being pursued by the Humanist Movement. You are entitled to your point of view about it, but you must permit me to have mine, and, if I think desirable, to express it with sincerity and force.

Your invitation to me to interest myself personally in a certain Miss Schofield, who is in need of a sympathetic visitor, is one which I must decline. Not, however, for the reasons you suggest. I am not concerned with burning churches, insulting parsons or other such stupid activities. Nor, as you suggest, am I concerned *only* with ideas. Quite the contrary. I regard *people* as much the most important concern of everyone—*all* people, regardless of their beliefs. If I am interested in ideas, it is by no means an academic interest, I assure you, but essentially because the ideas are concerned with people and their welfare.

Helping people, as individuals, is always necessary. I am at present engaged with three people who have been victims of society. One is a convicted murderer recently released from jail after serving nine years of a life sentence for the murder of his mother. In truth it was the parents who 'murdered' the lad. He needs not financial help, but personal time and attention, which I am doing my best to give him. The other two people have not been so seriously hurt. But they also take up my time.

If, in writing to me as you have done, it was your intention, by a sneering challenge, to convict me of lack of concern for people, for individual people, you are way way off beam, brother. I find myself involved with people, people I don't know, who come to me for help, or whose paths of misfortune happen to cross mine. I am not less responsive than you are, I assure you.

But this does not lead me into the error of supposing that charity, compassion, and giving personal assistance to people will solve any fundamental problems. It won't. At best it alleviates. What is really needed is to change the society that makes such distressing circumstances so common: to create a new and more rational society with different values from the one in which we live. *This* is my real concern.

To return to Miss Schofield, it would, of course, be a simple matter for me to pay a visit to her. But what would this achieve if I were unable to sustain a real relationship with her? It could only disappoint her, and that would be very bad indeed. I don't know the woman. I've never met her. I don't know what the score might be. One should not start what one cannot finish.

> One of Bull's basic objections to religion was 'its dependence on indoctrination', which he traced to schooldays. 'The last thing religious organisations wish is that their dogmas and beliefs be examined rationally,' he wrote. 'They are concerned only to get them accepted. The only way this can be done is by the well-tried brainwashing technique. The Roman Catholic Church has the business down to a fine art. Catch the human being early enough, brainwash it effectively in childhood, and you have a Christian for life. No argument that this is an improper procedure or an offence against true education will prevail against it.'
>
> On the subject of schooling itself, Bull's disillusionment about his first career, as a teacher, grew complete; his lack of regard for the public school system was always apparent. He made it plain in his evidence to the Royal Commission on Gambling, referred to its consequences in his speech to the North West Racing Club, and expounded it in a letter, dated 11 January 1983, to John Conry, who had been taught by a Streatham colleague of Bull's:

I am, and always will be, strongly opposed to the Public Schools, for reasons which you would find in my writings and speeches, and also in Anthony Sampson's *Anatomy of Britain*.

I am not opposed to places like Summerhill and Dartington Hall, nor to John Aitkenhead's private school at Kilquhanity in Scotland. I knew A. S. Neill and I know Aitkenhead quite well. And I have many friends who are old Etonians. Sixty per cent of the Jockey Club are old Etonians, and most of the rest are ex-public schoolboys, so I see the public school products at first-hand.

What I am concerned with is not merely the educational aspect of things, but with the divisive social consequences of the public school masonry, the inculcation of irrational beliefs and elitist attitudes, and such things as the charity status accorded to public schools and denied to other equal or worthier bodies, eg the British Humanist Society. It's a big subject, and I've no wish to bore you with my views.

Bull was familiar with the free-expression Kilquhanity School because his daughter Anne and son Ray were educated there—and according to one Timeform employee, they returned to Halifax knowing more swear words than a navvy might expect to use. Alexander Sutherland Neill was headmaster of a similar private school, which was evacuated to Ffestiniog during the second world war. It was to there that Bull and William Hill went when they sought an education for the two sons of the employee whom Hill had sacked for embezzlement but whom he still wanted to help.

When Neill and his challenge to traditional schooling, especially compulsory lessons, returned to Summerhill in Suffolk, Bull continued the contact, and in a letter dated 21 November 1972, shortly before Neill's death in 1973, Bull wrote:

You remember that play of Ionesco's in which all the characters one after the other turn into Rhinoceroses? An allegorical representation of the way in which the idealism and earnestness and concern of youth is seduced by the temptation to 'make one's way' in the world, by the pleasures to be gained from material success, and by the ease and comfort of social approbation that comes from accepting and adapting to the existing society instead of fighting to change it. Ionesco called his play Rhinoceros. None of the critics had a clue what it was about when it was put on in the West End.

Well that's what happened to me. That's how I came to exchange thinking and writing about life for thinking and writing about racing. It was during the war when I turned into the Rhino—about the time when I brought Billy Hill to see you. It was dangerous at that time to show any signs of non-Rhino behaviour or thought. You got locked up for it—as [Bertrand] Russell did in the first world war. And I'm afraid I'm not the stuff that martyrs or heroes are made of.

I read with a smile your remembered remark to Russell that you understood everything he said but couldn't understand what he wrote. Well, by comparison with some of the traditional philosophers I've tried to read, Russell is clarity and lucidity itself; yet I've a strong suspicion that on occasions he himself didn't understand what he'd written.

Philosophy is bedevilled by semantic confusions, faulty logic and mistaken aims and assumptions. [Karl] Popper promises to sort it out. I've not read all his books yet, but he rings the bell for me like Russell rang it in my youth. Popper is certainly right in his rejection of induction, and Russell's view is wrong. Incidentally, there's no reason to read Popper in German. All his books are now available in English.

I congratulate you on your good fortune in never having had your time wasted in reading Proust, Hegel, Kant, etc. About as useful an exercise as learning Latin at school. Except from an historical point of view, I guess they're as dead as mutton. Too much has been learned about growing potatoes since they were digging the garden.

> Bull's regard for the freedoms of Kilquhanity—after which he named one of his racehorses—and Summerhill could be traced to his oft-confessed fervour for egalitarianism. He expressed his thoughts, and the inevitable drawbacks, in a letter to George Wigg dated 25 March 1973:

I am by logic and conviction an *egalitarian* in the full, rugged, literal sense of the word. I do not mean, of course, that I think all people are equal, or could or should be equal. There are, in talent, and attainment by application, or in innate mental capacity, no equals to the Mozarts, the Shakespeares, the Einsteins, the Joe Davises, or the Cassius Clays. But I *do* mean that a man's innate genetic endowment, however superlative, or his superior skills, his greater capacities, whether innate or acquired by hard work and diligent application (however laudable these may be)—I hold firmly that none of these things entitle a man to lay claim to, or assert the right to, a pennyworth of the fruits of the earth more than a man less well endowed in these or any other respects is entitled to.

I am open to persuasion. But I shall need some persuading that a stronger, or more acquisitive, or more intelligent man has a right, by virtue of his strength, acquisitiveness or intelligence, to more reward, than has a man 6'5" tall or one with red hair, by virtue of his height or the colour of his hair.

I have considered the implications, and am aware of the impracticability of implementing egalitarian ideas in the real world in which I live.

Foolish people ask me, when I discuss the point, whether I would be happy to change places with the deprived African in a Biafran village. Of course I would not. But it is not a case of exchanging places. There are thousands of deprived Africans or Indians or Chinese for every privileged European in my circumstances. Nor would it be likely to make a Biafran or a Black South African labourer much happier to be put in my shoes. But these things are irrelevant. It's not a case of exchanging places, but of seeking to change society in the direction of egalitarianism. And *that* I am in favour of.

Of course I know the time scale involved. Not years, but centuries. And this is where I become appalled by the magnitude of it all, by the realisation that I have, at most, twenty years or so to live, that I am a western capitalist, conditioned to the affluent life, whose only concerns are that he is down to his last Rolls-Royce, can't afford to keep more than a few horses in training at £2,000 a year, is running out of wine and cigars, and may be mugged on a street corner if he is foolish enough to walk out in dark places at night.

I think I could well live on a piece of cheese, two eggs, three apples, four slices of bread and a quart of ale a day, in a room with a table, a set of chessmen, a few books, pen and paper and the company of my fellow man, and music—and be resigned and happy and content. But I would fear to have to try. I am too old, too conditioned to comfort and luxury and all the peripheral beneficences of western advanced society.

Nevertheless, I cannot escape from the logical conclusion that the only just organisation of society is an *egalitarian* one. I don't *wish* to escape from it. But it's all an academic exercise in the mind. There's no prospect of it in a hundred, or two hundred years, and I'll be dead in twenty.

Wigg, a Labour MP for twenty-two years and a member of Harold Wilson's government as Paymaster General, left Parliament in November 1967, was made a life peer and became chairman of the Betting Levy Board. After he completed his second term in 1972 and handed over to Sir Stanley Raymond, he had more time to correspond with Bull. Wigg examined Bull's points about egalitarianism in a letter dated 6 May, and begged to 'put it in a slightly different way'. He ended by saying: 'Unto each according to his needs, from each according to his ability is still a workable egalitarian philosophy.' Bull's response was both immediate and explosive, his target in a letter dated 10 May 1973 being the politics of democracy:

So! You're a practical politician, accustomed to considerations of national interest, security and so forth, to political manoeuvre, expediency and compromise. No doubt you will tell me where I'm wrong. Ethics and honesty and justice on the political plane are, it seems to me, always subservient to national self-interest. Not in Cuba perhaps, and perhaps not in China, but in the western world and the USSR.

You were a member of Wilson's Government. Socialist? Rubbish! Concerned not to substitute a socialist society for a capitalist one, but merely to try to make capitalism work to ameliorate its ills, not to cure them. More money for the lower-paid workers, a better social service and so forth—but NOT to change the form of the society that makes these ameliorative exercises necessary.

How do you think History will rate Wilson alongside Mao, Ho Chi Minh, Tito and Castro? History will consign him to the same box as Ramsey MacDonald, a devaluer of the socialist vision, without the courage to grasp a nettle—a political acrobat in the interests of expediency.

I am furious, inwardly, about these things. You politicians play around in your talk-shop, scoring points off one another across the floor of the House: at your best when you're contesting points of order, or convicting someone of prevarication or lying, while the real problems of population, energy, pollution, social organisation and economic justice go by default. And your alibi is that this voting-talking charade is DEMOCRACY. In my view it stinks! You think the Jockey Club and the way they run racing stinks. It sure does. But so does your clapped-out parliamentary democracy.

Now make no mistake. I'm a democrat. I believe in the democratic control and planning of society's activities. But NOT in what we are familiar with as Western Democracy. That is a farce, a charade, a talk-screen. American society, the American way of life (as you yourself describe it) and the hypocritical Christian sanctimony that goes with it, is a *disaster*.

I'll tell you one thing. There's a fairish chance that the Americans will solve the problem of the population explosion. When you have people like Kennedy and Nixon with their fingers on the button, it's no more than even-money that they won't do it with H Bombs. The Pentagon's understanding of the realities is no better than the Jockey Club's.

> Tony Benn was the next to feel the strength of Bull's views
> on democracy and his disappointment with the Labour party in
> Parliament. He wrote to Benn on 5 October 1976:

You belong to the socialist minority in the Labour Party, which wishes to see capitalism replaced by socialism. The majority in the Labour Party, who may properly be described as social democrats, are more concerned with 'democracy' (a means) than with 'socialism' (an end). Their policies—tagging along with the US; defence against communism; preservation of democracy and a 'mixed' economy, and so forth—are designed to remove the unacceptable face of capitalism, but not to remove capitalism itself: they seek not to change but to ameliorate.

You, however, wish to change society in a radical way, from capitalism to socialism, and you know well enough what this requires. I go along with you. But I remind you of Cheddi Jagan and Salvador Allende [Chile's Marxist ruler], and I suggest that your battle can never be won at the polls or on the floor of a debating chamber. If you win by the votes, the other side doesn't accept the defeat. The outcome is always a power struggle, and, regrettable though it is, power, as Mao put it, stems from the barrel of a gun.

Events are building up to a situation where this struggle will arise, and I see no signs on the Labour left that they are aware of the probable consequences. The faith of your Left-wing Labour politicians seems to be in democracy and the rightness of the cause. It didn't serve Allende in Chile, and it won't serve you in Britain.

The nearest we've been to a revolutionary situation in this country was in 1926. It came along unsought, not understood by those who had brought it about, and who were unprepared for it. All the signs are that the Left is still as ignorant of the realities of a political power struggle as it was in 1926.

No doubt you know all this. It's plain enough also that one can't have a socialist or an egalitarian society without a socialist economy purged of capitalist finance. But Callaghan, Healey, Jenkins and nine-tenths of the Labour Party don't seem to appreciate it.

The truth is, it seems to me, that domestic politics is trapped by global forces outside the capacity of anyone or any party to handle, and parliament is become little more than a charade, endlessly debating trivial issues, while maintaining a conspiracy of silence over the important ones that threaten the lives of everyone on the planet—membership of Nato, the consequences of nuclear war and so forth.

You're a politician as passionate from the head as Aneurin Bevan was from the gut. Would there were more of you! But don't let's kid ourselves. When you lead the Labour Party, as I daresay you will sooner or later, you'll not effect any radical changes in society by operating within the rules of this party political charade that passes for democracy.

Nearly five years later, in a letter dated 27 April 1981, Bull was back on the path to Tony Benn's door, which by this time opened on to the Opposition benches. The theme, however, was the same:

Your reply, in denial of my evidence and argument, did not impress me. Indeed it displayed a refusal or inability to face the facts. You put your faith in democracy in spite of the evidence.

Since then you have had on the global scene a further example: Michael Manley in Jamaica. He too put his faith in democracy, but the USA and the IMF destabilised his economy and he was kicked out of office in the recent elections in favour of Seaga and his misnamed Jamaican Labour Party. No accident that Seaga was President Reagan's first visitor to the White House after his election—in front of Thatcher and everyone else.

I warned Michael Manley just after he had won the election which put him in power, what the Americans would do. His reply made it clear that he *did* understand the realities. He knew the score. But he thought he could handle things. He was wrong. Another victim of a misplaced faith in democracy.

It is, as I said to you a few years ago: this is a power struggle; those who hold power are happy with the democratic process so long as it serves their ends: when it ceases to do so they couldn't care a bugger for democracy: if necessary they will bring out the guns and the tanks in the streets. Do you seriously think that things will be any different in this country because we happen to be British and have a non-revolutionary tradition? You kid yourself.

On a domestic level you are having the same sort of political problem. The democratic process is fine so long as it doesn't rock the boat, lines up the Labour Party behind Healey, with a Band-aid, better safety net for the victims of capitalism and not the slightest intention of changing society.

The 'Right' see you as a socialist who means business. So their press and the media villify you. They're dead set to keep you out. And the paler of the pale pinks in the Labour Party, and empty demagogues like Michael Foot, turn tail and run. You'll be well shut of them. They are Ramsay MacDonalds.

I sympathise with you, and I don't say it patronisingly. Far from it. When I wrote to you some years ago, it was in the hope of finding *someone* in the Labour Party with an understanding of the realities. But your reply to me before gives me no confidence that you appreciate what you're up against.

I'm now 71 years of age. I've observed this pre-adolescent stage in human behaviour for fifty years, and seen the Labour Party from Kier Hardie, through MacDonald, Lansbury, Cripps, Maxton, Henderson, etc, to Wilson, Callaghan and Foot, and the present situation. I've seen unions grow from the time of A. J. Cook to Scargill and Moss Evans. And all the other things from the time when Britain was an imperial power living off the backs of the blacks in its empire, to now when it is an impoverished island blessed by oil, a client state of the USA, pretending to be big, whose prime minister postures for orders for military hardware in the Middle East, where it used to be king!

All round, it has been a remarkable and highly instructive play. I wonder how much of it you have seen, buried in Westminster, where years ago my uncle Gabe Price, MP for Hemsworth, with the biggest Labour majority in the country, became so disillusioned that he eventually committed suicide.

Frankly, I don't know why I write to you. I have plenty of purposes of my own to pursue, apart from this overriding one of interest in life and humanity and where things are heading. And of course I have only a relatively short time left to me. But there it is.

> And there it was. Benn sent a short, hand-written reply, saying: 'Thanks. You may be right, but it cannot alter the main task, to win a huge majority to the support of socialism. That is both the way to a majority for a socialist government and against any attempt to overturn it.'
>
> Bull came back with a six-page letter dated 20 May 1981, which can be distilled into two sentences—'I think you are profoundly mistaken', and 'Come Tony: step out of your parliamentary strait-jacket, for once.' The correspondence ended on 7 April 1982, with Bull describing Benn's 'equating Jesus with socialism, or something of the sort' as 'tripe'. Bull went on:

In the last letter you wrote to me you said that the Establishment was ineffectual. That is your fundamental error. It is not. The power, when it comes to the crunch, is in its hands, in this country as in all the European and non-European countries in which the Military has taken over. Power is in the bullet not in the ballot box, as Lenin, Mao, Castro, Allende and innumerable other examples in South America and Central America are evidence.

On what side, in this country, if it came to the crunch, do you think the army would be? The question answers itself. But of course you don't think it will ever come to that in Britain, do you? You rely on our democratic traditions. Ah well!

You are the most articulate and lucid of all the political propagandists around. You listen and you reply. Maybe one day you will step outside the parliamentary charade and debate the real power realities with me, and the possible scenarios that may ensue. It's no skin off my nose if you don't. I'm 72 and I'll be dead soon.

Why I write to you I don't know. At my age I should know better.

> Bull had been concerned about his age for several years. In October 1969, he wrote to Ben Clements, former editor of *The Sporting Life*: 'The fact is, brother, I'm getting old. I remember the distant past, but I don't recall the immediate past. This is normal enough, of course, but a little early for me to fall victim to it. I'm not 60 yet.' Eleven years later, in December 1980, he wrote to Roderick Thomson at Bradford Grammar School: 'As I am already over 70, and have perhaps only another five years or so to live, I am little more than an impotent observer, without the purposive zest that would enable me to raise even a wee small voice about the way things are going.'
>
> Yet not too many months before, Bull had demonstrated much more enthusiasm. In a letter to Countess Bunny Esterhazy, he wrote:

I think life is a magnificent adventure. It is well to recognise its transience, and that there is an end to it ahead, but not well to dwell upon it—simply to get on with it and enjoy it.

There was a character in one of Shaw's plays, a young woman, in 'The Simpleton of the Unexpected Isles', whose motto was 'Let life come to you'. By which she meant, not to run away from it, but to embrace its offerings and opportunities. She was dead right.

Of course there is prudence. It is well to be prudent as well as enthusiastic; but certainly not to the point of inhibiting the enjoyment of whatever comes along. That's the way I look at it. Jump in and swim. What does it matter if one makes an ass of oneself occasionally? So long as one enjoys the swim, the journey, surveying the scenery as one goes along. Neil Diamond as well as Mozart, no doubt! And sharing the fun with the other fish in the stream, and fighting off the predators. Exploration, communication, sympathy and affection!

> He had written on similar lines at around the same time to Henrietta Tavistock:

We all of us find our own purposes *in* life. But there is no purpose *to* life; no transcendental purpose; no playing out of any celestial pattern to the satisfaction of the gods, or God. That's all cock and fairy-tale.

We are conceived, we're born, we live and we die, in a chapter of accident. We *weren't*; we *are*; and shortly we shall *not be*. That's *it* for us, as it is for all living things from fleas to dinosaurs. But, and this is the point, all living things are purposive. Purposive activity is what differentiates living matter from inanimate matter: indeed it would not be too much to say that life *is* purposive activity.

We find for ourselves our own purposes in life: for Mozart, music; for Shakespeare, drama; for Einstein, physics; for you the welfare of your children and your husband, your management of Woburn and your involvement in thoroughbred breeding and horseracing; for me philosophising, polemical writing, racing and breeding, and piddling around with timefigures; or even, at one time, seeking to win your regard and affection.

M OST men and women are either 'day' people or 'night' people. Phil Bull came into the latter category—and others suffered for it. When he was not racing, he would often make his entrance to the Timeform office after lunchtime and work through the evening. And when he returned home to The Hollins, he would continue working into the early hours of the next morning. He seemed genuinely surprised—and made little effort to apologise—when his late-night phone calls were answered by friends who had retired to bed. Early morning was also the time for Bull to answer his personal correspondence, written out longhand with a thick-nibbed fountain pen. A letter to Dan Prenn in September 1973 started typically: 'Two fifteen a.m., and I've finished the work I had to do. So there's time to drop you a line, and I feel I'd like to'.

As well as starting a flow of correspondence, Bull invariably answered personally anyone who took the trouble to write to him. He would pick up on any topic which interested him, usually as the result of something he had seen on television or heard on the radio or read in a newspaper. Joan Bakewell, the interviewer, was complimented; Sir Hugh Carleton Greene, the BBC director general, was criticised. Bull was not afraid of introducing himself to either.

The following extracts from a selection of Bull's correspondence between 1968 and 1988 illustrate that though he was probably at his most expressive when discussing horseracing, his comments and observations were not always devoted to this single source:

19 December 1968: to Raymond Guest, whose colt Sir Ivor won the Derby, Champion Stakes and Washington International that year but was beaten in the Eclipse Stakes.

It is increasingly difficult to recapture the enthusiasms of one's youth: the fine flavour of experience diminishes with the years. With horses as with women! The late Aly Khan once said to me that there were only two things in life worth worrying about: women and horses. Maybe what he meant to say was that women and horses are the most fruitful sources of worry! Either way I couldn't myself agree with him, but have certainly shared his enthusiasms in both directions.

As a boy I was captivated by the flying Mumtaz Mahal. As a young man I was lifted off the deck by Hyperion. Later there were Dante and Nasrullah. Over the years, there have been a dozen or perhaps a score of horses that have really exhilarated me. Ribot and

Sea Bird of course. Most of these fine horses I recognised for what they were long before their reputations were made. With Sir Ivor I was a bit late.

I didn't have the opportunity of seeing him as a two-year-old. It took the Two Thousand Guineas to alert me. And it was only when I watched him walking around the saddling paddock at Epsom before the Derby that the full realisation of what he was came home to me. Hyperion was a lovely little horse; so was Exbury; Nasrullah was a magnificent individual—a horse to fill the eye. Sir Ivor filled mine in the paddock at Epsom in just the same way. For me the Derby was already as good as over. I thought him then probably the most perfect specimen of a thoroughbred I had ever seen, and the most perfectly trained. It is an opinion which, retrospectively, I don't think I would wish to change.

I suppose if it comes to performance, the best in my lifetime was Sea Bird's Arc de Triomphe. Objectively one can't get away from that. But Sea Bird was no Sir Ivor in looks and conformation.

There have been times when the racing scene, the stupidities of our Jockey Club, and personal adversities too, have made me feel at odds with the game; jaded and out of humour with racing: when I have wondered why I spend my life involved in it, with all the richer panorama of human activity outside, and so many other things to command one's interest and energies. I felt a bit like that early this year. Sir Ivor rescued me! His performance in the Two Thousand Guineas, the Derby, the Champion Stakes and the Washington International—and the Arc, for that matter—rekindled my enthusiasm more than any other horse of recent years.

I think Piggott rode excellent races on the horse in the Derby, the Arc and the Champion Stakes (a mere formality—I could have won on the horse). But I can't feel the same about his riding in the other races. To me, he gave the horse an unnecessary amount of ground to recover in the Eclipse. Vincent [O'Brien] told me that the firm ground at Sandown was the cause of Sir Ivor's defeat. I daresay. I don't contest it. But for a horse that had already won the Derby, over one and a half miles, to be set to make up four lengths over the last quarter of a mile *on two known class horses* like Taj Dewan and Royal Palace over one and a quarter miles seemed to me to be asking too much. I could be wrong. As for the International, I am compelled to take the view that most American critics took: I believe that Lester rode a race that courted disaster. I'm not sure that I wouldn't put it that Sir Ivor won in spite of Lester, not because of him.

2 October 1969: to George Wigg, the former Labour politician then chairman of the Betting Levy Board, about David Robinson, the self-made industrialist but publicity-shy racehorse owner, after his colt Yellow God had won the Gimcrack Stakes at York.

I see David Robinson is going to make a Gimcrack speech after all. A short one, he says. Explosive? Contemptuous of those who have insulted him? It'll be interesting. But I can't like the guy. He has delusions of grandeur. No kindliness, or modesty, or doubt that perhaps the world might not be as he sees it. Puffed up with his success. Not stupid. But he humiliated his secretary in front of Reg Griffin and myself. A little Hitler or a little Stalin, I guess. Perhaps I'm wrong. I hope so.

6 October 1970: to freelance journalist Ken Hurren, who was preparing a feature article on Bull for the *Daily Telegraph* Magazine, about the world champion snooker player Joe Davis.

It'll amuse you to know that Joe Davis has just 'leased' me his cue indefinitely. When he was here for Doncaster, I offered him £250 for it, but he said it wasn't for sale at any price. To my astonishment, the following week at Ascot he said I could have it on lease! You wouldn't think, would you, that so much could lie in a little wooden stick less than five feet long!

1 July 1971: to Alastair Urquahart, who was compiling a book, *The Wit of the Turf*, and had the correct wording of one of his intended items pointed out; it is the most famous statement about horseracing attributed to Bull, but is rarely quoted accurately.

I have to confess I'm hooked on the darn game, but in the context of life as a whole, racing is a mere triviality.

1 July 1971: to Alastair Urquahart, Bull went on to offer 'other quotes you might fancy'.

Punters generally talk through their pockets: the Duke of Norfolk through his coronet.

A distinguished military career fits a man for a responsible job in racing about as well as a successful career on the Turf qualifies a man to command a regiment.

The fact that local stewards are appointed for social reasons does not mean that they are necessarily stupid or ignorant of racing.

> *30 December 1971:* to F. Murgett from Ramsgate, who approached Bull for advice because he was unsure whether he could make a living from backing horses. Bull began by addressing one of his favourite topics, luck.

On the matter of luck, I repeat that you should pay no attention whatever to it. Luck is, of course, a great factor in everyone's life; sometimes an overriding factor which seems to make nonsense of everything else. But the point is that it is something over which no-one has any control. There is nothing one can do about it, either to anticipate its consequences, take advantage of it in advance or defend against it. Fortuitous happenings are fortuitous: there's *nothing* one can do about them.

Of course, in the decisions one makes on logical grounds, the probability of purely fortuitous happenings affecting the outcome have *always* to be taken into account—that's what insurance is all about—but since you can never know in advance the good or ill fortune that may befall, this, the insurance aspect, is the only one you can consider.

When I said that you should ignore luck, I was speaking in terms of betting. My recommendation is simply this. When you are betting, you are concerned with known and partially known things and judgements and estimations based upon them. Luck will assuredly affect the outcome. But since you can't know how or when, nor can you exercise control over it, you must concentrate wholly upon the things you *can* weigh up or control.

I hope I make myself clear? No-one could be more aware of the fantastic difference to one's life that can flow from purely fortuitous happenings than myself. But all anyone can do is weigh the evidence, the facts, the probabilities and possibilities, and act on the best assessment of which one is capable.

Crystal balls, lucky days, charms, numbers, astrology and all the rest of the luck business is complete nonsense. Forget it! Take your luck as it comes, with equanimity, knowing that it's an imponderable you can do nothing about, and you will come to ignore it and eventually forget about it. That is how I treat the stars and jewels and slings and arrows of glorious and outrageous fortune.

> *13 March 1972:* to Quintin Gilbey, a longtime collaborator and author of *Fun Was My Living*, which Bull reviewed favourably

in *Books and Bookmen*. Tom Reece was a commission agent; the 'jockey concerned' was Gordon Richards.

There's one thing I didn't put in the review, for obvious reasons. I assure you Tom Reece used to bet in monkeys [£500] (frequently ante-post) with Billy Hill, always personally and by phone, and I was privy to some of the conversations. It wasn't his money, and you will have no difficulty in identifying whose money it was. Needless to say, the jockey concerned used to come up not infrequently and beat his own cash. Sorry to remove your last illusion!

I've yet to meet the jockey who's never had a bet. And, frankly, I'm not altogether persuaded that they shouldn't be allowed to—since you can't stop 'em anyway!

> *13 March 1972:* to John Hislop, breeder, and owner with his wife Jean, of the great Brigadier Gerard, following a complimentary letter to Bull on the three-year-old colt's essay-form treatment in *Racehorses*.

I think you were right to miss the Derby. It does come too early (as indeed do all the classics), and I've always held the view that Epsom isn't a suitable course on which to run the Blue Riband of the Turf. There is hardly a level square foot of ground, and there are all sorts of objections to it—none of which is to deny that the Derby at Epsom is a great race and a fine spectacle.

In the particular case of Brigadier Gerard, I'm with Joe Mercer [his rider]. I don't think the track would have suited him, even though some might have thought the same applied to Pinza, Coronach and others who have won the Derby.

> *23 March 1972:* to Norman Emblin, a friend in Halifax who wrote to praise Bull for his 'beautiful, lucid and sheer style' of writing in reviews for *Books and Bookmen*, and implored him to write his autobiography.

How very nice of you to be so complimentary about my prose. Some fifteen or twenty years ago a reviewer of one of my *Best Horses* books told the story of an Irish priest, who was a schoolmaster, catching one of his pupils surreptitiously reading *Best Horses* when he was supposed to be studying the scriptures. The lad had it out of sight and was reading up Dante, or some other horse.

The priest called him out in front of the class, and the lad was trembling at the prospect of what might befall him for reading a racing book when he should have been reading the Bible—what more heinous crime could a schoolboy in class commit! However, to the young lad's relief and astonishment, he was but mildly reproved, and then complimented upon his 'alternative' choice of literature. The priest went on to extol the virtues of my lucid prose and precision in the use of words, and expressed the hope that the offending youngster would learn to appreciate such things and profit thereby!

Write my autobiography? Well, the trouble is that to do so would seem such a presumption of self-importance that I do not feel. Of course I could write an amusing and entertaining book—indeed several—on my life and experience on the Turf and off it. Perhaps I should do, before they put me under it. But autobiography? That seems to me altogether too self-important and presumptive.

> *5 November 1973:* to Emile Littler, the impresario and racehorse owner, concluding a correspondence which Littler started after his colt Hello-Goodbye (bred and sold by Bull) had proved unsuccessful on the racecourse, unlike another of his horses, Irish Ball, who cost £13,500, won over £100,000 and was syndicated for £320,000. Littler suggested that in view of Hello-Goodbye's failure, Bull might like to consider handing over one of his stallion nominations to make up for the disappointment.

I appreciate that people who hit jackpots, as you did with Irish Ball, are frequently disposed, from all sorts of motives, to distribute to others a proportion of their winnings. And most people have pet charities which they support. However, you are not inviting me to share a windfall I have had, nor to make a charitable donation. You are inviting me, as the breeder and seller of a yearling that subsequently proved no good, to make a part-payment back to you (in the form of a free nomination) to mitigate your ill fortune in having bought a 'stumer' from me.

The purpose of my previous letter was to discover what might have been the other side of the coin, had Hello-Goodbye turned out to be a real top horse. As, for example, if he won this year's Derby and had been syndicated for a million. I wondered whether in that eventuality you would have made me a present of a £25,000 share in the horse, out of concern for my ill fortune in having sold a million-pound property for £30,000.

The third paragraph of your letter conveys the answer. You would not. It wouldn't have occurred to you.

I quote: 'I shared my success with Irish Ball with my trainer and with the man who bought the horse for me. As far as the breeder is concerned, he received the best price in the market, and he received the acclaim for having bred the horse'. So much for PB if Hello-Goodbye had won the Derby!

Well, if as you say the breeder receives the best price in the market for the horse he sells, the buyer on his side pays the market price for it. If a buyer makes a massive profit and feels no obligation to share it with the seller, if the same buyer should suffer a substantial loss, he can hardly expect the seller to share it with him. No, Emile, much as I regret your losses over the purchase of Hello-Goodbye, and with all the love and goodwill in the world, I don't feel disposed to offer you a free nomination to Brigadier Gerard, Zeddaan or Thatch in mitigation, nor indeed any free nomination.

> *20 March 1973:* to Gerry Oldham, the Swiss-based racehorse owner, on Bull's contributions to *Books and Bookmen*.

Phillip Dosse, who owns the magazine, ticked me off mildly for the use of exclamation marks in my previous reviews, and for writing in the first person and using the personal pronoun. So I've written him a piece without a single 'I' or a single exclamation mark in it—just to demonstrate that there's no difficulty in doing it. But it's bloody silly, really. The importance lies in what you say, not in convention-alities of style—in precision of expression of ideas, not in punctilities [*sic*] of grammar and language. And I am a purist where language is concerned!

> *20 June 1973:* to Jocelyn Hambro, on the death of his wife Elisabeth.

Elisabeth's death touched me with a particular sadness. It was ten years or more ago that I first met her. She was then the Duchess of Roxburghe, and it was a very formal occasion. Everything was stiff, and it was not, for me, an agreeable experience.

The Duke of Roxburghe was well known to me. Occasionally he had deigned to speak condescendingly to me on the racecourse; and he was without exception the most boorish and objectionable person I've ever met in my life. And on this occasion, which was to do with Cancer Relief, of course, I was not impressed by his Duchess.

But later, at the Timeform Charity eve-of-the-meeting dinners at York, Elisabeth relaxed and became a real person to Reg [Griffin] and me; we became friends and found ourselves with respect and affection for her, which, I venture to think, was not unreciprocated. Anyhow,

Roxburghe died, Elisabeth became your wife, and I remember saying to Reg at the time, what a break this was for her, and how well she deserved it, after years of suffering Roxburghe.

Then came Elisabeth's fight against cancer. Think of it: the monumental injustice of it! She who had done so much for the relief of suffering occasioned by cancer in others!

Jocelyn: there are people who believe in God—you may be one, for all I know—but how they square a belief in a supposedly benign deity with such an atrocity against a person like Elisabeth I cannot imagine or comprehend. All it elicits in me is anger: and that is what I felt when I heard of Elisabeth's death. Does it surprise you that I am an atheist?

> *1974:* a memo to staff at Timeform, though Bull was not always complimentary about Prof. Eysenck's view of the world.

Professor Eysenck's views on intelligence testing and some of the conclusions he draws from IQ statistics are by no means universally accepted, but the soundness of his thesis in this article would not be questioned. I recommend all handicappers and comment writers to read what he has to say regarding IQ inheritance, and think of it in terms of the merits of racehorses, in terms of Timeform ratings instead of Intelligence Quotients.

There is a close analogy between the two. Neither IQs nor ratings are capable of exact measurement, but merely of being expertly graded by comparative methods. And just as intelligence in humans (as measured in IQ tests) is only partly genetic in origin, and is much affected by environmental factors (education, social advantages, etc) so merit in the thoroughbred (as measured by our ratings) is also only partly of genetic origin, and is much affected by early stud life, competence of training and other environmental factors.

Qualities or characters that are controlled by single pairs of genes (e.g. coat colour, or colour of eyes) have a simple Mendelian inheritance pattern, but a quality like intelligence, which is the complex product of the effect of many pairs of genes, is inherited in a pattern which follows the 'normal curve of error' distribution. One of the consequences of this is what is known as 'regression towards the mean', which Eysenck explains as clearly as I've seen it explained anywhere.

Racing journalists are frequently surprised that a mating of a classic-winning filly with top classic stallions rarely produces a classic winner. There is no need for surprise. All matings are highly unlikely to produce classic winners: but the matings of top-class race mares with top-class sires are much the most likely to do so, even though the likelihood is low.

> *3 February 1975:* to Harold Bell, booking manager for Associated Tower Cinemas in Leeds, who had met Bull travelling by train to London, and followed up the introduction by inviting Bull to view a certain film, suggesting it would convince him 'that television is no match for the cinema as entertainment'.

No, no! Not if the film you commend to me is the best ever made could I possibly concede the point that television is no match for the cinema as entertainment. On the contrary: for every good film, so good that it's worth one's while to forego the comfort and convenience of one's home for the (relative) discomfort and inconvenience of going to a cinema—for every such tempting morsel you can offer, there are ten worthwhile programmes on television.

No, brother! Think me perverse, if you wish, but I'm not to be converted. I like my home and my comforts, and the ease and freedom it offers me to work as I wish or watch television when I please. I no longer have the desire to get out into the crowd. I have to do that (not without enjoyment) on the racecourse. The cinema, no! OK, so I miss some good films? So what? It's only entertainment. D'you think I don't have enough entertainment? Too much, my friend! I have work to do. Not nine-to-five work, but work at things I wish to pursue, and do pursue with pleasurable reward.

> *3 March 1977:* to Frank Beale, of the British Bloodstock Agency, who followed up a series of points Bull made in his submission to Rothschild's Royal Commission on Gambling. Bull's reply included observations on Beale's references to the Jockey Club and a proposed new racing authority.

Re the Jockey Club—no, no, I'm not less than fair. I don't like what I've had to write any more than you do. But it's an understatement nevertheless. In all respects. Don't misunderstand me. I haven't said a quarter of what I could have said about their performance in the 1940s and early '50s.

The British Racing Board ... You're right about the problem: finding the people. OK about [Lord] Howard de Walden. Not OK about the Leverhulmes or the Willoughby de Brokes or the Norfolks.

Let me put it in a nutshell: there are two chaps at York, John Sanderson and Lord Halifax. Halifax, however stupid he may be, is automatically a member of the Jockey Club. John Sanderson, however admirable he may be, couldn't be a member as things are—he's an employee! That's the answer to your remark about chip on the shoulder. I could name for you, off the cuff, half a dozen brains who would make the Bengoughs and the Jockey Club lot look silly—all disqualified by virtue of lack of social qualification.

> *22 August 1977:* to his racehorse trainer Barry Hills, illus-
> trating that Bull's racing accounts were studied down to the last
> detail.

Your account for July has been wrongly added up. The total before VAT and Yard presents amounts to £1,536.28 not £1,566.28.

Also, I cannot accept liability to pay 5% of place money over Fiordiligi at Sandown. Rule 194(ii) (b) on page 102 of Rules of Racing 1977 shows that, 1) The *owner* of the second receives 17% of the total prize money. 2) The *trainer* of the second receives 1% of the total prize money. 3) The *stable* of the second receives also 1% of the total prize money.

You and the stable have, therefore, together already received through Weatherbys, in respect of Fiordiligi's second place, 2% of the total stakes, which is 11¾% of what I received through Weatherbys. I think it is quite wrong that I should be asked to pay another 5%, plus VAT, on it. This is precisely what the prize money distribution scheme embodied in Rule 194 was designed to do away with.

Leaving the item of £39.36 out of your account makes the correct total £1,496.92. This, with VAT (8%) £119.75, and Yard presents £70, makes a final total of £1,686.67. My cheque for this amount is enclosed.

> *2 August 1978:* to Philip Oppenheimer, of De Beers, sponsors
> of the King George VI and Queen Elizabeth Diamond Stakes at
> Ascot, complimenting him on having 'the vision that identifies
> the right race to promote for the purpose'.

I did it with the Timeform Gold Cup—the only Group 1 race invented and promoted by a sponsor (before the Benson & Hedges Gold Cup)—and I did it in the face of Jockey Club resistance and opposition. By comparison yours was an easy ride. You were welcomed. I wasn't.

Do you remember the Duke of Norfolk's opposition to sponsored races? They'd never have them at Ascot. Over his dead body! It was infra-dig for Ascot to accept sponsors. This, from the Earl Marshal of

England, at a time when he was throwing open Arundel Castle to trippers at half-a-crown a head! It takes an aristocratic head to harbour such ambivalent attitudes without being aware of their inherent contradictions.

> *24 December 1978:* to longtime publishing associate Bob Charman. Bull uses Christmas Eve to catch up on his correspondence and thanks Charman for his gift of two paintings of birds.

There is no sense at all in the art world. They pay thousands for a load of bricks, or a red square with a black spot such as myself could produce in a couple of hours. These are beautiful, meticulous, truthful bird watercolours that embody skills that have taken years to acquire and hours of work in application—well, the comparison is really too ridiculous, is it not?

> *22 July 1979:* to Lord Ailesbury, after a persistent correspondence between the enthusiastic timefigure follower and members of the Timeform staff, including Bull's computer expert John Whitley.

Of *course* I realise that you don't get your copies of the timefigures the day after posting. Of *course* I have subscribers more rustic than you. Of *course* posting two days before the race barely meets the case. But we do NOT cut it fine. We post at the earliest possible time. Your complaints on late delivery should be addressed to the Post Office—where *ours* are sent. Not to me.

You seem to be one of those people who always has something to complain about, and who is determined to have the last word. Please take it. You exhaust my patience and forbearance. If you're dissatisfied with the service we're able to give, that's too bad. You have the option of not subscribing to it. Mr Whitley is helpful, you say. Of course he is. Why shouldn't he be?

For Heaven's sake stop niggling. Either take the service or give it up.

> *12 November 1979:* to Rolf Johnson, working for racehorse trainer Toby Balding and seeking to enlist Bull's aid to gain compensation for a jockey refused a licence on medical grounds. Bull had taken issue with an earlier proposition that jockeys are analogous to workers in industry—'They are not; there is no racing industry.'

Too often you find my views a matter of semantics? Oh, come off it. I use words with precision, and I think the same way. Those who use words in a slovenly or ambiguous way get their thinking loused up in consequence.

Sure, you and the lads in the yard are industrious. So are pupils at school, and their teachers. Does that make teaching or learning an 'industry', or the school an industrial building?

> *20 May 1980:* to Emma Forster, a Halifax sculptress who had seen Bull's photograph in a local newspaper, realised 'what a fine, powerful head this would be in bronze', and asked if he would consider sitting for the purpose.

I have sufficient vanity to be pleased by your suggestion, but not enough sense of self-importance to seek a fancied immortality in bronze. However, you're welcome to come to The Hollins for a chat if you wish.

There is a suggestion in your letter that you seek to hold on to the past. Can't be done, you know. Not in bronze or anything else. Was it Blake who put it that life is but 'a snowflake on the river—a moment white and gone forever'?

It's right anyway. As Voltaire and Bernard Shaw said, there's only one thing to be done about it—keep on cultivating your garden: you your sculptural cultivation, and me such little purposes as I may find myself involved in.

> *25 June 1980:* to Tristram Ricketts, as secretary to the Betting Levy Board, objecting to its taking a financial interest in Final Straw, at £25,000 a share.

The National Stud, as a subsidiary of the Levy Board, is not in business competitively with private owners of stallions. Nor should it be.

Its sole function, its only *raison d'etre*, as I see it, is the use of its financial muscle as a defence against the exportation of potentially superlative stallions, the loss of whose services might be regarded as having significantly adverse consequences for British bloodstock.

> *20 March 1981:* to Rod Fabricius, who while clerk of the course at Lingfield had continued to explore his fascination with 'biological clocks in living organisms and more particularly animals', and sought Bull's views about 'on and off days as exhibited by racehorses'.

I don't think I can help you. In over 50 years on the racecourse as owner, breeder and observer, not to say punter, I have seen not a scintilla of evidence to suggest that the vagaries of racehorse performance have anything to do with biological clocks.

May I add that I am also an observer of myself, and I have no evidence that I have such a thing as a biological clock. That is not to say that I dismiss the phenomenon as mere fancy. On the contrary there is evidence that it is a real phenomenon. But so far as I'm concerned I have no pattern of living. I eat when I'm hungry. I go to bed when I feel like it, at any time from midnight to 9am; I get up when I have to or when it suits me, and I cat-nap as does the cat. I'm a healthy person who pursues all the purposes he finds for himself, and the lack of pattern or organisation of my life has never bothered or impeded me in the slightest. On the contrary.

I can well understand that creatures of habit find themselves discomforted and out of sorts when the pattern of living they have established for themselves is ruptured or disturbed by events, but I take the view that much of what is supposed to follow from disturbance of the biological clock is nothing to do with biology or genetic endowment, but is to be explained in environmental terms.

My frank view, for what that is worth, is that if you seek to find evidence for the biological clock in the performances of racehorses, or to explain the latter in terms of the former, you'll be wasting your time.

21 May 1981: to Don Murphy in Australia, one of a stream of correspondents who have asked to use *Timeform* ratings for the purpose of scientific (and often unscientific) research.

You are welcome to make use of *Timeform* ratings (annual ratings as given in *Racehorses*, of course) in any way you think fit, but I should appreciate some information as to what you propose to do. I take it that you are well qualified in statistics.

I mention this because I'd like to be sure that you have a serious scientific purpose, are equipped to pursue it, and are unlikely to balls things up by drawing facile conclusions from inadequate data, or choosing your data to fit your preconceptions.

21 May 1982: to R. H. Goddard from Reading, a lifelong racing enthusiast who was writing to his 'idol' after being 'made redundant and thrown on the scrapheap at the age of 49'.

I can't myself do anything about that, you know, much as I wish I could.

We live in a pretty dreadful world, where profits of big business count for everything and people for nothing; and we are all, within the next few years, likely to be incinerated in a nuclear holocaust. Not much interests you, I guess, except racing (though I may be wrong about that). Probably you're not a political animal. I am. And have always been so, and I'm appalled and angry, furious at the way things are, yet conscious of my impotence to do anything about it. It hardly bears thinking about—but I go on thinking about it, all the same.

Racing—your prime interest—is a piddling little pond of no importance. Do you know that there are fewer people commercially and professionally engaged in horseracing than were employed in just one of British Leyland's factories, the one at Longbridge, before they started sacking them because they couldn't sell their cars? It's a fact.

Of the 20 million working people in this country no more than 16,000 are employed in racing. Plus another 50,000 or so in betting shops. It's really quite trivial. And yet, at 71 years of age I find that I, an intelligent man, have spent the best part of my life on it! I'm appalled by that too.

I am a very busy man, Mr Goddard, but not too busy to reply to a letter such as yours—though too busy to indulge in reminiscent correspondence for the fun of the thing. If I see you on the racecourse, and you remind me who you are, and of this letter, I'll buy you a drink with the greatest of pleasure.

PS: I send you a couple of my books just for the hell of it!

21 January 1983: to Teddie Beverley-Cottage, one of the singing Beverley Sisters, who had watched the TV documentary Citizen Bull, which followed its subject even as far as the bathroom.

You were always extremely fond of me? Yes? Well, I tell you you were always very smashing to me, and I've often regretted having met you so infrequently, almost always at Goodwood. Something should be done about it. Now that you've seen me in the bath, you have the advantage of me!

21 January 1983: to John Bratby, the painter, who inquired about Bull's view of the Tote chairman Woodrow (later Lord) Wyatt.

What do I think of Woodrow? The best thing he ever did was his interview of Bernard Shaw. He was always a political maverick. He's low on logic and high on self-display. He should have been an actor.

> *2 February 1983:* to Laurie Higgins, head of sport at Yorkshire Television, giving his views on the ITV presentation of racing, at a time when the channel covered seven races on a Saturday afternoon, and before Channel 4 took up position.

In general the flavour of ITV's presentation is unprofessional and trivialising by comparison with that of the BBC. There's too much persiflage and back chat and too little attention to the realities of the races being televised.

Your presenters seem to pitch their view of the intelligence of their viewers far too low. Thus, they make idiotic remarks about the chances of horse X being impaired by the fact that so-and-so has tipped it or backed it, when even a moron knows that the result of a race cannot be affected by what so-and-so thinks or what he's backed. Their chatting up of the viewer is full of this sort of rubbish.

The ITV's usual answer to this is, of course, that you are, in fact, talking to non-racing people, so the chat is appropriate. I don't believe it. This answer might be more appropriate to the BBC's coverage of racing which may be restricted by mixing with skiing, table tennis, and all sorts of other sports.

ITV doesn't normally do that. Its racing coverage is continuous over a two-hour period. Its viewers are therefore people who *are* familiar with and interested in racing. They are seeking nothing else. That's why they are watching ITV and not BBC. And what they wish to see and hear are things relevant to each and every race as it comes along. They are punters. They need information in the literal sense of the word, facts material to the outcome of the race; information about the runners; a *view* of the runners in the paddock, on the way to the post, and, of course, betting information.

However, it is perfectly obvious to me that, all this aside, racing is losing out on TV coverage, and its viewing audience is going down because of the increasing exposure of snooker, darts and other sports, which is cheaper from the presentational point of view. This is despite the fact that, according to the Report of the Royal Commission, three million people back horses. I do not see any way of reversing the trend. I think it is something that racing people are going to have to reconcile themselves to.

TV exposure is vital to any sport. The more exposure the more the sport is popularised, the more it enjoys the rewards of this popularisation. It is a sad thing that the Jockey Club has never understood this. If it were alive to this elementary reality it would be seeking new ways of ordering its racing programmes, its big-race betting features, in co-operation with TV with a view to making the most of things. I have long despaired of the Jockey Club.

> *3 April 1984:* to Abe Hewitt, an American horseracing historian.

All the breeding theories I've read about—'great' or otherwise—are equivalent to palmistry, phrenology, scientology, astrology, etc —all pseudo-intellectual excreta.

> *17 January 1988:* to Paul Casson, a onetime Timeform employee who struck up a friendship with Bull and continued to correspond after he went to work in America. This was Bull's last Christmas; he died in June the following year, aged 79.

I do not enjoy Christmas, which has become little more for me than an obligation to spend £1,500 giving presents to others and receiving from them reciprocal items, many of which I could well do without. Shades of Scrooge! But Christmas has become a big commercial bonanza to the accompaniment of Religious Crap.

Anyhow, I've not been too well either, and am very lacking in energy. My snooker has gone to pot, and I still have a pile of pre-Christmas letters to answer that I haven't yet managed to force myself to get down to. The best that can be said about getting old is that the alternative is worse.

D ESPITE expressing a loathing for Latin from schooldays, Phil Bull remembered sufficient of the vocabulary to dream up a personal motto for the 1982 documentary Citizen Bull. 'I don't have a motto,' he said, 'but if I did, it would be Labor, Tranquillitas, Amor. Which by my translation would be Work, Serenity, Love—the three most vital things I appreciate right now.'

Work was no problem, as long as it referred to the occupation of his time. Though he admitted he put most other pursuits ahead of work at university, he made up the deficiency in later life in his approach to betting and writing. The search for serenity and love, however, was more tortuous, and only rarely fulfilled.

Bull's sister May remembers his anxiety 'to be his own man'. It emerged as he left home in Hemsworth for university, and remained with him throughout his involvement with racing. No-one could doubt that he was endowed with an abundance of talent, was a good writer with sound mathematical ability, and had the flair and equable temperament to make a successful backer of horses. But there was an element of doubt about his self-assurance; it was not always as solid as he liked people to think, and he took care to encourage the image of bluntness.

Occasional glimpses of a chip on Bull's shoulder can probably be traced to his arrival at Leeds University. There, the teenager from the biggest Labour stronghold in the country was exposed to the public school influence for the first time. He recalled walking into university wearing spats, and very quickly was made aware he had committed a social gaffe. 'I didn't belong among the public school element,' he said. His distaste for the make-up of the Jockey Club—'ninety-six per cent public school educated'—had an early foundation.

Dick Whitford, who worked more closely with Bull than anyone else from 1945 to 1949, recalls: 'He cultivated his image of being "one of a kind", a blunt-spoken extrovert who cared nothing about what others thought of him. I think he saw himself as a latter-day George Bernard Shaw, though he lacked his wit and charm and sense of humour. But much of his pugnacious manner was an affectation: a determination to be noticed. No-one could ever have doubted that he had an exceptional mind or that his talents were anything but extraordinary. But there were always glimpses of an inferiority complex. He was fiercely anti-Establishment and would go scarlet with emotion when raging about the machinations of the "old school tie" lot.

'In his early days the Jockey Club was the root of all evil. In 1947 he had a three-year-old, Empedocles, that had been turned into a coward by a hard race on his debut. For two seasons he would cringe whenever the whips started cracking but Phil thought he could still be made a winner. Rather than pay his keep for the winter he agreed to lease Empedocles to a friend who was a jumps enthusiast. One morning Phil stormed into my office, absolutely crimson with anger, and thrust a letter from the Jockey Club across my desk. "Will you please inform us of your motive in seeking to lease this horse to Mr G. Cooper ..." it read. "Motive?" Phil said. "What do they mean—motive? It's insulting ... do they think I'm trying to do something crooked? I'll tell 'em what my motive is—it's to save shooting a thoroughly bad horse!"

'The Jockey Club only escaped a court case when Phil found that none of his dictionaries suggested that any slight was implied in the word "motive".

'In the racing community, especially in the early days, Phil was far from being well-liked. Sometimes, in the paddock or the members' enclosure, people would turn on their heels if there was a chance of meeting him face to face. I was never really at ease with Phil myself but I came to recognise when he was playing a part and when he was being himself.

'In later life, age and self-confidence mellowed him and he cultivated a cheerful outlook quite foreign to his manner of earlier years. His reputation was secure by then, and having acquired some of the social graces, he came to be accepted on friendly terms by most racing regulars, including many whom he had affected to despise when he was first making his way on the Turf. But he was making heavy weather of it when I was with him.'

Bull himself would admit to nothing less than total honesty in his attitude and outlook, but he did once concede: 'I have had too much concern with ideas and work and things, and too little concern with people.' He attempted to remedy the fault in his later years, but his closest friends remained his oldest, Billie Richardson and Horace Jarvis.

The three met when Bull began teaching in south London in 1933, living on a salary of £173 per year and occupying digs in various places until he found a flat in Balham. In notes prepared in 1969 Bull reflected on Life In London:

Varied and interesting. Attended courses at the City Literary Institute on economics, political economy and drama: founded chess club and soon became captain and ran the club. Spent weekends camping at Chertsey, Happy days, Played [imaginary] chess on Sunday mornings while swimming from Chertsey to Shepperton Lock. Came to conclusion had not capabilities and interests requisite to success as dramatist.

In a letter to the Yorkshire industrialist Bill Rooney, dated 5 November 1986, Bull recalled how the trio first met:

One evening, on impulse, I walked into the City Literary Institute in Holborn. My intention, having written two or three one-act plays, was possibly to join their dramatic society. As I walked through the foyer I noticed two chaps playing chess, and went to sit and watch for a few minutes. They were Billie Richardson and Horace Jarvis (a paper merchant's son), and so began three lifetime friendships. We pursued many activities together.

Richardson spent his childhood in Calderdale, where his father originally had a textile business, and he retained an attachment to this region of West Yorkshire, though he later lived in Harrow. Their friendship extended to Richardson's handling the advertising for *Temple Racetime Analysis* and *Best Horses*, and his being the registered owner when the Jockey Club prevented Lady Electra and Anne of Essex from carrying Bull's name in 1943. It even survived Richardson's conservatism—Bull's description— and an obvious difference in philosophical outlook, to which Bull referred in a letter to Richardson, dated 25 May 1984, enclosing a copy of a book by Jenny Pearce. He gives the clear impression that Richardson—ten years Bull's senior—would not be able fully to appreciate the gift:

I don't know how much you remember of the time when you and I and Horace Jarvis attended E. C. Fairchild's lectures at the City Literary Institute in the 1930s. I don't know what effect he had on you, but he educated me, economically. Since then my education has been influenced by people like Noam Chomsky, Tarik Ali and many others. And now by a woman, Jenny Pearce. Actually, she doesn't educate me, she merely provides me with the documentation that confirms and reinforces my previous education. Do you have the patience at 82 years of age to read these things? Do you retain any concerns about the exploitation of the Third World by American dollar imperialism? I suspect not.

Years ago you educated me. You told me once—and I have never forgotten it—that there were no imperatives which demanded of a man that he should fight for anything. If a man, you said, wished to spend his life contemplating his own navel, while lying on a warm beach, eating the fruit that fell into his lap, there was no categorical imperatives requiring that he should do otherwise. I was compelled to agree with you. But such acquiescence in a negative attitude to life (rational as it is) was never agreeable, never commended itself to me. And forty years later I feel exactly the same way.

Philosophically you were quite right. But while I'm alive, laddie, I'm still a purposive individual, and I can't divest myself of this purposive drive to make the world a better place to live in, even though I know damn well I won't be around to live in it. That's the difference between us, you see. I'm built and conditioned one way, and you the other. In fact we are still playing out the hands that we were dealt when we were young, still playing them out as we were conditioned to do.

On returning to Yorkshire, Bull saw Richardson regularly and made various attempts to see that he was cared for after his wife died in 1985. Contact with Horace Jarvis, before his death in the Seventies, was more sporadic but the friendship was no less soundly based, since Jarvis was both a chess fan and a socialist. However, Jarvis singularly failed to exert any professional influence on Bull in his role as a naturotherapist. He also practised osteopathy and physiotherapy and ran a school for these pursuits in Croydon.

Jarvis visited his old friend in Yorkshire for the first time in 1958. In a letter dated 24 November, he noted: 'To put it mildly you are to be congratulated on your amazing success. You certainly live differently from your early days of stormy adventures in London.' Then he delivered the professional diagnosis: 'Your health condition interested me. To put it bluntly and frankly, as one old friend to another, you might last three years with your present method of living—or if you got down to it as you are obviously capable of, you might have another 30 years to look forward to.

'One thing you would have to do is to get some dentures that would prepare your food for digestion, and save you from trying to live on refined foods. I've an old friend who lives as you do because without teeth he can't digest wholemeal bread and many other things, and he is thus cutting his life short, and living on a deficient diet. This has in your case partly led to diabetes (a condition in which the digestive system starts to break down). I would bet that no insurance company would accept you for a policy for three years.

'I suggest that firstly you get some dentures, and stop bluffing yourself and kidding others that you can get by. Then get down to a good natural diet that will build health and stop the rot which has set in and threatens to get rapidly worse. You are at the crossroads now and can't afford to wait a couple of years, for it might then be too late. I think that you can still revolutionise your life in this direction. You know enough about Nature Cure and diet to appreciate that the only thing that matters is what you do. Action is the only prayer that's answered.

'A few of my leaflets enclosed. If I can help you in any way, I will. If on the other hand you think that I am a crackpot and got it all wrong, then put this in the waste-paper basket and prepare for kingdom come thirty years before your time.'

Nature Cure was Jarvis's field; it held not the slightest interest to Bull, who despite his friend's direst warning continued to follow the same lifestyle, and still lived for another 30 years. Bull had had all his teeth extracted in 1952 and never bothered with dentures, and he managed to diet around his diabetes. He provided an update on his health a few years before Jarvis died, in a letter dated 11 October 1971:

My health seems good. At the last check-up my tame witch doctor expressed (with some surprise) the view that if my blood pressure was anything to go by, I'd live to be a hundred. I think there's a big genetic element in this. My father was the same. He died at 85. When the embalmer drained the blood out of his corpse, he said that on the evidence of the old chap's arteries he'd have lived another 20 years. It was his digestive system that packed up. That, I expect, is what'll kill me.

Mind you, I take good care of myself. I have cut out all violent exercise and stressful activities like chess. I smoke 15 cigars and drink two bottles of wine every day without fail. And just to keep the old blood pressure in order I occasionally have five or six thousand pounds on a horse, as I did yesterday. D'you know, it doesn't raise my heart rate a couple of beats! Frankly, I wouldn't know what I could do that would excite me, since I gave up chasing the other sex and playing chess.

And of course there's another reason for my good health. I don't have any teeth, natural or artificial. So I don't go to work on such things as raw carrots or nuts or dog biscuits or celery.

The same letter illustrated Bull's bluntness, his commitment to personal honesty which he felt others should share, whether they were willing partners or not. Jarvis had mentioned having written a pamphlet on pollution—'It cannot be solved under capitalism any more than can war, crises, unemployment and poverty in the midst of potential plenty'—but expressed disappointment that he had not been able to find a publisher. Bull replied:

You don't surprise me when you tell me that neither Gollancz nor the Fabian Society would publish your pamphlet. The trouble with you, where your writings are concerned, is not with your ideas, with what you have to say—you have plenty to say, and you can be humorous and witty about it—but you can't bloody well use the English language. You can't *write* effectively.

Now forgive me for being blunt about this. I should have said it to you years ago. Editors and publishers are begging for books and copy. Only last week I had three new books sent to me by a publisher asking for me to review them. I sent 'em back and told them I hadn't the time to bother with them. Just reflect for a minute. Malcolm Muggeridge, Peregrine Worsthorne, Bernard Levin and such twits could get anything they wrote snapped up for publication on the dot. Why? They can't even think straight. They haven't got any of your understanding. But what they can do is write interesting and lively copy in first-class English. You can't.

You've sent me a lot of things full of interesting ideas, wit and humour, but I couldn't contemplate publishing any of them. Why? Because every one of them would have to be re-written from front to back in good, skilful, effective English. When a publisher receives a manuscript from you, the shortcomings of your English jump out at him from its pages and put him off any further consideration of the copy. It's a great pity. But that's the truth of it, brother.

Bull's passion for chess started at an early age, and despite his expressing comments to the contrary at various times and to various people, he retained the interest till late in his life. In a letter to James Adams dated 29 October 1986, he explained:

I played chess as a boy. At university I ran, captained and played first board for Leeds University and second board for the Northern Universities against Oxford on the one occasion such a fixture was held. I recall I played a blind opponent and had to be content with a draw. When I left Leeds and went to London as a teacher, I joined the City Literary Institute, took over as first board and captain, playing in the London league. With a couple of friends [Jarvis and Richardson] we rented a chalet on the banks of the Thames at Chertsey, for week-ends, and every Sunday morning we made a practice of swimming down the Thames from Chertsey to Shepperton Lock, playing a 'blindfold' game on the way.

On one occasion at the City Literary Institute I played three games simultaneously blindfold, against weak players, of course, winning one and drawing the other two. I was a fair player in those days. But of course the war put a stop to things and from then on I was far too involved in racing, writing those *Best Horses* books, starting Timeform and getting involved with owning, breeding, the Racehorse Owners Association, the Thoroughbred Breeders Association, etc, etc, ending up with chairmanship of the Horseracing Advisory Council, which I relinquished after six months.

So, of course, I played no chess from 1939 until about six or seven years ago, when I joined the Halifax Chess Club and sought to put some snap and vitality into the Calderdale Chess Championship. I discovered two things: that my chess had deteriorated, and that the local chess people had no idea of organising or running anything. So nowadays I just amuse myself by playing against the chess computers. I've had half-a-dozen of them, and presently have three.

Chess computers will eventually be so good that only Grandmasters will have much hope of beating them. And obviously they will kill correspondence chess—if they haven't done so already. Personally I've never played a single game by correspondence, though one [Jarvis] of the two friends who shared the chalet at Chertsey before the war always had ten or a dozen games running with people in various countries. It never appealed to me.

> Though Bull believed he could have been good enough to become a professional chess player—just as, at certain times, he thought he could have been a professional playwright or snooker player, or made a living from the Stock Exchange—the evidence suggests he was up to decent club standard at best. Whether, as he said, his chess had deteriorated over the years, or he had simply over-rated his ability, is open to question. His support for the first Calderdale Chess Championship in 1980 included prize money of £1,000, ten times that which a local event would normally offer. He told a correspondent in a letter dated 17 February 1981:

It cost me, or Timeform rather, roughly £2,000 to put on the show, including a cocktail party for forty people at The Hollins. Now we're off again with the 1981 championship, with £1,300 prize money, which will cost my company some £2,500, all told. We have an exceptionally strong entry this time, nineteen of them, of which I'm one, participating in an all-play-all tournament which won't be concluded till next December. I doubt whether I'll be good enough to finish higher than fourteenth or fifteenth. Anyhow, it'll be a testing experience, not to be run away from. All rounds in the tournament are to be played at The Hollins.

Bull's interest, and Timeform's involvement, quickly waned and died when he finished on the bottom two rungs of the league-table ladder.

His grand schemes also extended to his second great sporting passion, snooker. Dick Whitford recalls how he reacted to entertaining the world champion Joe Davis at The Hollins: 'Phil had ordered a new tournament-sized table in honour of the champion, but when it was delivered three days before Davis was due to arrive, it transpired that the doors and hallways of the house couldn't be negotiated by such a huge object. So the granite frames and leaded windows of the main lounge had to be dismantled and re-installed at short notice.'

The table was bought in 1947 from a Leeds company owned jointly by another world champion, Willie Smith. It cost £176 (about £3,350 in today's terms) and was ordered before being used for a tournament at Leeds Town Hall, with Bull specifically requesting that it be delivered with a plate attached to indicate its matchplay origin.

Guests at The Hollins testify to the seriousness with which Bull—who presented his old school, Hemsworth Grammar, with a billiard table in 1945—tackled even the friendliest of snooker games. He would quickly pounce on the most innocuous and unintentional example of foul play. One onlooker recalls when Bull was playing the Racecourse Association chairman Brookie Brooks, whose tie innocently fell on to the table and brushed the black ball. When Brooks apologised, Bull replied: 'Never mind sorry; seven away, brother,' as he marked the score accordingly.

Joe Davis was a regular member of house parties at The Hollins for racing at York and Doncaster. He and Bull remained friends, though there were times when feelings between them were not the most sanguine. Davis was a keen punter and always anxious to discuss form; when Bull played snooker, he played to win. The stakes did not matter to Bull, as he explained in a letter to Hugh McIlvanney, dated 17 March 1975, when he complimented the *Observer* sports writer on a feature he had written about him. Bull added a comment about the newspaper's racing correspondent:

Dick Baerlein is wrong in his assertion that I'm a different player on the snooker table when the money is down. Nothing could be further from the truth. I play with the same concentration for peanuts as for pounds, ponies or monkeys. I play against myself. Really, I don't know what Dick was thinking about to miss this point.

Bull's dedicated approach appears to have been mirrored on occasions by Joe Davis. In a letter dated 21 September 1975 to the political journalist Peter Jenkins, who had been on the end of a practical lesson from Davis, Bull wrote:

Joe is a disaster in a snooker room. He's right, of course, about your cue hold—indeed, your whole stance and address of the ball need putting right—but to keep on and on about things as he does is exasperating. I've been on the end of it so often that I now slap down on him hard. On one occasion I told him I'd turn him out of the room if he didn't behave himself. He's the personification of the retired *prima donna*!

Despite the irritations Bull retained his great affection for Davis, and on his death in 1978 he wrote, in a tribute in *The Sporting Life*: 'Joe was my friend for forty years. He was excellent company. Many a night we've talked well into the small hours on all sorts of subjects.' Bull saw some of his own reflection in Davis. In an address at a memorial service for Davis on 19 September 1978, Bull said:

His father was a coal-miner in a little village in Derbyshire, who managed to get out of the pits, as did my father in Yorkshire: his mother, like mine, was hardworking, resourceful and enterprising. So Joe, like me, escaped the worst of the poverty of the early years of the century, when barefoot, bandy-legged children with rickets were a common sight, and many went hungry.

Joe was a fighter. Always in there to win: aggressive and determined; but without a scintilla of unkindliness about him. For me the wealth of one's life is in its personal relationships: my life has been immeasurably enriched by knowing Joe Davis.

Not all professional snooker players had the same effect on Bull, who got more than he bargained for when he invited another hardened racing fan, Alex Higgins, back to Halifax after the York May meeting in 1978. Bull made his feelings known in the course of a telephone conversation to trainer Barry Hills, who had been at York:

Hurricane Higgins—he's a wrong sort of guy: he's a hustler and a cowboy. All he was doing with me was trying to get money off me.

He didn't succeed. I was playing for a tenner but he wanted a bet and said £500. We agreed on £250. I was contemptuous about it and he beat me. He wanted to play again, double or quits, so I played him and beat him. Then he wanted to play a third time, six o'clock in the bloody morning, so I tore him off a strip. He sulked for twenty minutes and wouldn't speak, and when he saw he wasn't going to get another game, he went to bed.

He can play. Christ I've never seen anybody pot balls at the pace that he can. He hits the ball so hard it scares the life out of you. You think the ball's going to go up in the air and through the bloody ceiling. Absolutely fantastic, but a deplorable guy.

> Purchasing The Hollins was the achievement of a lifetime for Bull. Built in about 1810 by the Dearden family, it was described in the property section of the Halifax *Evening Courier* in 1990, when put on the market following Bull's death, as 'probably the nearest thing to a castle in Calderdale'. It was the third house on the secluded 27-acre site, the first having been erected in the 14th Century. The only sign of the previous houses is a massive stone fireplace, inscribed with the date 1632, in the billiards room. The name 'Hollins' is mentioned in a noted diary of 1672, and the house was besieged in the Civil War, with the Battle of the Hollins being on record.
>
> Bull bought The Hollins in 1946 from the Ramsden family, who owned the *Courier* newspaper; he paid £8,750 (around £174,000 in today's terms). He had returned to Yorkshire in 1945, still owning a detached house in Putney purchased for £1,300 in 1940, when property prices were depressed on account of the Blitz. Back in his home surroundings of Hemsworth, he paid £1,650 for Windy Nook, into which his sister May moved when Bull lighted on The Hollins, after he had inspected both Rillington Manor, in North Yorkshire, and Nostell Priory, near Wakefield. In March 1947, when Bull was negotiating a loan from the Hemsworth branch of Barclays Bank—'This is my first experience of running an overdraft with a bank, or with borrowing at all, and you may be assured I shall take steps to terminate it as soon as I am able to put horses through the sale ring next July or October'—The Hollins had already appreciated to an estimated value of £10-15,000. In a financial statement made to the bank manager at the time, his summary of assets, comprising three houses, furniture and bloodstock, stood at £71,100 (about £1.37 million in today's terms).
>
> Dick Whitford recalls the day that Bull settled on The Hollins: 'Phil had wanted the house for quite a time but he was

either unwilling or unable to meet the asking price. He bided his time, and one grey afternoon at Manchester races he set out to land a big win on the last two races. Both horses won, and gained him The Hollins with some to spare. On the way home we stopped off in Halifax and drove down the mile-long drive at The Hollins, where he shook hands on the deal with Mr Ramsden. He was full of himself, and much to Mrs Ramsden's astonishment he gave her a luck-penny of £500. From the look on her face she was not used to being handed bundles of used five-pound notes over her afternoon tea, but she didn't refuse them.'

Bull paid a ten per cent deposit by cheque dated 1 June 1946 and lived at The Hollins till his death. He delighted in explaining his version of the origin of the name, as in a letter to a correspondent in West Germany, dated 23 May 1982:

It means Holy-place. It's appropriately named. One of the earliest owners of the place, around 1680, was convicted of urinating on the gravestones in the local churchyard and went to prison for blasphemy in consequence. And I am, of course, an atheist. I'm quite happy to be living in a holy place!

Surrounded by crenellated walls, The Hollins was described by the estate agents handling its sale in 1990 as 'a castle-like building with a fine Norman tower'. An imposing front door at the base of the tower opens into a circular hallway, from which the main hall leads into a drawing room, library/study, billiards room and dining room, and beyond to a sitting room and the kitchens.

Up the winding stone staircase featured at the start of Citizen Bull, the first floor comprises eight bedrooms and four bathrooms, the majority bearing the names of significant horses in Bull's career as owner and breeder—Orgoglio, Philoctetes, Anne of Essex, Lady Electra, Anadem, Orinthia, Orienne, Aureoletta, Dionisio, Sostenuto and Pheidippides.

In the grounds the main entrance gates are flanked by turreted gatehouses. A stone-flagged terrace leads to a small folly with a semi-circular seat, and steps descend to a croquet lawn and tennis court. A cannon stood guard outside the house, and among the acres of woodland, orchard and permanent pasture there was a single bronze figure, the Thracian Falconer, known locally as the Iron Man. It was the work of a local sculptor, Joseph Bentley Leyland, who died in 1851. In 1927, after spending 60 years in the grounds of a house in Halifax, it was bought by a scrap dealer for a few pounds, but before it could be broken up, the figure was rescued and taken to The Hollins.

The mounting cost of upkeep and the vagaries of Bull's personal cash flow meant that essential maintenance was not regularly carried out on The Hollins. When the property was put on the market in October 1990, offers were invited around £500,000, and it was sold to a Bradford businessman for £480,000. His company subsequently collapsed, and the bank sold The Hollins—minus a number of its moveable features—to its present owner, who has expressed the intention to restore the house to its former glory.

As well as enjoying chess, snooker, bridge and, very occasionally in his earlier years, golf, Bull had a passion for music. In his autobiographical notes of 1969 he remarked: 'Suppose most important hobby now is the panorama of life and trying to understand all that is happening in the world.' He also noted: 'One shouldn't take one's hobbies too seriously'—which may surprise those who were asked to provide opposition at snooker—but he did mark down music as 'very important', adding 'Mozart, Haydn, Beethoven: play piano (rather badly).'

Bull's mother Dolly taught music at school and privately, and both Phil and his sister May learned to play the piano, though May recalls: 'Phil had only a few lessons; the rest he taught himself.' Bull also took violin lessons as a boy, and he and May, playing piano and singing, would entertain with duets.

Expanding on his 1969 notes, Bull wrote:

Music means much to me. The grace of Mozart, the power of Beethoven, the warmth, humour and humanity of Haydn, delight me. Mozart is the one person in history who has all my admiration. Flawless in character and in his music. A man who deserved far more from life than it gave him. For a marvellous person like Mozart to die, penniless at 35 years of age, hardly at the peak of powers, with such a wealth of music still to give—I can never think of it without a sense of infinite sadness.

Dick Whitford remembers how, on moving into The Hollins, Bull had the library stripped and fitted with racks to take his gramophone records. Whitford recalls: "He wanted "all the symphonies and all the concertos" of this and that composer. The shelves were soon ready but he had to find the records up and down the country. All those 78s must have cost a fortune, though I suppose to Phil it was "just another bet".'

Bull referred to some of the collection in letters, dated 4 and 26 November 1973, to the *Observer* columnist Kenneth Harris, who had presented Bull with a collection of Mozart's piano music on a dozen records:

Years ago I bought the whole of Schnabel's recording of Beethoven's piano music, on 78s, of course, and with all the surface noise and hiss. Collectors' items now, I guess.

I must have half a ton of classical 78s from the 1930s—stored away somewhere and never played.

While Timeform employees were encouraged, even implored, from time to time to visit The Hollins to play chess, snooker or tennis against Bull, the house was at its busiest when important race meetings were taking place in the locality and Bull would host house parties.

Most of his friends and acquaintances inevitably came from the ranks of those associated with horseracing. His pursuit of political truths did not always make for easy conversation; nor did his abhorrence of small talk. Reg Griffin recalls: 'If at a cocktail party a woman approached and sought a compliment about her perfume or what she was wearing, and Phil didn't like either, he couldn't do like most of us and make some inoffensive, diplomatic remark. He'd have to say, "No, I think it's awful", or, "No, it doesn't suit you." He couldn't bring himself to tell a lie.'

Even among his closest friends Bull rarely relaxed his guard. He regularly took winter holidays in Jamaica, where William Hill had a house at Montego Bay, but doing nothing under the sun was not his idea of a holiday. He hated being in the sun, for one thing. Griffin remembers Bull's outlook: 'Holidays were for other people; he wanted to be doing something. If there was a racecourse nearby, he'd go there; if there were studs to see, he'd go and see them; if somebody played cards or snooker, he did that. You didn't sit around doing nothing. And after we'd come back from the races and we would begin to think about dining out, he'd often say, "I'm not going, I'll have soup and cheese here". And he'd leave me to take his wife Patricia to dinner.

'One year William Hill invited him to Jamaica, and said he'd meet him in Miami, to go to the Flamingo Ball, before travelling on to Montego Bay. Phil agreed, but when I picked him up at the airport at the end of the holiday, he was very quiet. I finally asked him if he had had an enjoyable time, and his answer was, "No, I certainly did not. I find William Hill objectionable; I find the people he associates with objectionable, and I want nothing more to do with him." It looked like thirty years' friendship down the drain in two weeks, but later I heard the story from William Hill.

'They had gone to the ball and were at the bar. Whereas William Hill was socialising, talking to people, Phil spent the whole of the time playing with a handheld game at the end of the bar, manoeuvring metal balls into holes. That's how much he

305

contributed to the evening. Then when they went to William's place in Jamaica, he had to get Phil out of bed one night to join the other people staying there. Phil made straight for the swimming pool and began doing the backstroke, his cigar in his mouth, going up and down as if it was a marathon. He was obviously bored with the whole thing, bored with the people, and bored with the place. Knowing he had to put up with it for two weeks, he had decided he would make himself objectionable to everyone else, whom he thought were objectionable anyway.

'It made no difference to the relationship between Phil and William Hill. They soon carried on as normal. But of course William used to bait Phil, teasing him to see how he would react. And Phil always fell for it, even though he thought he knew William better than anyone else.'

Griffin believes Bull was a poor judge of character. 'And Phil would sometimes admit it,' he says. 'He would come up with the most extraordinary people and welcome them into his home. He would think they were wonderful, but the only thing they had in common were extreme Left-wing views. Some of them definitely took advantage of him. There was a couple he met when he spoke at Bradford University, and they would go up to The Hollins and be invited to his box at the races. They were supposed to be Communists but they didn't mind enjoying all the trimmings of capitalism that Phil could offer. No doubt Phil had an answer. He could explain logically almost any circumstance that came along. He would have been able to explain the fall of the Berlin Wall, the fall of Communism, the fall of the Soviet Union, even the fall of the Jockey Club, though he couldn't have imagined any of them happening in his lifetime. He had an answer for most things.'

Insensitive to some of those whose opinions he did not share, Bull was also more susceptible than most to a hard-luck story. His concern stretched to the limits of naivety at times, as in the case of a man who wrote to him in December 1968 seeking advice about employment in the racing industry. When Bull replied asking for more information, the man wrote back: 'What I have to say will, I am sure, automatically disqualify me from any further consideration. I have a conviction for murder and am at present completing a life sentence.'

Far from disqualifying the writer, his situation stirred Bull into making every effort to help him over the next ten years, even to the extent of suggesting to at least one Timeform director that he should be given a job in the office once he left prison. Bull was unable to appreciate that he could not keep the man's conviction from the staff. 'They won't know,' he said. And then, when told they would have to be informed, he replied, 'I'll close the firm before I'll be dictated to.' The threat soon passed, and Bull admitted in a letter to the man: 'If [the conviction] became known among my staff, it might possibly create difficulties with them.' But Bull entertained him at The Hollins for weekends, took him racing, and continued to correspond at great length when he left prison and settled in Bradford.

The consuming written contact survived the man's recall to jail, when a threat of violence against his wife was regarded as a breach of his probation. Bull continued to see the good side of him, encouraging him to look forward. 'Gird up the loins and get cracking—not welding, or screwing nuts on bolts, to earn the daily bread, necessary though it is—get cracking on something rewarding, pleasureable, something that gives you satisfaction,' he wrote. 'Find it! Enjoy life, young man.' But the welter of advice proved largely unfruitful, and eventually Bull terminated the contact since it became a nuisance he could well do without.

Just once—on record at least—Bull was taken in totally by a less than genuine approach to his good nature. In the summer of 1975 he was approached by 'Prince Faisal of Saudi Arabia', who asked if Bull could assist him with his betting, 'outside the normal services provided by your Timeform Organisation'. In a letter addressed to 'Faisal House, Ashtree Estate, Stevenage', Bull said he would be 'happy to explore things with you if you wish', and so began two months of growing interest from 'Prince Faisal', who was given Bull's personal attention on betting matters, as well as detailed advice on how to mount an approach to buy the William Hill Studs at Whitsbury and Sezincote, and the late Arpad Plesch's Dollanstown Stud in Ireland.

A proposed visit to The Hollins in August was cancelled at the last minute; 'Prince Faisal' had to go to Saudi Arabia for fourteen days, Bull was informed in a telephone call taken by his son. Not to be denied, Bull assured 'Prince Faisal' that 'the field below my back drive would present no difficulty to the landing of twenty helicopters'. He dispatched air navigation and Ordnance Survey maps, and details of beacon bearings and distances, for the pilot, ready for when a meeting could be arranged. There was to be no visit; in this case there was no 'Prince Faisal of Saudi Arabia'.

However, there was no shortage of visitors to The Hollins for the major northern racing festivals, and Bull enjoyed the hospitality of a growing circle as he travelled the country to attend major race meetings. He referred to the group he most cherished as the Woburn Club, since it centred on the well-known home of

Lord and Lady Tavistock. Among their closest associates at the time were Lord Chelsea and his first wife Philippa.

Bull was captivated by Henrietta Tavistock, Philippa Chelsea and the third notable female member of the set, Countess Bunny Esterhazy, daughter of Mrs Etty Plesch, and he carried on lengthy and deeply personal correspondence with both Lady Tavistock and Countess Esterhazy. 'You understand me,' he once wrote to Countess Esterhazy, 'better than anybody else does, probably.' She also appeared regularly on his list for late-night telephone calls.

Most of Bull's lasting acquaintances came from the racing connection. They included Harry Ely, an owner with horses trained mainly in France, who had to keep his involvement largely secret, for fear of incurring the wrath of his mother, and spent most of the year travelling around Europe. They first met in 1940, when Ely was invited by the jockey Brownie Carslake to visit Cecil Ray's stable, where Bull had his first horses in training.

Holiday visits to Jamaica resulted in lengthy associations with the Kingston solicitor Harry Dayes and bookmaker Frank Watson, both of whom regularly visited Bull to go racing during the English summer. And the betting business brought him into close contact with Danny Cooper-Smith, who from his home in London would cover the country acting as commission agent after it became increasingly difficult for Bull to place bets at what he considered 'value' prices.

In the last fifteen years of his life Bull reserved his highest regard for George Wigg, the Labour peer who became chairman of the Betting Levy Board and had almost as great a loathing for the institution of the Jockey Club as did Bull. Reg Griffin recalls: 'Phil respected a lot of people when he found they objected to the Establishment and he made a point of introducing himself. Phil respected George Wigg because he stood up to the Jockey Club and made it clear that the Levy Board would dispense its money how he wanted, and not how the Jockey Club wanted. Phil regarded most other Levy Board chairmen as tools of the Jockey Club.'

Bull expressed his admiration for Wigg in a letter to him dated 25 March 1973, the year after his retirement from the Levy Board:

The journey, for you, was a rough and forthright, fighting one, but there were pleasures on the way, and you have the satisfaction of knowing that you put such a lot of things straight and changed the racing scene in a way that no-one else could have done—changed it irreversibly for the good, practically single-handed, against heavily entrenched traditional attitudes and stupidities. Maybe you are glad to be rid of it all now, but it was a fight worth winning (in the little field of racing), and you won it. It's something to be pleased about—and there are a lot of people in racing who appreciate it, I assure you.

I don't know your successor, Stanley Raymond, except by observation from the sideline, but judging from that and from what I'm told, the outlook is dim. Lord Leverhulme will be no improvement on Gerry Feilden, who retires [as Jockey Club senior steward] in July.

Bull kept in close touch with Wigg in the following years. He updated his feelings—with the almost inevitable digression and critical personal observation—in a letter to him dated 24 May 1981, the year after Bull's brief chairmanship of the Horseracing Advisory Council:

I have enormous admiration for you. You are the best thing that ever happened to racing. You shook it up. You took the stupid Jockey Club by the scruff of the neck and showed 'em where they got off. Since you vacated the Chairmanship of the Levy Board the Jockey Club has regained command and they are again lousing things up right, left and centre. I had a bit of a chance to fight 'em when I took on Chairmanship of the HAC, but I wasn't equal to the task. I couldn't carry the HAC with me. I haven't your political skills. So I turned it in, and opted out. And I did it in the mildest and gentlest way, so as not to rock the boat and not to embarrass my successor, General Bernard Penfold.

I was wrong. I should have gone out with a bang and made an issue of it—I should have done things in such a way that the bang would have been heard in the Home Office. Truth is I'm not cut out for internecine fighting. I'm too old for it. And, most of all, I recognise that, by comparison with what is happening in the world at large, the whole racing thing is a triviality. It's my pond. I know all about it (excuse the exaggeration). But really, towards the end of my life, it's too small and unimportant a pond for me to get myself fashed up about, if you know what I mean.

Let me get back to you. And bear with me while I say what I have to say, and don't take it to heart. Take it to head, not to heart. We are both of us old men, well able to bear frankness.

As a parliamentarian you have no superiors that I know of. In the House of Lords you are the only person who knows the score about racing and can spell it out lucidly and authoritatively. A lone voice, but a very, very loud and powerful one. Much depends on you.

But politically, in your view of world events and the way things are going you seem to me not to have got out of the third form. And philosophically, your so-called teleological view of life and belief in god—capital G if you like—is really too silly.

I don't regard this latter point as a side issue of little consequence. People tend to put their beliefs, especially religious beliefs, in little protected boxes, divorced from their attitudes to life and their motivations in the business of living. But in practice they don't stay there. They louse up their thinking about everything. It is not an accident that Christians and Moslems are killing one another in Northern Ireland and the Middle East. They've been crucifying and torturing people for two thousand years. Always the religious people are to be found aligned with repression, preservation of the *status quo*, on behalf of wealth and property.

Enough! Enough of that. You and I are presently engaged in the little racing scene. We're stuck with it, because our lives have got us involved in it, and we're too old to start afresh. It's been suggested that I should be the principal speaker at the St Leger dinner next September. I toy with the idea that I will accept the invitation: that I will reject my natural tendency to be good humoured and agreeable to everyone, and will take up the sword against the Jockey Club and the Levy Board and mince no words, regardless of what enemies it makes for me. Would you be with me? Would you help me?

I have an alternative, you know. I can simply continue my retirement, decline the invitation, and say what I have to say later, in memoirs or Press articles. The chicken's way out? I suppose so. They offer me a platform—not the best platform, of course—but one I think I could turn to good account. You, I guess, would counsel me to take it. I probably will. But I'll certainly wish to have the benefit of your vetting and advice on what I would say.

There was no St Leger dinner that year: George Wigg died in August 1983, and Bull's fire had already begun to be extinguished. Even his 'chicken's way out', through Press articles, was rarely used, and his memoirs strayed no farther than a collection of handwritten notes, detailing the sub-headings of his life and the main works he had produced. However, he continued to observe the passage of the outside world through increasingly critical eyes, and among those he entertained at The Hollins were the locally-based businessmen Lord Kagan, the Lithuanian-born producer of the Gannex raincoat so favoured by his foremost

admirer Harold Wilson, and Bill Rooney, founder of the Spring
Ram kitchen manufacturing company.

Joe Kagan was also a student at Leeds University, four years
after Bull had left for London. Caught by the Germans on his
return to Lithuania for a holiday in the early days of the war, he
escaped back to England in 1946, shortly after Bull had returned
to Yorkshire, and founded Kagan Textiles a few miles from
Halifax. Bull met Kagan—a chess player and fellow Labour
supporter who had made money in a capitalist society—in
November 1975, and in thanks wrote:

It is not often one is invited to someone's home for the first time
and finds oneself unconstrained and at ease. Says much for the host!

Re your question: Am I a socialist? The short answer is yes. My
father was one of the founders of the Labour Party. He used to chair
meetings at which Ramsay MacDonald and Philip Snowden were
speakers. I know some of the present-day politicians—Foot, Wigg,
Howell and trade unionists like Ray Gunter, Vic Feather, etc. And
others, of course, but not Harold Wilson.

The following year Bull came up with a proposition—'and
it's for serious'—which he put to Kagan in a letter dated 5 July
1976:

How about the pair of us taking a three weeks' trip to Cuba this
winter? I want to find out for myself about these new efforts to
restructure society on a non-capitalist basis. Russia is out, China's
too big and there are other objections: but Cuba shouldn't be too
inaccessible, and it seems to me the right ideas and attitudes are there.
Not a place for millionaires or comforts, of course—but that isn't the
issue. What about it? You should have no difficulties arranging visas,
and perhaps access to the old revolutionary [Fidel Castro] himself.
I'm serious. I'll go if you will: in fact, I'll go if you won't, and fend
for myself. But I'd much rather go with you as an argumentative
companion. If we run out of disputation, we could always play chess!

Winter passed without the trip taking place; four years later
Kagan was in prison. In December 1980 he was sentenced to ten
months' imprisonment on four charges of theft and three of false
accounting, personally fined a total of £56,000, and his company
ordered to pay a £375,000 fine for evasion of Corporation Tax and
Customs duties. Bull wrote to Kagan in prison, apologising that
'I have been negligent in not making a forthright effort to get to

see you', suggesting he was 'much too tough and realistic a guy to be oppressed unduly by a temporary deprivation of liberty', and keeping him up to date with the latest news of Bunny Esterhazy and Philippa Chelsea, and the Calderdale Chess Championship.

As an aside to this friendship, when Kagan died in January 1995, details of his private life were given greater publicity than had been the case previously. They included an affair with a woman journalist which resulted in the birth of a son, who was adopted at the age of three and prevented by law from contact with his natural father. A newspaper account of the liaison described Kagan as 'a sexual predator' who 'was later to boast of forty other lovers by the time he'd reached 60'. Some of the details were probably known to Bull. He would have been intrigued, since his own eye for a pretty and often much younger woman was well known, but whether he would have approved is doubtful, since he frowned upon a similar side to William Hill's character, describing his attitude towards women as 'deplorable'.

As for Cuba, Bull still hankered after visiting the island, and again talked of going there in March 1985. He promised as much to Hermes Herrera, the Cuban Ambassador in Britain, who dined at The Hollins in December 1984. Their correspondence illustrated Bull's lifelong devotion to cigars. After Herrera had specially arranged for a Cuban cigar-maker to produce a type he thought Bull would enjoy, Bull replied:

How very kind of you. The three I have smoked were very good, though somewhat on the thick side for my toothless gums! I much appreciate your having sought to find a cigar that might suit me. I have, of course, smoked hundreds of Cuban cigars of all the well-known brands, Upmanns, Montecristo, Romeo & Juliet and Partagas, mostly. Perhaps what I should do when I get to Cuba is to pay a visit to one or two of the manufacturers and obtain an assorted selection, with a view to importing a consignment of a thousand or more. There is, as I daresay you know, quite a demand among racehorse owners for Cuban cigars, though the rapacity of the British Treasury prices them out of the reach of most people.

Smoking the country's cigars proved to be the closest Bull got to Cuba. On 18 February 1985 he wrote to Ambassador Herrera:

Regretfully, circumstances and events over which I have no control have conspired to compel me to postpone my projected visit to Cuba this spring. I am extremely disappointed, not to say angered, about this: but it is, you may be sure, only a postponement.

It is, of course, very much on my mind that you will doubtless have written already to several persons in Havana regarding my projected visit, and I'm conscious of the trouble you must have been to on my behalf. For this please accept my most sincere apologies.

There is no evidence of 'circumstances and events' so serious that Bull would have been necessarily forced to cancel his trip. It was more likely another grand idea which simply did not materialise, and the postponement became permanent. However, Bull did continue to support Cuba's cigar industry, once telling a member of the Timeform staff—with little obvious regard for sensitivity or morale—that he spent more on cigars in a year than the employee received in annual salary.

Despite being one of the most instantly recognised personalities on the British horseracing scene, Bull cut a lone figure in the last fifteen years of his life. There was no shortage of support for his Timeform advice; many agreed with his views on racing, its administrators and its politics; he had a wide circle of social acquaintances. But he still searched for closer relationships. He referred to his situation in the midst of a nineteen-page, handwritten letter to Bunny Esterhazy in 1979:

I am 'alone' only in the sense that I have a view of the world that is not shared by anyone else I know—though it is shared by many people I don't know, whom I could name.

This aloneness does not distress me. I have long been accustomed to it and, I suppose, resigned to it. But not so resigned to have lost the hope of having meaningful communication with someone. This, essentially, was at the root of those long letters I used to write. Philippa told me, some time ago, that the recipient ran away from the sexual element in those letters. I don't remember the exact words used, but this was the content of them. It surprised me. The suggestion that there was something sexual about them. Not true at all, so far as I recall—love, yes; but not sexuality. And yet, of course, there must have been some sexual aspect to it.

Bull had referred to his 'being alone', also to Bunny Esterhazy, in a letter written a few years earlier, when he highlighted one aspect of his character which he felt might have let him down:

313

Someone once said that the trouble with me was that I was lonely. They were wrong. I'm not in the least lonely: but I am certainly alone, which is a very different thing. Alone, but far from lonely.

One of the things that makes me so is fastidiousness—physical and intellectual fastidiousness. I don't know whether it's a fault or a quality. I'm fastidious in innumerable ways. I can't bear my hands, or any part of my body, to be other than one hundred per cent clean, and to feel clean. I dislike untidiness in the office or at home; intellectually I detest slovenly argument, loose thinking; and where women are concerned I could no more fall in love with coarse features or a gross figure than I could swim the Atlantic, quite apart from the mental requirements.

Golda Meir [Israeli prime minister] might have had the best brain around (she didn't have, of course) but the mere sight of her would have made me want to run a mile in the opposite direction. When I look back on the girls I have loved, they have all been neat, elegant and clean—with one exception only, the mother of Anne and Ray [two of his children], who was neither neat nor elegant.

It is this fastidiousness which makes me so ridiculously antipathetic to such things as lipstick and heavy eye painting and artificial eyelashes [he would not allow his wives to wear make-up]. Angela Rippon I should find very attractive indeed were it not for the way she paints her face and, in particular, her eyes. This desecration of a nice face is, to me, hardly less than an aesthetic crime.

It is not that I have any objection to make-up as such. But its function (and I exclude TV requirements imposed by strong lighting) should be no more than the enhancement of beauty by the remedying of nature's mis-endowments. Lips that are redder, eyebrows blacker, eyelashes larger, eye-shadows darker than ever they are to be found in nature are an offence to me. All they do is to transform a human face into a conventional mask. They are just dirt on the face. There is simply no need for such over-accentuation.

And that came from a man who grew a beard at the age of 23 and became more publicly familiar as its colour lightened from flaming ginger to snowy white over his career in racing. He even suggested such a measure to a young man from Ireland, who wrote to him in 1977 explaining that he very seldom went out of the house because his face was 'a disaster, all deep-indented scars, spots and blackheads'. No cure could help him, and he asked Bull what staking plan would produce a profit of £20 per week from Timeform information so that he could 'save as much as possible to be able to have plastic surgery done in the not too distant future.'

Bull described the letter as one of the most distressing he had received, and in his reply suggested the young man should tackle his psychological problem first. 'A man is not his face: he's what's inside his head,' he wrote. Two days later Bull had a further suggestion: 'Your facial appearance might be less of an anxiety to you if you did as I did in 1933, and grew a beard.'

Bull's concern was typical of the kindly side of his nature. He tried to cultivate the characteristic, explaining in an impromptu letter, dated 23 June 1971, to Sir Hugh Carleton Greene, the BBC director general, commenting on an *Observer* article he had written about Lord Reith:

It was such a kindly and understanding appraisal of the man, as made me aware of my own shortcomings in respect of kindly feelings towards people whose views and attitudes I deplore. John Reith has always been filed alongside John Foster Dulles—two men personifying all the most bigoted, proselytising, reactionary characteristics of the true Christian.

I have always—well not always; not when I was young, but since I was 40, at any rate—I have regarded kindliness as the most important element in anyone's character. I do not regard tolerance as a virtue. No-one should tolerate genocide or grossly anti-social behaviour of any kind. But tolerance towards the person with whose views one violently disagrees (Enoch Powell, for example), I do regard as a virtue. And I do not feel myself well equipped in this respect.

Your appreciation of Lord Reith brought this home to me again. Of course I didn't know him as a man, and maybe this is a point. No doubt some who knew Hitler, or Goebbels, or even Himmler, as men, family men, might take of them a view different from that of the rest of us.

But this is really irrelevant. It is important to be capable of gentle, kindly, even friendly feelings, towards people to whose attitudes and actions one is diametrically opposed. Though this should not inhibit one from opposing those attitudes and seeking to defeat those actions with all the resources at one's command.

Bull returned to the theme in his 'fastidious' letter to Bunny Esterhazy:

I have long since learned to take people for what they are, valuing them for their qualities and doing my best to ignore or excuse their shortcomings. I was brought up by my father to be an idealist. And what the pursuit of ideals comes to, with anyone, eventually, is the pragmatic recognition of the possible and the attainable.

The principles were not always translated into actions, and Bull could lace vitriol with ridicule when he came across someone who had made a remark with which he did not agree. He did it once to the respected racing writer Vincent Orchard, reducing him to shamefaced silence before a group of racing people in Newmarket's Rutland Arms. One of those present recalls: 'We listened, cringing with embarrassment as Phil, grinning, plunged his verbal darts ever deeper. It was a truly awful spectacle, made all the worse by the fact that nothing he said could be contradicted. He was nearly always right about everything, or so it seemed until several minutes later, when you realised how he had loaded his arguments. Then it was too late.'

However, Bull himself was capable of being reduced to tears. He wept openly at Newmarket races when told of the death of William Hill; he broke down in the office in front of a member of staff when his wife Wendy left him, and he was deeply affected by the death of his jockey Don Morris in a car accident. When Alexander Elliott, son of Bunny Esterhazy, committed suicide in March 1985, he wrote to the Countess:

Nothing in recent years has hit me as traumatically, nor upset me so deeply, as the phone call that told me of last week's tragedy. Tears comes easily and not infrequently when one is young; but by the time you have reached my age you have learned to suffer emotional adversity too often to be thrown into crying it away. I thought I had. But I was wrong. The stab of pain and the surge of anger and impotent resentment were too much for me. And for the first time in many years I wept.

In April 1976, Bull told the Duke of Devonshire: 'I'm happier now than I've ever been. Such a wealth of marvellous friends (you appreciate 'em when you're 66) and so voracious an appetite for life.' The week before, he had entertained the Duke and a host of guests as chairman of the Saints and Sinners Club at a function in London's Dorchester Hotel, and the euphoria of the occasion still seemed to be with him. Other correspondence offered a counter perspective. To Dan Prenn, a sponsor at the Timeform Charity race meeting, he wrote on 4 September 1973:

You have enlarged my life by another person—two persons, counting Biddy as well. Most of my life has been spent in the pursuit of ideals and the chasing of goals. But as I have got older I have come to realise that both are really chimeras: the timescale involved in the former is too long for my little life, and as to the latter, I've had the satisfaction of achieving some of them and, having done so, the savour has gone from it all.

So I have been brought rather late in life to the realisation that it is people, and personal relationships, that make life worth living. We may pursue our ends, and perhaps achieve them, but without personal relationships that feed our needs there's an emptiness about the achievement. In the long run we are all very, very much alone. Death is a lonely business—a lonely event, from which even the presence of a friendly holding hand cannot remove the loneliness.

Do not take this as a morbid reflection. It isn't. It's a rational appreciation of the reality. But there is comfort in the holding hand, and in going through life with people from whom one has sympathy and affection and understanding.

When I was young, vigorous, revolutionary and iconoclastic, I hardly appreciated these things. I do now. I value people. I still pursue the ideas: still seek to smash the idols, and revolt against the injustices, iniquities and stupidities inherent in society. But in a sense that's a losing battle—a never-ending contest that can't be won. People! People are what matter. Especially young people. To give them joy, and release from confining conditioning: to give them understanding and warmth. That is my pleasure nowadays.

Of course I have old friends—people I met before the war, with whom I was in accord then, and with whom I am again in instant accord now, even though we meet only at intervals of a month or a year or so. Strong, intelligent, worthwhile people. But it is with the young that my sympathies lie, and with them that I am concerned. Young children, adolescents, young adults embarking on life with that same revolutionary fervour and concern that I had when I was young—these are the people I love.

Why do I write to you in this strain? I believe that you, too, understand. You value intelligence, as I do: but you wouldn't rate it above concern for people and affection and kindliness. That's the point.

You and I are mere acquaintances. You don't know me, and I don't know you. Talking in terms of background, that is. But short though the acquaintance may be, I know bloody well that you're a right guy who belongs in my world. Not in the world of the Billy Grahams, Mrs Whitehouses, Lord Longfords, Malcolm Muggeridges, Nixons and the rest.

Five years later, in December 1981, Bull was still concerned by the subject of kindliness and the search for personal relationships. In a letter—packed with grander overtones than the facts might suggest—to the Yorkshire businessman and racehorse owner Jack Hanson he wrote:

I get so involved with causes of one kind or another—the Horseracing Advisory Council, running the Calderdale Chess Championship, arguing the political case with people like Michael Manley or Tony Benn and others, building up the self-regard and self-confidence of other people's children, especially those who are victims of domestic break-ups—that I am ashamed of my neglect of my own personal relationships with people, both inside Timeform and outside it.

Take Guy Reed [another Yorkshire owner], for instance. For years I've been going to create a meaningful relationship with him. And I've done damn all about it. And deeply I regret it.

One gets slower as one gets older. You see the days, and the years, slipping away, and one's remaining span diminishing. Zest and energy to do things diminish too. And the feeling that whatever one may seek to do, it's pretty pointless in the end, is always increasingly in the back of one's mind. That's what happens when you're getting into your seventh decade.

I don't make New Year resolutions: but if I did, I think mine for 1982 would be to spend less time and thought pursuing purposes and more time on people and personal relationships.

Appreciation of the fault was not new. It had been apparent to Bull when, if not before, he compiled his autobiographical notes in 1969. Under the heading What Things Do You Regret In Your Life, he wrote:

My own faults and shortcomings: too much concern with ideas and work and things, and too little concern with people. That, I'm afraid, made me a poor husband and not too good a father. My children deny this, but I'm not sure my wives would. People and human relationships are the most important part of life. My relationships have not been bad or unsatisfactory. But they could have been better.

Marriage and Bull were comfortable bedfellows for only brief periods. He was married three times; once to a fellow teacher, who bore him a son, and twice to women who joined Timeform as his personal secretary and assistant, with whom there was no child. His first marriage lasted nine years, his second nearly fourteen, and his third a month short of four, but none went the recorded distance. The first took place in 1935, when Bull was 25; the last was dissolved in 1967, and from the age of 57 till his death at 79 he sought comfort from a number of female companions. His deepest relationship—never formalised by marriage—came after his first marriage, and from it there were two children.

Bull married schoolteacher Doris Ashley at Islington Register Office on 15 June 1935, and they lived in north London. Four months later a son, David William Bernard, was born [Bull himself was born only seven months after his parents married]. Shortly afterwards the family moved south of the Thames to a terraced house in Veronica Road, Balham, but before David was three years old the Bulls had split up and in September 1938 Doris was granted custody of the child. Phil Bull was ordered to pay £1 per week towards the maintenance of his son, but the order was discharged thirteen months later on an application that he had 'wilfully neglected to provide reasonable maintenance' for his wife. A new order was obtained, requiring Bull to pay £1 per week to his wife and the equivalent of 50p per week for the child. Bull remained at the house in Veronica Road, while his wife and son moved about a mile away. By the time that Doris petitioned for divorce in March 1943, she had moved to Stourbridge in Worcestershire, Bull was living in a detached house at Howards Lane, Putney, with another teacher, Eleanor Oxley, and they had had a daughter, Anne Marjorie Bull, born on 4 December 1942. Two of Bull's earliest racehorses were Queen Eleanor and Anne of Essex.

Doris Bull, who much later went to live in Paignton, sought the divorce on the grounds of her husband's 'frequent adultery' with Nell Oxley, with whom he had lived since September 1940. The divorce was made final on 19 June 1944, and a little under eight months later, on 26 February 1945, Bull and Miss Oxley had a second child—Bull's second son—Raymond William Oxley Bull. When Ray was born, Bull had completed his move back to Yorkshire, having bought Windy Nook in Hemsworth in 1944, but the newly-released grouping did not remain together. Bull's own female-dominated family viewed his marital, and non-marital, affairs with grave suspicion. However, Bull continued to support Nell Oxley and their children, providing a home for them at Scholes, near Leeds. His daughter Anne remained with Nell as she grew up, while son Ray lived at The Hollins with his father and went to school in Halifax, before both children were sent to the freethinking Kilquhanity School in Scotland.

319

A hurriedly-scribbled note from Bull to his printer Bob Charman, dated 31 October 1949, told of the next stage in the marriage story. It began:

I haven't forgotten about you, and I'm not hibernating or will o' the wisping, but—Nell and I have parted; Wendy and I get married on Friday.

Bull married Wendy Carter at Halifax Register Office on 4 November 1949. She continued to work for him at The Hollins and in the Halifax office when Timeform outgrew the Bull family home, and would accompany him to the races. However, in the middle of December 1954 Bob Charman, busy preparing to put the *Racehorses* annual together, received another brief note from Bull:

Wendy has left me, so all the light has gone out of my life. May not be able to do much on the book this year. Don't sympathise with me.

The significance of the last sentence did not come to light until much later, but in the meantime Charman received a letter, headed Confidential and dated 9 February 1955. It began:

Wendy and I are together again. Things are not perhaps quite what they were, but they may sort themselves out in time. Anyway, don't refer to it, because Wendy is a bit sensitive about it. I'm afraid I've neglected everything in the past couple of months and got quite out of the habit of work.

Though Bull and his wife remained together for a further four years, his apprehension was proved correct. They split up again, and in the rough draft of a letter written by Bull to Wendy while he stayed at the Westbury Hotel in London's New Bond Street, dated 15 March 1960, he raised the 1954 issue and outlined his current feelings. Curiously, he began by referring to dealing with Wendy's inquiry about photographs of the two-year-old colt Vivaldi, before moving to the subject of the divorce he was contemplating:

I'm not sure that I know what you mean when you say 'let's keep it clean'. So far as I know there's not likely to be anything dirty about it, though it is true that there is nothing so clean that the press cannot make it look dirty. You have committed adultery with David

[Bull's son] in 1954 and with Peter Haslam [a Timeform employee] in 1959. I can prove it conclusively in both cases. Nor have you ever denied it.

Either of these offences entitles me to divorce you. There are no counter accusations you can make against me, and so short of deliberate perjury, there is no defence available to you. You cannot blame me for wishing to divorce you, and you can hardly expect me to keep Peter Haslam's nose clean for him by waiting three years to divorce you on the grounds of desertion.

Do not misunderstand me: I do not feel ill-disposed towards you—quite the reverse. I wish to save you all the pain I can; and I shall always be very fond of you, and will always remember warmly the happy times we did have together.

Nor do I feel in the least vindictive towards Peter Haslam. I'm simply indifferent to his interests. If, as a result of my action against you, his wife divorces him, that's not my affair.

I am concerned about David and have always been worried by the long-term effect upon him of those events in 1954. He was little more than a boy at the time [around nineteen years old]. But you and Haslam are grown adults with full experience of life, understanding your responsibilities and capable of assessing the probable consequences of your actions. If I could protect David, I would do so. I cannot protect Haslam, and have no intention of trying.

Incidentally, Vivaldi, the two-year-old in whom Wendy expressed so much interest, was the second foal of Carteretta, who ran in her colours—distinguished from Phil Bull's only by a white cap—and won five races in succession as a three-year-old in 1954. Bull informed Wendy that Vivaldi could 'run a bit and should win a race'. He appeared twice within a month of Bull's letter. Third on his Manchester debut, drifting from 2/1 to 5/1 in the betting, he won at Pontefract, making all the running after being backed from 5/4 to 4/5. Barely two years old, he was immediately sold for export; it was the shortest time that Bull ever held on to one of his own horses. Whether that was the result of Bull's anguish over Wendy, or his desire to generate necessary cash flow, is not clear.

Wendy left The Hollins, but her new relationship was shortlived. The newspapers did indeed get to hear about the break-up, and for a time reporters from one of the nationals doorstepped the house: Bull called the Timeform staff together and instructed them not to speak to the Press, other than to say 'No comment'. The incident quickly passed, but Bull refrained from going through with what would have been a messy and public divorce. Instead, he let the matter lie and got on with his life. When he finally petitioned for divorce, it was on the grounds that Wendy had deserted him 'without cause for a period of at least three years'. The marriage was formally ended on 27 June 1963, and on 2 September that year Bull was back at the Halifax Register Office to marry Patricia Scott Finlay.

Patricia had replaced Wendy as Bull's personal assistant. She applied for a secretarial job at Timeform, and Bull happened to notice her letter, with its mention of a university education and degree qualifications, on the desk of one of his directors. Within a short time she was living at The Hollins and travelling with Bull to the races.

Before they were married Bull gifted to Patricia a two-year-old Grey Sovereign filly called Lanarkshire. By the first week in July 1963 she had run four times in Patricia's colours of white with a gold cap, winning twice. Each time she was odds on, as she was in between her victories, when—ironically in the light of subsequent events—she showed the first signs of a wayward temperament, refusing to line up and being left at the start. In 1964 Patricia suggested a level-weights match race between Lanarkshire and Phil's three-year-old Karelia. It took place as the last event on the card at Redcar on 19 May, and Patricia insisted that Lester Piggott should ride Lanarkshire. Bull's retained jockey Don Morris was on Karelia, who made all the running and won by a length and half at 4/5, to Lanarkshire's even-money. It was Karelia's second of three successes that season; Lanarkshire never won at three years and was retired to stud after being badly injured in a melée when she returned to race at Redcar that October.

It was not long afterwards that Patricia too moved on to new pastures. A newspaper report in 1965 noted: 'The third marriage of rich racehorse owner Phil Bull, 55, has gone on the rocks, hardly more than two years after he married the girl who was his personal assistant. And 28-year-old Patricia Bull has turned her back on the luxury life of Rolls-Royces and racecourse champagne for the love of handsome, fair-haired National Hunt jockey Tony King, also 28.' It went on to say, 'After twelve months things started to go wrong between the near-millionaire and the doctor's daughter from Middlesbrough. Said Patricia: "I know I had everything in the world, but things just weren't right between Phil and me. I couldn't go on".'

Just as in the case of Wendy Bull, Patricia left The Hollins but her new relationship lasted only a short time. Tony King subsequently committed suicide. Patricia went to live with her brother in Vancouver, from where she corresponded with Bull. He visited her and for a short time she returned to The Hollins, but there was no future in the relationship. On 4 October 1967 they were divorced, on the grounds that Patricia 'had been guilty of adultery with a man, service upon whom has been dispensed with', though Tony King was named as co-respondent.

For several years Bull kept in touch with and occasionally met Patricia, who moved between Scotland and Middlesbrough and for some time was working in the cocktail bar of the Drummond Arms Hotel in Crieff. She wrote letters which began 'Dearly' and ended 'Toosh', and talked of 'thriving and growing more beautiful and talented daily', of 'desperately trying to find time to get some drawing and writing done', and of 'living a "semi-settled" life'. Colleagues at Timeform remember her as a girl with a talent for surprise. 'She used to say that unlike Phil, who was an atheist, she was a pantheist, she believed in everything,' says one. 'You were never amazed by what she said or did, even when she sat in the middle of the floor making daisy chains.' Another says: 'She came out with some very odd thoughts, such as saying, "There are too many people in this world; we really could do with killing off some of them".'

In 1972, writing to Norman Emblin, a friend in Halifax, Bull said with obvious sorrow: 'I wish I'd had your good fortune in marriage. To have solid love in life, proof against all disagreement and fundamental philosophical differences of opinion, is, must be, a marvellous thing.' And writing to one of his 'unfortunates' in January 1975, he explained: 'All healthy men pursue women, some with more ardour than prudence, and some with more prudence than ardour. I was in the former class.' On Christmas Eve 1978, replying to Bob Charman's discussion of seasonal gifts, he wrote: 'You suggest I have no material wants? True enough. For who among us, who sees that he is soon to depart the stage, is bothered about material things? I have enough suits. I'm not going to go hungry: wine, cigars—I'll get by with them too. What I don't have is a hand to hold on the way. There you have the advantage of me. You have the reality, I have to make do with the pretence and the fantasies!'

Bull's second and third marriages were to women much younger than himself; he married Wendy Carter at the age of 39 and Patricia Scott Finlay at 53. When both were attracted to men of their own age, Bull's lack of attention caught up with him. Described by those who observed him closely at the time as very selfish and inconsiderate towards his wives, he devoted less time than he should to the common decency of a normal husband-

and-wife relationship of looking after them. When other opportunities arose, the inevitable happened.

In May 1966 Bull signalled the arrival of a companion to replace Patricia when he advised Weatherbys that the ownership of his three-year-old gelding Paisiello was to be registered as a partnership between himself and Miss Inge Sanders, in whose name he would run. Sadly, Paisiello proved himself to be 'of no account', in *Timeform*'s words, that year and was sold at the end of the season for 100 guineas. Inge stayed on for some time, alternating between her home in Green Hammerton, near York, and The Hollins. But eventually she married her boyfriend, and Bull was left to resort to advertising for a female secretary or personal assistant.

Reg Griffin recalls: 'He used to send out a questionnaire to those who replied, asking several very personal questions such as, Do you believe in sex before marriage? or Do you believe in birth control? or Are you religious? He didn't seem to bother that the tabloid press might have got hold of a copy and splashed it across their headlines. I remember being told that one girl answered the advertisement, was given a job, and travelled with him to the races. They stayed overnight in a hotel, Phil in a big bedroom, her in a single room. During the night she went to the bathroom and returned to find this little bearded man in her bed, expecting her to get in, which she refused. Another time, we were coming back from the races at Epsom; I was driving and Phil was in the back with a woman. We hadn't gone more than a mile down the road when I heard a voice say, "Get your dirty hand off my leg". Phil's response was, "My hand's not dirty".'

Bull's last companion was his most loyal, Jennifer Dawson, a near neighbour who could expect a call from him to herself and family at any time of the day and night. When Jennifer's mother and father died in quick succession and she split up from her husband, she and her three children moved into her parents' cottage near The Hollins. She would drive Bull to and from the races, his sister May in the back seat, and eventually the task was formalised with a financial commitment from Timeform.

Jennifer Dawson and her children were among eighteen beneficiaries named when a legal wrangle over Bull's will—raised by Reg Griffin—was sorted out in court in November 1990, seventeen months after Bull's death. Bull's principal will was dated 28 July 1986, but two further versions were dated 20 February and 3 May 1989, after he had suffered a stroke and shortly before he died. Beneficiaries of the three were brought together under an action resolved before Master Munrow in the High Court.

Apart from the Dawsons, and Edgar and Irene Stott, Bull's housekeepers, who received £2,000 each, the remaining twelve beneficiaries were members of his family: his sister May Watson-Gott, her daughter June Paxton-White and her two children Jill and Michael; his sister Connie Stead; his son Ray and his son Damon; his grandaughter Nadine Ahmed, her daughter Natalie and son Ashley, and step-daughter Rianne; and his grandaughter Donna Pearce.

As a family, this largish group hardly overwhelmed Bull with happiness in later life. The name of his one legitimate—but ostracised—son David was missing, and of his other two children only Ray survived their father. Phil and Ray remained close, though not as close as some father-son relationships. Bull was proud of Ray's achievements. In a letter to a contact in New York, dated 25 March 1963, shortly after Ray's eighteenth birthday, Bull wrote:

Ray is studying hard for his A-level physics and maths, and is doing pretty well. He recently took his advanced motorist test and got a first-class pass—one of the youngest motorists in the country to do this. This will serve, no doubt, to build up his self-confidence, though I hardly think it needs much building up.

The following year, on 6 August, Bull wrote to his former stable jockey Edgar Britt in Australia:

Ray has made a fine young man, very self-reliant and inde-pendent—so much so that I'm afraid I don't see very much of him these days.

Ray remained with his father at The Hollins when the relationship with Nell Oxley ended. He left home to join an air training school in 1964. When Ray qualified as a pilot, Phil Bull would delight in pointing out the fact to his companions if they travelled on a plane being flown by his son. Ray got married but within a fairly short time of his son Damon being born, he split from his wife Carol and returned to live in a cottage on The Hollins estate. An example of Bull's fastidiousness, even towards his own son, emerged when Ray planned to buy and renovate a cottage belonging to his father. In a confidential note to Ray, Bull remarked:

I'm in the dark about what modifications and alterations to the existing property you have in mind. Architects' plans and planning approval may be fine, but I have to consider how they affect me before I can approve them. This means that I have to have your specific proposals, spelling out in detail exactly what you wish conveyed to you. Boundaries, rights of way, maintenance responsibilities and all the rest of it have to be identified, not only in my interests and yours, but as they may affect any third party to whom I might sell The Hollins.

These things are a minefield of potential friction and dispute. For that reason I'm employing Anthony Blaza [surveyor] to advise me and later, of course, a solicitor to handle the conveyancing. The last thing I wish is to find myself at cross purposes with you. For this reason, though I'll discuss things with you if you wish, I will agree to nothing verbally. Everything has to be in writing to Blaza, who will deal with things on my instructions.

I hope this doesn't sound too formal, but I want things done in a manner that minimises the risk of my becoming involved in possible disputes. Frankly I think you must be mad to want to buy a property that needs so much doing to it and is situated in an area like this, with its climatic and other drawbacks. But that's your affair, laddie.

Bull's daughter Anne—born in December 1942, and just over seven years younger than his son David from his first marriage, and a little more than two years older than Ray—stayed with her mother when the relationship broke up but she frequently visited The Hollins on leaving school. Bull indulged her as a child, paying for her to take piano lessons with the best teacher in Halifax before going on to the Manchester College of Music. She failed to complete the course, as she did with several examinations and driving lessons. In her late-teens she married a local shopfitter, Frank Pearce, and very quickly they had two children—daughters Nadine and Donna. But equally quickly they separated. It was said that Anne had no idea about keeping house, or looking after children; she had been taught neither.

Left alone to bring up two young children, Anne began drinking and inevitably joined Alcoholics Anonymous. She appeared to benefit, so much so that when Bull wrote to Bob Charman on 20 December 1970, he noted:

Anne and Ray seem to be dealing with life pretty well. Anne is no longer an alcoholic: she has taken herself in hand astonishingly well, and is now, or seems to be, much more capable, much happier in herself, and able to cope with life. She's discharging her responsibilities to her two daughters much better than one could have hoped.

But Bull's optimism did not last long. On 16 November 1975 he wrote to Joe Kagan:

Anne has not been well—she never really will be, for she's incapable of facing the realities of life—and, regrettably, though I've tried hard, I simply can't get through to her. And now my patience has worn thin and I've thrown in the towel and fallen out with her. She's impossible; though really all she needs is a man in bed with her. Unfortunately she doesn't know how to be agreeable to anyone, and only an idiot would entangle himself with her.

Over the next nine years Anne's mental and physical condition fluctuated wildly, mainly getting worse. Bull could not give up on her altogether, and in a late-night phone call which Anne made in July 1979, he told his subdued daughter, 'You have a bit of a cross to bear, don't you. Just relax, don't distress yourself about me. I'm okay, and I love you. Don't worry about that.' Bull himself was worried, and in a letter, dated 18 September 1979, to Bob Charman he wrote:

Anne has been in the psychiatric unit of St James's Hospital in Leeds, having ECT. The other day when I went to see her, I found her suffering from delusions. She accused me of trying to kill her and her two children by putting lead in her water supply, and of making money by selling pornographic photographs, and warned me that she wasn't going to have me taking porno photos of herself and Nadine and Donna. Of other things too.

These delusions are, of course, a direct result of the ECT. But, of course, she can't understand that. No use arguing with Anne. She's incoherently irrational. It's a worrying situation.

A month later Bull was in better spirits, reporting to Jess Charman that 'Anne is a lot better'. But he admitted it could not last. 'The cycle will recur,' he wrote. 'She's not very stable, and not very capable of dealing with life. Not much I can do about it.' His grandchildren took on most of the home chores and became accustomed to looking after themselves. Nadine married and took on a step-daughter before she had two children of her own; Donna went to Belfast University. Bull had strong views on each. In a letter to Bob and Jess Charman dated 19 January 1982 he wrote: 'I'm a great-grandfather now, and wish I weren't. Nadine can't support herself, and I imagine neither can the child's father. Nor is Nadine equipped to bring up children.' And of Donna he later wrote: 'She is a self-willed person who, like Anne, tends to reject the help and advice that other people seek to give.'

A fortnight before Christmas 1985, Anne committed suicide. She was 43. Bull was shaken, but not surprised. He told Billie Richardson, in a letter dated 21 December 1985:

Anne had been a trouble and a trial to me and to everyone else almost all her life, so she will leave behind no-one suffering from the loss of her companionship. She had no friends. She alienated almost everyone she had anything to do with, including myself. I spent 20 years (far more if you go back to her childhood) trying to help her, and it ended up with her telling me she didn't want anything more to do with me. I don't know whether the fact I haven't been able to sleep well since this happened betokens some subconscious feelings of guilt in me, but I shall be glad when Monday [Anne's cremation] is over, when I've sorted out things with her daughters, and I can put it all behind me.

In a more factually detailed letter to John Aitkenhead, the principal of Kilquhanity School, dated 7 January 1986, Bull wrote:

You'll remember my telling you that Anne became an alcoholic and was a chronic schizophrenic. I might have added that she had made three or four attempts to commit suicide, one serious one from which only the fact that Donna was on hand saved her from death.

I'm sorry to tell you that three weeks ago she threw herself from a bridge and fell forty or fifty feet into the main road below. She was taken to Leeds Infirmary with multiple injuries, including a double fractured spine, a broken leg and broken ribs. Had she survived she would have been confined to a wheelchair for the rest of her life, but after a week, during which she was conscious only for short periods, she died.

I'm afraid I can't help thinking that it was a merciful release for her, and I am in no doubt that had she survived, the real victim of the tragedy would have been Donna. Anne had already done great damage to Donna's prospects for a happy life, and I'm very doubtful whether she can rescue herself from the agrophobia (which is the form her schizophrenia has taken); but at least she will now have a better chance of doing so.

Bull died three and a half years later, on 11 June 1989, aged 79. He had been referring to the eventuality for nearly twenty years, working out the genetic probabilities along the way. He came from a family packed with stamina. His paternal grandfather lived to the age of 93, when he walked through the fog in Sheffield, mistakenly fell into a canal and drowned. His father died at the age of 85, and his mother at 87. He was survived by his sisters Connie, who died in 1993 at the age of 79, and May, who was 84 in July 1995.

He was so concerned about the effort of writing *Best Horses of 1946*, which appeared many months after its expected publication, that on 10 November 1947 he told Bob Charman, in utmost seriousness: 'Should either of us peg out between now and the end of the 1948 season, this letter will confirm to our executors that I still hold £100 of yours as your investment in my betting for another twelve months (Flat racing only).'

Much later his health and an apparent lack of energy cropped up more frequently in his letters. They came after the end of his third marriage, and at times appeared to be a convenient excuse for failure to apply himself. In April 1971 he told the wife of a former Timeform employee who was living in Bangkok:

Your letter is one of the nicest things that has happened to me this year. There's no exaggeration about that. I've been very low all this year, in health, in zest, in interest in living. Life, the past, and what I can see of the future, has lain heavily upon me; and it does so still. Your letter seems to throw a shaft of sunlight through the scene, lightening it all and offering promise of some more sun perhaps to come.

Little over a year later lack of interest was again evident. On 18 September 1972 he wrote to the Blackpool solicitor and short-story writer John Budd:

I'm interested in writing, but I find it very hard work and am very conscious of my ignorance of the subjects I'm most interested in. Regret to tell you I'm not really interested any longer in horse racing, so I wouldn't have much enjoyment from writing about my involvement in it these last thirty-five years or so. Of course I have a story worth telling. Everyone has, if only he could tell it. But I think I'd find it an irksome task telling mine—the horseracing side of it, anyway.

On 25 September 1975 he wrote to the journalist Peter Jenkins:

For far too long I've been bothering myself with racing, and lacked the whetstone of intelligent argumentative opponents to sharpen my understanding of the world. And I haven't much time. I'm 65.

> He was still concerned about concentrating on racing, and even more concerned about the ageing process, when he wrote to Jess Charman on 29 October 1979:

The grey cells are deteriorating. I'm slow. I don't attend to things as I should. And I don't attend to my own affairs: I attend to other matters, racing politics and so forth. But at the cost of loss of control of Timeform and the things that should be of personal concern to me.

It is a reflection of growing old and of continuing to operate according to the pattern of behaviour established in the pursuit of goals of earlier years. And I'm damned if I know what to do about it. The problem is how to accept and accommodate oneself to one's own deterioration and increasing inefficiency. What is it they say, 'You're as old as you feel.' That's half the coin. You can't feel when you're 70 what you felt when you were 40.

I don't resent these consequences of increasing age. I don't like them. But I know they are natural and inevitable. So where would be the sense of resentment or annoyance or anger? We can't get back into the cradle, or the first, fine, carefree bed. We're getting old. We are old. We're *en route* to death and non-existence. It's for everyone. So what is there to be done except understand it and accept it as the inescapable reality, with as much grace and lack of anticipation as we can muster?

> Bull had not long finished with the councils of the Racehorse Owners Association and Thoroughbred Breeders Association; he was involved with the Racegoers Club; and he was soon to become bound up in the business of the Horseracing Advisory Council. Yet he still expressed a hankering after wider interests. The HAC experience seemed to strengthen his feeling, though he could not cut himself off from racing completely. On 16 January 1981 he wrote to John Macdonald-Buchanan, the Jockey Club senior steward:

I doubt you'll see much of me on the racecourse this year. I've more or less retired from the fray. I lack the incentive to battle with the bookmakers and the tax; and my experience with the HAC persuades me that I must spend the last ten years or so of my life (if

I'm fortunate enough to have so long) on less frustrating pursuits. But I daresay I'll be at Ascot, Epsom and Newmarket occasionally. Long-established habits die hard.

> He was not far out in his lifespan prediction, which he used again in a letter, dated 14 September 1984, to a 21-year-old correspondent asking if he could give advice about his future 'or maybe put me in touch with a few of your friends'. Bull did more than offer advice; he summed up his own personal outlook:

You are asking the impossible of me. I am an old man, 74 years of age, with the life expectation of a mere seven or eight more years to live. And I have much work to do, many pressing problems to deal with, and many, many people around me, working for me, with whom I am inextricably concerned, or who are dependent upon me for help with their own work and problems.

Surely you will understand that I cannot drop these things—cease my affairs and concerns—in order to apply myself to helping you, and all the other young and admirable people who are always knocking on my door, or writing to me in much the same terms as you have done.

Much as I should like to help you I do not have the time. Time is what I am short of, to do all the things I want to do. You are young, you think you have plenty of time, I know I haven't, and you'll have the same realisation when you are my age. No, laddie: you will have to row your own boat as best you can—as everyone has.

If there is one piece of advice I can give to you, it is this. You have a journey through life. It is a short journey, from birth (before which you are unaware of anything) until death (after which you will no longer exist). Seek to enjoy the journey as much as you can, savour the scenery and the people you meet *en route*. For it is all there is.